TROUBLEMAKER |

A Personal History of School Reform since Sputnik

TROUBLEMAKER

Chester E. Finn, Jr.

PRINCETON UNIVERSITY PRESS | *Princeton and Oxford*

Published by Princeton University Press, 41 William Street, Princeton, New Jersey 08540

In the United Kingdom: Princeton University Press, 3 Market Place, Woodstock,

Oxfordshire OX20 1SY

Library of Congress Cataloging-in-Publication Data

Finn, Chester E., 1944–

   Troublemaker : a personal history of school reform since Sputnik / Chester E. Finn, Jr.

    p. cm.

   Includes bibliographical references and index.

   ISBN 978-0-691-12990-7 (hardcover : alk. paper)

   1. Education—United States—History.   2. Educational change—United States—

History.   I. Title

  LA209.2.F54 2008

   379.73—dc22   2007038263

British Library Cataloging-in-Publication Data is available

This book has been composed in Bembo

Printed on acid-free paper. ∞

press.princeton.edu

Printed in the United States of America

10 9 8 7 6 5 4 3 2 1

For Emma, with love and expectation

For Dad, with love, remembrance, and appreciation

For Emma, with love and expectation

For Dad, with love, remembrance, and appreciation

CONTENTS |

INTRODUCTION |

The education system that my much-adored granddaughter Emma entered in 2006 and will exit around 2025 is different from the one I began in 1950 and light-years from those commenced by my father in 1923 and my grandfather around 1896. Worse in some ways, better in others, it's undeniably an object of greater angst and agitation.

American schools have changed from within as educators introduced new ideas and nostrums and altered their priorities and practices, but they've changed far more from without, as a more demanding (and more egalitarian) society and quickening international economy placed new stresses on them and as parents, community leaders, public officials, philanthropists, and innumerable experts and blue-ribbon panels sought to reshape them. They also bear the imprint of shifting demographics and wider cultural and technological developments. The schools that Emma will attend, for example, will likely import some of their instruction electronically from curriculum providers across the country and teachers on the other side of the planet. She'll be able to log on to her lessons from home or the beach. She could live in Rome or Bangkok and "attend" the same school. I had no such options. Neither did my kids.

Yet technology is only the most obvious transformation. Two subtler but momentous developments in the policy sphere have also reverberated through U.S. education since I entered kindergarten at Fairview Elementary School in Dayton, Ohio.

First, Americans no longer take for granted that they will attend a district-operated public school in their neighborhood—and that their only real alternative is a private school that's hard to access if you aren't rich or Catholic. That's how it worked when I was a kid. Mostly you went where the system assigned you according to where you lived. For Emma's generation, however, K–12 education is a cornucopia of school options, and about one-third of U.S. children already study somewhere *other* than their local district school.

Second, while parents still tend to judge schools on obvious grounds—How big are the classes? How spiffy the building? How close to my commute? How many games did the basketball team win last season?—and educators are wont to gauge them by budgets, salaries, programs, and services, state and federal officials have clamped very different criteria onto contemporary schools: Are their pupils learning what they should? Are schools meeting performance standards? Are they properly accountable for their results? If they're not delivering the goods, what interventions are called for?

Advancing parents' right to choose their children's schools while holding schools to account for their students' academic achievement are the twin turbos of education reform in twenty-first century America.

A third motor also adds propulsion, though in a somewhat different direction. Call it "professionalism." It seeks to empower teachers and principals with authority to make key education decisions; to create vehicles for them to design or redesign their own schools; to ensure that they are properly trained and licensed; and to recognize and (occasionally) reward excellence among them.

This campaign, too, is altering American K–12 education, sometimes in harmony and sometimes at cross-purposes with choice and standards.

That three energetic reform strategies are simultaneously at work attests to mounting discontent among elites—leaders of industry, government, the media, higher education, and more—with the performance of U.S. schools; to deepening frustration among poor and minority parents; to the complacency of a suburban middle class that is reasonably satisfied with its kids' current schools; to the inertia of an education system that's neither good at nor fond of changing, yet must change apace with the society that it serves; and to the irksome fact that no single scheme or theory can successfully reshape so complex an enterprise.

It's also evidence of a high-stakes struggle for influence and control of an immense public endeavor with 50 million pupils, 6 million employees, and a half-trillion-dollar budget. Will big decisions about the direction of that vast and vital activity primarily come down from government in the form of results-based accountability and "systemic" reform, as in the federal No Child Left Behind Act? Will they flow up from the marketplace via millions of determinations by individual families about the educational arrangements that suit them best, as signaled by vouchers, charter schools, and other forms of school choice? Will they emerge from professionals within the field, peeved at being told what to do by outsiders and confident that they know what's best for children and how schools should operate? Will decisions keep coming, as they do today, from all these directions and more? And will the changes that they seek complement or confound each other?

How and why all this complicated reforming overtook the mostly tranquil, slightly fusty education system of my childhood is the saga recounted here. These pages offer a history and tour guide to U.S. education reform since midcentury and some lessons to be drawn from that journey—from its political developments, from initiatives that fizzled, strategies that turned out to be incomplete, and ideas that had to be altered; from institutional changes; and from arguments and clashes among theories, individuals, organizations, parties, and factions, all claiming to be looking out for the interests of children and the nation.

It's also a personal chronicle.

I've taken part in many of these developments in three ways. First, as a card-carrying if oft-dissenting expert, privy to the secret codes and arcane lore of the education cognoscenti, sometimes even a source of ideas—not all of them sound—bearing on the major reform strands. Second, as a participating policymaker with my share of insider knowledge and direct contact with movers and shakers in government, think tanks, and the profession—and a propensity to team up with those most likely to overturn applecarts and to tip a few such conveyances myself. And third, as a sometimes-demanding consumer, as student, parent, mentor, and grandparent (not to mention child, grandchild, and sibling). Like other Americans, I've also been on the receiving end of what other experts, policymakers, and educators have dished out. And, like other Americans, I haven't always taken it calmly.

My expert face can claim forty years in the field, a trifecta of Harvard degrees, a stack of books, tenured professor, think tank fellow, foundation president, hundreds of articles, a thousand conferences, commissions, and blue-ribbon panels, speeches beyond counting, confabs beyond measuring, intercontinental boondoggles, and innumerable media quotes.

As policymaker, I've worked as a junior White House staffer, assistant secretary of education, legislative director for a high-profile U.S. senator, aide to one governor and kitchen cabinet member for another, member of the President's Education Policy Advisory Council, chairman of the National Assessment Governing Board, counsel to the U.S. ambassador to India, and more.

In and out, back and forth, sometimes changing my mind as well as my assignment, impatiently asking why the best-laid plans seldom work as intended, gradually evolving from naïve idealist to agitator, pushing back against hoary assumptions and long-standing arrangements, never keeping a job longer than four years (until my present post), craving both the excitement of direct participation and the freedom to analyze and write about it—and hector others about what they should do differently.

Yet much of what I've learned about education hasn't come from ruminating in think tanks or finger-smudging in government. It's the result of growing up and getting educated, traveling the world, being a husband and brother, raising two kids, uncle-ing and mentoring dozens of young relatives and protégés, and recently joining the ranks of doting grandparents.

In the following pages, I examine U.S. education reforms (and resistance) since 1950 through those personal lenses.

I owe more thanks than this aging brain can recall, particularly to a loving, long-suffering, and highly accomplished wife, two terrific kids and their spouses, the world's most perfect granddaughter, and my own parents and grandparents. Several memorable mentors appear often in these pages, above all Frank Broderick, Pat Moynihan, Bill Bennett, and Lamar Alexander—bottomless sources of advice, example, and opportunity. My constant soul mate over a quarter century of education reforming has been Diane Ravitch, America's keenest education historian.

This book exists because the trustees of the Thomas B. Fordham Foundation generously granted me a "mini-sabbatical" to write the first draft; because Stanford's Hoover Institution graciously furnished me an ideal setting in which to scribble; because the Fordham team, capably led by Eric Osberg, Mike Petrilli, and Terry Ryan, rose to the challenge (and welcomed the respite) of having me 2,500 miles away; because Diane, Tony Bryk, Scott Hamilton, Bruno Manno, and two anonymous reviewers supplied perceptive feedback and constructive ideas; because Sarah Kim printed out a dozen drafts and organized hundreds of notes and permissions; and because Peter Dougherty and his terrific team nursed it (with much improving and refining) through Princeton University Press.

All had previously earned my gratitude. My debt to them is now immeasurable.

Part I | *Early Days*

Before World War II, education in the United States was far from universal, and "equality of opportunity" was unimagined. Though public schooling had been invented in Massachusetts a century earlier and state universities arose after the Civil War, the American education system circa 1900–1940 consisted of several paths that seldom crossed—and the one you took depended mainly on your family circumstances.

The upper class, prosperous and mainly Protestant, enrolled its sons and daughters in private schools like Groton and Miss Porter's or in a handful of elite public schools such as Boston Latin. Thence to Princeton and Amherst, their southern counterparts (Duke, Vanderbilt, etc.), and that western upstart with the odd name of Leland Stanford Junior University. The focus was indisputably on boys, but a handful of plucky women and foresighted men had launched Vassar, Wellesley, Smith, and such for a small number of fortunate and mostly wellborn girls.

The middle class attended public school near home. Pretty much everyone went to primary school, and those who wanted it—and whose families were able to withstand the income hit—could attend high school, so long as they lived in a city or town large enough to have one. (In 1908, when my grandfather was eighteen, Dayton opened its second high school because the first had grown too crowded.) State universities were available to good students who sought higher education and could swing it financially, but relatively few did. In 1910, when my grandfather hoped but could not afford to enter Ohio State, just 13.5 percent of the U.S. adult population had graduated from high school and only 2.7 percent had completed four years of college. Thirty years later, when my father finished Yale, the corresponding figures were 24.5 percent and 4.6 percent.

Farmers and factory workers typically attended elementary school, then stopped. Most states had "compulsory attendance" laws by 1900, but these called for little more than basic competence in the three R's—and attendance through eighth grade, if that. New York's 1874 statute was typical:

> All parents and those who have the care of children shall instruct them, or cause them to be instructed, in spelling, reading, writing, English grammar, geography and arithmetic. And every parent, guardian or other person having control and charge of any child between the ages of eight and fourteen years shall cause such child to attend some public or private day school at least fourteen weeks in each year.[1]

In rural and small-town America, one-room, multigraded school-houses were the norm, typically presided over by a young (unmarried) woman who had herself attended no more than high school or the semi-college teacher-prep institution known as a "normal school." Overseeing them were tens of thousands of local school "systems"—many of which contained but a single school. (As late as 1930, the United States had 130,000 separate school systems, versus today's 15,000.)

For black Americans, the picture was different and bleaker. "Separate but equal" was the law of the land, and across much of that land Jim Crow ruled and the emphasis was on "separate." There were, to be sure, a handful of fine schools and colleges serving "Negro" pupils. Washington's all-black M Street School, renamed Dunbar High School in 1916, educated many leaders of the black community in the nation's capital. John D. Rockefeller's General Education Board, founded in 1903, made grants to schools and colleges for black youngsters throughout the South. Still, reports a University of California research team, "In 1940, when statistics on the educational attainment of the population by race first become available, whites reported high school completion rates of 24.2 and 28 percent for males and females, respectively; the comparable numbers for blacks were 6.9 and 8.4 percent."[2]

Immigrants mostly attended urban public schools, which undertook their assimilation, acculturation, and Americanization as essential parts of public education's mission, while also imparting academics, deportment, and character. Waves of new arrivals sent their children to schools that proudly taught them English, U.S. history and civics, patriotic values—and sometimes basic hygiene. The kids brought home what they learned in school and thereby helped Americanize their parents, too.

Roman Catholics were the one sizable group that shunned the public schools on grounds that they favored Protestantism. Beginning in the 1840s, Catholics built their own schools in New York and a handful of other eastern cities, particularly where poor, Irish immigrants clustered. In 1884, meeting in Baltimore, the Church's Third Plenary Council, declaring the era's public schools a "danger to the faith and morals" of Catholic youngsters, decreed that every parish should establish its own parochial school. Thus began a long period of extraordinary growth in the Catholic school system that, despite much recent erosion, still comprises the largest segment of U.S. private education.

Religious prejudice was felt by more than Catholics. In 1922, Harvard president A. Lawrence Lowell instituted a quota limiting the number of Jewish students at his university. This sort of thing was widespread in private schools and colleges. Discrimination thus coexisted with purposeful Americanization in U.S. education, suggesting that the country had not quite sorted out whose version of America was suited for whom and showing, most painfully for the nation's black population, that it did not always practice what it espoused.

Prejudice aside, it wasn't hard to get into what we now view as highly selective institutions. You needed to complete the prerequisites and afford the tuition, but you weren't vying for scarce openings with a throng of equally qualified rivals. Nor was it essential in those days to get credentialed via higher education in order to pursue your chosen career. Plenty of ministers never attended divinity school. Thousands of primary teachers had gone no further than high school themselves. Scads of shopkeepers, bankers, and tycoons never heard of business school. You could become an attorney by "reading law"—apprenticing with a veteran lawyer—rather than enrolling in law school.

That the education system treated kids differently caused few palpitations. It had its nasty side for sure: segregated schools and discriminatory admissions, as well as skimpy provision for handicapped youngsters (though the Perkins School for the Blind had been around since 1829 and Helen Keller enrolled there in 1888). But it had some pluses, too, such as the opportunity for motivated students to speed up, even to skip entire school grades, and to gain admission to the college of their dreams. If you had the desire, the talent, and the money, you could cobble together a first-class education. If you didn't, you mostly settled for the basic kind.

| By the time I appeared in 1944 in the maternity ward of Columbus, Ohio's old Grant Hospital, the Finn family had half a century of experience with U.S. education. My paternal grandfather, Samuel Finn, arrived in Ohio, a babe in arms, from Russia in 1891.[3] His younger sister and brothers were born in Dayton, where their mother sold fruit from a horse cart. Their father was learned in the Talmud but unworldly. In time he started a "bag and burlap" company that his sons turned into a decent business. (Many decades later, when I married a woman who had spent part of her childhood in Calcutta, my father

recalled that the family factory made its burlap bags with jute from Bengal.)

My grandfather attended the Dayton public schools, graduating from Steele High School in 1907 and intending to move on to Ohio State. His mother died soon thereafter, however, after a long illness that left the family too poor to pay for college, much less law school. So he went to work for the Hewitt Brothers Soap Company, traveling Ohio's roads with a satchel of soap samples in one hand and, says the oft-repeated tale, a valise of law books in the other. He "read law" with a senior Dayton attorney, passed the bar exam, and at the age of thirty teamed up with a pair of young colleagues to launch the new firm of Estabrook, Finn & McKee.

Craving a better education for his own two children, and thinking beyond the public schools of Dayton, he began exploring alternative options when my father (born in 1918) was a little boy. He wanted his son to attend "prep school," and his law partner, Roland McKee, suggested that my grandparents acquaint themselves with Lawrenceville Academy, the establishment prep school in New Jersey that he had attended.

That laudable plan ran afoul of the era's religious prejudice. Family lore says that my grandparents, after a grand tour of the academy, asked Lawrenceville's admissions director if their being Jewish would matter. He reportedly looked at his watch and said, "Mr. and Mrs. Finn, if you leave now you can catch the next train back to Trenton."

Rebuffed but undeterred, my grandfather again asked McKee and a respected Dayton judge for suggestions and was encouraged to check out Phillips Exeter Academy, a well-known boarding school in New Hampshire. Which is where my father found himself in 1933, aged fifteen. He had to repeat tenth grade, but his parents anticipated this by first sending him to the "Make Time School" operated by the Dayton Public Schools, where able youngsters could combine eighth and ninth grades into a single year.

Though the Great Depression was wreaking economic havoc across the land, Estabrook, Finn & McKee came through in decent shape, which enabled my father to go from Exeter to Yale, then to Harvard Law School, where he arrived on the threshold of World War II. His younger sister, meanwhile, graduated from Oakwood High School, located in a well-off suburb that kept its schools open even when Dayton went broke and had to shut its down. (Families with the means were welcome to pay tuition to

Oakwood.) She then attended Wheaton College in Massachusetts and, after raising her children, went back to earn a master's degree in library science from Simmons.

This was a classic immigrant tale, upwardly mobile, arising from the steely resolve of parents to obtain for their children the best possible education at whatever cost in money, sacrifice, even (as in the Lawrenceville tale) humiliation. No government program offered financial aid. No Office for Civil Rights fretted about discrimination. The public school system cooperated as best it could in fulfilling a family's dreams. There's no denying that my grandparents were fortunate. But determination, pluck, and hard work also figured in this sequence of events. Just three decades after my Yiddish-speaking great grandmother peddled produce from a wagon, my father matriculated at Yale.

| My mother's parents, too, sought the best education they could find for her and her brother. They moved from Lancaster, the small central Ohio town where my grandfather had a business, to Columbus primarily because of the superior schooling options available in the state capital. But the Depression hit them a bit harder. My mother had to change (private) schools because the first one cost too much, and though she was admitted to Wellesley College in 1937, her parents could not afford its tuition. So she spent her freshman year at the University of Illinois, then (with financial help from my grandmother's most successful brother) transferred to Wellesley, where she majored in English and became, among other things, a deft and witty writer. Following the custom of the day, she soon married and started a family. This was complicated by the war, of course, as my father interrupted law school to join the navy and served on a succession of ships in the Pacific, while my mother waited in West Coast ports and, once pregnant with me, back at her parents' home in Columbus.

By today's norms (including those of my wife, sister, and daughter), Mom's life was professionally incomplete. But she distinguished herself in a host of volunteer and community activities and devoted herself with gusto, skill, and patience to raising me, Natalie, and Sam—and later, while she lived, *our* kids. She and nine Wellesley classmates formed a "round-robin" letter-writing group to stay in touch after graduation. It continues today, though few of "The Inkspots" remain. Several of the ten were career women. The rest deployed their first-rate (and single-sex) education in less formal pursuits that were not necessarily less worthy or rewarding.

1 | Schoolkid in the Fifties

Through pastel lenses, many recall the Eisenhower era as the good old days of American education, when things were less complicated, frenetic, fractious, and fraught. Others, donning different spectacles, deplore the injustices and complacency of that era.

Both are partly correct.

U.S. schools bulged in the 1950s as the postwar baby boom hit. K–12 enrollments soared from 25 to 36 million. Just building enough classrooms and hiring teachers to staff them was ample challenge.

America was also beginning to expect all its children to attend high school—and to scorn as "dropouts" those who failed to complete it. During the fifties, the ratio of high-school graduates to seventeen-year-olds in the U.S. population rose from .59 to .69, close to where it is today. College, too, was more widely sought and, thanks to the GI Bill and similar financial aid schemes, more widely affordable. Postsecondary enrollments ballooned from 2.3 million to more than 4 million, and upward of half a million degrees were awarded in 1960. (When my father graduated twenty years earlier, the number was 220,000.) In 1948, a presidential commission urged creation of an entirely new institutional form, the "community college," to offer more tertiary options to Americans, and hundreds of them opened in the fifties and sixties, alongside dozens more of full-fledged colleges (including former "normal schools") and state universities.

The public schools of the day were old-fashioned in many respects, not yet jarred by desegregation, big federal and state programs, or technology (though they had mimeograph machines, overhead projectors, and public address systems). Their classrooms were ruled by no-nonsense teachers, many of them fifty-something Depression-era single women possessed of great ability and a solid education for whom this had been the best available career opportunity.

Once the classroom door was closed, it didn't much matter to the teacher what experts and critics were fussing about on the outside. Overhead, however, a philosophical air war raged between devotees of "progressive" or "pragmatic" ideas about curriculum and pedagogy, many of them followers of William Heard Kilpatrick, whose views held sway in colleges of education, and "essentialists" such as Robert Maynard Hutchins, Mortimer Smith, and Arthur Bestor, who founded the Council for Basic Education in 1956 to reclaim what Bestor termed America's "educational wastelands."[4]

On the ground below, most people attended neighborhood public schools. The biggest exception was Catholics, who were likely (and, said the Church, supposed) to attend parochial schools, staffed primarily by unpaid members of religious orders and thus tuition-free or nearly so to parishioners. At their apogee in 1960, Catholic schools enrolled one youngster for every seven in the public schools. Today's ratio is about one to twenty.

Many wealthy families still pursued private (mainly "independent") schooling for their daughters and sons, though this was more common in the older cities of the Northeast and mid-Atlantic than in the South or West. Burgeoning suburbs—Levittown dates to 1947—added options within the public sector. Towns like Bryn Mawr, Brookline, Winnetka, and Shaker Heights had long boasted "good" public schools, but when the population surge of the 1950s intersected with the increasing metropolitanization of American society, suburban school systems boomed as their communities offered green grass, fresh air, new housing, safety, and amenities.

Many Americans, however, still spent their lives in the towns where they were born, not infrequently working in their father's trade, often at a job—assembly line, agriculture, heavy labor—that didn't demand a great deal of formal education or elaborate training. Yet demographic upheavals were palpable—and not only the return of World War II veterans and the tsunami of babies. Family farms were starting their long fade, and rural America was losing population as opportunities centered in the city. Mobility crept into U.S. society as never before. Not least was the continuing movement of rural southern blacks northward to Detroit, Chicago, and other mighty municipalities of the industrial heartland—and into their public schools, which were segregated by neighborhood if not by law.

The growth-oriented education scene of the 1950s was jarred by two major-league surprises. The more profound was the Supreme Court's 1954 *Brown* decision, outlawing de jure segregation in public schooling. Second was the 1957 launch of Sputnik, the Soviet satellite that signaled to Americans that the country's scientific edge was dulling.

Both events drew Washington deeper into education. As the federal judiciary reshaped the racial and institutional contours of public schooling in the aftermath of *Brown*, federal funds, federal attorneys, federal laws and policies, even federal troops made their way into K–12 education, and America's long-standing if not always honorable tradition of "local control" was threatened.

Though the first U.S. satellite went into space just four months later, Sputnik angst fostered the National Defense Education Act (NDEA) of 1958, which sought via federal funds to strengthen training in math, science, and foreign languages. Most of the money went to universities, but some dollars sluiced into the K–12 system to purchase equipment, renovate classrooms, train teachers, and develop tests and guidance programs. With that revenue came new rules and restrictions.

For a while, America fretted that it had an education quality problem. *The Pursuit of Excellence*, an influential 1958 Rockefeller Brothers Fund report spearheaded by John W. Gardner, argued that the nation must earnestly strive to develop its human capital and that it could pursue excellence without forfeiting equality.

Even pre-Sputnik, Gardner's own Carnegie Corporation of New York had engaged former Harvard president James B. Conant to undertake a series of studies of K–12 education. The first of those, *The American High School Today*, appeared in 1959, urging wider propagation of "comprehensive" high schools featuring distinct "tracks" (college prep, vocational, etc.) for different types of students, who would be steered toward particular tracks according to their "aptitudes" and life plans. Far from equipping every young person with a broad, general education and thus spurring social mobility and equalizing opportunity, this view of the high school's mission would help boys and girls "adjust" to whatever hand fate had dealt them—and keep them off the streets.

Historian Jeffrey Mirel explains that Depression-era joblessness and the accompanying influx of young people into school had fostered

> a profoundly important shift in the nature and function of high schools. Increasingly, their task was custodial, to keep students *out of* the adult world (that is, out of the labor market) instead of preparing them for it. As a result, educators channeled increasing numbers of students into undemanding, nonacademic courses, while lowering standards in the academic courses that were required for

graduation. . . . In 1928, nonacademic courses accounted for about 33 percent of the classes taken by U.S. high-school students; by 1961 that number had increased to 43 percent. . . . Despite the sharp decline in the share of academic course taking, indeed, *because* of this decline, education leaders in the 1940s and 1950s declared that significant progress was being made toward equal opportunity for education. Pointing to growing high-school enrollments and graduation rates as evidence of the success of their policies, education leaders reiterated that getting diplomas in the hands of more students was far more egalitarian than having all students educated in discipline-based subject matter.[5]

A few Cassandras warned of catastrophe ahead. Perhaps the most articulate was Bestor, who said U.S. schools lacked serious content and rigor and neglected the core disciplines.[6] Yet such criticism cut little ice with practitioners and policymakers. Their student numbers and graduation rates were soaring, and Conant's much-discussed report reassured them that their school models were working fine. His book, Mirel asserts, "effectively ended the debate about the quality of American high schools for the next two decades."

Meanwhile, the country fared well enough. Despite the deepening Cold War (and, in Korea, a hot war), the economy was robust. The streets were peaceful. Eisenhower presided calmly. The education system seemed to be meeting the nation's needs.

Barely noticed at the time, however, the fifties also sowed the intellectual seeds of today's "school choice" movement. Though one can trace the idea to John Stuart Mill, even Adam Smith, on American shores the father of market-based approaches to schooling was, by common consent, the late Milton Friedman, a Nobel Prize–winning economist then at the University of Chicago. He broached this idea for the first time in a 1955 article, "The Role of Government in Education." In it, he pictured a system in which

Government, preferably local governmental units, would give each child, through his parents, a specified sum to be used solely in paying for his general education; the parents would be free to spend this sum at a school of their own choice, provided it met certain minimum standards laid down by the appropriate governmental unit. Such schools would be conducted under a variety of auspices: by private enterprises operated for profit, nonprofit institutions established by private endowment, religious bodies, and some even by governmental units.[7]

| I attended the Dayton public schools from kindergarten through ninth grade, benefiting from "Miss McCleary," "Miss Reynolds," "Mrs. Scibilia," "Miss Kramer," and a dozen other competent, decently educated, hard-working, gray-haired women who knew their stuff, taught us well, and brooked little nonsense. They were, in fact, practiced craftspeople and consummate professionals. Though they did not enjoy the status of doctors and ministers, they commanded respect as honorable practitioners of, even experts at, a vital community responsibility. So far as I could see, they did not dwell overmuch on their own "professionalism." But neither did they belong to trade unions like the thousands of blue-collar workers in Dayton's sprawling General Motors and National Cash Register plants.

Jefferson School, into whose district my family moved when I was in second grade, was a sizable K–8 neighborhood school with large classes and unabashed division of reading groups into "blue birds" and "red birds." For me and many classmates, this yielded effective-enough delivery of basic skills and knowledge without a lot of frills. I had phonics in first grade, memorized the multiplication tables in (as I recall) fourth grade, wrote lots of book reports, and absorbed plenty of history and geography from Miss Reynolds in seventh- and eighth-grade social studies. The only tests we took were the "nationally normed" kind, on which one's scores were reported according to what grade (and month) one's attainments in a given subject most closely matched.[8]

Schoolwork was by no means entirely academic. We also took art, music, and gym—and boys and girls alike sampled both home ec and shop.[9] With ample parent help, I made my share of papier-mâché dioramas, read hundreds of comic books (that's how Mrs. Scibilia rewarded kids in her third-grade class who finished their work early), and sang off-key in costumed Christmas pageants and school plays.

The teachers, though, were glad to help me learn as much as I wanted, and the system made it possible to accelerate and diversify. I took algebra one summer, seeking an academic leg up on the boarding school experience to follow, and learned touch-typing the following summer. I was a diligent student and fast learner (as well as a nerdy, unathletic, braces-and-glasses-wearing kid who would sometimes wake up early to read the encyclopedia), but Dayton offered no "gifted and talented" programs as such.

Everyone lived within a few blocks of school, and nearly everyone walked there twice a day, going home at noon to find Mom waiting with chicken-noodle soup and grilled cheese sandwiches, then back to school for the afternoon.

Once a year, my mother invited our teachers home for a relatively dressy, slightly stilted lunch. (I loved the shrimp salad and warm Parker House rolls, hated the tomato aspic.) No doubt she was doing her part to foster good teacher relations on behalf of her daughter and sons, but she and many other parents also supported the school itself in myriad ways. The active PTA held well-attended meetings and sponsored an annual "spring festival" to raise money for school extras.

Public school was not my whole life. I had Saturday or Sunday religion lessons at Temple Israel and ransacked the children's room at the nearby public library. (Particular passions included Bomba the Jungle Boy, the Hardy Boys, even Nancy Drew, and the excellent biographies published under the "Landmark" and "Signature" labels.) Far from making trouble during childhood, I was a dutiful Cub and Boy Scout—Mom was a den mother and Dad went on weekend camping trips—and spent innumerable after-school and Saturday hours at the YMCA taking gym and swimming lessons. For a time, I delivered morning papers to earn spending money, babysat, mowed lawns, and raised hamsters thinking that I might make a small fortune in animal husbandry. (Aware that hamsters were used for medical research, I eagerly phoned the Aero-Medical Laboratory at nearby Wright-Patterson Air Force Base to see what they might pay for the six or seven specimens I had accumulated and was crushed to learn that the Pentagon purchased its research hamsters by the thousand.) My father and I also went through a phase of getting "ham radio" licenses and learning Morse code before breakfast.

Summers were mostly fun, particularly the two years I spent at a rustic, canoe-centric "sleepaway camp" on the shore of Cass Lake in northern Minnesota; the family station-wagon trip "out west"; and the time my grandparents took a cousin and me to Europe by ship.

At home, we went to Saturday matinee double features (with cartoons) whenever we could and occasionally to children's concerts by the philharmonic. But television occupied only a small corner of our lives. The house had one set in the "den," and I watched a sequence of cherished programs (*Gunsmoke, Dragnet, Perry Mason*) on Saturday evenings, particularly when a sitter was in charge. During the week, however, the TV was seldom on—

save for the *Mickey Mouse Club* and occasionally the *Howdy Doody Show*. Instead, I used a flashlight to read under the covers after bedtime and built a "crystal set" radio so I could quietly listen to *The Lone Ranger* in the dark.

In September 1958, just turned fourteen, I began to walk a few blocks farther to attend ninth grade at Colonel White High School, which could have come right off Conant's pages. A standard-issue "comprehensive high school," it had something for everyone, including Friday evening football under the lights. Though the culture of the place was rah-rah, there were plenty of decent courses on offer and a smattering of first-rate teachers. You did not have to take those courses, however. One could easily enroll in a nonacademic track, and even the college-prep students could get by without much heavy lifting.

In retrospect, this Mayberry-like upbringing didn't serve everyone well. I knew that Dayton's "colored" community lived mainly on the "West Side" but scarcely noticed that the schools I attended were segregated in fact if not by law. I had no more than a couple of classmates who were black and few who were disabled (and then only mildly). Yet I and many others got a satisfactory education at relatively low cost in no-frills public schools that were rooted in their community, staffed by competent professionals, and backstopped by parents. A youngster who was able and eager could take extra (or harder) courses during the year or in summer school and could speed up his education to his heart's content, without fancy programs or specialized schools. On the other hand, few students were stretched, and not a heckuva lot was demanded of us. Our schools were not visibly "accountable" to anyone for their results—though education-minded families who could afford it might move into or out of neighborhoods according to their schools' reputations—and had no particular "standards" to follow other than preparing their pupils as they thought best for what would follow.[10]

2 | *Into the Sixties*

This chockablock decade spanned two eras in education and American life. It opened as an extension of the placid fifties, but JFK's death and the country's deepening involvement in Vietnam triggered huge changes that, as 1970 neared, racked college campuses with protests and radical ideas that percolated into high schools and beyond. The effects linger today, indeed are so pervasive that we've pretty much stopped noticing them. Above all, an enormous fraction of the senior teachers and professors of 2007, as well as those who train them and lead their schools and colleges, are men and women who came of age in the time of revolution.

From the "free speech movement" at Berkeley to Black Panthers toting rifles across the Cornell campus to the University Hall "bust" at Harvard, authority, tradition, and civility were assaulted in our educational institutions, traditional venues for the young and rebellious. (European universities underwent similar traumas.) The dual 1968 assassinations of Martin Luther King, Jr., and Robert F. Kennedy, accompanied by Nixon's election and stiffening antiwar protests, fed the flames of urban riots far beyond the campus, and deepened the sense that things were falling apart.

Though the Progressive Education Association had shut its doors in 1955, even as the Council for Basic Education was organizing, arguments still seethed in the K–12 world between "progressives" and "essentialists," with the latter viewing themselves as a beleaguered minority. They weren't wrong, E. D. Hirsch insists. "Subject matter" had been in eclipse for so long in U.S. education that its absence was no longer even felt, save by a handful of critics.[11]

Then came "open education." At the political or philosophical level, it resembled the antiauthoritarianism sweeping the campuses, and at the pedagogical level it was congenial to educators who already believed that students were better able than their teachers to determine what they needed to learn. Here is Ravitch's account:

> The open education movement . . . took off in 1967 after publication of a series of articles by Joseph Featherstone in *The New Republic*, which created a sensation among educational leaders. Featherstone [then at the Harvard Ed School, now an emeritus professor at Michi-

gan State] described British activity-centered infant schools as "a profound and sweeping revolution in English primary education." In the British primary schools, the routine of the day "is left completely up to the teacher, and the teacher, in turn, leaves options open to the children." . . . Teachers in the infant schools believed that "in a rich environment young children can learn a great deal by themselves and that most often their own choices reflect their needs."

. . . Unfortunately, many American converts to open education did not realize that the schools lauded by Featherstone enrolled children between the ages of five and seven and that they were not necessarily an appropriate model for youngsters of every age. Educators who had been raised on the tenets of progressive education hailed "open education" as the best approach for every stage of schooling. Its hallmarks were familiar to American progressives. An open school emphasized projects, activities, and student initiative. Its teachers were "facilitators" of learning, not transmitters of knowledge. . . . Multi-age groupings and individualized instruction were typical. Classrooms were arranged by activity centers, not by desks facing the teacher.[12]

Featherstone wasn't alone. A. S. Neill had published *Summerhill* in 1960, celebrating naturalistic learning and lauding schools that scrapped discipline, foreswore standards, and encouraged children to learn what and when and how they wished. By decade's end, Ivan Illich was urging the "de-schooling" of society, and Charles Silberman (in *Crisis in the Classroom*) also celebrated Britain's child-centered, "open education" methods as an antidote to the "mindlessness" of U.S. schools. In between, Paul Goodman wrote his influential *Compulsory Mis-education,* and Jonathan Kozol (in *Death at an Early Age*), Herbert Kohl (in *36 Children*), and Nat Hentoff (in *Our Children Are Dying*) deplored the dehumanizing nature of urban schools.

The revolutions of the day also altered some of the structures of public education. The sixties opened with a painful teacher strike in New York City, followed by the first-ever collective-bargaining contract for teachers (1962), then by strikes and contracts in cities across the land. Teaching began its gradual transformation from respected vocation to public employee union, and the relationship between teachers and administrators began shifting from collegiality to labor versus management.

Nor was unionization the end of New York's peculiar role as lab for new education experiments that sometimes exploded. Led by McGeorge Bundy and in the spirit of the War on Poverty, the Ford Foundation underwrote a test of "community control" of public schools in three neighborhoods, beginning in 1967–68. The project in Brooklyn's Ocean Hill–Brownsville turned ugly when local activists in charge of the governing board engaged in racialist and anti-Semitic invective while also firing thirteen teachers and six administrators for what the board said were efforts to sabotage the decentralization experiment. Union head Albert Shanker demanded due process, and an epic fight erupted between those siding with the community board and those supporting the union's argument that teachers had been denied their rights.

The United Federation of Teachers responded with a protracted strike in autumn 1968 (and Shanker went to jail for two weeks). Yet Mayor John V. Lindsay pushed ahead with school-system decentralization. Although Gotham's high schools remained under the central administration at 110 Livingston Street, the elementary and junior high schools were entrusted to several dozen locally elected district boards—an arrangement that lasted, for the most part unhappily, until Mayor Michael Bloomberg persuaded the state legislature in 2002 to vest control of the system in city hall.

Nationwide, enrollments still surged: U.S. public schools added 10 million more pupils during the 1960s and by decade's end had almost attained their present scale, while higher education appended five hundred campuses and more than doubled its student count. But the Catholic school system began its long, slow decline, shedding nearly 900,000 students and 1,500 schools between 1960 and 1970, a result of rising tuitions (occasioned mostly by a sharp decline in religious "vocations") plus the flight to the suburbs of many white ethnic families.

Even as America's largest network of private schools fell on hard times, the conceptual base for school choice grew more robust. Friedman's seminal *Capitalism and Freedom* appeared in 1962, and six years later a kindred approach to education reform floated out of the profession itself, from the pen of none other than Dean Theodore Sizer of the Harvard Graduate School of Education. In "A Poor Children's Bill of Rights," published in *Psychology Today*, he and graduate student Phillip A. Whitten urged that low-income students be provided with sizable federal "coupons" that they could redeem for education in schools of their choice—public, private, whatever.

Though the word "choice" during the sixties mainly evoked schemes for avoiding integration, by decade's end multiracial "alternative" schools, soon dubbed "magnet" schools, were established in a few cities. And in 1970 the federal Office of Economic Opportunity began casting about for locations to mount a voucher "demonstration."

On this and many other fronts, the sixties saw Uncle Sam plunge into the education enterprise as never before, centering on the provisions of four sprawling and ambitious statutes. First, 1964 brought the Economic Opportunity Act, the centerpiece of LBJ's War on Poverty and locus of such high-profile programs as Head Start, Job Corps, Upward Bound, and Volunteers in Service to America (VISTA). That same year, Congress enacted the epochal Civil Rights Act, barring racial discrimination in public facilities and the workplace and establishing the principle that federal dollars could be withheld from miscreant projects and institutions.

In 1965, Congress passed both the Elementary and Secondary Education Act (ESEA) and the Higher Education Act, directing unprecedented sums of federal aid into schools and colleges—and tying more strings from those institutions to Washington. Thus began a four-decade entanglement of mounting complexity, regulation, and interdependence cum mutual frustration—as well as the distribution of tens of billions more dollars—the latest stage of which is 2001's No Child Left Behind Act.

The federal courts, too, dug deeper into K–12 education. Although the *Brown* decision had called for the end of de jure segregation, in 1968 the Supreme Court (in *Green v. New Kent County*) struck down "freedom of choice" policies that did not lead to actual integration. As Ravitch explains, "The Court required the local school board to develop a plan that 'promises realistically to work now,' one that would produce 'a system without a "white" school and a "Negro" school, but just schools.' The Green decision was a landmark; the Court for the first time . . . specified that actual racial mixture was required to eliminate *de jure* segregation."[13] The result, in short order, was court-mandated race-based "busing plans" in many of the nation's once-segregated school systems. Backlash predictably followed—including "white flight" and further erosion of America's habits of neighborhood schooling and local control.

Coleman's Earthquake | Buried in the Civil Rights Act was an obscure mandate that yielded the decade's most consequential education study, also nominally about race but reverberating in many directions these past forty years. Congress instructed the U.S. commissioner of education—before creation of a cabinet-level department in 1980, this was the federal government's senior education post—to "conduct a survey and make a report . . . concerning the lack of availability of equality of educational opportunities for individuals by reason of race, color, religion, or national origin." Commissioner Francis W. Keppel (Sizer's predecessor as dean of the Harvard School of Education) entrusted this study to a Johns Hopkins research team co-led by the sociologist James S. Coleman, whose 737-page report was quietly released over the Fourth of July weekend in 1966 and little noticed at the time.

Once its startling findings began to be understood, however, the earth began to shake. Barely a year had passed since LBJ signed ESEA into law, promising to alter education outcomes and close achievement gaps by investing more money in schools. But here came the largest social-science study ever done, bearing word that school "inputs" had relatively little bearing on school results—and that pupil achievement depended more on race, income, social class, family background, and peer group, all of which are far harder for schools to affect and for public policy to alter.

This was stunning. As Christopher Jencks wrote in the *New Republic* a few months later, Coleman's "diagnosis of what makes students learn is at odds with almost everything legislators, school board members, and school administrators have believed in recent decades."[14] Not to mention presidents and members of Congress.

But was it true? Daniel Patrick Moynihan, newly arrived on the Harvard faculty, and several colleagues persuaded Carnegie to fund a yearlong seminar to reexamine Coleman's data. That symposium, which eventually grew to seventy-five eminent scholars and a host of graduate students on whose careers it had lasting impact, concluded that the report's core findings were essentially correct: that student achievement varied as much within schools as between them and that school differences were far less consequential than people had long assumed, particularly when placed alongside the influences of home, socioeconomic status, race, and peers.

Moynihan and the eminent statistician Frederick Mosteller later framed the significance of Coleman's study in these words:

> The findings constitute the most powerful empirical critique of the myths (the unquestioned basic assumptions, the socially received beliefs) of American education ever produced. It is the most important source of data on the sociology of American education yet to appear. It was the most complex analysis ever made of educational data in such

quantity. And, again, it is more than that. . . . [I]t is a document of profound significance for the future of racial and ethnic relations in America.[15]

While it abuses Coleman's analysis to say "schools don't matter," what he and his colleagues found was that, contrary to the assumptions of the education profession—and those behind LBJ's shiny new programs—school resources and services don't reliably translate into school results. Investing more in a school (more money, teachers, books, facilities, etc.) is no sure way to boost its pupils' achievement. So many factors shape a school's educational impacts, and so many forces influence the skills and knowledge that a child (or group of children) acquires, that the oldest and most straightforward remedy for low-performing schools, if it were a drug, would likely fail to win FDA approval on grounds that its efficacy is unproven. In Mosteller's and Moynihan's 1972 words, "Henceforth it is likely we shall find that increasing the 'supply' of education for schools that are going concerns by merely increasing gross 'inputs' will not have any great effect on gross 'outputs.' This seems clear."[16] As economist Eric Hanushek recently noted, "Up until that time, very little attention was paid to student outcomes. . . . The importance of the Coleman Report was that it changed the perspective to concentrating on student performance, and that has endured."[17]

Coleman had no way of knowing this, but today we realize that, even as he and his associates commenced their analysis, the academic achievement of U.S. high-school students was cresting—and that by the time his report was published it had begun its long downward slide to *A Nation at Risk*.

The evidence was found in Scholastic Aptitude Test (SAT) scores—a flawed indicator but the best available from those days. Though the College Board kept this news to itself until 1975, in fact 1964 marked the pinnacle of average SAT scores among college-bound U.S. high-school seniors, which slowly sagged thereafter.[18]

By 1966, in other words, the K–12 achievement time bomb had begun to tick—it did not fully explode for seventeen long years—even as an immense social-science study signaled that the path to stronger educational results was far twistier than either educators or lawmakers supposed.

| My own engagement with education during the sixties ran from callow tenth grader to callow White House aide, with several stops between.

High School | In 1959, I moved from Ohio's Colonel White High School to New Hampshire's Phillips Exeter Academy, following in my dad's footsteps. At fifteen, I had no idea that, save for holidays and vacations, I wouldn't really return to Dayton for almost four decades—and would then come back to a changed city in a very different role.

On a hot September day, my father and grandfather helped me move into a tiny, stuffy, dormered single on the fourth floor of aging Webster Hall. Then, eyes welling, they said good-bye and headed back to Ohio. I didn't know a soul.

Soon, though, I met dorm mates, classmates, and my faculty adviser, history teacher Francis L. (Frank) Broderick, who dwelt with wife and kids in a rambling apartment on the dorm's first floor and became the premier influence in my education until Pat Moynihan entered my life eight years later.

In those days, Exeter remained a boys-only institution in the classic mode of New England (and British) prep schools: jackets and ties in classroom and dining hall, six days of class a week (only till noon on Saturday, however), mandatory sports, movies in the gym on Saturday evenings (after franks and beans in the dining hall) unless there was a stilted, prearranged dance with a girls' school, bland and repetitive food (Sunday night's soup we dubbed "the vegetables of the week in review"), unbending discipline, and a sink-or-swim stance toward student performance.

I was a tenth grader ("lower middler" in academy parlance) and swiftly had to figure out what made this place tick while also figuring out what made me tick.

At fifteen, I fancied myself a bold individualist, lapping up Camus, Salinger, and Elie Wiesel and thinking overmuch about the different drummer I imagined that I heard, though in reality that meant little more than heading off to the woods with a book, orange juice, and cookies on warm Saturday afternoons while others played ball. No athlete, I struggled with crew (my father's sport), squash, and tennis before settling for desultory rounds of inept golf during fall and spring.

Intellectually, however, this was the most demanding regimen of my life—and I learned more at Exeter than anywhere else. By senior year, I was awakening at three a.m. most days to study. (A similarly driven dorm mate and I would meet to brew tea in my illicit electric pot.) "Mr. Broderick" was my adviser and mentor, and he and his kindly, no-nonsense wife, Barbara, became lasting friends and confidants. (I served as den chief for their son Tom's Cub Scout den and a decade later found myself bunking for a time in their Boston town house.) He taught me Advanced Placement (AP) Modern European History, too, with a college-level textbook, weekly research papers, and fast-moving class discussions. English teacher John Heath also labored over my prose—and any facility I possess in putting words on paper is their legacy. His senior-year course included nightly writing assignments ("a theme a day"), returned at the next class covered with his markings.

I struggled with physics and chemistry, however, and dropped an introductory Italian course because my curricular plate held more than I could chew. Exeter classes were small—a dozen, sometimes fourteen students—and mostly conducted around big wooden tables (the "Harkness Plan"), which made for universal participation and helped hardworking teachers (who also coached, advised, and stood duty in dorms) cope with all those student writing assignments. Like many elite private schools then and now, its pedagogy was more conversational and Socratic than didactic. But class size and lively argument were only part of the education package. The academy took lofty academic standards for granted and cut nobody much slack. Each term some boys flunked out and were ignominiously sent home. Our Exeter experience was also highly competitive, though we never saw an outside test other than SATs and AP exams and the school had no external "accountability" except to the parent marketplace and the demanding Ivy League colleges that most graduates went on to. It was, however, a 24/7 learning environment that offered few alternatives to studying. And the faculty abounded with gifted, passionate, hardworking instructors who had mastered their fields—many of them authored textbooks, and Broderick (who later became a Peace Corps country director and college president before deciding late in life to attend law school) wrote half a dozen well-reviewed historical monographs.

It may be that a great teacher on one end of the log and a willing student on the other are all that's needed for a world-class education. But tough standards and hard work also pay off. I was able to skip my freshman year of college thanks to AP credits earned at Exeter. Still, this blend of devoted all-round instructors, rigorous expectations, and a paternalistic education culture was not confined to upper-middle-class kids in elite prep schools. Something like it was standard practice in Catholic schools serving working-class children. And I see it working wonders today with poor and minority youngsters in the Knowledge Is Power

Program (KIPP) and other all-enveloping schools—provided, that is, that both educators and parents get past modern hang-ups about "changing the kids' culture."

Outward Bound | The summer I graduated from Exeter, I went through the brand-new Colorado Outward Bound School, high in the Rocky Mountains. Outward Bound had originated in England during World War II when celebrated educator Kurt Hahn observed that British sailors whose ships were torpedoed by German U-boats tended to give up hope and drown without struggling hard to survive. To foster strong character, self-reliance, and a sense of responsibility toward others, he founded an "outdoor education" program. Outward Bound slowly spread through the Commonwealth and, in the 1950s, caught the attention of American educator Joshua L. Miner, himself an Exeter graduate then teaching at Andover. Miner recruited allies and financial backers and, in 1962, launched the first U.S. Outward Bound program in ruggedly gorgeous terrain near the hamlet of Marble, Colorado.

Frank Broderick challenged me and a close Exeter friend to take part that first year. For most of the summer, I worked as a counselor at the Dayton YMCA day camp and mowed lawns to accumulate the Outward Bound tuition; then my friend and I crossed the heartland by Greyhound bus from Ohio to Denver. When we reached the mountains, we found ourselves amid a very odd mix of "students." About a third of us were eastern preppies. Another third were youthful offenders sent by a Denver juvenile judge to expiate their crimes and recalibrate their lives. The final third were newly recruited Peace Corp volunteers—JFK was still president—preparing for their assignment in Nepal. (Not knowing how best to train them, novice Peace Corps bureaucrats settled on replicating the topography of their future posting as faithfully as could be done within the continental United States.)

My tent mate was a young but practiced auto thief. When, at the outset of our initial four-day mountaineering expedition, he ate our entire food ration on the first day, I began to appreciate the value of "deferred gratification." Then he raided an abandoned miner's cabin for canned goods during the 48-hour "solo survival" while I dutifully plucked watercress from a burbling spring and rationed my secret roll of Life Savers. Mainly, though, for a chubby, bookish type, the Outward Bound experience—more than three straight weeks of it—was a physical challenge at every level: trudging slowly up 14,000-foot peaks (panting at the top of one, I haplessly swigged a mouthful of white gas from the wrong canteen); climbing ropes and walls, with much help from my mates; and jogging breathlessly down miles of stony road on the "marathon." It was humbling, but—as intended—getting through it intact built one's confidence.

I also began to see that there's more to education than book learning—and people who are really good at the other kinds of learning deserve respect, too. I was used to being an intellectual leader, but those who distinguished themselves at Outward Bound had physical prowess, street smarts, character, stamina, and the ability to forge and lead a group. These skills have societal value, too, of a sort not often tallied by contemporary "school accountability" schemes.

College | I entered Harvard that September (1962), continuing my privileged, parent-funded education in elite institutions and beginning what turned out to be nearly seven years in Cambridge. Arriving on campus with "sophomore standing," I had immediately to select my major: U.S. history. Studying, however, was not my top priority. Finally liberated from the discipline of home, boarding school, and Outward Bound, I took a liking to gin-and-tonics, dated some Radcliffe and Wellesley students, and had my share of good times. But mostly what I did was volunteer. At eighteen, I was a budding social reformer.

A year earlier, Jane Jacobs had published *The Death and Life of Great American Cities*. My first year of college brought *The Other America*, Michael Harrington's passionate exposé of U.S. poverty, and Herbert J. Gans's *The Urban Villagers*, documenting the human damage inflicted by urban renewal efforts in Boston's West End, just across the river. President Kennedy, after admonishing us to ask what we could do for our country, had launched the Peace Corps to help the needy in other lands. And I was ready to pitch in.

That first year, I spent Friday evenings fetching and carrying—and bandaging and occasionally suturing—in Boston City Hospital's frenetic emergency room, and leading a group of housing-project boys one afternoon a week at an old-line settlement house in East Cambridge led by the charismatic Elsa Baldwin, a chain-smoking, tireless, compassionate socialist, community organizer, and unbending poverty warrior. The umbrella for this and more was Harvard's Phillips Brooks House Association (PBHA), the country's oldest and largest student-led volunteer organization.

In time, I found myself heading one of the PBHA programs, then—pushing against conventional wisdom for perhaps the first time in my life—asking why we undergraduates couldn't do on our own at least as well as the professionals were doing. At Roosevelt Towers, a Cambridge housing project largely outside the purview of existing tutoring and recreation programs, a bunch of us persuaded the manager to lend us a cellar room, then went door-to-door recruiting families for an ever-expanding list of activities. We hustled grant dollars from local foundations, hired our own part-time social worker to lead "training groups" for volunteers, devised summer programs, and with all the smug self-assuredness of Ivy League youth were soon running a sizable operation.

The Roosevelt Towers experience helped to transform PBHA from a place that supplied volunteers for other people's institutions into a collection of self-propelled programs. In keeping with the slow radicalization of the era, it also helped turn a cadre of Harvard undergraduates from traditional do-gooders into would-be change agents. And it left a lasting mark on me. I found myself leading others, administering complex projects, analyzing and writing about them, raising money, and challenging university administrators and adult professionals. I was brash and cocky, for sure, and rubbed some folks the wrong way. But I also found that I was pretty good at what I was doing—and enormously liked doing it.

Sometimes I even attended class. Harvard had a peerless faculty, of course, and I took some fine lecture courses from the likes of Oscar Handlin, Robert McCloskey, and Paul Freund. One day, Edward Banfield brought in as guest lecturer to his Urban Problems course a young assistant labor secretary from Washington named Moynihan to talk about LBJ's new War on Poverty—my first glimpse of the man who would become my most important mentor and teacher. But few professors ever knew my name—the graduate-student "tutors" did—and I didn't do much to capture their attention. My grades were mainly Bs. My parents expected me to apply to law school and follow grandfather and father into the family firm in Dayton.

Yet that was not to be. Education was beckoning. Besides tutoring Cambridge and Boston youngsters, I had helped teach summer school (back at Exeter) while in college; I was seized by the passion of education tracts by

Kozol and others; Kennedy was dead (a stunningly emotional time on the Harvard campus); and Johnson had placed education front and center on the national agenda, insisting that it was the surest and most direct way to end poverty, combat urban blight, and equalize opportunity in America. That sounded like something I needed to be part of.

3 | *Becoming an Educator*

The summer I graduated from college (1965), I began the Master of Arts in Teaching program at the Harvard Ed School, specializing in social studies, in which field Massachusetts certified me as a secondary teacher. After a hasty summer of practice teaching, I was placed at Newton High School as a full-time intern teacher for the 1965–6 school year. Despite my previous tutoring, camp counseling, and summer classroom gigs, this was my first big solo teaching job. And I wasn't much good at it.

I had just turned twenty-one. My students were all seniors, mostly eighteen-year-olds from the wrong side of the (Newton) tracks. Although this was (and remains) one of America's most esteemed public schools in a predominantly upper-middle-class, education-obsessed Boston suburb, as well as a regular research venue and practice-teaching site for Harvard educationists, it was also a Conant-style comprehensive high school. Which meant that, besides a strong honors track for bright students (such as my twin cousins, also seniors that year), it had a full measure of less able, less motivated, and less fortunate youngsters whom it accommodated in different courses. My four classes were part of "curriculum II," which by twelfth grade meant that my students were mostly putting in time until they could grab their diplomas and head off to work, the army, or the nearby community college. Many of the boys were bigger, and nearly all of them tougher, than I. The girls misbehaved less, but that didn't mean their minds were focused on the Problems of American Democracy course that I struggled to teach.

It had no set syllabus or textbook, and I had almost no experience. I was assigned a "master teacher" whom I could consult for tips (but who otherwise ignored me). The "house master," a suave and well-turned-out Iowan who desperately wanted to be taken for a proper Bostonian—he lived on Beacon Hill and was even named Adams—was on call when, as often happened, I encountered problems with what educators politely term "classroom management." But I was left to devise my own curriculum and pedagogy. Though "P.A.D." served as the traditional senior-year civics course, nobody much cared what I taught or what, if anything, my students learned. And there were no external exams or other ways of finding out.

Sometimes my classes went okay. The Social Studies Department's book room was well stocked, and I stayed up late many evenings in my little Cambridge apartment, devising ambitious lesson plans. But often as not, between discipline problems and overwrought (or underdeveloped) instructional notions, things slid off track. One memorable day, teaching *Lord of the Flies* and nearing the part where the marooned boys cut off the pig's head, place it atop a stake, and engage in a form of primitive worship, I drove to an old-fashioned Italian butcher shop in Boston's North End and bought an honest-to-God pig's head—the gnarliest, bristliest, one in the store. Then I found a stick somewhere. After horrifying my faculty colleagues by briefly stashing this chunk of porcine anatomy in the teachers' lounge refrigerator (where else in a high school could one store a large piece of raw meat?), I triumphantly introduced my "prop" to my students. Alas, the lesson I had planned to impart was quite lost upon these flabbergasted teenagers who couldn't stop muttering that "Mr. Finn brought a pig's head to school."

I came to understand that teaching is hard and that being smart and well educated doesn't necessarily mean one will be effective at it. I also learned vividly that even the most acclaimed schools have "kids left behind," youngsters getting an inferior education while their age mates get a good one. For most of my students, I was the third consecutive "intern" teacher in their three years of high-school social studies. They never had an experienced instructor in this subject. The education system that had served me well as a student in Dayton just a few years earlier was mistreating these kids in Newton. Someone needed to make more of a fuss about it.

Part of what I learned that year were the simple classroom realities that ed schools don't dwell on but novice teachers must figure out: how an instructional gimmick can overpower the lesson plan, how little gets learned if the room is out of control, and so on. But my big discovery, even as successful teachers won my lasting respect, was that "retail" work in the classroom was not where I belonged over the long haul. If I were personally going to make a difference in American education—especially in relation to its hoary practices, outdated assumptions, and mixed-bag performance— I would have to find a perch in the wholesale world. Yet as Finance Committee chairman Russell Long was wont to remark during my later stint on the Senate staff, even a blind hog finds an acorn now and then; even a mediocre instructor can sometimes enjoy a bit of the gratification that keeps good teachers going. Thirty-five years later, one of my Newton students tracked me down via the Internet to tell me that I had changed her life and that she had been trying forever to locate me so that she could thank me.

Ed School | After my challenging bout with Newton High School, I returned to the Harvard Ed School and spent the next three years on campus, first completing the MAT degree, then a design-your-own doctoral program in education policy. As in college, I encountered some superb professors and fine courses—and plenty of nonsense.

For all the talk of equality, civil rights, and urban problems, elite schools of education such as Harvard's were far more engaged with public education in leafy suburbs like Newton and Brookline than with the inner-city schools they fretted about. An odd schizophrenia separated many professors' stated concerns from where they plied their trade.

Faculty members and students alike were buzzing with the fashionable nostrums that dominated U.S. education discourse in the late sixties, including Featherstone's fascination with Leicestershire's "infant schools." These hewed to the recommendations of the Plowden Report, a comprehensive look at British primary schooling that was solidly grounded in Piaget's notions of child development and urged greater curricular freedom and heightened attention to individual differences.

Freedom and individual differences were in the air. That's also the message that educators had long drawn (none too accurately) from the teachings of Dewey and his followers. And that's what fired the imagination of "open" educators and "de-schoolers," as well as the more alarming moral relativists and "values clarifiers" who insisted that it was not the proper role of educators to impart morals or virtues to children, but rather to help them "clarify" their innate values.

I succumbed to a bit of this, but it wasn't my main interest. A brilliant instructor named Richard Light did his best to teach me statistics. Education anthropologist John Herzog invited me to join his research projects—which actually dealt with urban schools. In a memorable seminar with political scientist Martha Derthick, I undertook an ambitious historical study of rising Irish influence in Boston's public schools over several decades. To help me gauge which school committee members were indeed Irish at various points in time, I recruited a veteran janitor at Phillips Brooks House, where I was moonlighting as graduate student adviser. He reviewed endless lists of names for me, ticking off those that qualified as

Irish in the ear of an Irishman. I proudly turned in my lengthy and, I thought, sophisticated analysis to Derthick, only to have her observe that I had reached precisely the opposite conclusions from what my data showed. I rewrote the paper, while absorbing a lesson about the precariousness of social-science research.

My most life-changing event started with repeatedly parking myself outside the office of Daniel P. Moynihan, the new director of the Harvard-MIT Joint Center for Urban Studies. Perhaps the nation's foremost "urbanologist" (a neologism of the day), he appeared on the cover of *Time* magazine in the summer of 1967, aged forty, as Newark, Chicago, and other cities endured riots and arson. But he was also a recent refugee from the Johnson administration, which he had left amid sparks struck by his celebrated, controversial, and much-misrepresented report on "the Negro family."

An ed school professor at the time (later stints at Harvard found him in the Government Department), Moynihan as yet had no doctoral students—and I desperately wanted him to be my adviser. The only real requirement of my design-your-own degree program was to persuade a senior professor to okay it. I suspect that Pat finally judged it less bothersome to consent than to keep putting me off. In any case, that decision yielded an extraordinary if sometimes difficult mentor over a fifteen-year period, three riveting jobs, and an unparalleled berth on the U.S. policy train through the 1970s.

It also yielded an immediate window onto one of the most stimulating education events on campus: the Carnegie-funded Coleman seminar that Moynihan and Mosteller were leading along with Thomas Pettigrew, Sizer, and other Harvard professors. The attendance roster reads like a directory of movers and shakers in U.S. education policy from the sixties to today. I was more observer than participant, but for a graduate student to place even a toe into those policy waters was exhilarating—and made me want to wade deeper.

Meanwhile, I was also moonlighting, both to earn tuition dollars—my parents still helped with room and board—and because being a graduate student doesn't really qualify as full-time work. I oversaw and advised PBHA's undergraduate leaders and also worked part-time for the Cambridge "community action program," the local battalion of LBJ's assault on poverty. (In 1970, Moynihan would expose the internal contradictions of that program in a seminal book, *Maximum Feasible Misunderstanding*.)

In 1966, while teaching in Newton, a couple of grad-student colleagues and I had persuaded Sizer that Harvard should apply for a grant from the

Office of Economic Opportunity to run an Upward Bound program. Another element of the War on Poverty, it sought to take "deprived" high-school pupils and boost them into college via a summer immersion experience followed by tutoring and counseling during the school year.

Our proposal succeeded, and in short order I found myself co-leading the hastily cobbled-together project with several dozen low-income Cambridge kids. The summer phase on the Harvard campus was as energized, imaginative, and earnest as such things can be, and we did our best to keep up with its adolescent participants when they returned to public school in the fall. Several of us formed lasting ties with our tutees and mentees. But as the Coleman seminar was affirming, counterforces at work on nearly all these kids were stronger than the modest propulsion we supplied. Our Upward Bound teens lived with tattered families, poverty, drugs, gangs, crummy schools, early pregnancy, and more. By the time we got to them, they were already burdened by the disorder that many faced at home and in the neighborhood, as well as years of mediocre schooling. We didn't do them any harm—but I don't think we transformed any lives.

This early "mugging by reality" cast the first shadow over my romance with the Great Society assumption that big federal "social" programs could vanquish poverty, redirect education, and change people's fate on a large and lasting scale. It also accelerated my transformation from idealist to troublemaker.

White House Bound | Soon after Nixon's 1968 election victory, his associates contacted Moynihan about a senior role on their new White House team. On December 10, the transition office announced that Pat would join the administration as "assistant to the President for urban affairs." He promptly began to plan his return to Washington, surely relishing the personal vindication, albeit this time in a GOP administration. By Christmas, when I flew off to tour the game parks of Kenya and Tanzania with a close friend—a fellow Outward Bound alum—who was there with the Peace Corps, I wondered whether Pat might ask me to tag along.

Our relationship had deepened over the previous eighteen months. Besides taking a couple of seminars from him and auditing the Coleman sessions, I served as a teaching assistant in his undergraduate course and began to attend movie nights and other well-lubricated social events at Pat and Liz's big house in the lovely, tree-lined faculty precinct of Francis Avenue.

(The John Kenneth Galbraiths lived a few doors down the street, the Nathan Glazers a couple of blocks away.)

I had also completed my doctoral course work. What lay ahead were a "qualifying paper" and dissertation, obligations that now competed with my mounting desire to leave revolutionary Cambridge and immerse myself in larger affairs.

Soon after my return from Africa, Pat did indeed ask me to join his White House team, but—he was still my adviser, after all—we agreed that I would first complete my qualifying paper. It hurt to picture the heady goings-on in the West Wing during the early weeks of the new administration, but I kept my part of the agreement, wrote the requisite paper, and, in early March, packed the contents of my small grad-student apartment into my red Chevy Nova and sped down the interstate to Washington. With a few interruptions, I've never really left.

Part II | *The Seventies*

This was American education's most painful decade. Perhaps it was fated to be, considering how the whole country ached from Watergate, the wrenching end of the Vietnam War, stagflation, gas lines, Jimmy Carter's malaise, and Soviet conquests hither and yon around the globe.

"To be blunt," *U.S. News* education correspondent Thomas Toch wrote in a perceptive 1991 book, "the 1970's left public education in a shambles." [1]

School performance was deteriorating. Even before the College Board revealed the long-term sag in SAT scores in 1975, the customers were complaining. [2] Employers grumped that the high-school graduates they were hiring lacked basic skills. Remediation crept into higher education (particularly after the City University of New York adopted "open admissions" in 1970), seeking to equip new—often "nontraditional"—college students with the literacy and mathematical facility that they should have acquired in school. Military brass and drill sergeants protested that recruits to the "all-volunteer army" (the draft ended in 1973) couldn't grasp training materials written at the ninth-grade level.

The stakes rose, too, as larger economic forces buffeted America, including stiffening competition from Germany and Japan, the OPEC oil embargo, and blue-collar jobs starting to move offshore. This inevitably echoed back into the schools, both because the domestic U.S. workforce needed to become better educated and because we have a long-standing if naïve tradition of expecting our schools to solve just about every societal problem—and thereby letting others off the hook.

Good education data were scarce, comprehensive achievement statistics scarcer still. The most-watched indicators had to do with "attainment": getting more special-needs kids access to more school services, seeing more minority youngsters enroll in college, arranging for more black students to attend the same schools as white students, and so forth. Though the National Assessment of Educational Progress (NAEP) began in 1969, its original design—the result of hard-won compromises with state education chiefs and other powerful public-education interests—intentionally veiled academic performance trends and comparisons.

Yet anecdotal evidence of weak achievement was mounting, and in the hands of a few plucky analysts, such as Barbara Lerner, some of it was more than anecdotal. Signs that some high-school graduates could not read their own diplomas, much less handle the challenges of jobs and college, also prompted one legislature after another to enact "minimum competency" requirements: mandatory basic-skills tests that high-school students had to pass before they could graduate.

As Chris Pipho recounted that sequence,

> Minimum competency testing (MCT) burst onto the state education scene with great excitement in the mid-1970s. An education reform mandated by noneducators, it was based on the notion that a minimum level of achievement should be established for the basic skills, and all students should be expected to attain this level of competency to move through school and graduate.
>
> At the time, the idea was viewed with alarm by educators because it seemed to call into question the teacher's authority over classroom instruction. Policymakers viewed this concern with suspicion, assuming teachers were simply opposed to teaching basic skills. Some legislators then pushed the idea even harder, saying MCT laws would "at least force teachers to teach something." Teachers countered by saying that a failing student would not be taught to read by a test, and that teacher judgment over instructional matters was crucial.
>
> But policymakers were so sold on the idea of minimum competency testing that they moved quickly, often with only brief hearings, to pass simplistic one-page bills and state board resolutions. Between 1975 and 1978, more than 30 states enacted MCT mandates.[3]

Despite such legislative bustle, which may be seen as foreshadowing today's standards-based reform efforts (and educators' wariness toward external performance gauges), academic achievement ranked low on America's education priority list during the 1970s. Other matters drew far more attention, above all the extension of new rights and services to groups that, with varying degrees of justification, laid ever greater claims on K–12 education.

The Education for All Handicapped Children Act became law in 1975, conferring on disabled youngsters the federally assured right to "a free public education" in the "least restrictive environment" and inaugurating the age of "special" education throughout the land. It created much-needed opportunities for kids who had been unwelcome in school, commonly kept at home (or institutionalized) by their families, and who, when enrolled at all, were frequently denied the extra help that many needed. Like all such initiatives, however, this law (now the Individuals with Disabilities Education Act) also brought new rules, procedures, disputes, and controversies as well as the temptation (among educators, parents, attorneys, etc.) to classify as "disabled" millions of children who might have been better served by simpler interventions, such as more adroit teaching or stronger discipline. When signing this measure, President Gerald R. Ford shared his own misgivings in a statement noting that "[T]his bill promises more than the federal government can deliver, and its good intentions could be thwarted by the many unwise provisions it contains."[4]

The Bilingual Education Act dates to 1968. At first it was permissive, conferring smallish federal sums on local "demonstration" programs. This changed dramatically after 1970, when the Office for Civil Rights of the Department of Health, Education, and Welfare (HEW) determined, in Diane Ravitch's words, "that discrimination against children who were 'deficient in English language skills' violated Title VI of the Civil Rights Act."[5] This prompted federal guidelines (affirmed by the Supreme Court in 1975) that required school systems to mount special bilingual programs to "rectify the language deficiency" of non-English-speaking pupils. Besides placing new curricular, instructional, and budgetary challenges before school districts, once this mandate was interpreted by advocates and then by Washington to require continuing instruction of children in their native languages, it gradually reversed the century-old understanding that a core duty of public education was rapidly to transform immigrants into full-fledged, English-fluent Americans.

Title IX of the Higher Education Act, mandating gender equality in college sports, became law (with Nixon's signature) in 1972. Two years later, Congress passed the Women's Educational Equity Act, based on an Office of Education report alleging that women were being subjected to educational "exploitation and exclusion" akin to that experienced by "ethnic minorities, the handicapped and the poor."[6]

Federally sanctioned "affirmative action" spread through universities, public employers, and, via mandates affecting firms that did business with government, private employers, too. In 1978 the Supreme Court handed down its *Bakke* decision, which said—never mind the civil rights legislation of the previous fourteen years and the "color blindness" of *Brown*—that race *could* play a role in college admissions decisions.

Meanwhile, the desegregation steamroller continued its ponderous flattening of the K–12 terrain, causing drastic changes in many southern communities and now also reshaping education in northern cities that had never practiced de jure separation.[7] Here, too, color blindness gave way to color consciousness. As Ravitch explains,

> By 1972, the kind of racial segregation that had existed before the *Brown* decision had nearly been eliminated. . . . However, this standard was no longer relevant. [The new standard] . . . redefined "segregation" as racial imbalance or a predominantly black school. . . . [T]he *Swann* decision (1971) endorsed the use of racial redistribution as a remedy for previous unconstitutional segregation. There was no reason why the logic of *Swann* should be limited to southern school systems, and the *Keyes* decision in 1973 established that it would not be. . . . Having determined that segregation existed "in a substantial portion of the district," the Court declared that Denver was unconstitutionally operating a dual system of *de jure* segregated schools. Denver's claims that racial concentration resulted from its neighborhood school policy . . . were rejected.[8]

Soon the nation's urban school systems were burdened by court-ordered "busing" plans meant to combine black and white students in the same schools. Coleman declared in 1975 that his report was being misused to justify policies that actually fostered "white flight," but the buses rolled on, as did the backlash, which extended to some unlikely places. Although Chief Justice Earl Warren noted in *Brown* that segregation had ended in Boston's public schools in 1855, Judge Arthur Garrity's infamous 1974 ruling, insisting that the "Athens of America" take bold steps to integrate its school system, bred racial rancor and violence—and the exodus of many white families for private and suburban alternatives. Today, Boston's public school enrollment is 86% minority, compared with 35 percent when Garrity issued his decision—and is less than half its 1970 size.

As white students exited, as minority interests came to dominate many urban school systems, as demands for more services and special considerations poured in from all sides, and as teachers unionized, the civic and business elites that had long concerned themselves with public education in those communities tended to turn away. They no longer felt welcome in the urban education crucible, they didn't much like getting yelled at, and their own children and grandchildren were likely to be in school elsewhere.

In Washington, too, the driving theme of education policy through-out the decade was the quest for "equity" in myriad forms, as one group after another sought redress for real or imagined injustices—or simply to improve its status, visibility, or funding prospects. The Nixon and Ford administrations offered unexpectedly little resistance to all this, and the Democratic Party, well past its southern-based foot-dragging on civil rights and increasingly in political thrall to minority (and women's) as well as teacher-union causes, commanded the House of Representatives and held a majority of the Senate for the entire time.

ESEA and the Higher Education Act were dutifully reauthorized every six or seven years, and each renewal brought more programs, additional mandates, the promise of more federal money, and the harder-to-keep promise that schools and colleges would solve even more of society's problems.

When Jimmy Carter came into office in 1977, aided in that quest by the National Education Association's first-ever presidential endorsement, the hydra-headed equity movement was joined by a more energized, better organized, and hungrier public-education "establishment" than Washington had previously seen.

Yet money hunger doesn't fully explain why teachers unionized and joined other education interest groups in demanding more from the public fisc. It was a time of profound change in virtually every sector of American life and nowhere more so than in the schools. Ill-prepared (and largely white) faculties were expected to deal with a host of new and different students, many with special needs and unfamiliar demands, and to keep kids in school even when their home lives pushed in the opposite direction. The conflicts in urban communities often walked right through the school (and school board) doors, and those who previously had little voice frequently proved demanding and disrespectful. All this transformed the teacher's work in powerful ways that school-system bureaucracies were none too skilled in helping their staffs to address. Union membership offered sanctuary and solidarity plus, for some, the added support and training that they craved.

Simple demographics posed a further challenge as well as possible job losses for teachers. The baby boom having passed, U.S. public schools *shed* 4 million pupils between 1970 and 1980—while the beleaguered Catholic system lost another million and a quarter students and shut more than 1,700 schools.

The unions grew more militant as well as political. The Bureau of Labor Statistics tallied a thousand strikes involving a million teachers between 1975 and 1980 alone. "Indeed," writes Toch, "when Philadelphia's 22,000 teachers manned picket lines for fifty days in 1981–82, it was the eighth time they had shut down the city's schools in thirteen years."[9] Besides inconveniencing the children and families immediately affected, this pattern of behavior—more like that of steel- or autoworkers than doctors and lawyers, even nurses and social workers—undermined the notion that teachers are, and should be viewed as, education "professionals." Though Americans continued, by and large, to revere their own kids' instructors, teachers as a collective were positioning themselves as a self-absorbed adult interest group.

And every year brought more of them. Even as student cadres shrank, America's teacher corps added 200,000 members during the seventies, an expansion made possible because school spending surged from $3,849 per pupil in 1969–70 to $5,214 (in constant dollars) a decade later.

Although anxiety about pupil achievement had little impact on congressional actions, it led states to adopt the aforementioned minimum-competency tests that anticipated today's "standards-based" reforms. The seventies also brought much talk, more writing, and a bit of movement on the school-choice front. Part of the impetus was to test the heretical notions of Milton Friedman, Theodore Sizer, Christopher Jencks, and (in 1978) John Coons and Stephen Sugarman by equipping poor parents with the purchasing power to select schools that suited them. And part was to rescue Catholic schools from creeping oblivion. Noisy showdowns in Congress yielded little help for private schools, but the Office of Economic Opportunity launched its voucher "demonstration" project between 1972 and 1977 in the dusty precincts of Alum Rock, California. Unfortunately, it was so bobtailed that it demonstrated very little. Limited to a handful of schools, all public, it was far from a road test for vouchers as Milton Friedman pictured them.

4 | *White House Days*

I presented myself at the iron gates of the White House on a chilly March day in 1969, eager to start my heady new job as staff assistant to the president of the United States. This was a big deal for a twenty-four-year-old graduate student—and at $10,000 per year I was also going to earn considerably more than before.

My balloon wrinkled a bit when it turned out that nobody had told the Secret Service to let me in—and nobody had readied the payroll paperwork, either. The frenetic Moynihan office reacted along the lines of "Oh, it's you, we were wondering when you might turn up." And instead of sitting me down to craft national policy, Pat's secretary promptly dispatched me to fetch his shirts from a nearby laundry. (Liz and their three kids remained in Cambridge during his White House stint; hence he had nobody around to help with the nuisances of daily life.)

In time, I did get to assist with policy development, but at first I functioned mostly as general aide to Moynihan: drafting correspondence, briefing him before meetings, doing research for his speeches, writings, and memoranda, and helping a bit with logistics of the cabinet-level Urban Affairs Council, whose director he was.

Pat's happy few were first-rate. Deputy Stephen Hess had been an Eisenhower aide and, in the years since, has been one of Washington's keenest analysts of politics, the presidency, and the press. Longtime Moynihan pal Leonard "Story" Zartman came down from Eastman Kodak. Attorney John Price arrived from the Ripon Society. Also plunging in were two recent Harvard grads and Moynihangers-on, even younger than I: Christopher DeMuth (now president of the American Enterprise Institute) and Richard Blumenthal (now the attorney general of Connecticut). Our summer interns included Harvard undergraduate Frank Raines, later a Rhodes Scholar, who went on to distinguished service as Bill Clinton's budget director and a troubled stint as head of Fannie Mae.

During his first year in the Oval Office, Nixon organized his domestic aides into rival fiefs that jousted for the president's attention and his blessing for their proposals. In addition to Moynihan's moderate-to-liberal "urban affairs" team, the economist Arthur Burns, who carried the august title of "counselor to the president" (and would move on a year later to chair the

Federal Reserve Board), assembled a band of more traditional conservatives, including Martin Anderson, Roger Freeman, and Richard Burress. Investment banker Peter Flanigan and a couple of sharp lieutenants focused chiefly on business-type concerns. And presidential counsel John Ehrlichman and a team of smart thirty-something campaign veterans, mostly lawyers new to Washington, often had the president's ear when the jousting ended.

Moynihan's great interest was welfare reform, and this was the territory where he had the most dramatic influence on administration policy. Nixon's "Family Assistance Plan" was, in effect, a national guaranteed-income scheme, an astounding proposal from a putatively conservative GOP White House that was supposed to shun Great Society–style schemes. (Pat responded that equipping the poor with purchasing power was a far cry from hiring organizers to disrupt communities and redistribute political power.)

Yet nearly every domestic issue had some tie-in to "urban affairs" and thus made its way to Moynihan's desk—which of course he relished, eagerly inserting his nimble typing fingers into innumerable policy pies.

My main assignment, besides all-purpose helper, was staffing the education issues coming down the pike—and those that the White House dispatched up the highway. Topics ranged from the future of Head Start, to how best to finance public and private schools (Procter & Gamble chairman—and former defense secretary—Neil McElroy chaired a blue-ribbon commission on that knotty matter), to the spreading plague of campus unrest.

Education occupied no lofty perch on Richard Nixon's personal priority list. He didn't pay a lot of direct attention to the federal government's relatively small role in a very large territory that he believed was the proper work of states and communities. Sometimes, as with the sticky wicket of southern school desegregation, education policy commanded his notice, but mainly he focused on international affairs and economics. Insofar as he and his closest advisers dwelt on domestic social policy, reforming welfare got most of their attention. In late May 1969, however, the president followed Moynihan's suggestion and formed an education subcommittee of the Urban Affairs Council, chaired by HEW Secretary Robert Finch and filled with cabinet heavy hitters.

A week later, they spent an evening with Moynihan on the presidential yacht. I wasn't invited aboard but helped prepare their briefing book, which ranged across the landscape from the philosophy of liberal education to the "dusty, smelly" condition of city schools, from the policy implications of the Coleman Report to the appropriate level of federal higher-education spending.

Nothing much resulted from the cruise other than plenty more staff work, but by fall it seemed that the education subcommittee was finally ready to set a policy agenda. The staff churned out more memos. In early November, however, an earthquake hit: Nixon restructured the White House domestic apparatus.

The contending-power-centers approach no longer suited him and his inner circle. The Urban Affairs Council would continue on paper but was superseded by a new Domestic Council under the direction of Ehrlichman, who emerged as de facto policy czar. Moynihan was promoted to cabinet rank and acquired the lofty "counselor to the president" title but was more or less stripped of staff support and eased outside the chain of command. Wrote Moynihan biographer Douglas Schoen:

> There are a number of possible explanations of Nixon's reorganization. First, he had been disturbed by the conflict that had developed over the formulation of the Family Assistance Program, and Ehrlichman could be expected to make policy making more bureaucratic and to perform in a low key. Second, Moynihan's UAC had been effective in the early days of the administration in developing policy innovations such as welfare reform and Burns's revenue-sharing proposal, but now Nixon sought a more broadly based body that would encompass all domestic policy and be responsible for the implementation of policy already formulated. The reorganization indicated that Nixon considered that the bulk of the innovation for his first term was over and that it was time now to put the new programs into effect. Finally, the reorganization was testament to the growing influence of H. R. Haldeman and John Ehrlichman in the White House power structure.[10]

With other Moynihan aides (and junior staffers from other policy fiefs), I was ushered into Ehrlichman's office and told that, if I wanted to stay, I would henceforth be part of his consolidated operation, assigned specifically to Edward L. Morgan, a youngish, Arizona-bred lawyer and trusted Ehrlichman lieutenant who would assume responsibility for education and much else.

I liked the quick, droll Morgan and wasn't ready to exit the White House, whose occupants were only beginning to focus on my chief policy interest. But I worked out a side agreement with Ehrlichman and Moynihan that allowed me also to continue assisting Pat with matters of mutual interest and projects where he wanted help.

During his and my remaining year at the White House, that included ample attention to federal education policy, the twin centerpieces of which were Nixon's dual messages to Congress on education, dispatched to Capitol Hill in March 1970.

Both emerged from "working groups" convened by Morgan and consisting of assistant-secretary-level folks from HEW, Labor, and other cabinet agencies, plus Moynihan and other units within the Executive Office of the President (e.g., Science Adviser Lee DuBridge). Most of the staff work was done by me, by capable careerists in the education and manpower section of the Office of Management and Budget (called the Bureau of the Budget until 1970), and by the staff of Education Commissioner James E. Allen, Jr. (Formerly New York State's education chief, the earnest, pensive, proud Allen was fired in June 1970 because he disagreed with the White House on both Vietnam and school desegregation. The following year he and his wife tragically perished in a plane crash while touring the Grand Canyon.)

Allen's top aide was Gregory R. Anrig, who went on to a brilliant career as Massachusetts commissioner of education and head of the Educational Testing Service. We became friends as well as colleagues—his wife, Charlotte, was a terrific cook and warm hostess—and devised an active "back channel" between the Office of Education and the White House that kept papers flowing and problems getting addressed even when our superiors were at odds over one thing or another. After Allen's dismissal, Greg wanted out of Washington, and I had the pleasure of introducing him to Frank Broderick, then chancellor of the University of Massachusetts at Boston, which led to a campus post that enabled the Anrigs to relocate to Massachusetts and Greg to relaunch his career.

Schools | The working group on K–12 education cranked up in autumn 1969, partly in response to the House of Representatives appropriating $1 billion more for education than the administration wanted. Knowing they could not fight something with nothing, Finch, Allen, and Moynihan sought to speed development of a pro-active education policy statement in advance of the Senate appropriations hearing. They had less than two weeks.

As often happens in government, even at the top, this deadline was missed—and then some. Congress went on to add the additional billion to the fiscal 1970 Labor-HEW appropriation bill, and Nixon went on, in January, to veto it. (This was, notes Oxford historian Gareth Davies, the first time any president vetoed the education appropriation—and the first of seven Nixon-Ford vetoes of that measure over an eight-year period, most of which Congress overrode.) [11] Early in 1970, the White House and Congress agreed on a revised figure that was just $600 million more than the administration wanted, but the big Washington education story was that Capitol Hill Democrats (and more than a few Republicans) were more generous to poor kids and their teachers than the tight-fisted Nixon.

The White House craved to change that impression, and one way to do so was to redirect attention from how much was being spent on education to how effective it was. This impulse meshed perfectly with Pat's desire to focus the country on educational outcomes à la Coleman and what it would take to strengthen them.

By March, the president's belated message to Congress on K–12 education was ready. Its centerpiece was a Moynihan-inspired proposal to create a "National Institute of Education" (NIE) within HEW to "begin the serious, systematic search for new knowledge needed to make educational opportunity truly equal." Its mandate was to "set priorities for research and experimentation projects and . . . develop criteria and measures for enabling localities to assess educational achievement and for evaluating particular educational programs."

Thirty-five years later, a new R&D initiative seems no big deal, scarcely even deserving of presidential attention, but in fact the NIE proposal was the tip of an important conceptual shift and hoped-for policy breakthrough—as well as a shrewd way to highlight education's bang rather than its bucks. As the president put it, in words drafted by Moynihan,

> We must stop letting wishes color our judgments about the educational effectiveness of many special compensatory programs,
> when . . . there is growing evidence that most of them are not yet measurably improving the success of poor children in school. . . . We must stop congratulating ourselves for spending nearly as much money on education as does the entire rest of the world . . . when we are not

getting as much as we should out of the dollars we spend. . . . Apart from the general public interest in providing teachers an honorable and well-paid professional career, there is only one important question to be asked about education: *What do the children learn?* [12]

Less than four years after Coleman's big report, his central finding had made its way, via his premier "reanalyst," to the nation's foremost bully pulpit and had become the basis for a substantial White House initiative. "What makes a 'good' school?" the president's message asked rhetorically.

> The old answer was a school that maintained high standards of plant and equipment; that had a reasonable number of children per classroom; whose teachers had good college and often graduate training. . . . This was a fair enough definition so long as it was assumed that there was a direct connection between "school characteristics" and the actual amount of learning that takes place in a school. Years of educational research, culminating in the Equal Educational Opportunity Survey of 1966 have, however, demonstrated that this direct, uncomplicated relationship does not exist. [13]

And yet, observed Nixon in words italicized for emphasis in the White House document,

> [W]e know that something does make a difference. The outcome of schooling—what children learn—is profoundly different for different groups of children and different parts of the country. Although we do not seem to understand just what it is in one school or school system that produces a different outcome from another, one conclusion is inescapable: *We do not yet have equal educational opportunity in America.* [14]

Three decades before George W. Bush put the "achievement gap" and the "soft bigotry of low expectations" indelibly onto the national agenda with his No Child Left Behind Act, Richard M. Nixon was deploring the same thing, linking equity concerns to weak academic performance, decrying the education system's proclivity to focus on inputs rather than results, and insisting that schools instead be judged on the basis of their students' achievement. He even demanded that the NIE devise "new measures of educational output" by which "accountability" could be assured. "School administrators and school teachers alike are responsible for their performance," the president's message asserted, "and it is in their interest as well as in the interest of their pupils that they be held accountable."

He also tiptoed onto the treacherous terrain of national standards without quite calling for them. "For years," Nixon said, "the fear of 'national standards' has been one of the bugaboos of education. . . . The problem is that in opposing some mythical threat of 'national standards' what we have too often been doing is avoiding accountability for our own local performance. We have, as a nation, too long avoided thinking of the *productivity* of schools."

Almost all of this proved to be ahead of its time. The Ninety-first Congress, far more interested in outspending Nixon on education, ignored his policy initiatives. . After the White House resubmitted its plan in January 1971, however, the Ninety-second Congress took the NIE proposal more seriously. Representative John Brademas, an Indiana Democrat who cared passionately about education and chaired the Subcommittee on Select Education, held extensive hearings—Moynihan, then a civilian again, was lead witness—and the idea elicited some bipartisan support and little opposition. It was enacted the following year in roughly the form that the administration originally suggested.

The Colemanesque reasoning about education, however—the emphasis on results, standards, and productivity—had no discernible impact on public opinion or the guts of federal K–12 education policy, which continued for two long decades more in the mode of LBJ's Elementary and Secondary Act. Nor did the broader education field pay much attention to the presidential bully pulpit. This was the seventies, after all. Money struggles and desegregation challenges were more compelling. Educators had no love for Richard Nixon and, in any case, were consumed by their equity agenda.

And Colleges | The president's second 1970 message to Congress dealt with higher education. It emerged from a parallel, Morgan-led working group and engaged a similar cast of characters. Its centerpiece was an un-Republican plan to widen federal grant and loan aid for low-income college students. This would emerge from Capitol Hill two years later as Basic Educational Opportunity Grants (now called Pell grants), an array of subsidized and unsubsidized loans, and a "secondary market" (later known as Sallie Mae) meant to add liquidity to the student-loan credit market.

The sleeper in the higher-ed message, however, was another Moynihan-inspired proposal for yet another new federal agency: a "National Foundation for Higher Education" to support "excellence, new ideas and reform in higher education," its specific grants to be determined "on the basis of the quality of the institutions and programs concerned." Additional foundation mandates included strengthening colleges and programs "that play a uniquely valuable role" (i.e., historically black campuses) or that face "special difficulties," and providing "an organization concerned, on the highest level, with the development of national policy in higher education." [15]

Pat was troubled by the deteriorating situation on American campuses—he fretted about educational quality and institutional integrity as well as the spreading virus of unrest—and strove to persuade his colleagues that Uncle Sam might lend a helping hand. He didn't like organizational meltdowns and occasionally quoted Yeats to the effect that "Things fall apart; the centre cannot hold." If Washington could assist in averting such an outcome in so vital a domain as higher education, in his view it should.

Months earlier, he had unsuccessfully floated the idea of a cabinet-level Department of Higher Education and Research. When that balloon popped—Jim Allen, for one, was keen on a full-fledged Education Department—Moynihan chanced upon a recent proposal from Clark Kerr's Carnegie Commission on Higher Education for a noncabinet agency, located outside HEW and cast along the lines of the National Science Foundation.

This device enabled the working group to incorporate several other pressing concerns, including aid for black colleges and OMB's desire to consolidate a mounting pile of narrow-gauge programs into a larger and more flexible spending authority.

The list kept growing. By late February, Moynihan had identified eleven separate purposes that the new foundation would be "authorized and directed" to fulfill. His enthusiasm had plainly got the better of him, overriding his own insight that Johnson's community action program had collapsed under the burden of incompatible missions and competing theories of action.

HEW's brilliant assistant secretary for policy and evaluation, Lewis H. Butler, plainspoken and normally gentle, saw through this fog of wishful thinking. Two weeks before the presidential message was to be dispatched to Capitol Hill, he sent a stern memo to his working-group colleagues: "The proposed Foundation," he wrote, "is a superficially appealing idea which, when analyzed—at least by me—turns into mush." He urged them to recognize the "fundamental differences among us" and the folly of "turning them all over to a Foundation and abdicating to that institution these decisions on Federal policy." [16]

Pat pushed back, however, and, in time, the working group informed the president that its members were split on this issue. But Nixon bought the National Foundation idea and appeared to accept Moynihan's underlying view that future higher-education policy should be tied to two pillars: aid for low-income students, and a mechanism whereby the many federal dollars gushing into the universities themselves (for scientific research and a hundred other purposes) would not undermine academic self-determination or subject campuses overmuch to Washington's shifting priorities.

Congress, however, was fixated on student aid and let the devil take the hindmost with respect to how other moneys reached college coffers. The higher-education lobbies were lukewarm toward the foundation proposal, protective of the "categorical" programs that OMB wanted to consolidate and (futilely) hopeful that some form of unrestricted institutional aid might be extracted from Congress. Even so, a pale shadow of the National Foundation idea made its way into the 1972 Higher Education Act in the form of a new Fund for Improvement of Post-Secondary Education, firmly lodged within the Department of HEW and focused exclusively on "innovation."

| My job was consuming. Many evenings I returned after dinner to the Old Executive Office Building and stayed until the wee hours. My assignments sometimes went beyond education—I worked, for example, on White House "population" policy—and not every education ruckus reached my desk. Billion-dollar budget battles, veto strategies, and school desegregation conflicts were above my pay grade. The latter were mostly handled by the lawyers and political types who were simultaneously crafting the administration's "southern strategy," though this is another domestic domain where Nixon typically gets a bum rap. In fact, writes historian Raymond Wolters, after courting southern white voters via the (failed) Supreme Court nominations of Clement Haynsworth and Harold Carswell,

> his administration moved vigorously to impose integration. In 1970 more than one hundred U.S. attorneys, federal marshals, and other civil rights enforcers were sent to the South to monitor integration,

and the Department of Justice instituted a spate of suits against school districts that were clinging to free choice and resisting racial balance. As a result of this vigorous legal offensive, more racial mixing was achieved during Nixon's first two years in the White House than ever before.[17]

Plenty came my way, however. After all those years in school and college in New England, I relished my grown-up responsibilities as well as the chance to explore the nation's capital. Most days, I walked to work from my one-bedroom apartment near Thomas Circle. The city was smaller then, a bit more laid back, not so posh and pretentious as today, not so overrun by lobbyists and influence peddlers, and, while it was plenty partisan at the top—and getting more so, even as I watched—at my level the mood was congenial enough that Sam Halperin (a Democratic alumnus of the Johnson administration) led an outstanding multiyear seminar for education aides from both parties (and both executive branch and Congress), under the aegis of a Ford-funded group called the Institute for Educational Leadership. It featured interesting speakers, candid discussion, good meals, and informative field trips. And it fostered networks and communication among people whose bosses might be at loggerheads.

When I grew discouraged by government or politics, I would take myself to the Lincoln Memorial late in the evening, when Daniel Chester French's splendid statue of our greatest president is beautifully illuminated and where, from the top of the steps, a clear view can be had past the Washington Monument to the Capitol gleaming at the Mall's other end. I usually paused long enough to reread the Gettysburg Address and Lincoln's Second Inaugural, both permanently inscribed on the memorial's walls, and recharged my patriotic batteries.

Back in the Old Executive Office Building, some of my miscellaneous assignments were odd, occasionally exhilarating, and once in a while hilarious.

■ Soon after reaching the White House, along with Frank Raines and another Moynihan intern, I briefed the president and cabinet on "youth policy," a session precipitated by uncertainty over the proper federal response to campus unrest as well as puzzlement about what was happening to young America as the decade neared its end.

■ I was dispatched one dawn on an air force jet to fetch the entertainer Art Linkletter, who had recently and painfully lost a child to drugs and was coming to address a White House conference on drug abuse. This expedition turned into a comedy of errors when the military pilot, assuming I was fully briefed, asked me at *which* of two nearby Florida airports Linkletter and his wife would be waiting. Clueless, I guessed wrong, necessitating a short flight from the first to second airfield, where we fetched a peeved and humorless humorist.

■ In November 1969, as buses ringed the White House complex to wall it off from massed antiwar protesters, Dick Blumenthal and I found ourselves in a bizarre "communications link" that involved the Secret Service and the marchers themselves. The goal was to maintain an open channel with mobilization leaders and quash rumors before they led to clashes. In that era before cell phones and instant messaging, Blumenthal and I roamed the District of Columbia, walkie-talkies in hand, communicating as fast as we could. This was made easier by the fact that several protest leaders were bunking at the capacious home of wealthy Democratic congressman Dick Ottinger and his wife Betty Ann, friends of Blumenthal's who had also become friends of mine (and whose flagstone-rimmed pool on Tilden Street was one of my favorite swimming holes.)[18]

■ After dozens of colleges erupted in the aftermath of the Cambodian "incursion" in May 1970, including tragic deaths at Ohio's Kent State and Mississippi's Jackson State, White House public affairs hierarchs decided to send a dozen young aides to visit campuses in a sort of fact-finding and pacification effort. The Nixon staff abounded with under-thirties—another "Kiddie Corps" member and major player in my later life was Lamar Alexander, whose job with congressional relations chief Bryce Harlow resembled mine with Moynihan—and our seniors thought we might have some success in mollifying angry students.

This struck me as far-fetched but, seeking to make lemonade, I seized the opportunity to visit parts of the country I had never been to. My reception at Oregon's rambunctious Reed College was frosty; at the University of Washington Law School it was lukewarm; and at Montana State University it was positively cordial—though I soon slipped away to pay my respects to Yellowstone National Park in its snow-covered late-spring majesty.

Returning to Washington, I sent John Ehrlichman a memo seeking to explain the "current student phenomenon" ("non-rational" but widespread, not confined to "radicals or extremists"); warning that the country's future was cloudy if many of its young people "lack that element of trust in the future and in the society itself"; and apologizing for us youthful emissaries "wasting the President's time" in our debriefing session—one of the rare face-to-face meetings that most junior staffers had with Nixon. Ehrlichman passed my two-page note on to him and received it back covered with Nixon's famous jottings—declaring that he had found the meeting "useful" and righteously opining that "staffers should never feel nervous when they come to see the President or disappointed after they do. It's an experience that they should remember with some sense of fulfillment." [19]

My more conventional work both benefited and suffered from having two bosses. Though Moynihan and Morgan liked each other and frequently agreed on policy matters, they argued, too, and more than once I found myself crafting a rejoinder for one to send in response to a memorandum I had drafted for the other. The dual reporting arrangement also made for extra work and more late nights.

After being "kicked upstairs," Pat kept busy with his previous issues and more. He struggled to keep the Family Assistance Plan alive on Capitol Hill. He pressed for a "national urban policy." He lobbied NATO to concern itself with environmental issues. He stayed immersed in the education working groups. He spearheaded a White House conference on food and nutrition. Joined by his old friend and drinking buddy, the eminent architect Nathaniel Owings, he persevered with the redevelopment of Pennsylvania Avenue, a passion since his days in the Kennedy administration. And he continued to fuss over myriad race issues, which led to the stormiest chapter of his two years on Nixon's staff: a February 1970 memorandum advising the president that the overheated issue of race in America might benefit from a period of "benign neglect."

As had happened with the "Moynihan Report" five years earlier, he was right—indeed he was presciently perceptive—and got into big trouble as a result. In the words of biographer Doug Schoen, "[T]he civil rights leadership . . . had distrusted him on account of the black family report and because he was working for their avowed enemy, Richard Nixon—and now he was saying that their problems should be neglected!" [20]

Of course he was saying nothing of the sort. Rather, he was recommending a sort of cooling-off period after several tense years—and was subtly urging the administration to ease back on its "southern strategy" and the inflammatory, race-laced speeches that Vice President Spiro Agnew was given to making. The memo itself envisioned "a period in which Negro progress continues and racial rhetoric fades." But when the leaked document surfaced on page one of the *New York Times*, Schoen recalls, "calls and protests poured into the White House."[21]

Who leaked it remains a mystery. But it was a body blow to Moynihan and further diminished his influence in White House circles. Indeed, by the time of the Cambodian incursion a few months later, Pat told Nixon that he should return to Harvard. The president, however, asked him to stay long enough to see the welfare reform plan through Congress. (Hope for it ebbed in October and November—and Moynihan exited soon thereafter.)

My other boss, Ed Morgan, was affable, wry, and very smart. A party animal, too, he became an occasional drinks-and-dinner companion as well as a considerate superior. I wasn't privy to all parts of his job, however, and later was crushed to learn that (in his lawyer role) he had knowingly misdated some presidential documents. He thereby ran afoul of the Watergate prosecutors, served time in prison, and never rebounded.

Morgan and the rest of his team were card-carrying Republicans. I still thought of myself as a "Moynihan Democrat," which meant I was no fan of the congressional leadership or the McGovern-led wave that swamped the party in 1972 and thereafter. Yet I had misgivings about a few Nixon policies. Cousins and friends were among those protesting the Vietnam War outside the White House gates, and I used my presidential staff position to persuade my Dayton draft board that I was too valuable to be sent into battle. (In retrospect, I'm thoroughly ashamed of that chapter, albeit glad to be alive and whole.)

Mostly, though, I thought the administration was forward-looking in its approach to domestic policy—the source of much heartburn among true-blue conservatives—and most historians agree that Nixon's first two years were a time of unexpected creativity and ferment in this area.

In truth, I was too close to the policy action at the time to appreciate how surprising some of his initiatives were, from welfare to affirmative action to college-student aid to education reform. Nobody can fully explain what made Richard Nixon tick, but several elements seem clear. Though averse to spending billions on LBJ's programs—appropriations battles with Congress raged throughout his presidency—he fretted that outright undoing of big chunks of the Great Society or the civil-rights revolution would lead to criticism by the elites whom he both vilified and craved approval from. (It cannot be coincidence that he installed Harvard professors Moynihan and Kissinger in key West Wing roles.) Many of the policies that he advanced showed the influence of cabinet members and staff aides who were, in varying degrees, pragmatic, moderate, even liberal. During 1969 and 1970, at least, the president himself was open to imaginative innovations. His memoirs recall that, to overcome "our public image as a 'negative' party," and to erase the labels of "reckless and racist," Republicans "needed to leapfrog the Democrats on the Great Society issues and get ahead of them."[22] What's more, some important lessons about "big government" had not yet been learned and thus could not be grasped by Nixon and his team; these mid-sixties programs were still too new for their track records to be appraised.

It's true that Congress ignored or rebuffed many administration ideas.[23] It's also true that, in hindsight, I can glimpse a few troublesome precedents being set, such as the "Philadelphia Plan," advanced by then–labor secretary George Shultz, which pioneered the use of racial quotas in federally funded construction projects. And, as I would later come to appreciate in connection with the National Institute of Education, I contributed my bit to the administration's naïveté regarding Uncle Sam's capacity to solve societal problems and change the direction of major institutions.

This was, however, an amazing first job as well as a singular way to finish graduate school. I kept a monthly journal and periodically flew to Cambridge to debrief with my doctoral committee. Pressed by a couple of concerned and impatient deans, and encouraged by Moynihan, I scribbled a quasi dissertation on "presidential education policy-making," derived entirely from my White House experience. After an exceedingly well-lubricated Saturday lunch in a Cambridge restaurant, Pat and I and the other two committee members adjourned to Francis Avenue for a perfunctory "oral exam." And in June 2000, Ted Sizer handed me my degree.

In November, Nixon flirted with naming Moynihan ambassador to the United Nations, and Pat and I talked about me accompanying him to New York. (I recall examining the floor plan of the ambassador's grand suite in the Waldorf Towers.) But this did not come to pass, and Moynihan instead returned to Harvard before his two-year leave of absence expired. It was time for me to depart, too.

It had been a tough period for the nation but an extraordinary opportunity for me, and I felt good about my few contributions. Despite the late nights and short weekends, it was sometimes a real kick—lunching in the White House mess, walking through the woods at Camp David, asking the fabled White House switchboard to ring up friends and relatives. (My mother loved to recount the time I then came on the line not to seek counsel on national affairs but to request her fudge-cake recipe.) My eighty-year-old grandfather visited and, after touring the Oval Office and cabinet room and being introduced to Pat, remarked that my place of work was "a long way from Rogge Street," recalling the decrepit neighborhood where he and his immigrant parents had first lived in Dayton. I relished his pride in how far the family had come.

I also learned a lot, not all of it uplifting. I saw how clumsy and weak are Washington's instruments for effecting changes in education; how seemingly good ideas, once translated into legislation and bureaucracy, often end up not working; how much easier it is, even near the pinnacle of government, to prevaricate, argue, and block change than to accomplish things; yet also how steady goals and perseverance can matter over the long haul. Moynihan's multi-decade pursuit of several causes (Pennsylvania Avenue redevelopment, welfare reform, education) was a bona fide inspiration. So was he, of course. As with Frank Broderick back at Exeter, I also saw the value of *having* a mentor, which left me more disposed later to *be* one.

5 | *Out of Washington*

With a loan from my folks and a few contacts and rest stops in faraway lands arranged with the help of White House friends, I spent the first half of 1971 circling the globe solo. Travel has always been a personal passion, and I feared such an opportunity might not recur. Though education was not my focus on this expedition, I managed to visit schools in such remote locales as the New Guinea highlands, Ethiopia, Malawi, and rural Afghanistan, as well as slightly more conventional spots like Sydney, Kuala Lumpur, and Bombay. I took a bus through the Khyber Pass, crossed the Pakistan-India border on foot (vehicles weren't permitted), and hitchhiked down the eastern half of Africa. It cleared my brain, gave me a bit of perspective on the White House, got me through several thick James Michener novels, and left me a tad lonely.

In midsummer, after receiving word in Nairobi of the devastating death during heart surgery of a much-loved seven-year-old cousin, I cut my journey short, wired my parents to expect me, and returned to the United States to take up a prearranged job in Boston as "policy director" for Robert C. Wood, then president of the University of Massachusetts. Wood was a well-regarded political scientist, LBJ cabinet member, and energetic university chief, but for me this turned out to be a mismatch. It was, in fact, the only big job mistake I've made so far.

After a month or so of unemployment, I joined the staff of Massachusetts governor Francis W. Sargent, a Republican of the "moderate northeastern" sort, a rare breed today, as his education aide. The Bay State had America's longest tradition of public education but was roiled by most of the hot-button issues of the day. Though Boston's school system was not yet traumatized by Judge Garrity, race relations in that city were tense, and politicians such as Louise Day Hicks were exploiting the situation.

One bright day, the parents of disabled kids across the Commonwealth marched on the capitol to demand special education programs for their children—the federal law was still several years away—and I was sent out to reason with them on the venerable State House steps atop Beacon Hill. This turned out to be a big mistake. They didn't want to hear what I had to say on the governor's behalf, and I wasn't able to deliver what they wanted. I learned then and forever that parents look out mainly for the interests of their own kids, not for larger public-policy considerations—and if their children are disabled, the parents, themselves exhausted, frazzled, and often guilt ridden, are especially adamant and single-minded. (Two years later, I, too, would find myself a demanding, child-centered parent.)

My colleagues were talented and busy. Besides state policy challenges, a host of "new federalism" programs were starting. The first General Revenue Sharing check arrived in the mail one day to the puzzlement of gubernatorial aides, compounded by the fact that it was made out to "Francis W. Sargent, Governor." There were so many jokes about how he could decamp with those millions to someplace warm that the banking day nearly ended before anyone thought to run down the street to deposit the check so as to reap the overnight interest for the Commonwealth.

Frank Sargent was one of the first governors to seek greater control of his state's education system by restructuring it at the top. Since Horace Mann's day, Massachusetts had a constitutionally mandated board of education, which hired a commissioner to preside over the K–12 operation. But the commissioner didn't work directly for the governor and, in the event, had nothing to say about the state's burgeoning, multiheaded, and costly higher-education system. So Sargent named a "secretary of education" (former Harvard Ed School professor Joseph M. Cronin) to his cabinet to oversee and make sense of all this. As the governor's education aide with a parallel portfolio, I enjoyed a slightly strained relationship with the Cronin office—but not nearly so strained as that enjoyed by Bob Wood, my former employer, who strove to preserve his university's autonomy and fiscal independence from gubernatorial efforts to centralize and subordinate it.

In my spare time, I put pen to paper. Two years after the Nixon education messages that I had helped craft, the fates of the administration's twin "institutional" proposals—the NIE and National Foundation for Higher Education—were finally being settled on Capitol Hill. (Both were swept, with much else, into the 1972 HEA reauthorization.)

In February 1972, beginning my own evolution from drafter of internal memos to author of published works, I wrote in glowing, almost jubilant terms of the bright future that awaited the new National Institute of Education, grandiosely terming it "the most important addition to the federal government's education efforts in this century" and again linking its mandate back to Coleman and the rich-poor achievement gap: "Put simply, poor kids don't learn as much as unpoor ones, at least not as much of the things that seem to lead to success and happiness in our society. Until we understand this process well enough to affect it, the persistent gap . . . will gnaw at the vitals of society as surely and as fatefully as a carcinoma." [24]

I was right about the gap and the problems that it posed—still poses— for American society. I was wrong about the new institute's capacity to do much about it—and partly wrong in believing that ignorance about education itself was the central problem in need of solution. Such ignorance is indeed a challenge, but one dwarfed by the system's refusal (or inability) to deploy the knowledge that we already possess about how kids learn and what works in classrooms.

If I was guilelessly hopeful on the NIE front, I was sorely disappointed by the fate of the proposed National Foundation. "Death of an Idea" was the subtitle of my angry March 1972 essay in *Change* magazine. Though I faulted the administration's handling of congressional relations, acknowledged the internal contradictions that our White House working group had let creep into the initial plan, and noted that the version resubmitted to Congress early in 1971 was much diminished from the original proposal, mostly I blamed the higher-ed community and its Washington lobbyists for their lack of vision, their greed, and their knee-jerk animus toward the GOP administration. "Whether by simple incompetence at the legislative process," I stormed, "or a prior determination that Richard Nixon was out to do them in, the spokesmen for American universities displayed a failure of imagination so total that a promising idea was lost, and a lack of political sophistication so stunning that one might conclude he would be better off with no spokesman at all." [25]

Most of the time, however, I benefited by being hundreds of miles from Washington and by daily reminders that, in matters of education, what transpires in state capitals is more consequential than decisions made on the Potomac's shores.

India and Principals | While struggling to make sense of state policy and politics—and living over an Italian deli in Boston's North End, a source of delicious eggplant-parmesan subs and close enough to walk to the State House—I also found myself back in the Moynihan orbit. A Harvard professor again, living with Liz and their three children in the big house on Francis Avenue (its third-floor apartment rented by a parade of graduate students that included David Stockman, then in Divinity School, later Reagan's first budget director), he taught a popular undergraduate course in which I lent a hand. I dined and drank, ran the occasional errand, and generally hung out. Though irascible and long-memoried when crossed, Liz was warmly gracious and helpful, even motherly, to me and other young Pat protégés.

Pat also stayed active on the fringes of federal policy, testifying on bills he cared about, sending the occasional memorandum to Nixon, and serving, at the president's behest, as U.S. representative to the United Nations' "third committee," which deals with humanitarian and cultural affairs.

Although nominally neutral in the 1972 election, that September Pat published an essay in *Life* magazine that sympathetically depicted what a second Nixon term would bring. As biographer Schoen noted, "Such an article could only be seen as an implicit endorsement of Nixon's candidacy, and an examination of Moynihan's language reveals his obviously warm feelings for Nixon and his goals." [26]

Soon after the president's sweeping victory over George McGovern, he asked Pat to go to New Delhi as U.S. ambassador to India. (Schoen says Moynihan had a summertime premonition that this might happen.) And soon after that, Pat called to ask if I would consider tagging along.

The State Department permits noncareer ambassadors in major overseas posts to take an assistant from outside the Foreign Service. I had supposed that my month on the subcontinent during 1971's round-the-world tour—including a few nights as then-ambassador Kenneth Keating's guest in a spare bedroom at Roosevelt House, the cavernous Edward Durrell Stone–designed residence beside the Delhi chancery—would be the only time I would ever see India. But it didn't take much to rekindle my wanderlust.

Indian-American relations were dicey. The United States had taken Pakistan's side in the 1971 Indo-Pak war. Officially and outspokenly "non-aligned," in fact Prime Minister Indira Gandhi was gradually sliding her vast nation under the Soviet umbrella and, though American intelligence was oblivious to this, was also developing a nuclear capability. Rubbing salt in the relationship, America "owned" a large fraction of India's currency, the legacy of generous but ill-conceived aid schemes during famines of the fifties and sixties when we lent India the wherewithal to purchase U.S. crop surpluses.

Yet this embassy was a prestigious posting previously held by such eminences as Chester Bowles, John Sherman Cooper, and fellow Harvard professor Ken Galbraith. (En route to Delhi, we devoured his *Ambassador's*

Journal in search of pointers about the exotic venture on which we were embarked.) Pat was also ready to get out of Cambridge again. Harvard had not welcomed him back as warmly as he'd hoped, antiwar demonstrators had trashed the Moynihans' house one spring evening in 1972, and he was increasingly interested in international affairs.

Though Watergate had been in the news since June, it had not yet inflicted major damage upon Nixon himself, and no dishonor attached to representing him and the United States in the capital of the "world's largest democracy." Pat easily won Senate confirmation to this post.

So I said farewell to the Sargent squad, again packed my apartment, and reported to the State Department for processing.

On February 20, 1973, the Moynihans and I disembarked the big Pan Am jet at Delhi's Palam airport in the three a.m. darkness that always accompanies such comings and goings. In a reprise of my unexpected arrival at the White House gates four years earlier, the State Department had not bothered to inform the embassy that I, too, was coming. But after a couple of nights back in one of those extra bedrooms at Roosevelt House, the embassy's competent administrative staff arranged a two-bedroom duplex for me in the American-style compound behind the chancery. Real Foreign Service officers lived in pleasant homes scattered across New Delhi's nicer "colonies," looked after by lots of servants. One was plenty for me, however, and I loved being able to stroll to work—and to Roosevelt House, its swimming pool, and a social life that, at least at the start, revolved around the Moynihan family. (Two kids accompanied them to Delhi while the eldest enrolled at Exeter.)

The twenty months I spent in India were riveting and transformative, not least because I returned with a wife and two small children. But most of the job—we called me "counsel to the ambassador," because the "executive assistant" was a career officer and the "special assistant" was the CIA station chief—had little direct bearing on education. Besides pitching in on sundry foreign policy issues—Pat was determined above all to forgive India's rupee debt, but he and Secretary of State Kissinger rarely saw eye to eye—I worked on USIA exchange programs, helped arrange for visiting speakers and scholars, called on Peace Corps volunteers in remote villages (yielding many insights into what made Indians and Americans tick, plus a bout with amebic dysentery), accompanied Pat on innumerable expeditions across that sprawling and diverse land, and escorted Liz and the kids on several high-altitude escapes from Delhi's torrid summers.

The more I traveled and got to know Indians, including the large industrialist family whose youngest daughter I would marry, the clearer it became that India had a two-tiered education system and no immediate prospects of changing it. The upper classes fared well enough in long-established British-style private schools, then in highly competitive, government-subsidized universities. The education system, in fact, served them better than did the national economy into which they emerged. India at the time was full of degree-bearing, English-fluent elevator operators and clerks. The more fortunate (unless their families had established businesses to join) took poorly paid government jobs. Indeed, on our second date, my future wife, Renu, then a young physician in a government hospital, would not let me order a bottle of middling wine that cost the equivalent of her monthly salary. (The Indian stuff we drank instead was heinous.)

Many ambitious Indian graduates headed overseas in search of better prospects, a sensible move for them, albeit a major contributor to India's hurtful "brain drain." For years, Renu's medical school classmates, products of a sound, government-financed education at Delhi University, held their reunions in New Jersey.

That's changed of late as India's more open economy has boomed and a reverse brain drain has begun to draw doctors and other "nonresident Indians" back to the subcontinent, where opportunities now await.

What has not changed is the miserable education available to India's immense underclass in tens of thousands of rural villages and urban bustees. With few exceptions (e.g., the state of Kerala), the public schools are unreliable, woefully equipped, and staffed by civil servants who can make more money by cutting class and spending their time tutoring kids at parents' expense. As partial antidote, a fascinating but little-known array of low-priced private schools, many of them for-profit and some of them unlicensed, has sprung up in the slums of many Indian (and other third-world) cities, affordable even by poor families and yielding academic results that rival those of government schools.[27] All this despite innumerable government schemes and billions in foreign aid and development assistance.

Technology and prosperity may eventually alter this bleak prospect. For now, however, as three decades ago, it's easy to understand why so many citizens of this enormous land are illiterate even as millions of others are so well educated that Americans are losing jobs to them.

In 1973–4, my primary K–12 assignment was serving as the ambassador's representative on the board of the American Embassy School, a private institution that educated the children of most U.S. families in Delhi plus dozens of other expats and a smattering of upscale Indians. (Though pricey by local norms, the highly regarded school welcomed Indian pupils. However, the government of India, as part of its policy of keeping America at arm's length, threw multiple enrollment roadblocks across the path of its own nationals.)

The longtime school director resigned during this time and, as the only education specialist on the board, I was asked to return to the United States to vet candidates to replace him. Thinking myself expert in such things, I welcomed the assignment—the prospect of a visit home was also appealing—and clambered back aboard a Pan Am jet to New York.

After interviewing several prospects prescreened by the State Department unit that assists overseas schools with such things, I returned to Delhi with a recommendation, after which my top candidate came for a visit and was duly offered the post. Alas, I had chosen wrong. Wowed by the man's provocative ideas, I didn't pay sufficient heed to his actual track record as an education executive, nor did I check with enough references or probe them as hard as I should have. Though the "effective schools" research of the 1970s still lay in the future, I sensed that having the right principal was key to a successful school—and nowhere more so than in a faraway private school that had to be largely self-sufficient. But while I knew plenty about education policy, I had too little experience in the trenches to know what to look for in that vital role. The fellow I picked was not a disaster, but he was no success either and didn't last long. (The school continues today, larger than ever.)

Think-tanking | Once it became clear in early 1974 (after my parents traveled to Delhi and passed muster with her family) that Renu and I were going to wed, that her dowry included a daughter and son, then turning four and three, and that we would live in the United States, I began to fret about what to do next. Parking Arti and Aloke in June with my folks in Dayton, while Renu hunkered down with her doctor sister in Nashville to study for the demanding exam that foreign-trained physicians must pass, I spent several weeks checking out my stateside options. Most appealing by far was an offer to join the Brookings Institution in Washington as research associate in governmental studies, there to work on higher-education issues. I owed this opportunity to the good offices of Steve Hess, Pat's White

House deputy four years earlier, who had remained a friend and had guest-lectured in India while we were there.

After several more months back in Delhi, the State Department's approval of my marriage plans (I was still in the Foreign Service, and negotiating such permission was standard procedure for those marrying non-Americans), a wedding in my parents' living room in Dayton, and a brief honeymoon in South Carolina—we arrived in a rainstorm at Hilton Head the evening Nixon resigned—by midautumn we were living in a rented house in outermost Bethesda, Maryland. Nursery schools, neighborhood playmates, wet beds, and a driver's license for Renu were among our preoccupations when I came home from my long bus commute to Dupont Circle. Adios bachelorhood and walking to work.

In the midseventies, higher-education policy was more interesting than K–12. While school enrollments shrank, the postsecondary sector was booming. Its student count soared by 2.5 million during the first half of the 1970s alone, and two hundred more institutions opened. The 1972 HEA reauthorization had ignored Moynihan's "National Foundation" scheme but overhauled and greatly expanded federal student assistance while rebuffing the universities' plea for "institutional aid."

With the end of the Vietnam War (and Nixon's exit from the presidency), U.S. campuses were quiet. But private-sector tuitions were fast inflating, and government aid did not begin to keep pace even as billions went into public-sector growth. The result was a gradual shift in the student balance from private to public. As recently as 1965, private campuses had enrolled one-third of all students; by 1975 their share had fallen to 21%. This clouded the future of a major national asset, threatened to put private college beyond reach of all but the rich, and rested on economically irrational state policies that generously subsidized the (public) higher education of families that could easily pay more in tuition.

As for Uncle Sam, after close examination, Brookings economist (now University of Virginia Ed School dean) David W. Breneman and I wrote in 1978 that "the stipend levels for these various federal [student aid] programs are unresponsive to the wide price range found within American higher education—a range that generally locates private institutions at the upper end. A program designed to afford a student access to postsecondary education may be far less helpful in providing him with choice."[28]

Though "school choice" was not yet a hot issue at the K–12 level, choosing one's college from among varied options was a hallmark of American higher education—nothing like it could be found overseas—and its eclipse, we judged, was not good either for students (especially needy ones) or for institutions. But crafting solutions was no cakewalk. "[O]ne of the ironies of the dual system of control in higher education," we observed in cautious Brookings prose, "is that the private sector has been forced in part by the presence of the public sector to request public aid; and yet if the private sector succeeds too well in this quest, it may cease to be private, independent and unique."[29]

The obvious remedy was to narrow the "tuition gap," which in theory policymakers could do by letting student aid vary with college fees or—less likely—by subsidizing private colleges directly (unconstitutional in some states) or—still less likely—by reducing state subsidies to public campuses and forcing them to charge something closer to their true costs or—least likely—by devising means to curb the escalation of private-sector prices.

In the end, we punted and called for "statesmanship"!

Simultaneously, I was crafting a solo book on federal higher-education policy, which Brookings, in its leisurely way, also published in 1978 (a year after I left) under the title *Scholars, Dollars & Bureaucrats*. It mapped the Washington terrain, paying as much attention to regulatory issues and cost-benefit conundrums as to prices and dollar flows. Undergirding the analysis was what I termed a "subtle but fundamental question: is the national interest in higher education adequately served by the present arrangements, manifold but messy, that entwine the federal government with colleges and students?"[30]

Two hundred pages later, I concluded that "The patient is not very ill" and "[I]t would be a mistake to prescribe too much." The biggest problem was that "[T]he federal government lacks any reliable mechanism or structure for making 'higher education policy' or of appraising the effects of diverse programs and actions on higher education as a whole." Echoing a theme that Moynihan had Nixon articulate six years earlier, I fretted that the absence of any overarching policy apparatus meant nobody was responsible for the vitality of higher education per se.

Ironically, a few months later, I stood at Moynihan's side on the Senate floor as the junior senator from New York argued eloquently and earnestly *against* creation of a federal Education Department primarily on grounds that vesting so much authority in any one place was risky and that disorganization and decentralization kept both colleges and primary schools safer from government mischief.

Children of My Own | I was also beginning to navigate the education shoals for my instant kids, functioning as a consumer for the first time since my own days in school. Renu and I slid onto the private-school pathway for four-year-old Aloke, mainly because the Montgomery County public schools wouldn't take him until he was five. Then we started feeling guilty about Arti, who was in the nearby public-school kindergarten, a perfectly okay place but how dare we send our male child to private school and our female child to public school? (My mother gently underscored that question—my late and much-missed mother, the world's finest grandmother, on whose lap Arti and Aloke became fluent in English within weeks of leaving Delhi for Dayton.) In the event, both children wound up spending their early grades in one of Washington's more acclaimed private schools, though we could ill afford it on my Brookings salary. At first, Renu had no income, then a resident's meager pay. When I did the family's weekly marketing at Safeway on Saturday morning, it was with $25 in my pocket to spend. Our kids drank a lot of powdered milk.

Loans from my folks helped ease our cash flow crunches and made it possible to cover the tuition bills when checks had to be written. Although it would have been terrific if a government program had paid for our children's education, I took for granted that making personal sacrifices for this purpose was the right thing to do. But school options have to be there, both decent institutions worth choosing among and, for most Americans, help in covering their costs. Soon I would rejoin the political fray and do my bit to persuade government to widen the opportunities for more families.

6 | The Politics of Aiding Private Schools

Having taken a two-week leave from Brookings to help Pat with his Senate campaign in 1976, I returned to his orbit in early 1977, beginning four years on Capitol Hill that culminated as his legislative director. I also began, for the first time, to take an interest in the twenty-somethings who reported to me, resolving to work them hard, set high standards, teach them all I could, set an example, and, for those who rose to the challenge, attend to their subsequent careers. Thus started an alumni/ae club that has grown for three decades and of which I'm exceptionally proud.

Moynihan always attracted smart, interesting, and creative types to his staff, men and women not unlike himself. Because he was headstrong and mercurial, however, apt to rewrite everything himself, and given to keeping eccentric office hours, working for him was exasperating as well as stimulating, which made for a lot of turnover. But his first-term Senate team was as strong as any I've ever been part of: it included Tim Russert, now host of *Meet the Press*, and Elliott Abrams, who had a stormy tour in Reagan's State Department during the Iran-Contra era and who, as I write, is deputy chief of George W. Bush's National Security Council. Half a dozen of us became good friends, thrown together by cramped working conditions—three or four aides per room—and because, we said half jokingly, we had a "common enemy" in a senator whose extraordinary intellect and policy acumen were not always matched by legislative discipline.

One morning he overslept in New York, thus missing a subcommittee hearing in Washington that he had called—and at which various of his friends, academic peers, and former colleagues were to testify, all of them invited by me on his behalf! He airily suggested by phone from the Carlyle Hotel that I ask Senator John Danforth to chair the session, which that gentlemanly, thoughtful, and sobersided Missouri Republican graciously did. Because the Moynihan team were also among the few neoconservative Democrats on Capitol Hill, on many matters we were more apt to find ourselves making common cause with moderate Republicans—of which there were still plenty—than with McGovernite Democrats.

Pat had talked his way onto the Senate's powerful Finance Committee, which became the focus of most of the domestic policy work in my purview, so many projects involved topics like welfare, adoption, and New

York City's fiscal crisis. But two looming education issues held deep interest for the new junior senator and emerged as sizable chunks of my work: saving parochial schools and resisting creation of a cabinet-level Education Department.

Parochial Schools in Jeopardy | Catholic schools were closing right and left. Demographics were one factor, as the U.S. population of school-age children shrank in the seventies after two decades of unprecedented growth. Many Catholic families joined the middle-class exodus from blighted communities where parochial schools were plentiful to grassy suburbs where they were sparse. And Americans in general were slowly migrating from the industrial Northeast, with its long tradition of Catholic education, to western and southern states where this was a more exotic practice.

The changing Church also caused trouble. The liberalization—one may fairly say slackening—of religious practice that set in after Vatican II left many U.S. Catholic parents with a diminished sense of obligation to educate their kids in parochial schools, and the fall-off in people entering religious vocations made it far harder and costlier to staff those schools. As tuition levels crept up to match escalating expenses, Catholic education grew less affordable for families, even as cost-cutting measures undertaken by the schools led to large classes, deteriorating buildings, and a paucity of enticing new programs, technologies, and extracurricular offerings. The remaining parochial schools were also apt to be found in declining neighborhoods inhabited by fewer families (of whatever faith) with the means to pay rising tuitions. Many suburban parishes, though proximate to plenty of middle-class Catholic families, felt no obligation to establish, underwrite, and operate their own schools or to press church members to register their sons and daughters.

Larger changes in American culture undoubtedly inflicted damage, too. Insofar as revolting against authority was the fashion in education, why would one want to attend, or send one's children to, some of the most authoritarian and dogmatic schools of all, especially when that meant shelling out sizable sums from one's own pocket? Besides, there was as yet no general awareness that the free public schools were providing anything but a satisfactory education. (In 1981, the prolific James Coleman would publish the first significant scholarly finding that Catholic schools were more effective.)

Yet it was evident that urban parochial schools were competently serving a growing share of disadvantaged and frequently non-Catholic youngsters—insofar as such families could afford to enroll in them or parishes could subsidize them.

The rising prices and thinning ranks of Catholic schools thus posed two policy problems for American education, in addition to the dilemmas they caused for the Church. First, middle-class families who wanted their kids to attend parochial schools—and who dutifully paid property and other taxes to support public schools—were caught in a cash crunch. And second, poor families, proper objects of the era's concern with educational equity, found much to like in these schools (including safety, discipline, and attention to character development as well as academics), schools that were increasingly willing to serve non-Catholics and had space to accommodate them—yet escalating tuitions often priced this option beyond such families' reach. (This despite the fact that Catholic schools' *operating* costs, even with more salaried teachers, have always been lower than those of public schools.)

How government should treat religious schools had been a political briar patch for ages because of the "Catholic issue," because of ceaseless brawling in the church-state intersection, and because in the post-*Brown* era some private schools—often dubbed "segregation academies"—functioned as refuges for white families that did not want their children to sit next to black youngsters in class.

Catholic and other long-established private schools were not tarred by the segregationist brush but had their own political and legal problems. Besides the embers of nativism and anti-Catholicism, public-school partisans, including increasingly militant teacher unions and now joined by such advocacy organizations as Americans for Democratic Action and Americans United for Separation of Church and State, objected to using government funds to assist church-affiliated schools (or private schools of any sort, some of these groups insisted).

As early as 1960, when Congress began to wrestle with the idea of generalized financial assistance to primary-secondary education (versus the narrow funding categories of the National Defense Education Act), the issue of "parochiaid" heaved up—and capsized the entire measure.

As America's first Roman Catholic president at a time when that was a very big deal, JFK was understandably wary of promoting government programs that could be described by critics as carrying water for the Vatican.

(In a celebrated campaign speech in 1960, he had assured the Greater Houston Ministerial Association of his commitment to "absolute" separation of church and state and to "an America . . . where no church or church school is granted any public funds.") Indeed, Kennedy bent over so far backward that his chief aid-to-education proposal was confined exclusively to public schools. This so upset the U.S. bishops that they joined with southern and GOP school-aid opponents to torpedo the plan. But when Kennedy sought quietly through backdoor channels to amend NDEA to assist private schools, word leaked out, and the *New York Times* thundered that the reauthorization process was "being used as a cover under which there is an attempt to slip through large-scale Federal aid to non-public schools." [31]

Things went from bad to worse. On Capitol Hill, in the powerful House Rules Committee one July day in 1961, recounts historian Hugh Davis Graham,

> Virginia's [Democratic congressman and committee chairman] Judge Smith teamed up with Mississippi's [William] Colmer and the Catholic [James] Delaney in a strange coalition to join the five Rules Committee Republicans in killing the public-school bill, the NDEA bill, *and* the college-aid bill in an afternoon of acrimony and slaughter. The Republicans wanted no bill at all, nor did the Southern Democrats Smith and Colmer. The Catholics wanted the NDEA "sweeteners" for parochial schools, but three southern Democrats . . . objected to such thinly disguised church aid in the unlikely name of defense. The key was Delaney, who reflected understandable Catholic fears that federal aid for public school teachers' salaries posed potentially ruinous competition for poorly paid Catholic lay teachers. The paralysis was complete.[32]

Though the next couple of years brought further proposals, dustups, and meltdowns in the name of federal aid to education, the political stalemate lasted for the rest of JFK's abbreviated White House tenure. In 1964, however, things loosened. That year's Civil Rights Act made clear that federal aid would not support segregated schools; the new Protestant president did not have to worry about being seen as pro-Catholic; and Lyndon Baines Johnson was not only a master legislative strategist but also believed that winning the War on Poverty meant aiding schools to do a better job of educating poor kids.

That shift in focus—from subsidizing teachers and schools qua schools to helping disadvantaged children use education as an escalator out of poverty—gave rise to the "child benefit theory" as a new basis for federal education spending, which in turn made possible a delicate public-private compromise that both shaped ESEA's Title I centerpiece and cleared a political path to that law's enactment. According to legislative chroniclers (and former congressional staffers) Eugene Eidenberg and Roy Morey, this brilliant bit of political craftsmanship stemmed from LBJ's insistence on finding a path to federal education aid that skirted the church-state thicket and from Education Commissioner Francis Keppel's successful secret negotiations with the National Education Association *and* the U.S. Catholic Conference. The key agreement, in Eidenberg's and Morey's words, was the "understanding" that "aid money would go not to private and parochial schools but to the children of nonpublic schools based on a formula that reflected the number of children in a school district that came from families with incomes of less than $2000 per year." [33]

Unfortunately, this Solomon-like settlement looked more promising for Catholic schools in prospect than it turned out to be in reality. As implemented, federal dollars never actually entered private-school bank accounts. Rather, their eligible pupils were to be tutored by personnel paid via the public school system in programs generally delivered off-site. This left fiscal control in the public system's hands and obliged parochial schools to jump through bureaucratic hoops to document which of their pupils even qualified for such assistance.

While all this was going on in Washington, a number of states were seeking to assist their Catholic schools with specific items such as textbooks and transportation. Indeed, this began in the late 1940s when the New Jersey legislature authorized Garden State school systems to reimburse parents for the bus fares their children paid to travel to the private and parochial schools that educated them.

Enter the U.S. Supreme Court, prodded by the public-school lobby and liberal separationist groups to find such schemes unconstitutional under the "establishment" clause of the First Amendment. The same groups were encouraging voters to amend their *state* constitutions to prohibit the use of public dollars for religious institutions and/or privately controlled schools. Dozens of states had done this in the late nineteenth century by adopting so-called "Blaine Amendments" but several had added, modified, or strengthened their barriers much more recently, notably Michigan in 1970.

Supreme Court jurisprudence in this area was tangled and inconsistent during the mid–twentieth century. Sometimes the justices said okay, sometimes they said no; most often they said "maybe," "yes, but," or "only if." As Antonin Scalia, now on the high court himself and then on the faculty of the University of Chicago Law School, testified in 1978, "It is impossible, within the time allotted, to describe with any completeness the utter confusion of Supreme Court pronouncements in the church-state area."[34] The same university's Philip Kurland termed the Court "thoroughly unprincipled in the area."[35]

One pair of decisions, for example, approved New York's lending (secular) textbooks to parochial-school pupils while barring two other states from providing such schools with maps. This led Senator Moynihan famously to wonder aloud how the Court would respond to a "book of maps," that is, an atlas. Another decision attempted to parse the reasons why government aid to church-affiliated colleges was permissible but financial assistance to parochial high schools was not. (It came down to a pseudo-psycho-legal distinction concerning the "impressionability" of students at different ages.)

The law, in short, was a perplexing mess but, especially in combination with the "Blaine amendments," it was enough to block most governmental aid to ailing Catholic schools both in Washington and in states whose elected leaders were inclined in that direction.

By the mid-seventies, however, with "equity" the siren song of U.S. education policy at every level, it began to be said that Catholic and other religious schools were discriminated against by government itself, thus possibly violating civil rights statutes, "equal protection" guarantees, maybe even the First Amendment's other religion clause, which bars government actions that impede the "free exercise" of one's faith.

Meanwhile, parochial schools were closing their doors, shedding pupils, and hiking tuition.

Uncle Sam to the Rescue? | In 1973, Treasury Secretary George Shultz testified before the House Ways and Means Committee in favor of a federal income-tax credit for families' tuition expenses in private schools. "The nonpublic school system plays a vital role in our society," he explained, but "education costs are rising, the enrollment in the nonpublic schools is declining, and an important American institution may be in jeopardy."[36]

The 1976 GOP platform urged "tax credits for parents making elementary and secondary school tuition payments." The same year's Democratic platform, in a plank drafted by Moynihan, endorsed "a constitutionally acceptable method of providing tax aid for the education of all pupils in non-segregated schools in order to ensure parental freedom in choosing the best education for their children."

Campaigning for the presidency that year, Jimmy Carter wrote in nearly identical language to the nation's Catholic school administrators that he was "firmly committed to finding constitutionally acceptable methods of providing aid to parents whose children attend parochial schools." Soon after Carter's inauguration, his new education commissioner, Ernest L. Boyer, echoed that sentiment, saying in a speech that "Private education is absolutely crucial to the vitality of this nation and public policy should strengthen rather than diminish these essential institutions."

One might suppose the bipartisan stars had finally aligned such that new forms of direct or indirect assistance to parochial schools would soon emerge from Washington. Which is exactly what freshman senator Pat Moynihan, teaming up with his friend and Finance Committee colleague, Oregon GOP senator Bob Packwood, tried to make happen.

In September 1977, they introduced S. 2142, to be known as the Tuition Tax Credit Act of 1977—and did so with fifty sponsors, ranging ideologically from George McGovern to Barry Goldwater and almost evenly divided between Republicans and Democrats. At first blush, this looked like a winner.

In its original form, it provided a 50% tax credit for tuitions up to $1,000 per child per year. In other words, a federal taxpayer could reduce his tax bill by fifty cents for each dollar of tuition that he paid on his own or a dependent's behalf to an "eligible educational institution," up to a maximum tax reduction of $500 per student. Colleges and universities were eligible—there was keen congressional interest in tax relief for higher-ed tuitions—and so were primary-secondary schools, both public and private, as long as the latter were accredited and nonprofit. The credit, moreover, was to be "refundable," meaning that low-income families with scant tax liability could also benefit from the maximum sums permitted under this measure.

Nothing happened that fall, but in January 1978 the two primary sponsors presided over three consecutive days of hearings before the Finance Committee's tax subcommittee, airing their bill and several kindred proposals. The transcript ran to 724 pages.

Witnesses presented predictably divergent views, as did the debate that began to seethe far beyond Capitol Hill. Advocates said this measure would be good for poor families, good for freedom, diversity, and choice, and surely good for schools, which would be better able to attract and retain tuition-paying students. Opponents raised church-state issues and economic efficiency arguments (namely, that if the goal were to assist low-income families and not those who don't need it, government should provide means-tested, scholarship-type assistance rather than wider-ranging tax reductions).

In its testimony, the Carter administration completely changed its tune from the candidate's 1976 commitment and Commissioner Boyer's disquisition on the value of private education. (Jimmy Carter's own bulky presidential memoir devotes just two pages to education and never mentions private schools.) The Treasury Department, now opposed to use of the tax code to offset education expenses, even for college, raised the additional K–12 specter that "a broad general tuition tax credit for private primary and secondary education would have rather radical effects on public schools education [sic] in this country." The HEW testimony amplified this dire prediction, asserting that a K–12 tax credit "could undermine the principle of public education in this country. It might encourage relatively more affluent families to enroll their children in private schools, leaving the public schools for the poor. . . . This could accelerate the enrollment decline already underway in our public schools."

An angry Moynihan accused administration witnesses of duplicity and "lying" and charged that junior officials had been sent into the Senate lion's den because their superiors were "hiding" from the issue, too embarrassed by their change of heart and newfound opposition to private schooling to travel a few blocks up the Hill to say so.

The spokesmen for public education lined up, too, from the unions, the school boards association, even the National PTA—which testified that tax credits not only posed an immediate fiscal threat to public education but also portended a long-term "weakening of political and financial support for the public schools at the local level."

The real issue was thus squarely joined. The battles facing the Packwood-Moynihan bill would not be fought over what it might do to sustain educational diversity, widen the options for low- and moderate-income families, and bolster a network of effective, economical schools. Rather, its foes did not want federal dollars used in any way that would loosen the quasi monopoly of the public school system. And the Carter administration, elected in part with NEA support and now more apt to view public employee unions than working-class Catholic "ethnics" as key parts of its political base, was not about to break ranks on this issue, no matter what the president and his education commissioner had said two years before.

In a 1981 memoir of his days as HEW secretary, Joseph A. Califano, Jr.—one of the senior officials that Moynihan charged with "hiding"— writes that the Packwood-Moynihan bill "stood traditional concepts of government support of public education on their head" and "could have a ruinous impact on public schools."[37] Califano says it was at his urging that the White House worked to sever the K–12 tax credit from the higher-education part by shrewdly rushing out its own proposal to assist middle-income college students via an expansion of grant-based aid. (Carter's version of what would become the Middle Income Student Assistance Act was sent to Congress barely a fortnight after the Senate tax-credit hearings.)

Later in 1978, after bitter debate, a Packwood-Moynihan-style tuition tax-credit bill cleared the House of Representatives, and a modified version was okayed by the Senate Finance Committee and scheduled for floor action, which occurred during three hot—and heated—days in August. South Carolina Democrat Ernest F. "Fritz" Hollings was chosen to lead the fight against the K–12 portion of this measure. Although Finance Committee chairman Russell Long, the legendary Louisiana lawmaker, was nominally responsible for advancing his committee's bills through the Senate, he delegated that mission to Moynihan and Packwood. (The Senate was strongly controlled at the time by Democrats, 62–38.) This also enabled Long, no great fan of tuition tax credits, to keep his own powder dry for later use.

A powerful orator and shrewd tactician, Hollings mustered every possible argument on behalf of his amendment to strike the K–12 provision from the tax-credit bill, which everyone knew would pass if restricted to higher ed. Standing at Moynihan's side during most of this, I personally came in for a bit of the Hollings invective. Perhaps his most telling point— doubly so when voiced in his thick southern accent—was that tax credits would assist private "segregation academies" to continue to block the nation's progress toward racial equality. But what was mainly going on in the background was the massed forces of public education and their political allies in the Carter administration and Congress struggling to repel this threat to their hegemony.

They had the votes, too, including more than a few senators whose own children attended private schools. It has always seemed to me hypocritical when public officials refuse others the same opportunities that they secure for themselves and their families, but at sixty-three I suppose I'm still credulous. In the event, Hollings's amendment passed, 56–41, meaning a Senate-House conference committee would determine whether the K–12 provision was in or out of the final measure. Negotiators deadlocked. Eventually Russell Long himself defected, arguing that he had to defend the Senate's position and therefore could not sign a conference report containing the elementary-secondary element. In a highly unusual act, however, the House rejected the conference report providing tax credits exclusively for higher education. The conferees then sought to compromise on secondary (but not primary) school eligibility, but early one Sunday morning the handful of senators present in the chamber voted to send that version "back to conference," effectively killing the entire tax-credit measure, including the higher-ed portion. This spared Carter twice: from having to veto a K–12 aid plan that was popular among Catholics and from having to veto a college tuition tax-credit plan that was popular almost everywhere except inside the administration and the university lobbies.

Meanwhile, the president's proposal to aid middle-income college students, duly amended, was clearing its own legislative hurdles on roughly the same timetable as the tax measure. Moynihan and Packwood moved to extend its grant aid to needy K–12 students, too—"baby BEOGs," these were dubbed—but Hollings and his allies would have none of it. Bottom line: middle-income college students won, while Catholic schools and poor primary-secondary pupils lost. The public school monopoly won big.

Moynihan's role in this fracas warrants comment. The freshman Democrat was not only opposing an administration that, for the first time in eight years, belonged to his party; he was also going squarely against the American Federation of Teachers (AFT), whose longtime leader, Albert Shanker, was influential in New York (and national) Democratic politics and whose support had been important to Moynihan's election less than two years earlier.

But tangling with the Carter team never fazed the senator, whose previous post had entailed tangling with the Soviet Union at Turtle Bay on behalf of a GOP president, and who by 1978, comments Godfrey Hodgson in an insightful Moynihan biography, "was comprehensively disillusioned with Jimmy Carter."[38] There was also something oppositional, even countercyclical, about Pat that tended to place him athwart the conventional wisdom and regnant political attitudes of the day. As a neocon Democrat, he was appalled by the administration's foreign policy, which he saw as defeatist and far too inclined to appease communist aggression. (He grew countercyclical in a very different way after Ronald Reagan's 1980 victory.) And he was doing near-constant battle with the Carter White House—and the Califano-led HEW—over welfare reform. (A reprise of this was audible in the mid-nineties when Bill Clinton occupied the Oval Office.)

As for the teachers' union, it must be remembered that Moynihan was himself a practicing Roman Catholic, that many of his constituents and more of his supporters were Catholics—more, even, than were public schoolteachers—and that he had a lifelong tendency to identify with working-class concerns. Harvard professor though he was, he also loved to poke at what he saw as elite theories and elitist hang-ups.

Above all, I think, he believed that government should play fair, level the playing field, and keep its promises and that, in the case of Catholic schools, it wasn't honoring the 1965 compact and was instead letting itself be used by those who didn't like his coreligionists or their "parochial" institutions.

The tuition tax-credit battles of the late seventies were not, of course, the end of the larger school-choice war, although at the federal level the tax-code approach was gradually replaced by voucher and charter-school proposals and the policy goal shifted from a primary focus on salvaging schools to creating more decent opportunities for needy kids. The most enduring value conflict in American K–12 education is between partisans of the public school *system* and advocates of pluralism, competition, and choice. When such conflicts reach the political arena, defenders of established interests have an inherent advantage over those who stand to benefit from changes that have not yet occurred. The former are crystal clear about what they stand to lose while the latter have trouble even picturing, much less getting aroused over, policies or programs from which they have never benefited.

7 | *A Federal Department of Education?*

Breaking education out of HEW and giving it a seat of its own at the cabinet table was an old idea with many supporters. Almost every session of Congress saw bills introduced to elevate education's status on the federal organization chart, but before 1976 none was taken seriously. Indeed, between 1953 and 1976, none even reached the stage of formal committee hearings.

Carter's election changed all that. After its contentious 1968 Chicago convention and Humphrey's loss to Nixon, the Democratic Party revamped its nominating process to place less weight on party bosses and more on grassroots participation. Changing campaign-finance laws also magnified the influence of "political action committees." This, plus Jimmy Carter's own populist instincts and insurgent-style campaign, created a perfect opening for the National Education Association to throw its heft around on behalf of his nomination and election. Having already shed its school-administrator ranks and emerged as a vigorous and unashamed union of teachers, it was now one of the largest, best-financed, and politically deftest interest groups associated with the Democratic Party. (It was never formally tied but most of the candidates it supported had a "D" after their name and most of the causes it pursued held greater appeal for Democrats than Republicans. That's still true today.)

The NEA had a long federal wish list, headed by more education spending and creation of a separate Education Department. Though the latter goal was almost always clad in rhetoric about it being good for education, the NEA's real motive was to gain greater sway over a cabinet member—a person presumed to have Oval Office access and Capitol Hill clout—than it could reasonably hope to wield over any HEW secretary. After all, the AFL-CIO (with which the NEA was manifestly not affiliated, though its rival AFT was) had *its* own cabinet member in the labor secretary's chair. The NEA wanted no less.

Carter fruitfully courted the NEA during the run-up to the 1976 convention, and the union dispatched to that convention the largest single bloc of delegates—172 of them—committed to his nomination. His selection of Walter Mondale as running mate cemented the relationship. The vice presidential candidate had long-standing NEA ties—his brother was a union official—and the NEA would go on to support his own run for the Oval Office eight years later. As senator, Mondale was also a longtime backer of a larger federal education role and budget, which dovetailed with the NEA's other great priority: boosting Washington's share of K–12 revenues from its historic 6–8% to a full one-third. Addressing the NEA's annual meeting shortly before the 1976 Democratic convention, Mondale declared that "The present structure of education at the federal level is a disgrace. . . . The time has long since past [*sic*] when we should create a new department called the Department of Education under a Secretary of Education."[39]

In September 1976, the NEA endorsed a presidential candidate for the first time in its 119-year history and mustered its large field operations staff and political action committees to rustle dollars and hustle votes for the Democratic ticket.

The teachers' union understandably wanted something in return, and it was far easier for Carter to commit to a cabinet Education Department than to billions more in federal aid. Indeed, he had previewed such a commitment in October 1975, when he told Iowa teachers—not long before their state's crucial caucuses—that "The only department I would consider creating would be a separate Department of Education." In February 1976, he repeated that a cabinet-level Education Department was the sole exception to his general opposition to "the proliferation of federal agencies."[40] His rationale was that it "would consolidate the grant programs, job training, early childhood education, literacy training, and many other functions currently scattered throughout the government. The result would be a stronger voice for education at the federal level."[41]

By election day, it was obvious both that Carter owed a debt to the NEA and that the likeliest currency for paying it off was a cabinet chair.

The politics were clear. The merits were another matter. And the scope of the new agency was unresolved. Dozens of education-related programs were scattered far beyond HEW's Education Division and its two main units: the hoary U.S. Office of Education, headed by a commissioner, and the vintage-1972 National Institute of Education, headed by a director. Over both was an assistant HEW secretary for education, who in the Carter administration was Mary Frances Berry, later the long-term, headstrong, and intensely partisan chair of the U.S. Commission on Civil Rights.

It was not, however, careless government housekeeping that had produced this messy sprawl. Rather, the many non-HEW programs were not simply *education* programs. They were simultaneously veterans' programs,

Indian programs, food programs, armed forces dependents' programs, child development programs, and so forth. Each was tied to more than one federal mission—and those other missions intersected with powerful constituencies that were markedly less interested in education per se. The child development people, for example, didn't view Head Start as primarily an education program but as a social service that should be housed and aligned with other children's programs. The military saw the Defense Department's network of schools as a key personnel benefit for far-flung servicemen and women. Native Americans regarded the Bureau of Indian Affairs schools as essential tribal institutions. Scientists believed that the curriculum projects financed by the National Science Foundation were needed to strengthen America's scientific infrastructure. And on and on.

These programs not only had boosters, advocates, and dependents. With time and money, they had also acquired their own bureaucratic turf in other agencies and their own networks of congressional committees, subcommittees, and staffers, all of which stood to lose status or power if the federal organization chart were seriously reshaped around the education mission.

Even a narrowly conceived Education Department—such as elevating the extant HEW Education Division to cabinet status—had foes, both outside government and within. The AFT's Shanker feared it would strengthen the rival NEA. Higher-education interests were alarmed that it would favor primary-secondary schools. HEW secretary Joseph A. Califano, a formidable Washington operator, did not want to lose a big chunk of his domain—and his earlier experience in the Johnson White House had convinced him that the fewer separate, interest-driven officials with direct access to the president the better, a point he forcefully shared with White House aides and Carter himself. Califano liked big departments whose secretaries would broker conflicts and rivalries before these reached the Oval Office. If HEW needed restructuring, he wanted a Pentagon-style arrangement in which the individual "service" secretaries answer to the secretary of defense.

Within the White House complex, the Office of Management and Budget also harbored long-standing objections to the proliferation of narrow-gauge programs and special-interest-driven agencies. OMB's mantra then as now was large, multipurpose units and flexible programs well suited to making trade-offs and adapting to new circumstances and altered priorities.

Such objections gave the White House pause, and for months after his inauguration it appeared that Carter might renege on his promise to the

NEA, as he had to the Catholic bishops. In June 1977, he directed OMB's government reorganization unit to examine and report on "whether or not it was feasible to have a separate Department of Education." During the summer, however, the NEA mounted a full-court press with the help of its White House allies, including Mondale and presidential chief of staff Hamilton Jordan, who said, as recorded by Califano, "I don't know anything about the merits, but I know the politics, and politically the NEA is important to us, and it's important for the President to keep his word."[42] In August, a senior NEA lobbyist stated that if Carter welched on his commitment, "We're going to have a hell of a lot of members who are going to feel double-crossed."[43]

By September, OMB staffers were meeting with the NEA to evaluate options, and in late November a "decision memo" went forward to the president. Here is how Califano recalled his own stance:

> After my first year of experience at HEW, I was even more deeply
> troubled by the idea of a separate department and I expressed my
> argument strongly. From the President's point of view, such a
> constituency-oriented department put yet another special interest
> directly on his back. . . . Inevitably, the Secretary of such a narrowly
> composed department would be less responsive to the President as the
> daily pressure of the constituencies corroded the relationship with the
> White House. The narrow interest situation would be aggravated
> because the special interests to which an education department would
> be largely responsive—the NEA teachers union, school administra-
> tors, groups protecting pet programs—were not the interests it was
> supposed to serve; its obligations were to the students. . . .[44]

Surprisingly, for a Great Society Democrat, the HEW secretary even played the "federal control of education" card more oft associated with conservatives. "With federal funds go federal strings," he wrote. "Against this financial and bureaucratic horizon, a separate education department looms as a truly dangerous specter to our tradition of intellectual freedom of inquiry and institutional autonomy."[45]

Others, however, were also whispering in Carter's ear, and in early January 1978 Califano and the rest of the cabinet and staff learned of the president's decision: to support creation of a separate Education Department and to construct a broad version of such an agency, amassing under one roof the education-related programs of multiple agencies. In his State of the Union message that month, Carter said: "[N]ow it's time to take another major step by creating a separate Department of Education."[46] In late February, he advised Congress that he had directed OMB and HEW to "work with Congress" to develop legislation that would "let us focus on Federal educational policy, at the highest levels of our government; permit closer coordination of Federal education programs and other related activities; reduce Federal regulations . . . and cut duplication; [and] assist school districts, teachers, and parents to make better use of local resources and ingenuity."

That was pretty nebulous, and enormous intragovernment fighting ensued over just how broad to make the proposed cabinet agency and what, exactly, to transfer into it. Meanwhile, Senator Abraham Ribicoff (D-CT), himself a former HEW secretary, longtime advocate of a separate Education Department, and now, as chair of the Senate Government Affairs Committee, well positioned to make it happen, had already scheduled hearings on his own version of such a measure.

Rather than draft its own bill, the Carter team opted to testify favorably on Ribicoff's version, then work with him to craft a mutually acceptable plan. Hours before OMB director James McIntyre appeared at the February 1978 hearing, the president told him to modify his testimony to widen the proposed department's scope. The hastily expanded list that McIntyre presented to Ribicoff contained some 167 extant programs drawn from seven agencies—much like the senator's own bill, though still far from a comprehensive ingathering of all federal education activities.

During the balance of 1978, after stripping off Head Start, school lunch programs, and Indian schools, whose constituents insisted that their cherished programs stay where they were, the Senate readily (77–11) passed a slimmed-down Department of Education Organization Act. The House of Representatives balked, however. Though its Government Affairs Committee reported out a bill, rank-and-file opposition was mounting. At the behest of the AFT, the AFL-CIO noisily opposed the measure; conservative members warned about federal control of the curriculum; and major newspapers editorialized against the bill. This was, in fact, one of the few policy issues in memory to elicit parallel criticisms from the liberal *New York Times* and *Washington Post* and the conservative *Wall Street Journal*. In urging House members to oppose the Education Department measure, the *Post*, for example, bitingly termed it "the inspiration of the NEA, an organization that has much the same relation to the public schools as the plumbers union has to the plumbing business." The *Journal* groused that "The new Education Department will be the product of old-style pork barrel politics plus the new-style tendency of legislators to try to create an impression of government in perpetual and vigorous motion. It is a bad idea."[47]

Lacking the votes to pass the measure and warned by foes that they would bring the chamber's business to a halt that election-year autumn, the House leadership didn't let the Education Department bill reach the floor in 1978. Whereupon the Ninety-fifth Congress came to an end and the Ninety-sixth had to start afresh.

The NEA regrouped, furiously working that fall for congressional candidates committed to the department concept and expending some $3 million in political action funds on their behalf. Seeking to mute the "payoff to the NEA" argument against the measure, it also mobilized a larger coalition of interest groups in support of the bill, evidently believing this would camouflage its own role. (The NEA did, however, retain firm strategic control of the actual lobbying effort.)

The Carter administration also stepped up its congressional-relations activity, assembling a high-level task force from across the executive branch to coordinate efforts with Ribicoff and his House counterpart (chairman Jack Brooks, D-TX) as well as with the NEA and other advocacy groups. After fresh bills were introduced in January 1979, Mondale reportedly spent part of every day on this issue, and some analysts say Carter himself devoted more time to lobbying for the Education Department bill than for anything else save the Panama Canal treaties.

By now the White House had scaled back its vision of the new department to little more than the extant HEW Education Division. That didn't do much for the broad, multi-agency coordination that the president and other backers once sought, but it meant the 1979 legislative process did not have to contend with such controversial add-ons as the school lunch program, Head Start, and Indian education.

The Senate took up the bill in late April. As it happened, Pat Moynihan emerged as leader of the Democratic opposition, and I again found myself by his side on the Senate floor. Though he had no qualms about working to neuter or defeat a Carter-administration proposal, he hated to go up against Ribicoff, who was a friend, Finance Committee colleague, and fellow alumnus of the Kennedy administration. But unlike the tuition tax-credit tussle a year earlier, on this issue he could make common cause with Shanker's AFT, which by now had catalyzed a broad-based if ineffectual "Committee

Against a Separate Department of Education" that contained many prominent education figures plus the Catholic bishops and, for once, the *New York Times*.

Partly because he was thin-skinned and partly because of that newspaper's wide influence in both New York and Washington, Pat always took the *Times* seriously though he often disagreed with it. In this case, the editorial writers opined that supporters of the proposed department "misunderstand the nature of American education, which is characterized by diversity. The legitimate centers of gravity are, and ought to remain, in the educational authorities of the states and the local communities for the public schools, and in the independent governing boards of the colleges and the universities."[48]

He was not, however, just doing the bidding of others. Moynihan was nothing if not a keen-eyed observer of politics and government, and his experience joined with his instincts to conclude that this agency was a bad idea, notwithstanding its kinship to the National Foundation for Higher Education that he had once talked Nixon into proposing. The Carter-style department, he judged, wouldn't work well. It would always want more money—and would pay scant attention to what the dollars bought by way of results. (This time, he and Califano held similar views.) As a narrowly conceived entity focused mainly on public schooling it would, he forecast, "drive the President crazy" with its demands for funds and attention, and in time presidents would refuse even to meet with their education secretaries. "In the Office of Management and Budget," Moynihan predicted, "they will keep a tab as to how much per minute it costs for the President to see the Secretary of Education."[49]

Such an agency, he foresaw, would be beholden to adult interest groups more than the concerns of children and parents. It would be hostile to private and parochial schools. It augured greater federal control of curricular matters and a diminution of academic freedom. He was also swayed by a letter from Harvard friend and colleague David Riesman, perhaps the most respected figure in U.S. higher education at the time, who wrote that "education is best served by being part of a much more powerful coalition. . . . It needs to have many diverse sources of support, combined with a certain precious obscurity."

Moynihan's floor strategy was puckish but instructive. He set out to kill the bill with kindness—by adding back into the proposed department all those non–Education Division programs and functions that others had stripped out, and turning it into a massive, comprehensive agency worthy of cabinet status, complete with crosscutting responsibilities, a broader base of support, more diverse constituents, and greater capacity to coordinate and set priorities for more than a handful of programs and institutions.

Accordingly, joined by California Republican S. I. Hayakawa, also a former professor, he submitted a complex amendment to transfer some eighty education-related programs into the Education Department from all over the federal landscape. These included not just the obvious candidates already tried by Carter and Ribicoff but also such whopping additions as the whole of the National Science Foundation and the National Institutes of Health. "If there is to be such a department," Moynihan explained, "it seems to me it is altogether desirable that it be a large department, a complex one, and one incorporating so many interests as not easily to be dominated by any one of them." That would be healthier than elevating HEW's Education Division to cabinet status in what he brutally termed "a backroom deal, born out of a squalid politics."

Pat never really expected his amendment to pass. (The *Washington Post* termed it "the Moynihan monstrosity.") But Professor Moynihan hoped to show his colleagues and the nation what it would mean to organize a federal agency systematically and comprehensively around education.

Ribicoff wearily responded that he liked and agreed with much of the Moynihan amendment and had indeed done his best to construct a broader-gauge department but this had proven politically infeasible, that half a loaf was better than none, and that perhaps the agency could be enlarged at a later date. The White House, meanwhile, didn't much care so long as it could declare victory and hand a scalp to the NEA. Hence, as Shanker wrote in his weekly *New York Times* column on April 29, "the Carter Administration is now busy staving off efforts" to assemble an Education Department much more like its original proposal, "because the Administration knows a bill which includes all will never pass." [50]

As expected, the Moynihan amendment lost, as did most others, and after four days of debate the Senate voted, 72–21, to create the new department.

The House of Representatives, however, again balked. After its Government Operations Committee approved the bill by a single vote, the politics grew ugly. Califano recounts a painful episode where, with Education Commissioner Boyer leaving government to lead the Carnegie Foundation, he sought to name Marshall Smith (later dean of the Stanford Ed School) as acting commissioner. Whereupon the congressional Black Caucus threw a fit, insisting that Mary Berry be given the post and objecting to Smith on grounds that he had once assisted Christopher Jencks with a book (*Inequality*) that questioned the efficacy of school desegregation in boosting the achievement of black students.

Califano recalls that "[Black Caucus chairman Parren] Mitchell threatened to lead a major assault against the Department of Education on the House floor unless the designation of Smith as Acting Commissioner was withdrawn."[51] This alarmed an administration already nervous about mustering enough votes for the new agency. In the face of strong objection by Califano and HEW undersecretary Hale Champion, Mondale insisted that Smith withdraw and Berry be given the post, which is what happened.

Remarking on that shabby business, the *Times* charged the vice president with behaving "shamelessly," using "cruel" tactics and caving before "absurd" charges. The Jencks book, the editorial board correctly noted, "is a serious treatise that no responsible person would condemn as racist. Those who hurl such charges and those who appease them should never be entrusted with education or scholarship in any setting."[52] (Califano lost his own job that summer, in part because of his lack of cooperation with White House efforts to carve this new cabinet department out of HEW.)

The legislative process dragged on. Not until July 11 did the House—barely—pass the Education Department bill, and matters almost came unglued again when a Senate-House conference committee produced the final version a few weeks later. But on October 17 Carter signed the Department of Education Organization Act, and the new agency, led by former federal judge Shirley M. Hufstedler, opened for business in May 1980, during what proved to be the final seven months of Carter's presidency. By midsummer, the Republican Party platform was calling for the department's abolition, and when Ronald Reagan strode into the Oval Office the following January, he had been elected in part on the basis of his pledge to put it out of its misery. With a GOP majority in the Senate for the first time in ages, it looked as if he might manage to do precisely that.

I learned plenty from this episode about government and politics. Congress yields few easy victories, and the more disruptive the idea, the more relentless the opposition. Nothing is harder than changing government structures—but that's probably a good thing, considering what thin justifications such changes often rest on. A reorganization as important as slicing education away from HEW and adding a chair to the cabinet table may be based on considerations as evanescent as a hasty campaign promise—yet campaign promises are often broken (as in the case of Carter and tuition tax credits) if the promise maker is deeper in debt to opposing interests. Even important ideas typically get so distorted during their passage through the legislative meat grinder that what finally squeezes between the blades lacks whatever savor held greatest appeal in the original idea.

I also learned a bit more about Pat Moynihan, whom I thought I knew well. He could be vain and thin-skinned, yes, not to mention quixotic and occasionally impish. In the grip of a strong conviction or powerful idea, however, he was resourceful, eloquent, and tenacious. And he never quite stopped being a professor. I suspect that his Senate colleagues didn't always enjoy his lectures, but he persisted, coming up with data, examples, quotes, bits of history, more data, and prescient forecasts the like of which few of them encountered anywhere else.

8 | Becoming a Republican

Despite serving the Nixon administration twice and occasionally vot- ing Republican (more often voting *against* unspeakable Democratic candidates), I had long viewed myself as some sort of Democrat. I entered the 1960s a youthful but earnest Kennedy-Johnson liberal, fired by JFK's vision for America and LBJ's commitment to vanquish the poverty that Michael Harrington and Oscar Lewis wrote about so movingly and that I saw up close in the housing projects of East Cambridge. Indeed, that's what drew me into the field of education. When President Johnson declared schools to be "our primary weapon in the war on poverty," I took note. When, two months before I graduated from college, he signed ESEA in front of the one-room Texas schoolhouse he had attended as a child, I was stirred by what it meant for America. Terming this "the most sweeping ed- ucational bill ever to come before Congress," Johnson depicted it as "a ma- jor new commitment of the Federal Government to quality and equality in the schooling that we offer our young people" and said that all who sup- ported it on Capitol Hill

> will be remembered in history as men and women who began a new
> day of greatness in American society. . . . By passing this bill, we
> bridge the gap between helplessness and hope for more than 5 million
> educationally deprived children. . . . As a son of a tenant farmer,
> I know that education is the only valid passport from poverty. As a
> former teacher—and, I hope, a future one—I have great expectations
> of what this law will mean for all of our young people.[53]

I was idealistic, half-formed, and eager to pitch in to make America a better, fairer place. I had not yet faced four classes a day of mostly sullen twelfth graders, ill served by one of the nation's premier school systems. I had not yet seen the Upward Bound program founder in its efforts to transform the life prospects of urban teens. I had not yet been exposed to ed school non- sense. Coleman's seminal report was a year in the future. And I had no expe- rience with the challenge of implementing grandly conceived federal laws.

Still, the prospect of deploying education as a powerful tool for social betterment was a life-changing, career-molding inspiration. This was a crusade I yearned to join. Perhaps I could even help to halt the "death at an early age" that Kozol depicted in the schools of poor and minority young-sters.[54] Maybe I could change kids' lives.

Though I scarcely noticed at the time, the Kennedy-Johnson vision of education was embedded in what some today term a "national greatness" view of America, which we now associate primarily with Republicans of a certain stripe. In the early and mid-sixties, Vietnam, urban riots, and campus protests had not yet jarred our self-confidence, and there was no sense—at least among civic, business, and political leaders—that education was about self-actualization or child-centeredness. Rather, it was part of what a muscular country did to assure itself a robust, prosperous, and se-cure future, while incorporating all its citizens into that future. Democrats actually talked that way forty-odd years ago, and meant it. Republicans of the day were more apt to murmur about local control and fret about federal interference. Given that choice—and insofar as I had any political consciousness—I was proud to think myself a Democrat. (Like not be-coming a Dayton lawyer, this probably also had to do with differentiating myself from parents who were then casting their ballots mostly for GOP candidates.)

Much of this changed, though very gradually, over the next fifteen years. Several developments fed my slow transformation into a Republican.

As a graduate student, I became acquainted with, and impressed by, the brilliant early leaders of what became known as "neoconservatism," people like James Q. Wilson, Nathan Glazer, Irving Kristol, Daniel Bell, and Nor-man Podhoretz—all of them Moynihan pals who were apt to turn up for lunch or drinks or movie night on Francis Avenue. The first issue of their flagship journal, *The Public Interest*, appeared during my senior year at Har-vard. Coeditor Kristol's recollection of those early days is worth noting:

> We certainly thought there was a role for government in moving
> people out of poverty—a much larger role than conservatives thought
> appropriate. But we did not believe that political activism (a.k.a. "the
> class struggle") could deliver people from poverty. . . . For the first
> seven years of its existence, *The Public Interest* was generally regarded
> (and regarded itself) as a moderately liberal journal. The editors and
> most of the contributors, after all, were registered Democrats. . . . It
> was the election of 1972 that precipitated the first political divisions in
> our community. . . . My Republican vote produced little shock waves

in the New York intellectual community. . . . Some of my best friends and close associates at *The Public Interest* did not join me in that heresy. The magazine continued to shy away from anything resembling partisan politics and concentrated on revisionist social science. . . . But we were never single-minded economists or social scientists. On the contrary, we soon discovered that behind the hard realities of economics and social science were the equally hard realities of morality, family, culture, and religion—the "habits of the mind" and "habits of the heart," as Tocqueville said, that determine the quality and character of a people.[55]

Years would pass before I wrote for Kristol's distinguished (and now sadly vanished) journal or for Podhoretz's *Commentary*, the other neoconservative flagship, but from nearly the beginning I found myself nodding in agreement with much that I read there. Yes, government should try to solve social problems. But noble intentions aren't enough. The programs also had to *work*—it was unhealthy for a society to be misled by its elected officials or duped by lofty pronouncements—and their implementation, besides invariably proving more challenging than expected, needed to be watched lest its unintended consequences do harm. While reading such thoughts on magazine pages, I was absorbing similar lessons from the best of my ed school courses and from widening encounters with real schools and government programs.

Reaching Washington in 1969, I still considered myself a Democrat, part of that peculiar den of Moynihan cubs in the Nixon White House. But except for half doubts about the administration's "southern strategy"—offset by its unexpected warmth toward affirmative action, which I then viewed as a good idea—nothing about the Nixon education agenda in 1969 and 1970 struck me as misguided. Rather, it seemed just what the situation called for. (To be sure, I had a role in shaping it.) In retrospect, however, I see that we, too, vested excessive hope in our own ideas for new federal ventures, almost as if we hadn't been reading *The Public Interest*. I was bamboozled, for example, by my own romantic vision for the National Institute of Education—and years had to pass before I recognized how meager an accomplishment that proved to be. Moynihan was deceived by his own lofty pronouncements about the proposed National Foundation for Higher Education.

We also underestimated the resistance of the education lobbies and the Democratic Congress to Nixon's proposals, especially when budget disputes were heated. Yet my growing awareness of those barriers to change—above all, the deaf ears turned to the president's plea to shift the focus from school inputs to results—fueled more doubts regarding Washington's conventional education wisdom.

The early seventies proved a sobering time as my dismay over the shambles and scandals of the administration I had recently left jostled with my deepening disaffection with left-leaning Democrats. "Neocons" grew ever less welcome in their company—post-Vietnam foreign policy was the big divide—and I observed a party ever more tightly tethered to groups that claimed to care about the education of children but in reality cared more for the interests of adults. I had not lost faith in education as solver of social problems, but at every turn I encountered fresh evidence that educators themselves, and the political figures they relied on, were principally concerned about themselves, their dogmas—E. D. Hirsch aptly terms it their "thoughtworld"—and their institutions. My stint at Brookings framed such a view of higher education, and my time on Moynihan's Senate staff left me disheartened by the extent to which a Democratic president and his congressional allies took their policy signals from the teachers' unions and other "establishment" forces.

I also discerned that the Democrats' main education agenda—"equity" in its infinite permutations—no longer addressed what was fast becoming the country's foremost education problem, namely weak pupil achievement. This gave rise, in March 1981, two years before *A Nation at Risk*, to my essay in *Life* magazine titled "A Call for Quality Education." In retrospect, it might even be termed prescient. At the time, it was just a heterodox, rattle-the-china argument that stated my own policy priorities.

Though still on Moynihan's Senate payroll, I agreed to provide quiet campaign advice to the Reagan campaign's "issues" staff—then as now, GOP education experts are scarce—and after the 1980 election was asked to join the "transition team" at the new Department of Education, where, really for the first time, I found myself working closely with Republicans and conservatives of various stripes—and without Pat as buffer.

After four years in the Senate, I was also restive, a tad bored, and ready for a change. Though moonlighting on the Reagan transition team cost me a family trip back to India that Christmas, it was stimulating to poke around the six-month-old Education Department and try to determine what a GOP administration might make of it.

Budget director Dave Stockman (whom I knew from when he lived upstairs at the Moynihans) drew me into deliberations about the new administration's education policies and budgets—sharp reductions is how he approached the latter—and, partly for that reason, incoming Education Secretary Ted Bell asked me to join his team. Here is how Bell's memoir recounts that painful episode:

> David Stockman, director of the Office of Management and Budget, suggested that the very competent Chester Finn be appointed deputy undersecretary for planning and budget in ED. Finn had served in the Nixon White House. I had known him from my Nixon-Ford years, and I knew that I could work with him. Given Stockman's support, I was hopeful that he would be the first one to break the [White House personnel] logjam. But despite this endorsement, Finn was promptly rejected by White House Personnel because he was currently serving on the staff of Democratic Senator Pat Moynihan. . . . That was enough to do him in. I failed to win clearance for Finn.[56]

Martin Anderson, who knew me in the Nixon White House and was now back in Washington as Reagan's senior domestic policy adviser, told me later that he personally vetoed my appointment because he "didn't want there to happen to Reagan what had happened to Nixon," which I took to mean that he didn't want Moynihan types—or neocons or Democrats—burrowing within a GOP administration that intended to be conservative. (I was not the only Bell pick blackballed by the White House.)

At the time, I wanted the Education Department job so badly I could taste it, so my early-1981 rejection felt devastating. Mercifully, before the election I had been courted by Vanderbilt University's new education dean, Willis Hawley, then taking advantage of Vanderbilt's absorption of the old George Peabody College for Teachers to rebuild his Nashville-based faculty. The university's small but respectable public-policy institute also signaled an interest in me, and when it turned out that Vanderbilt's Medical School was keen to bring Renu into its Pathology Department, we had to take this choice seriously. After all, how often in a modern two-career family does the same employer offer attractive opportunities to both spouses at the same time?

With Bell and Stockman beckoning, however, and being plenty busy with my Moynihan day job as well as the (unpaid) transition work, Renu and I equivocated about whether to travel to Nashville to check the place out and formally "audition" for these faculty berths. We almost canceled the trip, then said what the heck, we'd better have a look. Coincidentally, just minutes before my scheduled presentation to future colleagues at the Vanderbilt Institute for Public Policy Studies, Ted Bell tracked me down by phone to report that things were not going well at the White House and he was not sure he would be able to deliver my Education Department appointment. Crestfallen and upset, I treated my imminent lecture seriously—and the audience did, too. Renu was also well received at the medical school and increasingly ready for a job change herself. So we accepted the proffered faculty posts and started searching for a house in Nashville, selecting schools for Arti and Aloke, and preparing to move the family, which happened in the summer of 1981.

One of Tennessee's attractions for me, besides a flattering post as full professor at a well-regarded university at age thirty-seven—and an honorable escape from Washington, which contained both a job I was tired of and one that had been denied me—was that my quondam "kiddie corps" colleague from the Nixon White House, Lamar Alexander, was then governor and had placed education squarely in his policy bull's-eye. When I wrote that we were on our way, he urged me to get in touch upon arrival. In the end, that also helped keep me within GOP territory, notwithstanding the White House view that I was a dangerous Democrat. Only gradually did I realize that being rebuffed for the post with Ted Bell was, in career terms, a lucky break rather than a fatal setback. It led both to the independent credential of a professor and the opportunity to re-enter government four years later with Bill Bennett.

On reflection, my JFK-LBJ-style view of education's role in American society and the lives of its people didn't change much between 1960 and 1980, but the political world changed around me. What I valued—equal opportunity, color blindness, upward mobility via powerful schools with high standards, choices made by families rather than bureaucrats or judges, kids' needs given precedence over adult interests—still felt right (and does today). By the late 1970s, however, except for Moynihan and a handful of others, that wasn't the way Democrats viewed education. Republicans hadn't quite figured out what they sought in this domain—they were still better at saying what they opposed—but their values seemed closer to mine. My confidence in big-government programs was also waning as I watched close-up the Senate floor debates on such things, drank more deeply of post-Coleman analyses, and immersed myself in neocon policy journals. Above all, I saw that the "equity agenda" was spent. It had largely done what good it could for U.S. education and was becoming counterproductive. It was time to craft a very different plan—and probably necessary to make some waves.

Moving to Nashville and edging toward the GOP also meant moving out from under the Moynihan umbrella that had sheltered me for fifteen remarkable years. We remained personally cordial thereafter when we bumped into each other at big Washington events and happy or sad occasions (including Jim Coleman's funeral in Chicago in 1995), but it was never the same. In preparation for his 1982 reelection campaign, with Tim Russert's shrewd counsel and mindful of the many pitfalls in New York politics, Pat gradually moved leftward on a number of issues—which also suited his countercyclical tendencies, given that Reaganism had replaced Carterism as Washington's conventional wisdom. My friendship with Liz cooled, too, after I married Renu. I watched the remaining two decades of Pat's remarkable dual career with interest and admiration—George Will famously quipped that he wrote more books than most of his Senate colleagues had *read*—and with profound gratitude. His 2003 funeral service at an imposing old Catholic church in downtown Washington was packed not only with familiar political faces from both parties but also with eminent academics, respected journalists, and dozens of former staff members. Among the teachers and mentors who shaped me and gave me opportunities, he was by far the most important. I just wish I had found a suitable occasion during his later years to tell him that.

Part III | *The Eighties*

E arly in this decade, American education nervously began to turn a sharp corner. The big, symbolic event was _A Nation at Risk_, the 1983 report of the National Commission on Excellence in Education and chief catalyst of the "excellence movement" that still rocks us. This momentous shift from a fixation on equity and services to an obsession with student achievement and school performance followed logically from the Coleman-sparked realization that, if what you seek is better results, you cannot depend on fiddling with inputs to produce them. That this understanding took the better part of two decades to reach the policy mainstream can be attributed partly to the education system's sluggish reaction time but more to the slowness of the country's awakening to its schools' quality problem.

Stable enrollments also meant the United States could afford to focus on quality. Modest growth in the elementary grades during the eighties was offset by high-school shrinkage, even as per pupil spending escalated by 37 percent (in constant dollars).

As with Sputnik a quarter century earlier, what seized the nation's attention was anxiety that our well-being was jeopardized by inadequacies in our K–12 system. Americans may have been mostly content with their _own_ children's schools but were also starting to understand that the system as a whole was not delivering the goods. The propulsion behind the excellence movement was—and today still is—the foreboding that to leave that system unchanged was to court stagnation and decline.

Terrel H. "Ted" Bell was not an obvious choice for secretary of education in the new Reagan cabinet. Though a Republican who had served in senior posts during the Nixon and Ford administrations— including two years as education commissioner—he was also a card-carrying member of the public-education establishment who had testified in favor of Carter's plan to create the department that Reagan vowed to abolish. The president's conservative base viewed Bell with suspicion. That he was also a decent, honorable man didn't redeem him in their eyes— which would likely have looked sourly upon _anyone_ in this unloved post. Bell was, however, highly regarded by Richard Wirthlin, the president's trusted longtime pollster and a fellow Mormon, and by Utah Senator Orrin Hatch, also a Mormon and, after the GOP won control of the Senate in 1980, chairman of the Education and Labor Committee. In deference to them—and because Reagan advisers found slim pickings when searching for credentialed Republican educationists that the Senate would confirm—Bell was invited back to Washington. Presidential aides, however, placed him on a short tether.

Ronald Reagan knew education was important, but in the Oval Office in 1981 other things were more so. The president was preoccupied by the Armageddon that could result if the United States and the Soviet Union did not find a way to make the Cold War stay cold, maybe even end it. He also had to jump-start a stalled economy. Those ultimately successful missions absorbed most of his attention, leaving little for domestic agencies and their issues. If trusted by White House aides, the heads of such agencies enjoyed a fairly free hand, within budget limits. If not, the short leash left them little running room.

Reagan, moreover, while an activist president on selected fronts, simply did not believe that Uncle Sam had much direct role to play in education. His instincts said leave it to states, communities, and parents, and prevent Washington bureaucrats from meddling. His chief domestic adviser, Ed Meese, was bent on abolishing the Education Department, and his budget director, David Stockman, was keen to slash its spending (and much else).

It was hard enough for the new education secretary to defend the programmatic and bureaucratic territory he had inherited, much less find any backing (or budget leeway) for fresh initiatives. Partly in frustration, Bell soon opted to create a blue-ribbon commission to assess the current status of American education. His determination to launch such a panel also arose from his sense that America needed a Sputnik-like shock. In his 1988 memoir, Bell recalled:

> Although the president's popularity was high, the nation itself was not in happy shape in 1981. . . . The national mood was one of self-doubt and helplessness. . . . It was in the context of this pervasive decline . . . that I was hearing constant complaints about education and its effectiveness. . . . We needed to regain our confidence in the future. This had to happen on many fronts, but it had to begin with our schools. . . . We needed some means of rallying the American people around their schools and colleges. Educators also needed to be shaken out of their complacency.[1]

When the White House, only mildly attentive to education and wary of anything proposed by Bell, declined to appoint a presidential panel, the secretary resolved to name his own. For months his staff dickered with Reagan aides over the commission's charter and members, but by August he was able to announce its creation and composition. In October, the Excellence Commission held its first meeting. A year and a half later, its epochal report was finished.

Bell chose well. The eighteen-member group was chaired by David P. Gardner, then en route from the University of Utah (where Bell had come to know him) to a distinguished term as president of the University of California. Joining him were business leaders, another university president (Yale's Bart Giamatti), a former governor and congressman (Minnesota's Al Quie), some tough-minded state and local leaders, several practicing K–12 educators, two eminent scientists, and at least one true-red Reaganite: Annette Kirk, the charming wife of conservative icon Russell Kirk. The secretary's charge to them focused on educational quality. And, perhaps because the White House expected so little from this panel that it didn't meddle much, he was able to assure nervous commissioners that they would enjoy ample independence—and then make good on that pledge.

A Nation at Risk hit with a bang that still echoes. It spoke to the public in stark, dramatic language that flowed from the pen of Harvard physicist Gerald Holton:

> Our Nation is at risk. Our once unchallenged preeminence in commerce, industry, science, and technological innovation is being overtaken by competitors throughout the world. This report is concerned with only one of the many causes and dimensions of the problem, but it is the one that under girds American prosperity, security, and civility. We report to the American people that while we can take justifiable pride in what our schools and colleges have historically accomplished and contributed to the United States and the well-being of its people, the educational foundations of our society are presently being eroded by a rising tide of mediocrity that threatens our very future as a Nation and a people. What was unimaginable a generation ago has begun to occur—others are matching and surpassing our educational attainments.[2]

Yet responsibility for this dire situation sat limply in our own laps:

If an unfriendly foreign power had attempted to impose on America the mediocre educational performance that exists today, we might well have viewed it as an act of war. As it stands, we have allowed this to happen to ourselves. . . . We have, in effect, been committing an act of unthinking, unilateral educational disarmament.[3]

The essence of the problem diagnosed by the commission was that U.S. children weren't learning enough and their schools weren't effective enough. Every one of the thirteen "indicators of risk" cited in its report involved weak and often declining achievement. Its many remedies ranged from stiffer high-school graduation requirements to more rigorous standards to better-trained teachers. All of them, panelists insisted, rested on a demand for "the best effort and performance from all students" and the "beliefs that everyone can learn, that everyone is born with an urge to learn which can be nurtured, [and] that a solid high-school education is within the reach of virtually all. . . ."

After an initial off-key reception of the report, the White House was pleasantly surprised by the positive stir it created and quickly embraced the commission's verdict as if it had been a presidential initiative rather than something grudgingly tolerated. In the next eleven weeks, Reagan appeared with Bell at some eighteen education events, and his participation dramatically boosted the report's visibility. Newspapers printed its full text. The initial Government Printing Office press run sold out. Commission members held forth on widely watched Sunday TV shows. Perhaps most important, a number of governors (including future education secretaries Lamar Alexander of Tennessee and Richard Riley of South Carolina) welcomed the report, which was made easier by the firsthand briefing they received during the summer of 1983, when Vice President Bush invited members of the National Governors Association to a Kennebunkport clambake joined by Bell and his family, who were vacationing in Maine.

One should not, however, conclude that this sixty-five-page report single-handedly altered the course of American education. Years were to pass before much change was visible. Moreover, the soil had already been tilled and fertilized—and *A Nation at Risk* wasn't the only seed planted during the early 1980s. In fact, the Excellence Commission turned out to have plenty of company.

9 | *Quality Gains Traction*

Widening awareness that College Board scores were drooping and many high-school graduates were ill prepared for what followed had already triggered multiple efforts to trace the source of these ailments and suggest possible cures.

I had penned several sharply worded articles on the imperative of placing quality atop U.S. education priorities and the obsolescence of education's reigning "liberal consensus" (more on this below). By 1982, Diane Ravitch and I had formed the Educational Excellence Network (on which more below, also).

In 1981, the Southern Regional Education Board, a consortium of fifteen states mostly in the Old Confederacy, released a hard-hitting report called *The Need for Quality*, which urged wide-ranging reforms in the region's generally mediocre K-12 system, including more exacting teacher standards, a core curriculum for all schools, and reduced emphasis on vocational education. The following year, the Mississippi legislature—Mississippi!—"shocked the education world," as Thomas Toch put it, by enacting "the largest tax increase in the state's history to pay for a comprehensive package of school reforms."[4]

By 1981, Ronald Edmonds, an analyst working primarily within the New York City school system, had delivered several influential articles and speeches addressing both the urgency and the feasibility of transforming weak schools into facsimiles of those that were already effective. Rebuking those who had interpreted Coleman as saying "schools don't matter" because socioeconomic status and peer effects swamp the efforts of educators, he showed not only that schools matter plenty in how well and how much children learn but also that some schools are notably better at this than others. Pioneering what came to be known as "effective schools research," he identified five characteristics of such schools, including strong leadership, an emphasis on basic-skills acquisition, and high expectations for student learning.[5]

Other studies, task forces, exhortations, and analyses were under way on all sides, several of which coincidentally emerged within weeks of *A Nation At Risk*—and conveyed similar messages. The Education Commission of the States (ECS) released *Action for Excellence,* the product of a task force led by North Carolina's respected "education governor," Jim Hunt. The Twentieth Century Fund published *Making the Grade* (Ravitch and I served on that panel, staffed by political scientist Paul Peterson). The College Board unveiled *Academic Preparation for College*, which defined the skills and knowledge needed for high-school graduates to succeed in tertiary education. And in September a committee named by the National Science Board outlined a plan—*Educating Americans for the 21st Century*—that called for big changes in math and science instruction.

The notable feature of this flurry of reports, studies, and articles is that nearly all of them pointed in the same direction: toward a radical shift in America's education priorities, a fresh commitment to quality and a premium on stronger academic achievement. A synthesis by the Education Resources Information Center said their "common premise . . . is that the nation's global preeminence in science, technology, industry, commerce, and military defense is threatened by its mediocre education."

As has been the case with most waves of change in U.S. education, the real impetus behind this one came from outside the education sector and beyond our borders—from competition by the "Asian tigers" and the far-reaching societal transformations wrought by a globalizing, knowledge-based economy. It was no surprise that a public-education system designed for the agrarian and industrial ages was ill suited to meet this challenge or that it would need wrenching alterations. Still, the criticism rankled many educators. As Toch summarized the response of the major establishment groups, "The indictments of public education in *A Nation at Risk* and the other reform reports were overstated. And they argued that the critics' recommendations . . . were in many cases ill-conceived. . . . The solution to the crisis in the schools, the organizations argued (even as they denied that a crisis existed), lay not in a spate of reforms but in increased spending on education."[6]

Plainly, the Coleman insights of 1966 had not yet penetrated very deep into the profession itself, nor had the alarum sounded by the Excellence Commission or the more hopeful findings of "effective schools" analysts. When faced with demands for better results, what passed for the leadership of American education rationalized, temporized, denied—and pleaded for still more resources. I cannot count the number of times I have heard educators call for "a Marshall plan for the schools," which smacks of reconstruction, to be sure, but mainly of a hunger for billions more dollars to spend.[7]

Federal Fracases | The Reagan White House was pledged to eliminate the Department of Education, which hadn't been around long but so far showed few signs of fulfilling Jimmy Carter's boast that it "was able to give much better service, to provide a consistent policy, and to eliminate many of the legal disputes that had long plagued the system . . . combined with lower administrative costs and fewer employees."[8]

Ted Bell was understandably opposed to his department's demise and, to the frustration of presidential advisers, moved very slowly to develop such a plan. In August 1981, the same month the Excellence Commission was named, an interagency reorganization task force recommended that the department be turned into a freestanding National Education Foundation, akin to the National Science Foundation and reminiscent of several earlier ideas, including Moynihan's from a decade before. But the real intra-administration struggle involved the nature and scale of the federal *role* in education, not the name over the door.

Presidential aides Meese and Martin Anderson wanted to scrap most programs and functions—especially the now-despised National Institute of Education. At OMB, Stockman pressed to cut both taxes and domestic spending, to consolidate programs, and to turn over as much education responsibility as possible to the states in the form of "block grants." Bell pressed back, determined to retain as vigorous and visible a federal presence as he could—and a budget to match. There was stalemate. In the end, Congress assented to a one-year education spending cut of about 10%, far less reduction than Stockman sought. But neither Bell nor Reagan could persuade a single member of the Senate even to *introduce* a bill to abolish or downgrade the Education Department. Majority Leader Howard Baker said that, not only did he want nothing to do with filing such a measure, but he would actively oppose it. (There was never much hope in the House, where the Democrats ruled from 1955 to 1995.)

"Before I was done [making rounds in the Senate]," Bell recalled "I had gone to virtually every member. . . . The most optimistic estimate I could make was that nineteen Senators would support the president's bill to abolish ED and establish a foundation in its stead. Eighty-one would vote against it."[9]

As part of its 1981 "New Federalism" initiative, the administration did persuade lawmakers to consolidate two dozen specialized education programs into "block grants." (Bell's memoirs proudly recount his success in dissuading Stockman from trying to fold in such major activities as bilingual education and Title I.) In subsequent years, however, these amalgams were gradually undone, and most of the "categorical" programs reemerged as separate line items in the Education Department appropriation.[10]

Another White House priority during Reagan's first term was to revive tuition tax credits to assist families opting for private schools. This had been a prominent item in the 1980 party platform, and the president felt he owed it to his supporters—including lots of blue-collar families, many of them Catholic "Reagan Democrats"—to keep his word and at least make the effort. It also meshed with his visceral preference for empowering parents and weakening government control of education. This bill the administration managed to get introduced. Bob Dole filed the Senate version, which cleared the GOP-majority Finance Committee, and Ohio's Willis Gradison introduced a counterpart in the House. The initiative went no farther, however. The unions were implacable, and Democrats were yielding few victories to the administration. The federal budget was in deficit, and tax-credit foes screeched that OMB was slashing education programs. Reagan had honored his commitment to try. But it was not to be.

Stockman persisted on spending, however. Each year he set a budget target for the Education Department well below the previous year's appropriation. Each year, Bell sought to appeal to the president but made little headway. Reagan simply didn't believe that Uncle Sam should have much to do with education, and he, too, was keen to shrink the domestic government. Hence the administration's education budget request for fiscal 1983, for example, was $4.2 billion lower than the 1982 appropriation. But Congress simply scoffed. Except for the small one-time reduction contained in 1981's "budget reconciliation" measure, appropriators routinely ignored White House figures and (with some back-channel advice from Bell's team) substituted their own sums. In the end, funds appropriated for Education Department programs rose on Reagan's watch by roughly $1 billion a year—from $14.8 billion in 1981 to $19 billion four years later and $23 billion in 1989.

Governors Take Command | In a development more consequential than any scheme hatched on the Potomac's banks, governors were beginning to stir the education pot. Traditionally, they had played minimal roles in this field, leaving it to constitutionally separate state boards and commissioners and local school systems. Even in jurisdictions where the governor appointed a state's education officials, it was unusual for the chief executive to delve deeply into K–12 issues. (That's why I got a charge from assisting one of the exceptions, Massachusetts governor Frank Sargent, in the early 1970s.) Few of them viewed education either as a big problem or as something over which they had much control or specialized knowledge. What's more, they weren't welcome—though the state's money surely was. Educators clung to the Progressive Era belief that their noble work was too important to be soiled by grubby political fingers, and they cherished the separate governance structures of boards and superintendents, both local and state, that had arisen around 1900 to "keep education out of politics." They chose not to notice how thoroughly politicized and interest-group-dominated the K–12 policy arena had since become, preferring to view themselves as a professional priesthood into whose arcane rites and holy precincts governors and legislators were discouraged from entering. (Parents, too, entered only by invitation.)

By the early 1980s, this was changing. Education was becoming a broad societal problem and thus a challenge for elected officials. While consuming vast amounts of money—it has long vied with Medicaid for the dubious honor of being the largest item in state budgets—education was also the subject of mounting criticism: from employers, universities, even lawmakers puzzled about why their schools weren't producing literate graduates and why educators spoke such an obscure language. Washington's deepening involvements—both in civil rights and in a cascade of rule-bound spending programs—inevitably roped in state officials, too. School finance lawsuits and demands for more equal spending from town to town led to increases both in the portion of state budgets devoted to education and in the states' share of K–12 outlays, which climbed, on average, from 39 percent in 1970 to 49 percent fifteen years later.

A host of front-page issues—teacher strikes, school choice, federal regulation, special ed, textbook disputes—further propelled education into politics and drew politicians into education. More than one governor awoke to ask: if this is the biggest item in my budget, if people are complaining about it, if my state's future prosperity hinges on it, if everyone is fussing about how to fix it, and if the voters are willy-nilly going to hold me responsible for it, why do I have so little say about it?

Beginning in the South, long the country's poorest region, governors also figured out that if they were serious about economic development and social progress, they must overhaul their schools—and must therefore tangle with the education system's traditional fiefdoms, rituals, and beliefs. The economic recession that squeezed state budgets in the early 1980s strengthened their resolve. And the Reagan administration's "New Federalism" talk about returning education responsibility to the states got their attention, even if Congress assented only to bits of it. As Toch explains:

> Governors of both political parties from Mississippi to Maine began to champion school reform as part of an effort to bolster their states' failing economies. "Education is the keystone to economic prosperity," Texas Governor Mark White told the National Conference of State Legislators in 1983, and Governor Rudy Perpich of Minnesota warned his state that year that "knowledge will be the steel of this post-industrial society." [11]

Even before publication of *A Nation at Risk*, some governors were stirring, mostly in Southern Regional Education Board (SREB) states. Mississippi's William Winter was on the march by 1982. Tennessee's Alexander unveiled his wide-ranging "Better Schools Program" three months ahead of the Excellence Commission. But in the federal report's aftermath the floodgates opened. Clinton in Arkansas, Hunt in North Carolina, Riley in South Carolina, Graham in Florida, White in Texas—these and a few others formed the vanguard of the "excellence movement" and its single most potent force: smart, determined, politically agile leaders at the level of government with genuine constitutional responsibility for education as well as men who were not part of the school establishment nor afraid to challenge its practices, criticize its performance, and question its ideology. They served as examples for their peers and successors across the land, some of whom—including New Jersey's Tom Kean, Minnesota's Rudy Perpich, Wisconsin's Tommy Thompson, Ohio's George Voinovich, Michigan's John Engler—readily seized these reins. Many also went on to make their marks at the national level. And what Mark White launched in Texas in the mid-eighties, abetted by none other than Ross Perot, commenced a two-decade-long reform cycle in the Lone Star State that survived statehouse turnovers and party shifts and surfaced in Washington in 2001 when ex-governor George W. Bush proposed the No Child Left Behind Act.

Their proposals differed in specifics, of course, but shared a common theme: raise standards, particularly in high school; construct better gauges of performance; and ratchet up the quality of teachers and teaching. Above all, ask whether the state's schools are producing the results that it requires for the future and, if not, don't hesitate to take charge.

Consistent though it was with the shelf of reform reports that emerged in the early eighties, the governors' view of education—utilitarian, instrumental, practical—collided with the dogmas that ruled the ed schools and the adult-interest-driven priorities of the national associations. These institutions clung to permissive, child-centered, and equity-focused ideas and to pedagogies that trusted students to construct their own knowledge. Professors charged with preparing the next generation of classroom practitioners admonished them that their proper classroom role was to be a "guide on the side, not a sage on the stage." In other words, the teacher's job was not to impart specific skills and knowledge to her pupils, but subtly to assist them to figure things out for themselves.

At my alma mater, Harvard's Graduate School of Education, Lawrence Kohlberg propounded notions about children's moral development that many educators took as admonitions not to instruct their pupils in the difference between right and wrong. (Strictly speaking, he had a hierarchy of "values" but shunned "virtues" as overly behaviorist.) In *Frames of Mind*, published the same year as *A Nation at Risk*, his faculty colleague Howard Gardner advanced the theory of "multiple intelligences," the burden of which is that not all children are well designed for academic learning. Besides "linguistic" and "logical-mathematical" intelligence, which are typically tapped by standardized tests, he advanced five more kinds, including "bodily-kinesthetic" (dance, miming, etc.) and spatial ("thinking in pictures").[12] On the same campus, gender-studies expert Carol Gilligan, in *A Different Voice* (1982), suggested that girls develop psychologically in different ways than boys—that they are less selfish and judgmental. And campus after campus was chattering about left and right brains, claiming that if you happen to be born with a "dominant right brain," you are more apt to be intuitive and creative than rational and logical.

The ed schools weren't alone. Intellectuals and professors all over the place were falling under the spells of postmodernism and multiculturalism. The "search for truth" was overtaken by "it all depends on your perspective." Nondiscrimination in admissions and hiring was being replaced by the reverse discrimination of affirmative action, and the "core curriculum" was eroded by waves of ethnic and gender studies. More classrooms were used for propaganda, even as traditional notions of academic freedom crumbled under the burden of campus "speech codes" that barred "insensitive" acts and statements that "stigmatize."

Some academics stooped to using schoolchildren for political purposes. At a House committee hearing in 1983, for example, fervently antinuclear psychiatrists from Ivy League campuses, seeking to persuade Congress that Reagan's "arms race" was terrifying youngsters and should therefore be halted, trotted out carefully coached adolescents to say things like "It makes me feel sad and depressed when I think about a bomb being dropped. . . . I don't want to die alone." [13]

There was, to put it gently, a chasm between what governors and blue-ribbon commissions were urging for K–12 education and what many of that field's own leaders propounded.

In the Profession | Also visible by the mid-1980s was the beginning of a power struggle that endures today over the shape and control of the education reform agenda. Would leadership in setting that agenda rest primarily in the fingers of K–12 educators and their organizations or in the palms of elected officials, corporate moguls, and high-status panels of laymen? And would students and their achievement be the exclusive focus of those reforms or would the needs and concerns of educators get equal—perhaps even superior—billing?

The Excellence Commission's take on this was straightforward. While paying some heed to "professionalism," its core was an instrumental view of teachers as crucial workers in an underperforming industry, namely U.S. schools. Bold steps were needed to boost that industry's productivity, which naturally included attention to the effectiveness of its workforce. But the commissioners' conception of teachers was primarily as important means to a more important end, not as an end in themselves. They were seen as one key element of a production system that needed to be recalibrated—along with curriculum, standards, and the extent and uses of school time—in order to make schools more effective.

Such alterations would challenge the sturdiest bastions of the "education establishment": teachers' unions, colleges of education, and state bureaucracies. They meant training people differently, licensing them differently, paying them differently, judging them differently. That very little of this happened in the 1980s was due in part to simple politics and in part to the emergence of a different reform strategy within the education establishment itself. Call it the "professionalism" agenda.

It began to gain prominence in 1986 with publication of two much-discussed reports. *Tomorrow's Teachers* emerged from the Holmes Group, a loose consortium of ed school deans keen to strengthen the professional training of teachers within the nation's major research universities. (The successor Holmes Consortium continues today.)

More prominent was *A Nation Prepared: Teachers for the Twenty-first Century*.[14] This had no official standing yet carried considerable weight. Its sponsor was the Carnegie Corporation of New York; its authors were members of a Carnegie-appointed "Task Force on Teaching as a Profession," chaired by Lewis Branscomb, then IBM's chief scientist (now an emeritus Harvard professor); and it was unveiled at a high-status soirée at San Diego's fashionable Del Coronado Hotel.

This report's most noteworthy feature was a subtle yet profound change of focus: from teachers as instruments of school improvement to teachers as *shapers* of school improvement. From teachers as means to teachers as ends. From teachers as key employees in an education system run by others, to teachers as key decision makers about the purpose and operations of the system itself. One might almost say from teachers as workers to teachers as bosses.

Though the task force didn't spell this out, the backdrop for its shift of emphasis included educators' self-inflicted *loss* of professionalism and forfeiture of status over the previous twenty years. When the United Federation of Teachers called its first strike in 1968 and the NEA expelled administrators from its ranks and began to press for collective bargaining, the two national teacher organizations began to emerge as true trade unions, chiefly concerned with the compensation and working conditions of their adult members. While that is standard practice for organized labor, it's a far cry from what people expect of "professionals," and it sapped public respect for teachers. By the mid-eighties, they yearned to have their cake and eat it, too: enjoy the political clout and organizational security of a union while recapturing the trust, esteem, and authority of professionals.

This meant recasting the key education challenges facing America. The Carnegie task force acknowledged the need for stronger student achievement but added a second challenge that it deemed equally important: "creating . . . a profession of well-educated teachers prepared to assume new powers and responsibilities to redesign schools for the future."

A Nation Prepared thus restated the country's central education problem as a dearth of properly empowered teachers and crafted its solution in terms of making this occupation more "professional." Its authors sought to shift authority away from "those who would improve the schools from the outside" and confer it upon educators themselves, including the power to create and revamp schools to their own liking and in accord with their own beliefs.

The panel did not remark on how teachers, over the preceding two decades, had sacrificed their inherent professional standing on the altars of collective bargaining and political power-brokering. It overlooked how completely the K–12 establishment had missed—and was still denying—the achievement shortfall that the Excellence Commission and others had diagnosed. Understandably if perhaps hypocritically, task force members now sought to piggyback their case for more-professional teachers on a campaign that by mid-decade had obvious traction with governors, CEOs, federal officials, and public opinion: the quest for better schools.

Thus began the third strand in today's education reform enterprise, born within the system, advanced by leaders of the system, devoted to boosting the stature, influence, compensation, and autonomy of the system's employees and insistent that this will yield better results for the kids.

A Swelling Chorus | In 1983, the same year as *A Nation at Risk*, former education commissioner Ernest L. Boyer, a respected senior figure who then headed the Carnegie Foundation for the Advancement of Teaching, published *High School*, which sought to chart a new course for U.S. secondary schooling. Cautiously phrased, it lit few fires, but from deep in the establishment it underscored the Excellence Commission's insistence on a stronger high-school core curriculum and introduced the novel thought that every student should be prepared for both college and the workplace.[15]

A year later, Theodore R. Sizer, ex-Harvard dean and Andover headmaster, published *Horace's Compromise*. Subtitled *The Dilemma of the American High School*, it introduced a likable fictional teacher named Horace Smith and depicted the many ways that high-school norms and external pressures kept him from evoking the best from his students. In Sizer's words, "Horace has to compromise what he knows will work in order to meet the demands of the system." Also coming from a prominent mainline educator, this evocative book helped build the case for change in K–12 schooling and paved the way for multiple efforts to empower educators to design schools to their liking.[16]

Almost concurrently, John I. Goodlad, former dean of the UCLA Ed School, published *A Place Called School*, a ponderous, gloomy book that brimmed with the "complexity" of schooling but that also developed both an agenda for "improving the schools we have" and a tantalizing depiction of how future schools might differ.[17]

The accelerating "excellence movement" gained momentum from these pleas for change from heavyweights within the profession. As Toch explains,

> Bell, Boyer, Sizer, Goodlad, and other prominent reformers them-
> selves contributed to the wide dissemination of the reform message by
> actively promoting their recommendations to educators and policy-
> makers. Like modern-day circuit riders, they barnstormed the nation,
> exhorting, scolding, challenging—in effect, selling reform. . . . Bell
> alone made 140 speeches in the twelve months following publication
> of *A Nation at Risk*. . . . the Carnegie Foundation . . . produced a
> documentary film version of its report, *High School*, [that] was nomi-
> nated for an Academy Award.[18]

Though not as achievement-fixated as *A Nation at Risk*, this tide of re-formism among card-carrying K–12 leaders helped the waters of change flow through the field. Yet America's opinion elites probably paid greater heed to criticisms and advice from outside. The year 1987 brought two best-selling books, both denounced by educators and academics for their alleged conservatism, that lent powerful support to the excellence movement: Allan Bloom's *The Closing of the American Mind* and E. D. Hirsch's *Cultural Literacy*.[19]

Hirsch in particular kicked up a ruckus in the K–12 world with his sixty-three-page appendix listing "what literate Americans know" (adieu, Adirondack Mountains, adjective, Adonis, adrenal gland, etc.). He was charged with cultural imperialism, canonical tyranny, insensitivity, and more. But his book skewered the notion that specific knowledge is unimportant and that so long as one has a skilled and agile mind one "can always look it up." Instead he showed (based on impeccable research by leading cognitive scientists) that knowledge builds upon knowledge, that one must know things in order to learn things, and that disadvantaged youngsters, in particular, are gravely handicapped by schools that don't purposefully attend to their knowledge base.

Hirsch next formed the Core Knowledge Foundation (that being a less explosive term than "cultural literacy"), which created curricular guides and materials that parents and schools could actually deploy. Hundreds of schools have since registered as "Core Knowledge" schools (an affiliation that's especially popular among today's charter schools); the foundation provides them with technical assistance and moral support;[20] and several other prominent education ventures, including Bill Bennett's and Lowell Milken's "virtual school" K12 program, have patterned themselves on the Core Knowledge model.

Also published in 1987, though no best seller, was Ravitch's and my *What Do Our 17-Year-Olds Know?* It contributed hard data—based on the first-ever National Assessment of U.S. history and literature—to the debate on school performance and student achievement. Though nearly every high-school junior takes American history, we discovered that few could even locate the Civil War in the proper half-century. We decried constructivist educators' habit of pooh-poohing the acquisition of knowledge ("mere facts," "rote memorization") in favor of concepts and "learning skills." A false dichotomy, we termed it: "At best, concepts explain the facts of a given situation, while facts provide examples with which to illustrate or test concepts." We particularly deplored the tendency of social-studies educators to focus exclusively on "critical thinking." "It is fatuous," we said, "to believe that students can think critically or conceptually when they are ignorant of the most basic facts of American history."[21]

The following year brought Gerald Grant's perceptive and alarming profile of a real (if pseudonymous) northeastern high school, *The World We Created at Hamilton High*, which stressed the malign effects over the previous two decades of the schools' (and their teachers') "loss of social authority" and the mounting tension between the priorities of practicing educators and the values of what Grant termed the new "national managers" of education.

With perfect timing, 1988 also brought an important statement by two of those "managers": *Winning the Brain Race* by Xerox CEO David Kearns and education critic Denis Doyle argued that business leaders should join educators and elected officials in restructuring American K–12 education so as to maintain the country's economic edge. The essential elements of their six-point plan, including both standards and choice, would echo through many reform strategies in the years to follow—and in 1991 Kearns would himself play a leading role in reshaping federal policy.

Scarce Numbers | Those drowning in data today may scoff, but in the 1980s it was still hard to get clear statistics on educational achievement, particularly numbers that lent themselves to comparisons over time or across jurisdictions. The much-discussed SAT results were limited to college-bound students nearing the end of high school. They said nothing about the attainments of younger pupils or those not seeking entry to competitive universities. The "norm referenced" tests that most states and districts bought from commercial publishers—and that I had taken year after year at Dayton's Jefferson School—were clear and comparable as far as they went. Yet their "norms" were simply averages—nothing normative about them—and youngsters could be getting a mediocre education while clinging to, say, the 75th percentile (which proved only that three-quarters of the other kids were doing worse.) In 1987, an obscure West Virginia physician named John J. Cannell published a self-financed study, swiftly dubbed the "Lake Wobegon Report," which showed that nearly every state was using—or misusing—those tests to demonstrate that its students were "above average."

The National Assessment of Educational Progress (NAEP) was respected for its accurate national sample, its administration at three age levels (nine, thirteen, seventeen), and its psychometric integrity, but few understood what NAEP results really meant. Its "scale" showed ups and downs but had no standards by which to judge sufficiency. And its data were reported nationally and for four quadrants of the United States but not for states or anything else that was actionable by policymakers.

Responding to the governors' appeal for comparable performance data, Secretary Bell promised to see what he could do and returned to Washington from Bush's Maine clambake bent on producing usable statistics. That proved harder than he expected. In fact, he later recalled, "Gathering academic achievement test scores state by state turned out to be an utter impossibility." So he, too, settled for college entrance scores, using both the College Board's SAT results and those of the lesser-known American College Testing Program (ACT), which dominates the country's midsection.

In January 1984, the Department of Education unveiled its first "wall chart," containing lots of state-by-state comparisons. Bell described the response as "sharp and animated." Educators, by and large, hated the chart, but newspaper editors, state officials, and the general public welcomed it. For the first time, they could see how their own state stacked up against others—and against the country as a whole. The annual wall chart—it lasted four years—signaled that the Education Department, far from being a lackey to the NEA and the public-school establishment, could step away from its presumptive constituents and instead take the side of those bent on shaking up that establishment. For Carter, Mondale, Ribicoff, and others who struggled to create the agency and give its secretary a megaphone "on behalf of education," this must have begun to resemble a nightmare.

Support Groups | Alongside government officials and blue-ribbon panels, a few change-minded organizations pushed against the education status quo, above all the National Governors Association (NGA). Led by Tennessee's Alexander, it embarked in 1985 on a multiyear school-reform initiative—most unusual for an outfit that normally changes priorities as often as it changes chairs, that is, annually. The key event was the governors' release and endorsement, during their annual summer meeting in 1986, of an Alexander-inspired report called *Time for Results*.

The steamy, stylish resort island of Hilton Head, South Carolina, was the venue for this historic NGA conclave. Though the contented, prosperous atmosphere of golf, yachts, wide beaches, and gourmet barbecues did not evoke either an at-risk nation or an obvious concern with the plight of America's poor, the NGA's commitment to education reform in general and the message of *Time for Results* in particular were important on four fronts.

■ The governors embraced the post-Coleman reasoning that if stronger achievement is what's needed, policymakers should focus on the results they seek and how to extract those from the education system, willing or not.

■ They introduced a quid pro quo that foreshadowed charter schools and kindred structural innovations. Experts call it "tight-loose" management: being demanding with regard to outcomes but relaxed about how those outcomes are produced. In Alexander's more homespun phrasing, the governors declared themselves ready for "some old-fashioned horse-trading. We'll regulate less, if schools and school districts will produce better results." Such a swap, he predicted, "will change dramatically the way most American schools work. First, the Governors want to help establish clear goals and better report cards, ways to measure what students know and can do. Then, we're ready to give up a lot of state regulatory control … *if* schools and school districts will be accountable for the results."[22]

■ They committed themselves to school choice as a key element of comprehensive education reform.

■ They signaled to the nation, as had the Excellence Commission, that education reform did not have to emerge from the profession, that it was legitimate for elected officials to lead a makeover, and that strong medicine might be called for, even medicine distasteful to the priestly palate.

The NGA was not alone. The Atlanta-based Southern Regional Education Board also strove to hold member states' feet to the reformist fire. During his thirty years in leadership roles at the SREB (1975–2005) including sixteen as its president, Mark Musick prodded, cajoled, and invented new ways to induce overdue changes in the arc of states from Delaware around to Oklahoma. In dozens of studies, reports, state audits, resolutions, and policy papers, the SREB hammered its members on the need for data, comparisons, ideas, and backbone.

In 1985, for example, as NGA task forces were composing *Time for Results*, the SREB published an analysis of transcripts of thousands of graduates from seventeen prominent state universities, which showed that three-quarters of the schoolteachers emerging from those campuses had taken *no* courses in economics, philosophy, physics, chemistry, or foreign languages—and just half had studied any political science at all. Only 15 percent of all courses taken by elementary teachers were in English or math, though those subjects comprise most of the primary curriculum for which they would be responsible. The SREB didn't do a lot of butt kicking or sheer noisemaking. But it produced reams of alarming data.

Among its bravest moves was inducing member states, beginning in 1984, to join a pilot program whereby National Assessment tests would be administered to state-specific samples of students—and the results would be analyzed and compared. This was a revolutionary change for NAEP and one that laid the foundation for the state-by-state NAEP reports that we now take for granted. By 1985, inspired by the SREB example, annoyed by

Ted Bell's "wall charts," and fretful that the governors were stealing their thunder, the state superintendents, via their umbrella organization, the Council of Chief State School Officers, voted to conduct cross-state assessments of student performance, to make comparisons, and to report the results publicly. That was a very big shift and a crucial breakthrough.

We lived in Nashville from mid-1981 to mid-1985, while Arti and Aloke turned into teenagers and Renu became a major-league researcher in cardiac disease. Our lives were different in that smaller and relatively laid-back city, with its blend of southern charm and ambivalence toward newcomers—and just a trace of leftover race-consciousness. Our spacious house was minutes from campus, and getting around was easy. As a state capital, airline hub, and economic boomtown in the "new South," Nashville was also beginning to accumulate metropolitan amenities. There was a good bagel shop not far from our house, and I smiled hungrily when a "French bakery" opened in the nearby mall, bringing the prospect of real baguettes and croissants.

My work life had two halves: university teaching and research, and advising Governor Lamar Alexander on his education reform initiatives, which were numerous and plucky.

My Vanderbilt colleagues were friendly, but few of them saw the education issues of the day as I did. In that way, I felt lonely and isolated. In New York, Diane Ravitch was having a similar experience at Teachers College, Columbia, and, though we hadn't been close earlier, we now made common cause. (Her then-husband was part of Pat Moynihan's kitchen cabinet, and we had begun to compare notes while I was on his Senate staff.)

Diane and I each knew a few academics who agreed with us about the makeover that K–12 education needed, plus a smattering of sympathetic education leaders and state officials, but these people were scattered and seldom in touch. Sensing that there might be safety, camaraderie, and perhaps influence if we found a way to band together, we decided to create a "network" of like-minded folks. To distinguish ourselves from the priestly mainstream with its equity addiction, we christened it the Educational Excellence Network. Excellence was important to us—surely it was the most important thing—but two years before *A Nation at Risk* this remained an esoteric, even slightly suspect, prism through which to view education. In hindsight, we were fumbling toward what psychologists call a "support group," what politicians term an "advocacy group," and what in Revolutionary War days was known as a "committee of correspondence."

As Diane later recalled,

> The Educational Excellence Network was formed in 1981 at what may
> well be described as a dark hour in the history of American education.
> Test scores had gone through a long, steady decline and there was not
> yet any indication that the decline would end or level out. . . . High
> school graduation requirements were weak, and the word "standard"
> had long been banished from the education profession's lexicon. When
> a hardy band of dissidents gathered in the Grace Dodge Room at
> Teachers College, our overriding concern was the low state of educa-
> tional achievement in K–12 education, as well as the apathy that
> sustained low standards with which so many people seemed to be
> content. We agreed to form a network of like-minded souls and to
> issue a regular publication to rally all those who sought high academic
> standards in our nation's schools.[23]

The John M. Olin Foundation, led by the visionary Michael Joyce, gave
us a small seed grant, as did the Andrew Mellon Foundation. We didn't need
much. At first, besides phone bills, duplicating costs, and occasional plane
tickets—there was no Internet or e-mail—the "network" consisted of dozens, then a few hundred, individuals around America who more or less
shared Diane's and my beliefs, which in time we codified into a network
credo. We sent them a monthly compilation of articles and studies, xeroxed,
collated, and mailed by my part-time research assistant at Vanderbilt.

Over the next couple of years we grew more ambitious, and the network's activities expanded to include conferences leading to a pair of books
that Diane and I coedited. These were funded by the National Endowment
for the Humanities, headed by William J. Bennett, who was new to K–12
issues but spunky, eager, and superquick to learn, willing to break china (in
ways that Ted Bell, for example, was not), and instinctively sympathetic to
our views. One of those NEH-supported conferences led to Hirsch pen-
ning *Cultural Literacy* after Diane and I heard him deliver an illuminating
talk—we hadn't previously known him—about why poor kids would remain behind the education eight ball until their schools equipped them
with a solid base of knowledge as well as skills. "You should write a book,"
we said to Hirsch. And so he did.

The network was never a formal organization with officers or bylaws. But
it espoused a clear, strong set of education precepts, and into it came many of

the brain trusts of the dawning "excellence movement." Here is how Thomas Toch, that movement's foremost biographer, described what was going on:

> In an extensive body of articles, books, reports, essays, and other writings that formed the philosophical blueprint for the excellence movement, the intellectual leaders of the movement [he names seven people] attacked educational utilitarianism and its underlying premises, and advocated in its place a new philosophical foundation for public secondary education, with educational excellence—a high level of *intellectual* training for *all* students—as its cornerstone.
>
> Through prolific writing . . . ; as contributors to many of the major studies of public education in the early 1980s; as consultants to governors and state legislators; and by virtue of their roles within the Reagan administration or the visibility their work received from the federal government under Reagan, these critics of public education played a key part in shaping the reform movement.[24]

Bill Bennett was not just a financial backer of other people's projects via the Humanities Endowment. He was also a Washington mover-shaker trusted at the White House in ways that Bell was not, and hungry to understand what was awry in the schools that aggravated problems he had previously observed in higher education. Though NEH had done little in K–12 education before he arrived, it thereafter did a lot—and Bennett became a frequent dining companion during my trips from Nashville to the nation's capital. Along with good food, we chewed over both the intellectual and instrumental cases for better elementary-secondary schooling in America and the barriers to realizing this.

Back on campus, I was amazed by how little real work a tenured professor had to do—a bit of teaching was most of it, once I deduced that faculty committee meetings were a waste of time and vacations seemed to occupy more of the year than class days. This must be one of the comfiest jobs on the planet, a virtual retirement home for those who would rather snooze, fish, or garden, yet a peerless opportunity for those moved to make something of it. I welcomed the freedom it gave me to write, attend (and host) conferences and workshops, manufacture the occasional bombshell, kibitz on federal policy, and advise the governor's team.

I poured myself into op-eds and magazine articles, as I had begun to do in my latter days on Moynihan's Senate staff. Two months before the 1980 election, I wrote in *Change* magazine that "the liberal consensus that has shaped national education policy for the past fifteen years is turning sour." While saluting the core principles of that "consensus"—equality, experimentation, innovation—I faulted its inattention to quality, its animus toward accountability, and its aversion to educational "pluralism and diversity" (by which I really meant school choice). Then I sketched a new agenda that, I averred, resurrected the original credo of a liberal consensus that had since deviated from it: "colorblindness instead of quotas as the symbol of equality opportunity, aid for those who need it rather than for all who want it, a premium on excellence and achievement, a minimum of government interference, and a maximum of individual and family choice."[25]

"Concern for the quality of American education is becoming respectable," I wrote in the *Wall Street Journal* in June 1981, before driving to Nashville, as if asserting this might make it true. "For the better part of two decades, the arbiters of educational fashion have given the nod to just one goal: . . . If it did not foster 'equity' it was not legitimate. But now there is widening acceptance of the view . . . that excellence is as valid an objective and quality as sound a criterion by which to gauge the worth of a school or educational policies."[26]

To the consternation of ed school dean Bill Hawley, who sped to my office door, eyebrows raised, a few weeks after my arrival on campus, I published (as the maiden back-page "commentary" of a brand-new journalistic venture called *Education Week*) a defense of Coleman's novel comparison of public and private schools and charged his critics with using methodological concerns to disguise their real objection, which was to his finding that the latter are more effective.

In January 1982, I said the battle in Washington over whether to keep the Department of Education was a red herring, and what people should be arguing about was Uncle Sam's proper role in education, not the name or status of the agency housing that role.

Why recount those ancient musings? Simply to indicate that I and Diane and a slowly widening circle of friends and allies were alarmed by much of what we saw about us and increasingly willing to engage in a war of ideas that, we hoped, might help to shift the direction of U.S. education.

| This war had an international dimension, too. My one-time Moynihan Senate colleague Elliott Abrams was now assistant secretary of state for international organizations, which included America's participation in

UNESCO. He asked me to join the U.S. delegation to an education conference in Paris in April 1983.

The cavernous UNESCO headquarters on the Left Bank was a spooky place, bureaucratic, corrupt, and often used by the Soviet Union and so-called "nonaligned" countries to make life difficult for the United States, its Western allies, and their values. This was the era of the proposed "New World Information Order," a Moscow-sparked initiative to license journalists and manage the flow of information in ways that would radically curb press freedom and make it easier for governments to control what people learned.

The education conference was full of bad ideas and horrendous resolutions on a host of topics that the United States and its allies usually lacked the votes to alter or block. The Soviets played it like a harp. In one appalling episode, our delegation could not even muster a majority of conferees to re-dedicate UNESCO to the "Universal Declaration of Human Rights" that had been one of the UN's proudest achievements during the late 1940s. (It failed this time because of the declaration's references to the free movement of people, which implied that unhappy residents of Soviet-bloc countries and other dictatorships should be able to emigrate without hassle)

After a session where my fellow delegate Charles Fairbanks (now a distinguished professor at the Johns Hopkins School of Advanced International Studies) made a particularly spirited defense of freedom, a burly Soviet representative, likely a KGB agent, who had been monitoring the proceedings came up to me, pen in hand, and demanded to know the identity of the American who had been speaking. I declined to tell him, but this reinforced the spookiness of the whole experience.

After the *New York Times* Paris correspondent, E. J. Dionne, and I lunched together, he perceptively wrote (to the consternation of the U.S. mission to UNESCO, which thought Ambassador Jean Girard deserved whatever press attention was to be had) that I found UNESCO "a place where words entirely lose their original meaning and then reappear, monstrously, meaning something completely different. It is also a place where, Mr. Finn says, the United States is faring very badly indeed and where the Soviet Union plays the game far better." [27]

I came back to Nashville and knocked out a fervent article that *Commentary* titled "How to Lose the War of Ideas." Months later, the United States withdrew from UNESCO. I was proud of my tiny contribution to that momentous decision, which typified the Reagan administration's brash but principled approach to the world beyond our borders.

Reforming Tennessee Education | The gubernatorial part of my life was more attuned to the world of policy and politics in one specific place, namely Tennessee, at a time when that state needed and was beginning to emerge from the South's static, low-wage, low-skilled, semiagrarian economy into a modern industrial and postindustrial era. Though the state often elected Democrats to office—Albert Gore père and fils, for example—it was an innately conservative place that resisted abrupt change in established ways of doing things.

Lamar Alexander became governor in 1979—he served for eight years—and when I reached Nashville in 1981, he was beginning to focus on education. As the SREB was pointing out and his peers in other southern states were discovering, a backward economy—made worse by the stagflation of the time—was doomed to stay that way until its people gained stronger skills and greater knowledge. "Better schools mean better jobs for Tennessee" became his education reform mantra, and he probably uttered it a thousand times. To a politician, that's not instrumentalism; it's realism.

Alexander's "Better Schools Program" was presented to the legislature in January 1983 as the centerpiece of his second-term agenda. It had multiple elements, of which the boldest and most contentious was a "career ladder" for teachers—in effect, a merit pay plan.

No legislative strategist, I was thrilled to be a member of the governor's brain trust, batting out memos, drafts, talking points, explanations, and questions-and-answers on my Vanderbilt typewriter, and joining innumerable meetings at the statehouse and executive mansion. (We worked on his NGA agenda, too, and began the *Time for Results* sequence.) I also relished introducing Lamar to Al Shanker—we lunched at the Baltimore airport during a day trip via state plane—who responded with interest to the governor's "master teacher" plan, wrote supportively about it in his *New York Times* column, and invited Alexander to address the AFT convention later that year in Los Angeles. (Reagan spoke there, too.) Shanker had a venturesome mind, was a bona fide education reformer, and, within the limits of his position, was bent on distinguishing *his* union from the NEA. He was never afraid to listen to and argue with people whose views he did not necessarily share.

After much arm-twisting, compromising, and revising, Tennessee legislators agreed to key parts of the "Better Schools Program," including the contentious career ladder. Lamar thus won his spurs as an "education governor," among the first such. But neither of us fully appreciated the rubber-band-like nature of K–12 policy and how it yearns to snap back into its previous shape as soon as the tension eases. Once Alexander's term ended, the Tennessee Education Association and its political allies, now including a Democratic governor, began to "revise," "improve," "make fairer," and generally erode the performance-pay scheme and other prickly parts of his plan. Here is how Lamar recalled his gubernatorial reform efforts in a 1998 interview (while unsuccessfully running for president):

> We became the first state to pay teachers more for teaching well, but I ran into the teachers' unions trying to do that. We created a number of programs for gifted students in the summer—governor's schools for teachers of writing, and for students in history and mathematics and science, and those are still there. And we created Centers of Excellence at the universities and Chairs of Excellence and those are still there, but in terms of completely restructuring our schools, remodeling them, getting rid of the overhead, setting higher standards, giving parents more choices of schools, that was the most intractable problem I ran into and it's still a problem. . . . Al Shanker . . . actually supported my idea of paying good teachers more for teaching well, but the National Education Association, the dominant union in our state, fought it tooth and nail.[28]

Any lasting policy change in education, I was coming to realize, must include a vigorous "war of ideas" because the broader political culture either subscribes to obsolete beliefs or has delegated responsibility to a priesthood that stubbornly clings to them. Just as important, however, is Alexander-style political leadership—astute, brave, goal driven, results oriented, and relentless. Yet even with those assets in place, a leader's boldest reforms are apt to prove transitory once he/she leaves the scene and the establishment strikes back.

12 | *Inside the Beast*

B y 1985, the message of *A Nation at Risk* was more audible, even if many education groups still wore earplugs. Governors were on the march. The economy was again humming. Except in Nicaragua and Afghanistan, the Cold War was fairly cool. Reagan had been overwhelmingly reelected, and the GOP clung to a slim Senate majority. SREB member states were preparing to have their academic achievement compared. Ted Bell had, rather bitterly, returned to Utah. And the brainy, irrepressible Bill Bennett was beginning his three-plus years as U.S. secretary of education.

Unlike Bell, he enjoyed considerable running room within the executive branch, and the Department of Education under his leadership was largely self-propelled. He made the most of his extraordinary podium-cum-articulateness, visited schools across the land, went into classrooms and taught lessons himself, celebrated great teachers and their pedagogical successes, insisted that the department disseminate reliable information about "what works" in education, placed content, character, and choice—the "three Cs"—at the top of his K–12 agenda, and, again unlike Bell, was a fixture on TV interview shows and newspaper front pages. (Tugging bulldog-like on elementary-secondary issues, however, he didn't spend much time on other parts of the Education Department's portfolio, such as special ed, voc ed, and higher ed.)

Bennett was determinedly, even proudly, *not* a member of the education establishment and didn't care what it thought of him. He regarded its Washington lobbyists as greedy feeders at the public trough, advocates for adult interests, and Reagan haters. (Asked what he had eaten one day when he could not avoid lunching with a self-important higher ed representative, he told his staff that the bill of fare featured "poached shark.")

Through his force of personality, eloquence, and adroit use of the Education Department's sparse discretionary dollars—Congress continued to appropriate more money for the agency than the White House sought but gave the secretary scant leeway to spend it as he saw fit—Bennett got a fair amount done and made plenty of noise, thereby boosting the excellence movement. But with rare exceptions, the administration's legislative agenda fared no better during Reagan's second term. The House of Representatives ignored, killed, or totally rewrote most proposals, and administration allies in the

Senate were seldom able to do more than contain the damage. Sometimes they compounded it. (The slim GOP majority in that body hinged on such conspicuously non-Reaganite members as Connecticut's Lowell Weicker.)

Most conspicuously, the Bennett-Reagan plan to "voucherize" the big Title I program—turning the compensatory ed money over to parents instead of school systems—went nowhere on Capitol Hill. (Congress, in fact, dithered over that ESEA reauthorization until Democrats regained control of the Senate in 1986.)

Outside Washington, however, school choice was making modest inroads. Since 1976, New York City's local District 4 in East Harlem had been fruitfully creating new middle schools around various themes and specialties—and giving students the right to select among them. Beginning in 1981, Cambridge, Massachusetts, permitted its students to pick their public school via a "controlled choice" system meant to foster racial integration. This idea soon spread to Rochester, Buffalo, and Prince George's County, Maryland. Indeed, voluntary choice programs of all sorts—including the appealing "magnet school" idea—were fast replacing "forced busing" as the standard approach to desegregation. (In 1974, the Supreme Court's *Milliken* decision had blocked involuntary transporting of students across city-suburb lines, and popular resistance to compulsory busing even within cities—and the resulting white flight—led civil rights advocates to seek less draconian means of encouraging white and black youngsters to attend the same schools.)

The governors endorsed school choice in *Time for Results*. While shunning talk of private schools or vouchers, the NGA's task force on parent involvement and choice, led by Colorado Democrat Richard Lamm, sought via several forms of public-sector choice both to empower parents in dealing with schools and educators *and* to stimulate the creation and renewal of schools themselves, thus fostering stronger pupil achievement. The task force set forth an ambitious (and literate) image of what U.S. education should become:

> If we first implement choice, true choice among public schools, we unlock the values of competition in the educational marketplace. Schools that compete for students, teachers, and dollars will by virtue of their environment make those changes that allow them to succeed. Schools will, in fact, set the pace. . . . Choice, and the ensuing competition it will produce, is the force we need to ensure meaningful

reform in education into the 1990s. If our children are to be competitive in the international marketplace . . . we must be competitive here at home. . . . As William Shakespeare said in Hamlet, "He may not, as unvalu'd persons do, carve for himself, for on his choice depends the safety and health of the whole state."[29]

The Committee for Economic Development, a sixty-five year old organization of corporate chieftains, also lauded choice, noting that achievement was stronger in schools that families selected. Then the idea went statewide, beginning in Minnesota, which had long afforded taxpayers a deduction for dependents' education expenses, including tuitions paid to private schools—an approach that the U.S. Supreme Court okayed in 1983. In 1985 Minnesota lifted the ceiling on that deduction, and Democratic governor Rudy Perpich also proposed an "open enrollment" plan under which youngsters could attend any public school in the state. The legislature wasn't quite ready to go that far but okayed a "postsecondary options" program whereby advanced high-school students might take courses on college campuses.

Though true vouchers—public funds to enable youngsters to attend private schools—remained politically taboo, the intellectual and social-scientific underpinnings for this form of school choice were strengthening. Drawing on a remarkable federal data set called "High School and Beyond," which began in 1980 to accumulate information on tenth and twelfth graders, analysts were able to compare the effectiveness of public and private secondary schools. Led again by the indefatigable Coleman, pathbreaking studies showed that private schools were generally more effective in advancing their pupils, particularly poor and minority youngsters, on several dimensions, including academic achievement.[30] Though data seldom trump organized interests on such hotly contested issues, for a country troubled by weak school performance in general and an achievement chasm for poor and minority youngsters in particular, it was getting harder—and more nakedly self-interested—to explain why needy students shouldn't be helped to attend schools that would do them more good.

Excellence Movements | Most mid-decade reform action was on the "excellence front," not the choice front—and most of it occurred beyond the Washington Beltway. Bell proudly recalled in his memoirs that by April

1986 "forty-one states had raised their high school graduation requirements, thirty-three states had initiated student competency testing, and thirty required teacher competency tests. Also, twenty-four states had initiated career ladder salary programs." All the latter, he noted, were "mandated and funded by legislative action. Not one state at that time had initiated performance-based pay through the action of a state board of education."[31]

The reform drive, in other words, was indeed gaining traction in the states but was coming from outside the traditional education policy apparatus. In most places, in fact, it was being imposed upon a reluctant school establishment.

In a few cities, business and civic elites that had abandoned public education during the previous decade were reengaging. They saw that the schools weren't doing the job their communities and companies needed. Anthony Bryk recalls, for example, that by the time he joined the University of Chicago faculty in 1985, that city's prestigious Commercial Club had formed a "civic committee" to find ways of energizing the local economy and it quickly embraced education reform as an essential component of any such renaissance. By 1988 it had spun off an influential, business-backed advocacy organization called Leadership for Quality Education. David Rockefeller's New York City Partnership played a similar role, pushing for education reform as a vital ingredient of economic development, the more so after Frank J. Macchiarola left his post as chancellor of the city school system in 1983 to head the partnership.

Most business-led groups preferred to "partner" with school systems, however, rather than to confront them. They tended both to trust educators to chart a worthy course and to shun controversy, mindful, too, that their own leaders were wealthy and (mostly) white people who often sent their own kids to private or suburban schools.

Governors and legislators, once they caught the education reform virus, were less diffident. Yet conscious of the need to cushion blows to the system—and placate if not win over as many educators as possible—they put additional money on the table even as they laid down new mandates and standards. "State spending on public education," Toch reports, "rose dramatically following the onset of the reform movement: by 46 percent in Tennessee between 1983 and 1987, by 69 percent in Minnesota, by 46 percent in New Jersey, by 65 percent in California, by 48 percent in Indiana, by 54 percent in Arkansas and by 56 percent in South Carolina," while inflation added just 14 percent.[32]

To be sure, the U.S. economy was thriving in the mid-eighties, and lots of states enjoyed surpluses. Nor was all of the added education spending earmarked for "reform." Public school outlays in America have risen for as long as anyone can remember, and most of the increase, like most of the underlying budget, goes for staff salaries, with or without changes in the ground rules. After 1975, a sizable fraction went into the costly new venture known as "special education."

Still, it's notable that policymakers were willing to coat their bitter reform pills with the caramel of more money for schools and educators—taxes were increased in state after state as part of school reform packages—and that they weren't pressing the Coleman-style analysis to a politically suicidal point by demanding big changes without any sweetener at all on the "inputs" side.

Return to Washington | In mid-1984, after three years at Vanderbilt, Renu was selected to chair the Department of Cardio-vascular Pathology at the Armed Forces Institute of Pathology, located on the Walter Reed Hospital campus back in Washington. We agreed that she would return to the D.C. area while Arti, Aloke, and I spent the 1984–85 school year in Nashville before joining her. I made plans to relocate the Educational Excellence Network to Vanderbilt's unprepossessing Washington office. Before those plans jelled, however, Bill Bennett called and said, "I know you're already planning to return to Washington. You have no reason not to join me at the Education Department." He offered an irresistible dual position: line responsibility as assistant secretary for research and improvement, plus "inner circle" duties as counselor to the secretary. In short order, I was asking Vanderbilt if I could arrange a leave of absence. No problem, came the answer.

This time around, White House clearance posed no problem, either, save for the reams of obligatory paperwork. Marty Anderson had returned to California. I was four years away from my last Moynihan link and had forged an identity of my own. More important, Bennett was allowed to select his own Education Department team as Bell had never been.

It turned out to be one heckuva team, especially when playing offense. Gary Bauer was undersecretary (the post of "deputy secretary" had not yet been created) and served as liaison to the "old Right"—we called them paleocons, to distinguish them from neocons like Bennett and several of the rest of us. Bill Kristol, fresh from the Harvard faculty, became chief of staff.

John Walters, now the nation's "drug czar," was deputy chief of staff. Two senior staffers at the Humanities Endowment came across town with Bill: take-no-prisoners Bruce Carnes to manage budget and planning, and the deft Marion Blakey, now federal aviation administrator, to emcee public affairs. Wendell L. Willkie II left the White House counsel's office to become the department's general counsel. Also in the inner circle were several superb young researcher/speechwriters, including Peter Wehner, John Cribb, and Eugene Scalia.

It was an all-star cast, on par with Moynihan's first-term Senate team, and Bill treated it like a nonstop seminar. We would pile into his big corner office several times a day, sometimes over lunch—the secretary merited a private dining room and "steward," though we were billed for meals and the food was just passable—and discuss what to do about the latest crisis or opportunity. He was more cheerleader, inspiration, and friend than boss, open to others' ideas, secure enough to welcome smart people into his circle, willing—unlike so many Washington figures—to share the limelight, and eager to play touch football on Sunday afternoons with all and sundry. Watching Bennett in action, I came to appreciate (as earlier with Moynihan and Alexander) what a difference it makes to have clear ideas and forcefully articulate them. The "bully pulpit" has real value. But how quickly one gets into hot water when those ideas clash with the established wisdom. (How willing one is to be in trouble, versus going with the flow, may be the truest gauge of courage in public life.)

First, though, the Senate had to approve me. Although I could function as a consultant to the department during the interim, I was admonished by White House congressional-relations aides not to "make any decisions" until confirmed and sworn in. That meant I could join Bennett's skull sessions and hold conversations in my own spacious, sunny (but airless) corner office about fifty feet from his, but capable career civil servant Emerson Elliott served as "acting" assistant secretary. (I had known Em since he, then at OMB, and I worked together on Nixon's education policy fifteen years earlier.)

In 1985, the Office of Educational Research and Improvement (OERI) consisted primarily of the thirteen-year-old National Institute of Education (NIE) and Uncle Sam's ancient but struggling little education data unit, the National Center for Education Statistics (NCES). Indeed, under that structure, the OERI assistant secretary—my predecessor was Donald Senese—had little to do except watch over the NIE director (then Manuel Justiz).

By now, NIE had dashed the hopes I once held for it, had its budget slashed time and again, and was mistrusted both by the administration and by many in Congress. In a 1983 article, I said it had developed three "fundamental failings": its research agenda was ruled by ideology; its organizational workings were "bureaucratized and politicized"; and most of its shrunken appropriation was earmarked for a band of greedy but well-wired R&D organizations known as the "labs and centers," leaving institute leaders with few dollars to do anything new or different.[33]

At NCES, meanwhile, the nation's primary font of education data was starved and neglected. (Emerson was its administrator, too, as well as acting NIE director after Justiz was sacked.)

Bennett and I resolved to overhaul OERI and try to give it a new lease on life. Though I couldn't yet do anything official, others began quietly devising a new arrangement while I "consulted" with them.

Senate confirmation proved relatively painless. I never had a real hearing. Instead, staffers attached to Education and Labor Committee members informally grilled me, and I responded to myriad written questions. One tense moment occurred when an aide to Senator Weicker fished out of his briefcase a sharp-edged "manifesto" that a band of heterodox academics had issued on the topic of special education and, in full McCarthy mode, said something like, "I have here a memorandum that you are alleged to have written." Fortunately, I recognized it as the product of a group-think effort that I had quit when it headed toward positions that I didn't share. Nobody pressed the matter or gave me grief about anything else.

Like any White House nominee for an "advice and consent" post, however, I was expected to make courtesy calls on senators who asked to meet me. This led to a brief but bizarre session with Ohio Democrat Howard Metzenbaum, who wasn't very interested in educational research but did represent my home state. He looked up from my résumé and asked, "Are you really Jewish?" (I think the name Finn gave him pause. Or perhaps he thought he knew every Jewish Buckeye.) It occurred to me that this was a wildly inappropriate question, one that could be interpreted as an unconstitutional "religious test" for public office, but I calmly assured the senator that indeed I was Jewish by birth and upbringing, albeit not very observant (and married to a Hindu). That seemed to satisfy him.

With no further ado, I was unanimously confirmed in July and sworn in, Renu and the kids proudly at my side.

Before leaving Nashville to return to Washington in 1985 with two teenagers, I wrote the school superintendent in Montgomery County, Maryland, where we still owned and were renovating a house, asking if we could have our choice of schools in that sprawling suburban system. I was keen to give our kids at least a few broadening years in public schools instead of returning them to the elite private-school world they had inhabited since kindergarten. The public schools near our home were good, but better ones were to be found a few miles away. I was on a first-name basis with superintendent Wilmer Cody after attending scads of conferences, seminars, and panels with him, and I hoped for a positive response. Many weeks passed, however, before I received a long and thoroughly bureaucratic letter, the gist of which was that only if moving from one school to another would improve the racial balance would Montgomery County permit it. Our daughter and son went back to private schools as I ruefully concluded that even an "enlightened" public school system was marching to its own well-intended but user-unfriendly policy drummer.

The OERI reorganization proved far easier than I expected. The NIE's authorizing law was about to expire and, aside from the labs and centers and a handful of academics, it was friendless. Moreover, the Department of Education's organizing statute had empowered the secretary to make wide-ranging structural changes in his agency, including authority to "alter, consolidate or discontinue" entire units within it, so long as he gave Congress ninety days notice. That's what we did, announcing a plan to fold NIE, NCES, and the department's public-library aid programs into a reconfigured OERI with five divisions. The NIE itself—and its controversial policy body, the National Council on Educational Research (on which I had served during the Ford-Carter years)—would disappear.

Congressman David Obey (D-WI) briefly objected, indicating that if Bennett went ahead with this restructuring he might seek redress via the department's annual appropriation, but he found scant support on Capitol Hill. Thus, notwithstanding the general waxing of partisan obstructionism in Washington, the NIE simply died. And so, with amazingly little fuss (other than the inevitable bureaucratic shuffles), the new OERI was born. Which meant we could focus on its agenda rather than its organization chart.[34]

Offices | I spent most of my time in the main Education Department building with a few aides (including super executive assistant Patty Hobbs, who left the White House to join our little team, and my "personnel person," Louise Oliver, now ambassador to UNESCO, which the United States rejoined in 2002), but most of OERI's nearly five hundred employees worked across town, beginning with senior careerist Emerson Elliott (who continued to head the statistics operation) and several topflight recruits to the OERI leadership: chief of staff Bruno Manno, previously head of research at the National Catholic Educational Association; research chief Sally Kilgore, a longtime Coleman associate; *Nation at Risk* orchestrator Milt Goldberg; and Jim Bencivenga and Mitch Pearlstein, who arrived from Boston and Minneapolis to help us communicate with the larger world.

They were all housed on several floors of a new office building owned by, of all things, Shanker's American Federation of Teachers, space that the government leased for OERI's use. It so happened that about the time I arrived back in Washington, the longtime landlord of the old NIE decided to renovate and raise the rent on his prime downtown location at Nineteenth and M. So the federal education researchers had to leave. The General Services Administration proposed to relocate them to a remote spot called Buzzard's Point where nobody wanted to work. I said nothing doing. It also happened that the AFT and a couple of other unions were erecting a huge complex only steps away from easily accessible Union Station and urgently seeking tenants. It further happened that my old Moynihan Senate colleague and friend, Judy Bardacke, then a senior AFT official, eagerly introduced me to the union's top business manager, who made the government an acceptable lease offer. The quarters proved fine and the location workable, though Washington gabbled for years about the strangeness of Reagan's Education Department renting office space from Shanker's union.

13 | *The Quest for Better Information*

Bennett's foremost goal for OERI was to produce credible, accurate, usable research that would help teachers and principals do a better job. Two years after *A Nation at Risk*, the country was hungry for proven ways of boosting student achievement.

My own priorities were to beef up the statistics operation and turn the National Assessment of Educational Progress into a more useful tool by which to monitor and benchmark school performance.

We plugged away on both fronts. With the important exception of NAEP, Congress was allergic to everything we proposed that required legislation—and was bent on advancing a number of interests that we had little use for. But we made decent progress anyway.

At Bennett's insistence and with skilled leadership by OERI staffers Milt Goldberg and Susan Traiman, we set out to distill reams of education research into straightforward lessons that practitioners and parents could apply. The main product was an eighty-five-page booklet titled *What Works: Research About Teaching and Learning*, the first edition of which (March 1986) contained forty-one "findings." [35] (We later added more.) Each laid out in plain language a robust, actionable conclusion based on multiple studies and vetted by experts in the field. In the "home" section, for example, we reported, with five footnotes: "Children who are encouraged to draw and scribble 'stories' at an early age will later learn to compose more easily, more effectively, and with greater confidence than children who do not have this encouragement." In the "classroom" section, we declared (again with five scholarly citations): "Students will become more adept at solving math problems if teachers encourage them to think through a problem before they begin working on it, guide them through the thinking process, and give them regular and frequent practice in solving problems." And in the "school" section, we explained (six footnotes this time): "A school staff that provides encouragement and personalized attention, and monitors daily attendance can reduce unexcused absences and class-cutting."

Such conclusions may look obvious, even banal, but in fact it was unprecedented for the federal education research agency to treat teachers, principals, and parents as key clients, rather than targeting its products at academics and policymakers.

Copies flew off the shelf, more than half a million during the first year. We heard a little carping from the research community that we had "over-simplified" and a bit of whining that several findings had a Bennett tilt (such as serious talk about history and character). Mostly, though, those who examined *What Works* applauded it. The problem was that, despite all the trees and postage sacrificed to its dissemination, it had little impact on its primary audiences.

I figured this out six months later in San Diego, where I was being shown around by then-superintendent Tom Payzant, one of America's leading urban educators. He organized a lunch discussion with his high-school principals, and there, mainly as a conversation starter, I held up a copy of *What Works* and asked how many of them were acquainted with it. Only one raised his hand, and it wasn't clear whether he had actually read it.

Sobering. Half a year had passed. We'd exhausted the department's discretionary budget to paper the land with this reader-friendly, timely, and practical book. Yet here I was talking with the cream of the practitioner world—high-school heads in one of the best-led school systems in the land—and they didn't even know it existed.

The lesson was not only that American K–12 education is sprawling, decentralized, and loosely coupled but also that few of its practitioners strive to "keep up with the research" (as my wife's medical colleagues might put it) and even fewer translate research results into changed classroom practice. There's a staggering dissemination challenge here, yes, but the larger problem is cultural: educators may revise what they do on the basis of direct experience but tend not to change on the basis of "evidence" supplied by others, certainly not by scholars, analysts, and evaluators. No matter that something "works." That's not how we've always done things here in the schools of River City.

| We fared better on the statistics and assessment fronts.

If you can shape what gets measured and how it's reported, you can have a profound, if indirect effect on what is done. That's as true in education as anywhere. But U.S. education data were nowhere near what they should have been.

Part of it was just money. NCES had been "level funded" for years—from 1981 through 1986, its budget never topped $12.5 million—which meant its purchasing power was waning. Data came out late. Some essential statistics weren't even collected. Important but costly forms of data gathering, such as longitudinal studies, were going undone. The staff, though reasonably competent, was understandably dispirited.

NCES definitely needed more cash. Yet its woes went deeper than budget. A panel of the National Academy of Sciences, invited by my OERI predecessor to evaluate the statistics unit's work, issued a scathing report in 1986:

> We wish to emphasize the seriousness with which we view the [statistics] center's problems. We believe that there can be no defense for allowing the center to continue as it has for all too long. . . . Without strong and continuous commitment and demonstrated determination to undertake wide-ranging actions to change both the image and the reality of the center, we are unanimous in our conviction that serious consideration should be given to the more drastic alternative of abolishing the center and finding other means to obtain and disseminate education data.[36]

The academy accompanied its criticism with scads of recommendations, not all of which made sense to me. But I was in full agreement that we needed to bolster the data-gathering and reporting function. How could a "nation at risk" repair its schools if it lacked good information about them?

Bennett concurred and, much aided by his stalwart backing for this cause, which had few animated constituents in the outside world (but also mercifully few adversaries), each year the president's budget sought more for NCES than Congress had appropriated the year before—and, within whatever budgetary slack we had in OERI, I steered the lion's share to NCES. This naturally peeved the heads of OERI's other four units, but they understood the secretary's and my priorities.

It worked, too. The NCES appropriation grew from $12.2 million in 1986 (including NAEP) to $31.1 million three years later (and by 1991 had doubled again). Commissioner Elliott and his associates accelerated the analysis and release of key annual data, and we launched some worthy new studies. Morale improved, and we began to have a semblance of the grownup education statistics agency that America needs.

Reinventing the National Assessment | Changes on the NAEP front were more dramatic still. Planning for the National Assessment of Educational Progress had commenced in the mid-1960s, spearheaded by Commissioner Frank Keppel and underwritten at first by Carnegie. Federal funding began in 1968, and by 1972 it was entirely financed by Uncle Sam but administered via the Education Commission of the States (ECS). The assessment itself was first given in 1969, but the underlying political compromises meant that (a) students were tested by age, not grade level; (b) results were reported either as percentages of test takers getting individual questions right or (starting in 1984) on a psychometric scale that included no benchmarks, standards, or "cut points"; and (c) the "units of analysis" were the entire country and four big regions but not individual states, let alone districts or schools.

When Bennett and I arrived on the scene, Uncle Sam was spending some $5 million per year on NAEP, and its management had shifted from ECS to the Princeton-based Educational Testing Service, which administered the tests—and made most policy decisions—under the terms of a government contract. Yet the limits that had both made possible and hobbled NAEP at the outset were still in place, locked there by statute, tradition, and the terms of the ETS contract. Though nicknamed "The Nation's Report Card," in reality NAEP's reports were none too informative.

By the mideighties, the country craved more and better achievement data, and the governors, in particular, wanted comparative performance statistics for their states. Both their exasperation with Ted Bell's "wall chart" and the relatively smooth sailing of the SREB's state-level NAEP pilot project caused the "chiefs" to withdraw their opposition to state-specific NAEP testing.

The time for a change had come, but Congress wasn't likely to go along if a Republican president proposed it—nor was it a slam dunk *within* the administration for the federal government to expand its role in education in a way that could lead critics to murmur about the "camel's nose" or "first step toward a national curriculum."

So we decided to appoint a blue-ribbon panel of our own to examine NAEP and recommend changes. Lamar Alexander, then in his last year as Tennessee's governor, agreed to chair it so long as someone else did the heavy lifting. In that capacity—titled "vice chairman and study director"—we were fortunate to recruit H. Thomas James, president emeritus of the Spencer Foundation and a revered senior figure in the education-research universe. The National Academy of Education (NAE) agreed to serve as fiscal agent for the panel's work and to supply a "commentary" on its recommendations, which further insulated the project from accusations of politicization or undue control by Ronald Reagan's dark forces. Several major private foundations (including Exxon, Ford, Hewlett, and MacArthur) consented to cover the costs, and a terrific cast of twenty-two individuals agreed to serve, including Hillary Rodham Clinton, then the first lady of Arkansas; Stanford professor Michael Kirst; California schools chief Bill Honig; several academics and K–12 practitioners; a prominent businessman; even an AFT vice president.

Bennett announced the NAEP "study group" in May 1986, and ten months—and forty-six background papers and nine subgroups—later its report was released. During that time, Emerson and I were much involved behind the scenes, and Mike Kirst volunteered for vital drafting. Four of the panel's recommendations were key to NAEP's future utility:

■ Student achievement should be sampled and reported at key "transition grades," namely fourth, eighth, and twelfth grades, in addition to age levels.

■ More subjects should be assessed, spanning the curricular core.

■ A diverse, bipartisan, and independent board should be appointed to oversee NAEP policy, "buffered from manipulation by any individual, level or government, or special-interest group in the field of education."

■ Achievement should be tallied and reported for states (and cities) as well as the whole country. Indeed, this should be done "in such a way that a state or locality can readily produce similar data at the community or even neighborhood level. These data in turn can be compared with data from other communities, the entire state, or the nation, both now and over time."

State-level NAEP reporting elicited mild concern from the NAE reviewers, who fretted that undue attention might be given to an Olympic-style ranking of states on the basis of their scores and insufficient heed paid to the "many factors" that influence such scores. The reviewers also added a suggestion of their own, that in "each content area, NAEP should articulate clear descriptions of performance levels, descriptions that might be analogous to such craft rankings as novice, journeyman, highly competent and expert. Descriptions of this kind would be extremely useful to educators, parents, legislators, and an informed public."[37]

Secretary Bennett embraced all these recommendations, declaring in March 1987 that he "certainly intend(ed) to move forward with legislation and to seek authorization to put an improved report card into the nation's hands." He also agreed to "find whatever monies we can" to meet the price tag attached to the study group's recommendations, estimated to rise from $5 million to $20–30 million per annum when fully implemented.[38] (NAEP's 2006 appropriation was more than triple that prediction.)

States would not be required to take part in NAEP, but Bennett predicted that most would. "There is very great public interest," he remarked, "in this question of 'How are we doing? What are our children learning?'"

The Alexander-James report, combined with the NAE's qualified endorsement, Bennett's zeal, and a parallel proposal from the Council of Chief State School Officers to use NAEP as the vehicle for state comparisons, amounted to a sea change. As Kirst commented, "What is being discussed today wouldn't even have been considered 20 years ago. Anyone who had proposed it would have been laughed out of the room."[39] Though the Alexander-James panel was not nearly as visible as the Excellence Commission four years earlier, and while its function was more consensus forging than alarm clanging, its recommendations symbolized both a coming of age for American education—a real readiness to confront and compare school outcomes—and an essential foundation under the standards-based reforms to follow.

Few objections were voiced at first. Shanker commented that while revamping NAEP didn't top the education lobbies' agenda for the ESEA reauthorization cycle then under way, strengthening the assessment system was "one of the most important things we can accomplish in this round" of federal education legislation.[40]

OMB and the White House erected no obstacles, either, meaning the real action would occur in Congress, which had been fussing over the ESEA reauthorization since early 1986. The NAEP overhaul doubtless benefited from arriving late in the process and becoming just one more car on a mile-long legislative train.

At the end of 1987, both chambers passed their respective ESEA bills. The House version paid scant heed to NAEP, but the Senate incorporated nearly all of the Alexander-James recommendations.

How that happened illustrates the kind of backstage bipartisanship and teamwork that's still possible in Washington, though far rarer in today's polarized politics.

Massachusetts Democrat Edward M. Kennedy chaired the Senate Education and Labor Committee in the One-Hundredth Congress. (The GOP lost its majority in the 1986 midterm elections.) He and Bennett didn't agree on much, and Senator Kennedy was seldom keen to advance administration initiatives. His chief education staffer at the time, however, was an old friend and coauthor of mine, Terry W. Hartle (now senior vice president of the American Council on Education), who swiftly grasped the import of a NAEP overhaul and the wisdom of the Alexander-James recommendations. He and I worked closely and quickly behind the scenes to massage them into a legislative form that both Kennedy and the Reagan administration could endorse. Kennedy then became Senate champion for the NAEP reforms, including the key items on the study group's list—and for the enlarged budget authorization to pay for them.

The sledding got a bit rougher when Senate and House versions of ESEA met in conference in early 1988. A lobbyist for the National PTA declared, "This bandwagon of testing is getting ridiculous," and the American Association of School Administrators (the local-superintendents' group) complained, "The marginal good to educators of comparing data across state lines, compared with the cost, is not much."[41]

House conferees were apprehensive, too, particularly about interstate comparisons. This led to several compromises—notably designation of the new state-level NAEP as a "trial" rather than a permanent mandate—and a complicated dual-reporting structure that created an independent "governing board" to oversee NAEP while placing the assessment's administration under the commissioner of education statistics in a restructured NCES.

When the ESEA reauthorization was finally signed into law in 1988, near the end of the Reagan administration, its NAEP amendments did much to pave the way for standards-based, results-driven education reform. If I were clobbered by a bus tomorrow, this reinvention of NAEP would be among the very few public-policy accomplishments that I wish someone might put in my obituary. It was also proof that even in Washington one can sometimes effect worthwhile change by sticking with a project, winning others over to it, and gradually building momentum behind it.

Lynne Cheney and Chest Pains | In 1986, NAEP administered its first-ever assessments of U.S. history and literature to a nationally representative sample of eleventh graders. This was underwritten by a special one-time grant from the National Endowment for the Humanities, made while I was at Vanderbilt and Bennett was NEH chairman. Diane Ravitch and I had persuaded both the mandarins of NAEP and the Bennett NEH squad that it was crucial to find out just how much high-school juniors did or did not know about these two key subjects and that a NAEP add-on could accomplish this. Diane and I helped design the assessment and recruit the subject experts who assisted ETS in crafting suitable questions. We also hoped to write a book about the findings, though the data themselves would be in the public domain.

By the time the test results rolled in, I was working at the Education Department and Bennett was secretary. His NEH successor was Lynne V. Cheney, a strong-willed woman, author, and humanities booster, as well as Dick Cheney's wife.

Using the not-yet-released NAEP data, Diane and I wrote *What Do Our 17-Year-Olds Know?* which Harper & Row published in 1987. (As a federal employee, I took no royalties from its sales.) Cheney penned a foreword, accurately if mildly noting: "The results . . . show that while a few students did very well, most did not perform satisfactorily. Given the nature of this test and given that 78 percent of the students tested were taking U.S. history in the same school year as the assessment, the fact that only slightly more than half the test-takers answered a typical question correctly is cause for serious concern."

In fact, the assessment results were a devastating indictment of U.S. high schools. A third of test takers failed to identify the Declaration of Independence as the document marking the formal separation of the American colonies from Britain. Just 40 percent knew that *The Federalist* was written to encourage ratification of the Constitution. Presented with a timeline, fewer than three in five placed World War I in the correct fifty-year period. (A majority could not do that with the Civil War.) Barely half identified Kennedy's "ask not what your country can do for you" statement with the thirty-fifth president. And on and on.

As our book publication date neared, Cheney was completing her own NEH report, *American Memory*, a competent critique of the schools' failure to transmit knowledge of the past to U.S. youngsters. Seeking to maximize its impact, she elected to scoop Diane's and my book, scheduled for release a few days later, and put some of our major findings and choicest examples into her booklet.

The data, to be sure, had been paid for by the NEH, which Cheney now led, and in time would be available to all. Still, this scramble to get out ahead of us was, if not dirty pool, at least inconsiderate and offensive. Ravitch and I were mightily irked, and a prominent TV journalist dumbfounded Cheney by asking her on a national interview show if she had "plagiarized" from our book.

It was a stressful time for all concerned, the more so since NEH attorneys—possibly to cow me—were also questioning whether it was kosher for me to have used government typewriters and phones for my part of the book writing. And so it happened, one morning at the office, that, for the first time in my life, I felt chest pains. My wife the doctor instructed me to get out to the Walter Reed emergency room ASAP and she would have the cardiology team waiting. Just as assistant Patty Hobbs and I were walking out to my car, however, the phone rang. It was an irate Lynne Cheney, saying we have to talk about this problem and resolve it right now. I was too proud to tell her that I was having chest pains that she might have caused, so I drummed up the hasty excuse that a "family emergency" prevented me from talking with her right then. She didn't want to hear it, but I promised to call her back shortly.

At the ER, Walter Reed's top cardiologists quickly determined that whatever had caused my chest to ache was not a heart attack but insisted on following their standard protocol and keeping me overnight for observation. As orderlies wheeled me off on a gurney toward the ward where I would repose till morning, I said "Whoa, I need to make a phone call." I dialed Cheney's office and, still loath to tell her what had happened or where I was, made a date with her to talk about it all a day or two later.

In hindsight, Cheney's report attracted a measure of attention. Diane's and my book attracted more. Diane and Lynne both later served in the administration of the first President Bush and collaborated on several projects. Lynne and I have been on a dozen panels and seminars together in the years since. Today we enjoy a proper though tepid relationship, warmed slightly by the fact that our basic education values are similar. And I've had no more chest pains.

Other Projects | Midwifing the "new NAEP" and reviving the federal statistics operation are the two proudest achievements of my tenure at OERI (along with putting the NIE out of its misery), but my team and I also embarked—with less success—on several other worthwhile ventures.

Most federal grants and contracts for education research, as in other realms of government-supported R&D, are awarded through competitions among rival applicants judged by a "peer review" process. The rationale makes sense on paper: get experts in a given field to determine which projects have merit, and keep those decisions to the maximum extent out of the hands of bureaucrats and politicos.

The risk, however, is that the reviewers will hail from exactly the same groups, mind-sets, and institutions as the grant seekers, that "you fund me and later I'll fund you" will replace disinterested judgment, and that the presumptive beneficiaries of the research—in this case teachers, students, parents, and employers—have little say in what questions get asked or the methods by which answers are sought. Thus can the "research community" become a closed circle of self-interested scholars and institutions that do pretty much what they like with taxpayers' dollars in ways that may not meet the needs of those whose earnings are being spent or whose problems cry for solutions.

Over the years, that's what had happened to federal education research. A circle of academics associated with the American Educational Research Association (AERA) decided what would be investigated and where the money would go. Parents, teachers, policymakers, and other users and beneficiaries of such research had little say. Hence important issues went unexamined or were studied only from an "ed school perspective" rather than by, say, bona fide economists, political scientists, statisticians, or historians. And success was marked not by changes in classroom practice or pupil achievement but by the number of presentations that analysts made at AERA conventions and by the tenure decisions of ed school faculties.

While at OERI, I strove to open up the peer review process so that, when we planned new competitions or judged proposals on their merits, the consumers of education research would have a voice along with the producers. This ate up hours and hours—the career staff often had no idea where to find acceptable research "consumers"—and was controversial, as are all efforts to rethink the tenets of academic peer review. (Observe, for example, the big 2007 dustup over the Education Department's management of the peer review process for federal "Reading First" grants.)

Meanwhile, the "labs and centers" kept their hammerlock on most of OERI's research dollars. I tried every year to convince Congress to ease those earmarks. I used each cycle of lab-center grant renewals to bring new players into that cozy fraternity and struggled to inject greater consumer-mindedness into the work plans of those piggy feeders at the federal trough.

Politics rears its head, of course, whenever there are public dollars to be dispensed. One morning I was working at home when my phone rang and a pleasant woman said, "Good morning, Secretary Finn, the Speaker would like to talk with you." In a moment, the New England accent of Tip O'Neill boomed over the wire. He was putting in a good word for Boston College, which was a contender in one of the OERI competitions then under way. I assured him that I would give careful consideration to its proposal—and reminded him that in the end merit would prevail. He was fine with that. I suspect this was one of a dozen such calls to the executive branch that he made that day on behalf of constituents and friends. He didn't assume that his "recommendation" would change the outcome, but he did thereby ensure that the cognizant official would at least look at it—and he could assure the constituents that he had done his best for them. I have no problem with that kind of congressional intervention. It's the binding earmarks and merit-free pork-barrel projects, like the regional labs, that gall me—and waste many millions of the taxpayers' hard-earned dollars.

Because I was pushing back against lab and center funding *and* trying to change the in-group mode of proposal vetting, lab and center leaders cursed the ground I trod, and the AERA did not exactly worship it. Not only was I altering timeworn priorities and meddling with their cherished peer review process, I was also directing OERI's spare change into statistics and assessment rather than research.

After three years, I had made modest headway with my reforms, which of course crumbled soon after I was gone. I had also accumulated a lifetime's worth of contempt for the AERA, for the labs and centers that were (and remain) the politically nimblest players on the education-research field, for a congressional appropriations process that looked after adult interest groups at the expense of kids, parents, and practitioners, and for those Education Department bureaucrats who comprised the third side of Washington's infamous "iron triangle." (One of them leaked an undiplomatic e-mail in which I said what I really thought about the regional labs, causing minor havoc for months thereafter.)

The day I walked out of OERI, I vowed never to attend another AERA conference—as assistant secretary I was obligated to speak there annually—and nineteen years later that's been an easy promise to keep. (When Diane Ravitch concluded her tenure in the same post, peeved by insulting treatment at the AERA's hands, she, too, resolved to forgo that organization's companionship forever after.)

Winding Down | As the 1988 election—and Ronald Reagan's retirement—neared, Bennett made known that he was ready to leave, and so was I. For three years, I had lugged home an overstuffed briefcase each night and slogged through heaps of paperwork, trying to give my program directors and their lieutenants feedback the next morning. I had tussled with Bruce Carnes on the OERI budget, testified on three rounds of federal appropriations, failed to loosen the lab-center grip on our research dollars, flown on *Air Force Two* with the vice president and Barbara Bush, endured a month at home with a back-disk problem, buried my mother, testified in vain against federal support for the new National Board for Professional Teaching Standards, sent a teenaged Aloke off to boarding school, represented the United States at a half-dozen dull meetings of the education committees of the OECD (which at least gave me access to a decent sample of Paris's one-star restaurants), been the first Education Department official to visit China during the Reagan administration—and made my share of mistakes, including hiring a few individuals for key roles, sometimes because of their political credentials, who just weren't up to the tasks awaiting them.

While lastingly appreciative of the one-tenth or so of OERI's career civil servants who worked hard, strove to do a good job, and were open to new ideas, I was weary of dealing with the 90% who, on good days, just went through the motions, and on bad days sabotaged, leaked, and stonewalled. I was also tired of the internal roadblocks that the executive branch has erected lest some change actually occur. "The essential organizational fact-of-life in government," I wrote in *Education Week* shortly after exiting, "is that at least 237 people who work for the same President and mostly for the same Secretary but do not work for you are able to derail your initiatives."[42]

While the fourteen-hour, bureaucracy-laden days of an assistant secretary had their downside, being part of Bill Bennett's brain trust was always stimulating and usually fun. Visiting award-winning schools with him was a kick. A peerless troublemaker in his own right, he was endlessly quotable—and controversial—in the media. He found plenty in the education establishment that riled and amused him—this being a solemn and sanctimonious field where a lively sense of humor can get you in further trouble—and he didn't hesitate to speak his mind, telling the truth as he saw it, salted with apt quotes from Aristotle and Kant as well as second graders and moms and dads, with astonishingly little regard for the sacred cows of education and politics. Though most of the administration's legislative initiatives were doomed on Capitol Hill, he used such discretionary dollars and executive authority as he possessed to pursue his goals: good information, accurate data, candor about problems, respect for excellence, empathy for educators (but not their Washington lobbyists), and a steady focus on customers rather than producers.

When parents cornered him to ask about their own kids' education, he would say, "I don't do retail," yet he relished inviting successful practitioners in for a visit, getting to know them better, and giving them a pat on the back—and sometimes a meal. I fondly recall lunch with Jaime Escalante, the Los Angeles math instructor who was dubbed the "best teacher in America" and became the subject of the first-rate 1988 movie *Stand and Deliver.*

When Bill told a Chicago journalist one day in 1987 that that city's schools were the worst in the country, he urgently summoned me into his office and asked—I was the research guy, after all—if he was right. I thought fast and said, "Well, Chicago has some competition from Newark and St. Louis and Detroit, but you weren't wrong."

When Dr. Cannell issued his stunning 1987 report declaring that the commercial tests used by states and districts were subject to widespread manipulation and cheating, yielding the impossible conclusion that nearly everyone's scores were "above average," Bill asked if that could be true. We invited Cannell in, along with sundry psychometric experts and test-company representatives, and then asked the federally funded research center that focused on testing to review his data and methods. They reported back that Cannell was essentially correct.

Faithful to his long immersion in the humanities, Bennett had a keen interest in the content of education. Though the federal government was barred by law—an oft-stretched statute—from trying to control schools' curriculum, Bill couldn't see any prohibition against offering examples and advice regarding what they *should* teach. This led to the appointment of another "study group" to map a thorough overhaul of the early years of schooling (*First Lessons*, 1986), followed by model curricula for the high school (*James Madison High School*, 1987) and then the elementary grades (*James Madison Elementary School*, 1988).

A couple of times, Ken Baker (now Lord Baker of Dorking), Britain's education minister ("secretary of state for education and science") in the Thatcher government from 1986 to 1989, turned up in Bennett's office, journeying across the Atlantic with aides to compare notes on education reform. (The Thatcher-Reagan kinship transcended foreign and economic policy.) The Brits were getting ready to introduce a national curriculum, accompanied by student achievement standards at various "key stages," plus tests and school-level comparisons ("league tables"). They were simultaneously advancing several schemes for giving families more choices—and sapping the entrenched power of teachers' unions and local education bureaucracies. We were thinking alike—and we Yanks envied them the parliamentary system that made it so much easier to implement their promising plans.

Watching Bennett in action, multiplying the irritation to the education establishment that had been caused by Ted Bell's "wall chart" and earlier users of the secretary's bully pulpit, I again thought that the NEA, Mondale, Ribicoff, and other champions of the department's creation less than a decade back could not have pictured this role for their new cabinet agency. They had foreseen an education secretary who safeguarded educators' interests and pursued the equity agenda of the seventies. I doubt that their wildest dreams featured a feisty, conservative, Plato-quoting Republican who put kids and parents first, who was eager to say what was wrong (as well as what was sound) about schools and colleges, and who advanced such heresies as choice, character, and standards.

Not even the most extraordinary leadership, however, can transform a sluggish federal bureaucracy into a high-performance agency of change in three years. The Education Department was lucky to get its data accurate and its checks mailed to the right addresses. I came to realize that only those who had never seen it from the inside could expect it to remake teaching and learning in millions of classrooms as the No Child Left Behind Act now does. Government can alter the flow of dollars, yes, and can certainly influence priorities, provide information, and so forth.

But nobody who knows Washington well would ask it to change schools directly.

Perhaps I was growing cynical. In any case, it was time to move on. Vanderbilt had generously extended my leave and was again willing to take me and the Excellence Network (which Diane had run from Teachers College while I was in government) into its Washington office.

14 | *Goals, Standards, and Markets*

With the 1988 election looming and Republicans courting the Latino vote, the White House, prodded by presidential nominee George H. W. Bush, announced that Bennett's successor would be Lauro Cavazos, a Democrat and friend of Bush's who then presided over Texas Technical University in Lubbock.

Save for the precedent of placing on the cabinet a person of Hispanic descent, this was not a felicitous choice. His background was in higher education, yet Bush wanted to focus on elementary-secondary. Cavazos was gentle, courtly, and respectful, which was not only a vivid contrast to Bennett's temperament but a questionable asset in a domain where little changes as a result of affability. He also installed his wife in an Education Department office and seemed to defer to her on many issues.

I was glad to leave full-time government work—forever, as it turned out—yet loath to sever all links to the "new NAEP," which so far existed only on paper.

Bennett agreed that I should help turn it into reality. On his way out the door, he named me to a four-year term on the brand-new, twenty-three-member National Assessment Governing Board (NAGB)—I had helped him recruit the other twenty-two—and also designated me to chair it for the first year. (Cavazos and Deputy Secretary Ted Sanders extended my chairmanship to two years, and Lamar Alexander later appointed me to a second NAGB term.)

In short order, NAGB wrested policy control of NAEP away from ETS—a fundamental tenet of the Alexander-James report was that the government's assessment contractor shouldn't call its own shots—and began the knotty process of determining which decisions belonged to the board and which to the NCES commissioner. We also launched the "trial state assessment," which had its debut in 1990. And we embarked upon setting the "achievement levels" that today come as close as America has to national standards for K–12 education.

In the next chapter, I recount the achievement-level saga. As context, though, let me sketch what was happening under the broad headings of standards-based and market-driven school reforms.

In suggesting ways to mitigate the nation's risk, the Excellence Commission had focused on the high-school curriculum, spelling out how many years of English (four), math (three), science (three), and social studies (three) every young American should take in grades nine through twelve (plus half a year of computer studies). But it also recommended "that schools, colleges, and universities adopt more rigorous and measurable standards, and higher expectations, for academic performance and student conduct." It urged, for example, that colleges "advise all potential applicants of the standards for admission in terms of . . . levels of achievement on standardized achievement tests in each of the five Basics," and admonished schools to administer achievement tests "at major transition points from one level of schooling to another. . . . The tests should be administered as part of a nationwide (but not Federal) system of State and local standardized tests."

When, that same year, Arkansas governor Bill Clinton named his wife to head a new statewide Education Standards Committee, he was trying to move his state in the direction urged by *A Nation at Risk*. Addressing a special session of the legislature in October 1983, he said of the standards developed by Hillary's committee: "If implemented they will put Arkansas among a handful of states with the most precise, comprehensive, demanding standards in the country." [43]

Similar developments were under way elsewhere. In mid-1984, ECS tallied thirty states working on education standards, curriculum frameworks, or learning outcomes.

When the National Governors Association released *Time for Results* in 1986, it spoke of educators' "commitment to be held more accountable for results." But which results? In relation to what? Set by whom? Enforced by what authority? In some nebulous way, states were expected to work this out.

When eight SREB member states administered NAEP tests and the Council of Chief State School Officers called for state-level comparisons, they were groping toward a regimen of measurable results that, to be meaningful, had to be linked to some sort of standards.

A post-Coleman consciousness had dawned in the policy world and was finally glimmering on the horizon of the profession itself, most notably through Marshall Smith's and Jennifer O'Day's depiction of "systemic reform," a wholesale realignment of the education system around standards that spell out what schools should teach and children should learn and assessments that gauge how well this is being accomplished. A gifted scholar and policy shaper, Smith was himself an alumnus of the Coleman seminar two decades earlier at Harvard as well as a key education player in the Carter administration who later served as deputy secretary under Clinton. His unyielding insistence that standards should drive the K–12 enterprise gave this concept legitimacy among Democrats and academics that it otherwise may not have gained.

Charlottesville | Though partisan arguments continued (and still do) over whether standards should be set for students' "opportunity to learn" (i.e., school resources and services) as well as *what* they should learn, reformers of every political stripe were recognizing that the antidote to weak pupil performance was higher academic standards for schools, combined with some sort of measurement scheme and accountability system. But where would such standards come from?

A crucial step was taken in Charlottesville, Virginia, in September 1989, inaugurating a novel education partnership between the president and governors—and between Uncle Sam and the states—and signaling that education was too important for major decisions about such momentous matters to be left to educators. (It also signaled that Congress wasn't to be much involved, which led to later problems.)

George H. W. Bush not only hoped to be known for a "kinder, gentler" approach to governing than Ronald Reagan but also distinguished himself from his predecessor by wishing, as he declared in a January 1988 New Hampshire campaign speech, to become the "education president." "I want to lead a renaissance of quality in our schools," he said to the high-school students in his audience.

Lyndon Johnson surely coveted a similar title, but nobody who occupied the Oval Office between 1969 and 1989 deserved that designation.

During the campaign, Bush did not spell out what he had in mind but did declare his intention to meet with the governors to discuss education reform. Soon after election day, policy director Jim Pinkerton confirmed that the president would "convene an education summit of governors, college officials, and business aides."[44]

The NGA welcomed that initiative and directed its staff to frame various ways that the president and governors might jointly tackle education reform. Its preferred approach, says historian Maris Vinovskis, was "to have the governors work together with the incoming Bush administration to establish long-range goals and targets for reforming education."[45]

Once in office, White House chief of staff John Sununu, himself a former governor (New Hampshire), amplified the "summit" idea, turning it into a high-status event—with precedents set by both Roosevelts—and placing it in the town most identified with America's first "education president," Thomas Jefferson.

NGA director Ray Scheppach meanwhile proposed to the White House

> that the President and the Governors use their meeting to initiate a highly visible 9–12 month effort to establish long-range goals and targets for educational improvement. . . . This should be limited to approximately half a dozen areas which generally reflect the performance or outcomes of the system, rather than the level of resources or the nature of educational programs or practice.[46]

In July, Bush invited the governors to a September powwow, and both NGA and the Education Department shifted into high gear. The White House, nervous that the president might be publicly embarrassed by gubernatorial calls for more federal education spending, also set ground rules for the upcoming event, including the stipulation that sessions involving Bush himself would be off-limits to the press.

Emerging from a preparatory negotiation, Bill Clinton, then chairman of the Democratic Governors Association, informed his colleagues that "the White House has agreed to work with the governors to develop a set of national performance goals, for the first time in American history."[47]

All the governors turned up in Charlottesville, where, Vinovskis reports, "The key players were President Bush; his White House [domestic policy] advisor, [Roger] Porter; and the co-chairs of NGA's education task force, Governor Clinton and [South Carolina GOP] Governor [Carroll] Campbell. Secretary Cavazos was present but chose not to attend the late-night session at the Boar's Head Inn, where the final joint communiqué was crafted."[48]

Clinton's own memoir notes that Governor Campbell was "called home to deal with an emergency" and it thus fell to him "to work out the details of a summit statement" with the NGA and White House staffs. He says the president's aides were "afraid of committing him to a big idea that could get him into trouble by raising expectations of new federal funding," but "In the end, the White House came around. . . . Sununu convinced his White House colleagues that the governors couldn't go home empty-handed, and I promised to minimize public pressure from the governors for more federal money."[49]

Former Bush White House aide Charles Kolb, also present at Charlottesville, spins that tale a bit differently. "The conference almost fell completely apart over the issue of federal spending," he wrote. "Bush and Sununu wanted the focus on structural reforms—choice, flexibility, alternative certification, the need for high standards. . . . Democratic governors, prodded by their own constituencies at home, did not want to let Bush off the hook so easily when it came to resources. Bush won."[50]

In any case the summit didn't disintegrate, and the resulting communiqué was released to the world on September 28. Its key section said, "We believe that the time has come, for the first time in U.S. history, to establish clear, national performance goals, goals that will make us internationally competitive."

No specific goals were unveiled in Charlottesville, but a process was set in motion to do this by "early 1990." In fact, the president announced them in his January State of the Union message, after which they were lightly edited and re-released by the NGA in February. Six goals were enumerated, all targeted for "the year 2000," the symbolic end of the decade and millennium, a nice, round ten-year period and one that stretched safely beyond Bush's maximum term in office and those of nearly all the governors.

The goals addressed school readiness, high-school graduation rates, drugs, violence, and adult literacy, as well as the dreamy aspiration that America would become "first in the world" in science and math achievement. But the most important—certainly the most history altering—of them was goal three:

> American students will leave grades four, eight, and twelve having demonstrated competency in challenging subject matter including English, mathematics, science, history, and geography; and every school in America will ensure that all students learn to use their minds well, so they may be prepared for responsible citizenship, further learning, and productive employment in our modern economy.[51]

The second half of that statement—after the semicolon—admirably restated the purposes of K–12 education and the mission of schools. But the first half, worthy and concrete as it appears, raised three profound questions to which nobody yet had answers: Who decides what is "challenging subject matter"? Who defines "competency" and determines how it will be "demonstrated"? And what's the energy source—Uncle Sam? The states? The earth's rotation?—and behavior-altering mechanism for causing any of this to happen? In a country where primary responsibility for education is vested in the states and where Washington has historically played a minor role, what exactly does it mean to set *national* education goals? Sounds great, but unless they're actionable—and someone shoulders responsibility for that action—they won't yield much change.

The U.S. Department of Education was at low ebb. Never a firecracker, Secretary Cavazos seemed only minimally invested in what was soon termed the "goals process." Moreover, nobody really wanted the federal government to quarterback this game. It was to be a "partnership" between the president and governors, teamwork to be forged via some indeterminate machinery. How that developed we will examine below.

In the Schools | For all the reform ferment of the 1980s, student achievement remained more or less stagnant—at the low levels that had alarmed the Excellence Commission. NAEP trend lines for reading were horizontal, although math results improved a bit. (So did science achievement among younger pupils.)

On the closely watched Scholastic Aptitude Test, average math scores also gained—but verbal scores slipped further.

Such skimpy international data as existed were hard to interpret with regard to student achievement. Most of the big organizations involved with education—UNESCO, the OECD, and the World Bank, for example—shunned (or didn't know how to examine) school outcomes. But a low-profile, quasi-private outfit called the International Association for the Evaluation of Educational Achievement was beavering away at this, and data were trickling in—invariably showing American schools to be producing less learning than many of our allies and competitors. For example, a mid-1980s study of high-school science achievement in twenty-three countries found "consistently low levels of achievement for all three fields [physics, chemistry, biology]" among U.S. students. (Hong Kong, England, and Singapore led the pack.)[52]

In the pages of *The Public Interest* and elsewhere, the unquenchable Barbara Lerner plugged away, pointing out both how low were the "minimum competency" testing expectations set by most states and how much more was being achieved by youngsters overseas.

Americans were especially fascinated by the Japanese economic miracle and wondered how much of it might be attributed to their schools. Pioneering work by the University of Michigan's Harold Stevenson showed that Asian schools were indeed more effective than their American counterparts, starting in the early grades. U.S. educators tended to scoff, citing unbridgeable cultural differences far beyond the power of schools to counteract, but business leaders and government officials were tantalized. While I was at the Department of Education, we joined with Japan's Ministry of Education in examining each other's education systems. The ninety-page report produced by our team concluded that "Japan does a very effective job of providing a flexible and productive labor force for its economy, in large part because of the pivotal roles played by a high level of basic education, disciplined work habits, and group cohesiveness—all school based or fostered." [53] For their part, the Japanese were as intrigued by what they viewed as the creativity and resourcefulness nurtured in U.S. schools as we were by their country's lofty skill levels.

Time would show that Japan's economic policies and institutions lacked other elements needed to sustain the country's growth trajectory. But in the late 1980s, the Nipponese success story was, depending on where one sat, either an inspiration or a source of embarrassment for those engaged in U.S. school reforms.

On the planet occupied by the education profession, meanwhile, philosophical and curricular storms continued to rage.

Some of the studies that issued forth in the late 1980s seemed caught in a time warp, detached from the quest for higher standards and stronger achievement. An especially painful example was the 1989 report of yet another Carnegie-backed panel, this one focused on early adolescents. In *Turning Points: Preparing Youth for the 21st Century*, the Carnegie Council on Adolescent Development gave a boost to the emerging "middle school movement" and simultaneously set back the pursuit of educational excellence. It sought a "fundamental transformation" in grades five through eight on grounds that kids aged eleven to fifteen are beset by isolation, confusion, cynicism, and indifference. Its foremost recommendation was to replace "junior high schools" with "middle schools" focused on the whole child rather than specific subjects and more attentive to healthy development, self-confidence, and socialization than to academic achievement. Early adolescents were to be viewed as vessels brimming with hormones and angst whose personal challenges must be dealt with by teachers and schools and who ought not be expected to absorb much by way of formal skills and knowledge.

As Cheri Pierson Yecke (now Florida's chancellor of K–12 education) wrote, "The middle school concept that began to emerge in the 1970's and evolved through the 1980's had finally found its voice. In the early 1990's, life-adjustment, non-academic, and anti-intellectual philosophies came to gain ascendancy over all other viewpoints, driving the agenda for the middle-school movement for years to come." [54] At the very time when the country needed its middle grades to supply a strong foundation for high school, the middle school became the place, she said, "where academic achievement goes to die." [55]

As for the early grades, Harvard reading expert Jeanne S. Chall's seminal 1967 book, *Learning to Read: The Great Debate*, should have established for all time that beginning readers need, first and foremost, to "crack the code" and learn to translate print into words that they can read and understand—and that for most youngsters this means a hefty dose of phonics in kindergarten and the early grades. Yet advocates of the literature-based "whole language" approach held sway in most teacher-training programs and dominated the two main organizations of English teachers. They were undeterred by a strongly worded 1985 report from the National Academy of Education ("children who are taught phonics get off to a better start in learning to read"), and they won a big victory in California in 1987 when that state—freshly embarked on standards-based reform—adopted its new English standards. In an apologia written years later, state school superintendent Bill Honig ruefully declared that his efforts to promote literature as well as reading were "hijacked" by whole-language advocates. In time—after watching its NAEP reading scores plummet in the early 1990s—California would reverse course. [56]

A parallel tempest blew up in math education in 1989, when the National Council of Teachers of Mathematics (NCTM) released its own standards for U.S. schools, urging for this subject something akin to what whole-language advocates favored in reading: lots more attention to "problem-solving" and "real world applications" of math and correspondingly less emphasis on basic arithmetic. The NCTM felt, Ravitch has explained, "that students spent far too much time on computation, drill, and rote memory work. The organization wanted students to be taught to think mathematically, instead of using mathematics in an automatic, formulaic manner." [57] Its leaders were glad, for example, to have kids use electronic calculators for arithmetic, even in the early grades. And they didn't much care about youngsters getting precise solutions to math problems so long as they could "explain their work" and come up with plausible estimates.

The NCTM standards swept through the schools but eventually produced a backlash among mathematicians themselves, who said the teacher group misunderstood the structure of the discipline and the skills and knowledge that mathematically competent people need. As critics came to mock "fuzzy" and "rain forest" math, the NCTM would revise its position slightly in 2000 and more fundamentally in 2006. Yet instructional and curricular battles still rage in what laymen might suppose is the most straightforward of all school subjects.[58] It turns out that "setting standards" for schools is no walk in the park.

By the late 1980s, history was also sinking into turmoil, with traditional historians at loggerheads with cadres of professors, curriculum directors, and teachers, led by the National Council for the Social Studies, who sought to steer their subject toward relativism, multiculturalism, contemporary affairs, and political correctness.

The internecine disputes of individual disciplines seemed distant from the education trails being blazed by governors, the president, and assorted national panels and commissions. Soon, though, they would intersect. Redirecting U.S. schools to produce stronger results presupposes the capacity to say what those results ought to be. Few outside reformers could pull that off without help from educators within.

School Choice | Washington played only a tiny role in the school-choice developments of the late 1980s, mainly keeping the idea alive in government arenas via Bennett's bully pulpit and sundry White House initiatives that Congress spurned.

Still, the principles that parents should be able to select their children's schools, that schools could and should be different from one another, and that youngsters ought not be confined against their will in unsatisfactory schools all gained legitimacy during this eventful decade. So, too, did the idea that educators might design and launch their own schools.

In 1987, pathbreaking Minnesota held out yet more options for students who were faltering in traditional secondary schools. The following year it launched a phased-in "open enrollment" program under which kids might attend any public school in the state. Arkansas and Colorado joined in allowing K–12 pupils to transfer to public schools in other districts. By decade's end, Iowa and Colorado also permitted high-school students to take college courses at public expense.

The idea of "charter schools" surfaced in 1988, first in the writings of education thinker Ray Budde, then in a National Press Club speech by the highly visible Shanker, who returned from visiting an unconventional teacher-crafted school in Germany and asked why shouldn't U.S. teachers be able to devise and then run their own schools—and students be able to choose among them?[59]

Americans overwhelmingly believed that families should be able to select their children's schools. In 1987, for example, on the annual Gallup education survey, 71 percent of respondents agreed that parents in "this community should have the right to choose which local schools their children attend." A year later, a *Times Mirror* poll found that 49 percent of the public was more inclined to favor, and just 27 percent less apt to vote for, a presidential candidate who embraced vouchers.

Analysts also continued to probe New York's venture into public-school choice in East Harlem—and most of the studies yielded positive findings. The opportunity to create and diversify school offerings undeniably appealed to educators and parents alike, and the kids' academic results looked promising.

In an original historical analysis published in 1988 as *The Myth of the Common School,* Charles Glenn, then head of the Massachusetts Education Department's Bureau of Equal Educational Opportunity (now a professor and dean at Boston University), challenged the very notion that uniform public schools remained an essential nation-forging crucible and a beneficent eraser of difference. As he later wrote,

> State-sponsored schooling was intended to replace religious particularism (whether Catholic or Calvinist) as well as local loyalties and norms with an emerging national identity and culture. Enlightenment in this form was experienced by many as oppressive rather than liberating. . . . If we recognize that the attempt to achieve a government monopoly on schooling was intended to serve political purposes

during a period of nation-building, we can see that this monopoly is no longer appropriate—if it ever was.[60]

The decade's end brought a pair of momentous developments on the school-choice front.

Prodded by Democratic legislator Polly Williams and Republican governor Tommy Thompson, in 1990 Wisconsin enacted the first true school-voucher program of the modern era, ultimately affording thousands of low-income Milwaukee youngsters the opportunity to attend private schools with public dollars.[61] (See further discussion in chapter 16.)

That same year, Brookings published *Politics, Markets and America's Schools*, by political scientists John E. Chubb and Terry M. Moe. This blockbuster study, combined with Milton Friedman's earlier work, was to choice-based education reform what Coleman's 1966 study was to standards-based reform: a transformative event that altered the terms of debate. (Altering reality, of course, would prove infinitely harder.)

After studying four hundred high schools and the track records of twenty thousand pupils, teachers, and principals, the authors concluded not only that it does matter enormously to student outcomes whether a school is ineffective or highly effective, but also that the usual characteristics of successful schools can be identified. Above all, such schools are organized to succeed—with strong leadership, a coherent academic program, ambitious goals, and a professional staff imbued with team spirit.

Earlier analysts had sketched similar portraits of successful schools, but Chubb and Moe didn't settle for enumerating their elements. They went on to look for the settings in which such schools are most apt to be found—and discovered that freedom from external constraint is the vital ingredient. "[B]ureaucratic influence," they said, "is an important enough cause of school organization that it can make or break school performance all by itself."[62]

In what circumstances is school autonomy maximized? Where political control is weakest and market forces strongest, they concluded, freeing those who work in a school to make it as effective and appealing as possible, indeed compelling them to do so in order to retain clients, revenues, and status. That can't happen if platoons of assistant superintendents assign kids and teachers, administer programs, dictate curricula, select instructional materials, manage the funds, and keep the principal on a tight leash. "The institutions that govern America's public schools," wrote Chubb and Moe, "bear substantial responsibility for the bureaucratization of schools and the debilitation of their organization."[63]

What to do differently? Rely on markets instead of bureaucracies, they said, and America will have more effective schools. Remove schooling from the conventional engines of "democratic control"; empower those within a school to chart its course; and arm its clients with the means to shape its fate, much as private schools have always done.

The authors warned that existing bureaucracies will not voluntarily cede power. They saw no evidence that conventional experiments with "school based management" had actually shifted real and enduring authority. They also predicted that other popular education reforms of the day— more money, better-trained teachers, even externally imposed standards and "controlled" choice—were doomed. Even when such changes appear to succeed, they argued, the arrangement is inherently unstable and apt to shift with political winds and falter under the unstoppable temptation of bureaucracies and elected officials to add more regulations so as to prevent the occurrence of problems.

Instead, they said, America should embrace a nearly pure form of school choice, free from conventional political and bureaucratic controls. Public and private schools should participate. New schools would emerge. Some old ones would wither and die. And the invisible hand would determine their fate.

This message was grounded in social science, not just ideology or wishful thinking, and emanated from one of America's most respected think tanks. It had to be, and was, taken seriously. Indeed, it went a long way toward legitimizing school choice as a strategy for renewing U.S. education. But even important books don't change much on the ground, at least not quickly. No state or community has yet replaced its bureaucratic school system with one built to the Chubb-Moe design. And the many smaller forays that we've made into school choice have so far yielded mixed results.

To start with the happy outcome, today our son Aloke is a successful young clinician/researcher in cardiology who is terrific with his patients and periodically teams up with his mother on studies and journal articles. We enjoy a close, affectionate relationship with him and his new bride.

It was not always thus. That's why he attended five different schools between kindergarten and twelfth grade as we kept trying to tailor a suitable fit—and one of the reasons I believe so strongly that this right and obligation belongs to all parents, not just those who can afford private schools.

Though a sweet, bright, generous kid and competent soccer player, Aloke was a thoroughly unmotivated learner until halfway through college. The gentle Quaker progressivism of Washington's Sidwell Friends School did him no visible harm in the early grades, so when we moved to Nashville the summer before fifth grade we located a similar environment at a former lab school adjoining the Vanderbilt campus. After two years there, however, he didn't seem to be learning much, so we sought out Nashville's old-fashioned, boys-only, firmly disciplined, and thoroughly structured Montgomery Bell Academy for the remainder of his middle schooling.

This was a better fit for Aloke, a school with demanding teachers and a clear, rigorous curriculum consisting of knowledge and skills that the boys were expected to learn—and remember. Had we remained in Tennessee, he likely would have stayed there. But we were returning to Washington, where—after my failed effort to exercise choice within the public school system and after a frigid reception at Georgetown Prep, the Jesuit day school suggested by a professional counselor we had queried—our fourteen-year-old son prevailed upon us to let him rejoin his old chums at Sidwell Friends.

Big mistake. At the high-school level, Sidwell seems to work well for motivated and self-disciplined learners, but its lack of structure was exactly wrong for our unstructured and directionless son. He learned very little, his grades were mediocre—and if the school cared about any of this, nobody let on. He and a like-minded buddy would sometimes ditch class or skip school altogether. They weren't doing anything awful, just behaving like adolescents. His fretful father, meanwhile, was an assistant secretary of education, working long days telling the country how to educate its kids! Yes, it felt a bit hypocritical.

One school day I happened to come home unexpectedly—and found Aloke and his pal in our house, watching TV. I was livid—and our relationship began to deteriorate. Renu's and my nagging him to study was not only failing to turn him into a serious student; it was starting to alienate him. (My late mother, it must be said, never faltered in her confidence that her eldest grandson would turn out fine.)

When the end of tenth grade brought another round of lackluster (or worse) grades, we and Aloke were barely speaking, and I said to Renu that the time was at hand to look into boarding school. (Daughter Arti was already ensconced at Exeter.) With the help of a friend at the Secondary School Admissions Test Board, I learned that Mercersburg Academy was one of the solid residential schools still accepting applications in June. We drove up the interstate to bucolic south-central Pennsylvania, toured Mercersburg's lovely campus, and met the outstanding headmaster and his wife. Aloke had his interview, we filled out the forms, and in short order he was signed up.

I cannot claim that two years of boarding school turned him into a fervent intellectual, but putting those ninety miles between Aloke and his parents did much to salvage our relationship, and in due course he was accepted at Ohio's Kenyon College, where his sister was by then enrolled. Kenyon is swell, but Aloke coasted through his first two years there, too, playing a little soccer, pledging a fraternity, and having a grand time but, again, getting mediocre grades and heading nowhere in particular.

Finally we said, "You're wasting your time and our money. How about taking a break from college?" He was interested but clueless as to what he might do during what the British call a "gap year." The Berlin Wall had just fallen, and I, grasping for a constructive idea, said, "Why don't you go to Eastern Europe and teach somebody English?" Aloke liked that idea, and friends at the American Federation of Teachers steered me to a new crash program at the University of Warsaw to teach English—and civics—to future Polish schoolteachers, most of whom had been barred from studying the language during Soviet times.

Aloke had never taught anybody but this prospect inspired (or scared) him, and he spent the summer assembling instructional materials—including an entire civics "reader"—before heading off to Warsaw. We still can't explain (nor can he) what happened during that transformative year, living on his own in the bleak environs of newly free Poland's cold, gray capital city, but something clicked. Maybe it was teaching others. Possibly it was the influence of new peers, including some terrific U.S. Peace Corps volunteers with purpose in their lives. Maybe it was being a responsible adult. It likely included the arrival in his life of a couple of worthy role models (one of them a hard-charging medical student with whom he worked closely during a summer internship). Perhaps it was just maturity and independence. But he returned to the United States a different young man, vowing—to his mother's delight and my amazement—to become a doctor. During his final two years at Kenyon, he practically lived in the college library and earned straight As, scrambling to take the pre-med courses while majoring in political science. Medical school followed back at Vanderbilt, then a fine residency in Boston, and the rest, as they say, is history, albeit history still being written, most recently on the faculty of Emory's medical school.

Aloke is living proof that you must not give up on your kids. They really do mature at different rates and in different ways, for reasons that may remain mysterious and in response to stimuli that you cannot always glimpse. Much of that is innate, and parents can do little about it, but they can decide what's the best school for their kids at various stages. To exercise school choice effectively, of course, you need options among which to select, and you need decent information about them. (One's own hand does not work invisibly.) But you must also struggle to match school with student, being prepared to make another change when indicated. Some trial and error may be needed. Nor should parents shy away from intervening in their child's life if they have reason to believe it needs redirecting. Too many modern moms and dads are overly concerned with their kids' happiness—or too keen on being their pals—and diffident about pressing hard for midcourse corrections. Individual children may have as much need for such re-direction as do large school systems.

Part IV | *The Nineties*

The 1990s brought dramatic movement toward standards-based reform and added plenty of helium to the school-choice balloon while also advancing the teacher-professionalism and new-schools agendas. States began to accept the trinity of "standards, testing, and accountability," and George H. W. Bush, then Bill Clinton, applied some federal pressure, including enactment of the Goals 2000 and Improving America's Schools statutes of 1994, which nudged the states while paving the way for Bush 43's more forceful No Child Left Behind Act (NCLB).

There was resistance and backsliding, too, from both the education establishment and the political world, and plenty of ambitious schemes stalled or got derailed. Congress wanted no part of Bush 41's "America 2000" reform agenda (though key elements crept into Clinton's successful version). The Bush team also bungled its venture into setting national standards—and a few years later the Clinton White House botched its attempt to launch national tests. Both failures fed the belief in Washington that Uncle Sam must shun efforts to "nationalize" standards-based reform and led to some of NCLB's awkward compromises.

Yet the political environment was itself shifting. Though Clinton was indisputably the decade's towering (and sometimes tottering) political figure, as Reagan had been in the eighties, the nineties began with a Republican in the Oval Office and ended with the (contested) election of another one. At least as important from a federal policy perspective, the 1994 midterm election dramatically ended the Democrats' four-decade grip on the House of Representatives while also returning the Senate to GOP hands after eight years of Democratic control. Much the same thing was occurring at the state level, where Republican candidates won governors' chairs in record numbers and legislative majorities also tended toward the GOP.

Though upsetting to some educators, such political shifts were mostly good for school reform, at least for those genres that are typically imposed from outside the system and thus more apt to be pursued by elected officials less beholden to "the system" and its forceful labor unions.

That's especially true of school choice in its proliferating varieties. Though some forms of it, notably charter schools, can claim bipartisan parentage, it's long been the case that the average Democratic politician is more apt to go slow on school choice while the typical Republican is likelier to speed up. Hence the GOP political ascendancy of the late 1990s accelerated movement in this direction. But Clinton, Education Secretary Dick Riley, and several influential Democratic governors (e.g., Colorado's

Roy Romer) deserve credit, too. While balking at vouchers and other enlistments of private schools, they went a fair distance to advance public-school choice.

Whatever their politics, state after state enacted laws allowing charter schools to be born—thirty-five jurisdictions joined these ranks between 1993 and 2000—and the number of such schools jumped from 100+ in 1994–95 to 2,000+ by decade's end (450 of them opened in 1999–2000 alone). Because charters tend to be small, their national enrollment impact was slight—about 300,000 youngsters in 1998–89, for example—but their heavy concentration in certain states and cities (e.g., Arizona, the District of Columbia, Dayton) made for mounting influence in those places.

Total K–12 enrollments also swelled again in the nineties, from 46 to 53 million youngsters. Private schools clung to their market share (in fact edged up from 11.3 percent to 11.5 percent), with Christian fundamentalist schools mushrooming while Catholic enrollments stabilized (at about 2.5 million pupils) after three decades of shrinkage.

For the most part, sending a child to private school still meant that her parents paid tuition, but the Wisconsin and Ohio legislatures enacted publicly funded voucher programs for low-income children in Milwaukee and Cleveland, and several states modified their tax codes to give school-related deductions and credits to parents and corporations. By decade's end, serious private money was also going into scholarships for needy youngsters in many cities, some of it catalyzed by an extraordinary $100 million commitment in 1998 by billionaires John Walton and Theodore J. Forstmann to launch the nationwide Children's Scholarship Fund.

This was also a time of school invention, with "whole school" designs propagated by the New American Schools Development Corporation, with Chris Whittle seeking to do for schooling what Thomas Edison had done for lighting, with technology beginning to make it possible to enroll in a school without physically sitting there, with scores of unique charter schools designed by educators (and others), and with myriad new forms of public-school choice helping this to happen at state expense. Instead of the familiar two-flavor arrangement of neighborhood public schools and private schools, U.S. K–12 education was coming to resemble a gelato stand laden with plenty of unfamiliar taste treats, some of them yummy and some unpalatable.

Though America was prosperous and the world mostly at peace, a mass of international data raised red flags for the long term: our children were shown to lag those of other countries and, by some analyses, the longer they spent in school, the wider those gaps grew. "Globalization" sunk in, too, as people saw more jobs outsourced to distant lands and realized that the career opportunities most apt to be available to their children and grandchildren would hinge on education and brains, not brawn or mastery of routines. Future employment options for ill-schooled, low-skilled people would be few, poorly paid, and often unpleasant.

15 | *Bipartisan Reform in Action—and Inaction*

In early 1990, President George H. W. Bush and the governors set their six ambitious national goals for the year 2000, but how to attain them, how even to track the country's progress toward them, was a puzzlement. America had no framework for this sort of partnership between statehouse and White House in the education field. Scrambling for usable mechanisms, political leaders cobbled together a quartet of novel panels and commissions.

In July 1990, they agreed to form the National Education Goals Panel (NEGP) with representation from governors, the executive branch, and Congress. Its charge was to monitor movement toward the decade-long goals and prepare annual reports and studies.

At the White House, meanwhile, domestic adviser Roger Porter was frustrated by Secretary Cavazos's inertia and determined that Bush might truly don the "education president" mantle that he sought. So Porter created panel number two, the President's Education Policy Advisory Committee (PEPAC), comprising twenty-some eminent business leaders—Paul O'Neill of ALCOA, later Bush 43's treasury secretary, chaired it—as well as public officials and educators. Though it didn't do much but talk, its conversations advanced the idea of education standards and accountability, even broaching the possibility of national testing within the walls of a GOP White House.

Besides a series of rousing if inconclusive discussions, often involving the president himself, PEPAC served one startling strategic function for the Pentagon, though we didn't know it at the time: providing "cover" for the launch of Operation Desert Storm on January 16, 1991. An afternoon meeting with our education panel was the only event on Bush's public schedule that day, and promptly at two o'clock he joined us in the cabinet room. As domestic policy aide Charles Kolb recalls, he "also made sure that the White House press pool was summoned to photograph and videotape him, flanked by Paul O'Neill and Education Secretary-designate Lamar Alexander. The film footage ran on CNN throughout most of the afternoon."[1]

At one point, the president briefly excused himself, saying he had to make a phone call. Then he returned and again gave us his rapt attention. Until PEPAC members turned on their televisions that evening, we had no idea that cruise missiles were headed toward Baghdad even as we were meeting and that Bush's high-profile parley with us served the added purpose of maintaining the surprise for Saddam Hussein. How could the commander in chief be dispatching bombers if he was calmly conferring with his education advisers? Recalling that afternoon later, I was most struck by Bush's capacity to focus on our mundane domestic issues while also commencing a complex, risky military operation. Though I fancy myself a multi-tasker, when dealing with a major crisis I'm not good at paying simultaneous attention to other things. I guess that's something presidents learn to do.

America 2000 | In time, the Bush White House wearied of Lauro Cavazos, a decent, colorless, and apolitical man who was getting no traction in the K–12 education arena where the president wanted to make his mark. In December 1990 he was relieved of his duties, and to replace him Bush turned to none other than Lamar Alexander, who, since ending his term as Tennessee governor in 1987, had been traveling, writing, and making some money. Lamar's nomination was announced in January 1991 and, mindful that months would likely elapse before his Senate confirmation, he resolved to land running.

He called Bruno Manno and me and, with Scott Hamilton and a borrowed staffer from the Education Department, we convened an informal working group to help plan his transition. Most of that planning took place in Vanderbilt's unpretentious outpost on Sixteenth Street, where I was hanging my hat at the time, opposite the Russian Embassy and about five blocks from the White House. Joining us when he could was David Kearns, former Xerox CEO and one of the country's foremost businessmen-turned-education-reformers, whom Lamar persuaded to join his leadership team as deputy secretary.

Alexander had been as engaged as anyone with the education reforms of the 1980s, and he recognized that this president, especially—a would-be "education president"—urgently needed a plausible *strategy* to accelerate the country's progress toward the national goals that Bush had already helped to shape and publicize. So he moved swiftly to devise such a plan.

The result, delivered to the White House shortly before Lamar's March 1991 confirmation, was an integrated four-part plan that he dubbed "America 2000" and that he insisted was a "national strategy, not a federal program."

Alexander termed the first section of the plan "better and more accountable schools." Its fifteen elements included "world class standards" in the five core subjects; a "new (voluntary) nationwide examination system" to be known as the "American Achievement Tests"; an expansion of NAEP (state-level testing in all five subjects in all three benchmark grades); and incentives for states and districts to widen school choice.

Second came "a new generation of American schools." Stimulated in part by the thinking of fellow Tennessean Chris Whittle, who went on a year later to establish the "Edison Project," and in part by Kearns and the innovativeness of successful firms like Xerox, Alexander sought to reinvent the school itself as an educational institution. He proposed to do this outside government via a novel nonprofit outfit called the New American Schools Development Corporation (NASDC, later "New American Schools"), to be underwritten by private dollars. That entity would stage design competitions among R&D organizations eager to devise fresh models. Congress would then be asked to pay for the replication and installation of the best among these.

Third was a set of work-related skills for adults seeking new or better jobs. And fourth was creation of what Lamar dubbed "America 2000 communities," a Tocquevillian vision of cities and towns mobilizing private, public, and civic resources and pledging themselves to realize the national education goals locally, to undertake actions that would move them in that direction, and honestly to report on their own progress.

I accompanied Alexander and Kearns to the White House to vet the America 2000 proposal with the president's senior aides. It was fun to watch chief of staff John Sununu and budget director Dick Darman race to see which of those brainy, competitive egotists could first claim to have read his copy of the thick briefing books we handed them. They liked the plan well enough, and a day or two later I found myself in the Oval Office as Lamar walked the president through its key elements.

"This is the best thing I've ever seen," Bush commented, immediately warming to Alexander's strategy—and visibly pleased finally to have an education secretary with ideas, initiative, and energy who brought him something he could claim as his own.

The president unveiled America 2000 at an April 18 White House ceremony, replete with congressional leaders and ten national teachers of the year. There he noted that per pupil spending had risen by 33 percent over the previous decade but added, "I don't think there's a person anywhere . . . who would say that we've seen a 33 percent improvement in our schools' performance." "For too long," he admonished the nation, "we've adopted a 'no fault' approach to education. Someone else is always to blame. . . . It's time we held our schools—and ourselves—accountable for results."

Going where no president, certainly no Republican president, had gone before, Bush said: "Working closely with the governors, we will define new World Class Standards for schools, teachers and students in the five core subjects. . . . We will develop voluntary . . . national tests for 4th, 8th, and 12th graders in the five core subjects. . . . I'm determined to have the first of these tests for 4th graders in place by the time that school starts in September of 1993."[2]

It was an ambitious and fairly coherent package, and the energetic Alexander and Kearns crisscrossed the countryside promoting it. Congress, however, wasn't very interested—education was still not territory the Democratic House majority wanted to cede to a GOP administration—and the teacher unions opposed nearly all of these ideas. Truth be told, Bush and Alexander didn't work Capitol Hill very hard on behalf of America 2000. These were not ideas with great appeal for congressional Republicans *or* Democrats at the time.

Yet key elements of this plan could launch without congressional assent. The grassroots and bully-pulpit parts were obvious. NASDC was a private-sector initiative funded with philanthropic dollars—and in fairly short order Kearns and Alexander raised more than $100 million for this purpose (about half of their target figure).

The administration also took a stab at developing national standards using discretionary dollars available to the Education Department and other agencies.

Both of those components of America 2000 happened without Congress okaying them. Neither, however, turned out as well as Lamar and his fellow planners (me included) had hoped, though the Clinton administration was well under way before any verdicts could be rendered.

National Standards? | In 1991 and 1992, the Department of Education made grants to educator groups to develop "voluntary national academic standards" in each of seven subjects. (Lynne Cheney's Humanities Endowment co-funded a couple of these, as did the National Science Foundation.) It was a worthy but perhaps naïve undertaking that might have benefited from reflecting on why nationwide standards for the one subject that already had them (courtesy of the math teachers in 1989) had triggered so much controversy.

Diane Ravitch was then assistant secretary for research and improvement, working with Lamar in much the way I had with Bennett a few years before. Here is how she recalls the administration's thinking:

> The voluntary national standards were supposed to describe what children should be expected to learn in different grades in every major academic subject. . . . The organizations that received the federal awards were supposed to identify clearly and succinctly what students should know and be able to do. . . . When the federal grants were made, it was widely anticipated that Congress would create some sort of national board to evaluate the voluntary national standards and that this board would oversee an iterative process to review and revise the draft national standards.[3]

But no such board ever materialized, and the quest for standards was instead weakened by the credulous expectation that self-interested experts, mostly free from the discipline of consumers, parents, practicing teachers, and policymakers—and sometimes free from leading university scholars in their own fields—could successfully distill from their own cherished subjects the essential skills and knowledge that kids should learn in school, and could do so while (a) avoiding political correctness, (b) sparing schools from the savage internecine disputes within the field, and (c) producing a manageable document of essential curricular guidance rather than a kitchen-sink tome with the heft of the Los Angeles phone directory.

The dismaying results ranged from incoherent blather (English) to left-leaning political correctness (history) to immense, encyclopedic treatments (geography) that placed the authors' discipline at the center of the intellectual universe and made everything else revolve around it. The U.S. Senate voted 99–1 to condemn the history standards, and an early draft of the English standards was so vapid that Clinton's Education Department cut off further funding.

This fiasco left political Washington wary of national academic standards, not least because it exposed the chasm between what experts value and what ordinary parents and teachers (and elected officials) expect schools to teach their students. "The abortive attempt to create national standards," Ravitch later wrote, "revealed the deep fissures within academic fields, as well as the wide gap between avant-garde thinkers in the academic world and the general public."[4]

New Schools | The "New American Schools" initiative also proved disappointing, as school-level reform so often does. Again, a bold initiative hatched by energized laymen turned mushy when the same old experts got hold of it, the system resisted it, communities weren't sure they wanted it, and in time the political system diluted it.

The initial concept was exhilarating and harmonized with much that was happening in private industry, where many firms had their own R&D centers, "skunk works," and labs to invent fresh solutions to problems old and new. Alarmed that, at the end of the twentieth century, young Americans attended schools almost exactly like the industrial-era models in which their grandparents had studied, Alexander confidently predicted: "We will unleash America's creative genius to invent and establish a New Generation of American Schools. . . . These will be the best schools in the world, schools that enable their students to reach the national education goals, to achieve a quantum leap in learning. . . ."[5]

As intended, NASDC staged a design competition for innovative school designs and planned to underwrite development of the winners. The organization had a superstar board, chaired by former New Jersey governor Thomas Kean, and plenty of expert help. Perhaps that was its downfall. In any case, hundreds of applications flooded in, and in 1992 NASDC picked eleven for further work. In time, nine of those design teams were disseminating their education blueprints around the country, and by 2001 some 3,500 schools claimed to be following NASDC models, though many of these were inept or incomplete replicas.

Extolling the selected designs at the time, Kean was as bullish as Alexander had been, confidently declaring, "You are going to see massive changes in American schools. We are aiming at nothing less than a fundamental and dramatic change in education."[6]

Yet the industrial-era model endured almost unscathed. I'm not certain whether school-level reform "at scale" is an oxymoron that shouldn't even be tried or whether NASDC suffered from conventional thinking and weak implementation. In any case, little about the New American Schools turned out to be truly new or exceptionally effective. The experts and groups that were given the chance to invent novel schools settled for variations on the familiar. No molds were decisively broken. Here is how education historian Jeffrey Mirel describes what happened:

> By setting up the process in a conventional way, NASDC almost guaranteed that most of the winning proposals would come from established education reformers and their groups. . . . The traditional RFP process not only rounded up many of the usual educational suspects, but as a consequence it rounded up the usual educational ideas, too. . . . Moreover, few of these widely shared ideas really broke the mold in educational reform. . . . Even winning proposal writer Robert Slavin noted critically, "They [NASDC] almost demanded that you put into your proposal all the things that were considered hot right now. What they've done is frozen 1992 in amber."[7]

Yet a paucity of breakthroughs on the design side was only part of the problem. NASDC's underlying "theory of action" also proved unequal to the challenge of changing American K–12 education. Indeed, concluded the program's handpicked RAND evaluators after ten years of experience, "The initial hypothesis, that by adopting a whole-school design a school could improve its performance, was largely unproven. . . . Our general findings showed difficulties in implementation and lack of strong improvements in school performance."[8]

RAND was too circumspect to say why the new-school designs had failed to deliver on the high hopes invested in them, but the reasons seem evident: the system's familiar blend of inertia, incapacity, and overregulation had again triumphed, repelling reformers who wanted to do things a little differently. But this was not just the stubbornness of educators. As Chubb and Moe had explained a few years earlier, the K–12 system's governance arrangements—public education's engines of "democratic control"—also work to sustain the status quo. Not many states and communities rushed to adopt new school designs—heavy-duty marketing persuaded some—and far fewer did a conscientious job of implementing them. Borrowing the title of a 1985 book by Diane Ravitch, maybe America already had "the schools we deserve"—and little appetite for replacing them with anything very different.

NCEST | Although Congress didn't want much to do with America 2000—the House was so allergic to national testing that the administration never even filed a bill to create its "American Achievement Tests"—Alexander did persuade it to authorize a third new panel, the National Council on Education Standards and Testing (NCEST), known (always with a smirk) as "en-sest." Its mandate was to advise the government and public as to "the desirability and feasibility of national standards and tests" and to "recommend long-term policies, structures, and mechanisms for setting voluntary education standards and planning an appropriate system of tests." It was another commission in lieu of action, but it enabled Congress to get into the standards-based-reform action, it was bipartisan, and it kept some ideas alive.

NCEST was co-chaired by two governors, South Carolina's affable Republican Carroll Campbell and Colorado's hyperkinetic Democrat Roy Romer, and competently staffed by Francie Alexander, who had piloted California's standard-setting work and went on to serve as Ravitch's deputy at the Education Department. Pressed by the impatient Romer—forever jumping to his omnipresent easel and pad to draw diagrams that nobody else could understand—the council worked in record time, issuing its report in January 1992. But that report was schizophrenic, revealing uncertainty, ambivalence, and division within the panel, which mirrored—in both composition and arguments—the policy elites that had struggled with these issues in the eighties and would continue to do so in years to follow.

The NCEST report was long on rhetoric and rationale for national (but not federal) standards and a "national system of assessments," but vague about how this should happen. As if waving a wand and expecting something to materialize, it declined to assign clear responsibility. It sought subject-specific content standards that would "reflect high expectations" via a foggy process that "must involve the widest possible participation in the process from individuals and groups at the national, state, and local levels."[9] Nor could it unite around a single national testing scheme. Instead, it proposed multiple tests, supposedly to emerge from consortia of states and testing companies, all of them somehow "aligned" with the national standards and all magically to yield scores that could be compared with one another. (Debate continues today as to whether that is technically possible. Most experts say no, at least not unless the tests are so similar that they might as well be the same.)

As Robert Schwartz and Marian Robinson explain,

> To make such a mixed system of centralized standards and decentralized assessments work, some kind of central coordinating structure was necessary. NCEST recommended that the National Education Goals Panel . . . be reconfigured . . . and that a new council be created under the panel's jurisdiction that would certify both standards and criteria for assessments. This new entity, the National Education Standards and Assessment Council (NESAC), would be appointed by the goals panel to give it some political insulation, while still making it accountable publicly. NESAC's membership would be one-third public officials, one-third educators, and one-third other citizens.[10]

In other words, panel three said that panel one should beget a new panel four, which would bestow its seal of approval on standards and tests that it liked, all this occurring at arm's length from Uncle Sam, albeit paid for from his wallet. In proposing so clumsy a structure, NCEST was struggling to find a walkable path through a thorny—and enduring—political thicket: given America's tradition of state responsibility and local control of education, its abiding mistrust of Washington dictating curriculum, and the fact that the executive branch was in Republican hands while Democrats ruled Congress, there was no obvious machinery to drive a national reform strategy. Yet "the nation" was at risk.

NCEST also reached an awkward compromise on one of the knottiest issues before it: should the push for national standards include "opportunity to learn" standards, that is, criteria to assure that schools actually teach and students have a fair chance to absorb the skills and knowledge framed by the content standards and tested by the assessment system? This was in part a debate between pre- and post-Coleman thinking, but it was also a tug-of-war between Democrats and Republicans and, with a presidential election on the horizon, it all but paralyzed NCEST, which finally recommended that both "school delivery" and "system performance" standards be set but not nationally. Rather, they would be "developed by the states collectively from which each state could select the criteria that it finds useful for the purpose of assessing a school's capacity and performance."[11]

Messy and irresolute indeed, but a perfect hologram of arguments that still seethe, primarily between educators worried about having the wherewithal to produce the desired results and outsiders insistent that the focus on results not be blurred and wary of yet another costly, chimerical quest for more school resources.

The very day that NCEST delivered its report, four dozen prominent educators issued a long statement lamenting America's slide toward results-based accountability via standards and testing. They termed a "cruel hoax" any policy that would "establish benchmarks for achievement without creating equity in the educational resources available to children." Signers included my old friend Greg Anrig, then head of the Educational Testing Service (which continued to hold the NAEP contract); my former ed school dean, Ted Sizer, then at Brown University; John Goodlad of the University of Washington; Harold "Doc" Howe II, who had been commissioner of education under LBJ; Harvard's Howard Gardner; Donald Stewart, head of the College Board; Lee Shulman, president of the National Academy of Education; and, amazingly, two members of NCEST itself, NEA chieftain Keith Geiger and Marshall Smith, then at the Stanford School of Education. (Ravitch remarks that they "signed both the NCEST report and the statement criticizing that report.")[12]

In an interview at the time, Sizer deplored "the arrogation of authority over children by the central government, in the name of high standards and international competition." [13]

By the time NCEST delivered its conflicted report, however, and its critics registered their objections, the 1992 New Hampshire primary was at hand and election season was noisily under way. Congress was not about to enact major education legislation that year, even if the advice given to it had been less garbled. Yet the council's tortuous recommendations, combined with key elements of the Bush-Alexander plan, fed directly into the Clinton strategy that would be named Goals 2000.

Setting Performance Levels | Panel upon panel, it seemed, world without end. I served on PEPAC and NCEST, lent a hand with multiple projects of the new Goals Panel, and informally advised Porter and his White House colleagues on federal policy, as well as assisting Lamar to devise the America 2000 strategy, then functioning as a member of his kitchen cabinet. If I contributed anything of lasting value to standards-based education reform during this confused time, however, it was via the National Assessment

Governing Board, where instead of jawboning, we actually moved to set functional academic standards for American K–12 education.

This board was a first-rate collection of twenty-three individuals, genuinely bipartisan and reasonably representative of both educators (two principals, two superintendents, three teachers, etc.) and public officials (two governors, two legislators, two state superintendents, etc.) with a decent smattering of experts, academics, and the "general public." Members were appointed to four-year terms by the secretary of education, but at first the board also served as its own nominating committee, giving it an added layer of autonomy. Congress had made clear that this was to be a *governing* board for NAEP, not an advisory committee, and conferred considerable authority on it. Blessed with a resourceful, gutsy little staff and an initial crop of members who took this responsibility gravely, volunteered tons of time, and nearly always managed to transcend their "constituencies" in pursuit of the national interest, it was the finest board I've ever been associated with.

If the new national goals were to mean much, I reasoned, someone had to grab this bull's horns and define "competency" and "challenging subject matter," as well as put into place a mechanism for appraising student achievement vis-à-vis those definitions. NAGB, I concluded, had the capacity to do this, the requisite independence, and a usable measuring tool. All that was needed was for it to define standards of student performance on NAEP and then report NAEP results according to how many students in the nation or a state met those standards in a given year, subject, and grade level.

We had a statutory basis for proffering such definitions. Picking up on the National Academy of Education's suggestion (in its commentary on the Alexander-James report) that "NAEP should articulate clear descriptions of performance levels," the 1988 statute that overhauled NAEP and birthed NAGB also charged the new board with "develop[ing] appropriate student performance levels for each age and grade in each subject area to be tested under" NAEP.

One cannot definitively tell from the legislative history of PL 100-297 whether lawmakers truly expected the new governing board to establish standards. But the language of the law plainly allowed for this to happen—and the Academy had indisputably recommended it.

Even before Charlottesville, NAGB was wrestling with how to go about this. We never imagined that NAEP—which uses a method known as "matrix-sampling" whereby no student takes the whole exam—would turn into a "high-stakes" test or that it would yield results for individual children. I doubt that board members would even have agreed on the desirability of that kind of testing. But we were responsible for a well-regarded nationwide assessment that was already used to monitor the overall performance of large chunks of geography and big groups of children in key subjects. How much more informative and useful it would be if its results were reported in relation to standards rather than on a scale that meant nothing except to a handful of psychometricians.

But what was the best process for developing "appropriate performance levels"? Should there be just one standard or several? What should it, or they, be called? We solicited advice from policy experts, technical folks, and education groups, and scrutinized other fields that had engaged in standard-setting exercises. After Goal 3 was announced in January 1990, we accelerated our efforts. Shanker, among others, warned that a single, universal standard would inevitably be set low, more a gauge of basic skills than a full set of desirable knowledge and skills. Board members eventually concurred, and in May 1990 we decreed three student performance levels ("basic," "proficient," "advanced") by which future NAEP results would be reported. (Such reporting actually began in 1992.)

"Proficient," we declared, was the "central level," the one that all students *ought* to attain and the proper benchmark for American education. We defined it as "solid academic performance for each grade tested" and said that it would "reflect a consensus that students reaching this level demonstrated competency over challenging subject matter and are well prepared for the next level of schooling." [14]

Audacious, yes, but someone had to do it, and who better than a diverse, bipartisan, and independent board charged via fresh congressional mandate with setting policy for the "nation's report card?"

Controversy has since dogged NAGB's achievement levels, part of it technical, part political. In today's No Child Left Behind era, where universal "proficiency" in reading and math is the coin of a high-stakes education regime, state officials and educators complain that NAGB's "proficient" level is too demanding and that it's madness to expect all kids to reach it. [15] Gradually, however, over the past fifteen years those levels have gained acceptance as the closest thing America has to national education standards and reliable measures of performance. But I get ahead of myself.

U sually defined as an "independent public school of choice," a charter school exists via a license or contract (its "charter") that allows its operator (usually a nonprofit organization) to run a public school for a limited period of time, typically five years, at the end of which it is evaluated to see if it deserves to continue. The school operator is supposed to deliver the results spelled out in the charter, normally denominated in student academic performance gauged by state tests, plus other measures, and is also obligated, to follow applicable laws and properly tend the public dollars that support the school. In return, the operator is supposed to be free to choose its curriculum, select its own staff (preferably without regard to state "certification" laws), and expend its budget as it sees fit.

On the other side of the charter agreement is a sponsor, also known as an authorizer, which confers on the school its right to operate and is supposed to monitor its performance. Sponsors may include local school boards, state education departments, sometimes state universities, occasionally independent "chartering boards," and, in a few places, nonprofit organizations and municipal agencies that are empowered to perform this function on the state's behalf.[16]

Three traits make charter schools "public" even though they're privately operated. First, they are paid for with tax dollars and may not charge tuition. Second, with rare exceptions they are open to all comers and, if oversubscribed, use a lottery system, rather than admissions screening, to determine which children attend. Third, they are "accountable" for their results to duly constituted public or quasi-public authorities (i.e., their sponsors), which in turn are accountable to the legislature, governor, voters, and taxpayers.

Students always enroll in charter schools by choice, not by being assigned to them.

Some schools achieve charter status by seceding from their local school systems. Most, though, are new institutions started from scratch by teachers, parents, community groups, or national school-management organizations.

Charter schools come in many sizes and types. Some have fewer than fifty pupils while others enroll more than a thousand. Some of today's "virtual" charter schools operate statewide with more than five thousand students. (There is also a multicampus brick-and-mortar complex in Chicago, all under a single charter, that enrolls nearly six thousand.)

They also cover the spectrum of traditional and progressive curricula and pedagogies.[17] Some are schools for budding artists or scientists, some for at-risk or disabled students, some for ordinary youngsters whose families seek alternatives not to be found in district schools, at least not in that particular community. Some are intended to bring dropouts back into public education; others are for ex–juvenile offenders. Most, it turns out, serve youngsters who stumbled or were ill served in district schools but whose families cannot afford private schooling.[18]

In 1991, the Minnesota legislature, again pioneering in the school-choice territory, enacted the first state charter law, followed a year later by California. As the movement gained speed, Uncle Sam was drawn in, too, with Congress authorizing a federal aid program in 1994 to stimulate creation of more such schools.

State charter laws differ widely in their mechanics, funding arrangements, and the extent to which they make it easy to start new schools. That is partly a reflection of states' varied education cultures, but mostly it reflects political accommodations that charter advocates have made with their foes. Without exception, the teachers' unions and other elements of the public school establishment—Bill Bennett dubbed it "the blob," a term these groups despised but which stuck like a wad of bubble gum—have done their utmost to block enactment of such laws and, where passage seems inevitable, to keep them as weak and cramped as possible.[19]

Their motive is straightforward. "Chartering" a school normally removes it from the union's collective bargaining unit and often from the district's enrollment counts and test-score tallies. Frequently, the school is exempted from regulations by which other parts of the establishment cling to their near monopolies, such as teacher certification via colleges of education. Insofar as state, federal, and (rarely) local dollars follow children into charter schools, they are usually deducted from district budgets. While that pain is milder in growing districts—sometimes charters help them to accommodate soaring enrollments—in the stable or contracting school systems often found in the Midwest and Northeast every kid moving from district to charter school means $5,000 to $10,000 less in district coffers, which eventually translates into fewer jobs. Although charters nearly everywhere get "less than their share" of total public-school funding—and districts commonly wind up with *more* money per remaining pupil than they had precharter—any erosion of their total revenues leaves them sorely aggrieved. Like other public-sector organizations, school systems are infinitely better at expanding than shrinking.[20]

Surging charter enrollments are also an embarrassment, even an affront, to establishment educators because they demonstrate that, when presented with exit options, many families will vote with their feet and move their kids out of district-operated schools. Hence the tighter the lid on charter schools (the leaner their rations, and the more thoroughly they are subordinated to local boards and bureaucracies), the less menacing they are.

Considering how many charter schools have been launched and led by educators, and recalling Al Shanker's early vision of chartering as a rare opportunity for teachers to create and teach in schools of their own devising, the fierce opposition mounted by unions and their allies seems shortsighted and self-denying. How ironic that groups pressing for greater teacher professionalism and educator leverage are also hostile to one of the surest and politically most popular mechanisms for fostering such conditions. Nevertheless, their antipathy has meant that many Democratic governors and legislators have been charter-wary and most of the procharter energy has come from Republicans.[21]

Sometimes the opposition proved so intense that the resulting charter program was warped from the beginning, operating under oppressive caps (on the number of schools and/or pupils), allowing only local boards to "sponsor" charters (akin, say advocates, to letting only foxes sponsor hens), denying them capital and facilities funding, or refusing to waive regulations that cause charters to resemble conventional schools.

Sometimes, too, the opposition was so fierce that charter laws could be enacted only because establishment forces feared something worse (vouchers, usually) or because a public official offered an irresistible quid pro quo. A vivid example occurred in New York in 1998, when Governor George Pataki held a much-coveted legislators' pay raise hostage to their okaying a small charter-school program for the Empire State.

The Birth of Vouchers | Liberals and conservatives have quarreled for decades over publicly financed mechanisms to assist children to attend private schools by covering the cost of their education with tax dollars. Although such aid schemes are common elsewhere in the developed world, as late as 1990 little of the sort was visible on U.S. shores. A number of states assisted their private schools in limited and specific ways (e.g., textbooks, bus transportation), and Minnesota and a couple of other jurisdictions had modest tax breaks for parents incurring educational expenses. Under the federal special-ed law and the litigation that it invited, parents of disabled youngsters could sometimes get local school systems to pay their children's way into private schools. But the closest thing to conventional vouchers in K–12 education was the time-honored practice in northern New England whereby a few small towns that didn't want (or were not large enough) to run their own public high schools might "tuition" their teenage pupils into schools in nearby towns, occasionally including privately operated "academies."

Then came Milwaukee. Against a backdrop of long-standing public-school failure in that city's minority neighborhoods, black activists such as Howard Fuller joined forces with legislator Annette "Polly" Williams, who represented thousands of such families and was herself black and a Democrat, and with veteran Wisconsin GOP governor (and passionate education reformer) Tommy Thompson, to persuade the legislature to enact a voucher "experiment" in 1990. Quietly trickling in the background was a steady flow of expertly directed philanthropic dollars and intellectual encouragement from the Milwaukee-based Bradley Foundation, then headed by the low-profile but formidable Michael Joyce, who had determined that real reform of American education called for both excellence *and* choice.[22] From such bipartisan convergings of public officials, wealthy mover-shakers, energized activists, and needy kids are lasting changes in K–12 education most likely to emerge.

At first, Milwaukee's voucher program was confined to seven secular private schools with a majority of nonvoucher youngsters. The number of children receiving vouchers could not exceed 1.5 percent of the enrollment in the Milwaukee Public Schools (MPS), and recipients' incomes could not exceed 175 percent of the federal poverty level.

Five years later, the cap was raised to 5 percent of MPS students, and participating schools could enroll as many voucher-bearing pupils as they wished. In 1998, the cap was again loosened, religious schools were allowed to take part—and new private schools started launching to accommodate (and sometimes exploit) the additional students, indicating, as Economics 101 teaches, that enough market demand begets new supply. By 2004, more than 12,000 youngsters took their vouchers (up to $6,600 apiece) to more than one hundred participating schools, most of them religious, at a total cost to state and city of nearly $100 million. Early in 2006, after a long political tussle, the cap was lifted once more, this time to 22,500 students, and the family income ceiling was raised to 220 percent of the poverty line.

Polly Williams's reasoning—and her anger and determination—are notable because, while untypical of African-American Democrats holding elective office, they do evoke the energy behind the spread of school choice in the nineties. This excerpt is from an interview with her in *Reason* magazine:

> *Reason:* What obstacles did the education establishment throw up to stop your choice plan?
>
> *Williams:* They tried everything to stop me. After they were convinced choice couldn't be stopped, they tried to hijack the issue and came up with their own version of choice. . . . This fake choice plan was the product of a white, do-good liberal legislator. . . . Liberals backed her; they weren't for my bill. We finally won when we got 200 parents to testify for three hours in favor of my bill. In good conscience, my colleagues could not vote against those parents. . . .
>
> *Reason:* Why do white liberals insist on busing instead of choice?
>
> *Williams:* It's more feel-good politics for them. They think their kids are having a neat cultural experience by going to school with African-American kids. But they don't want to really relate to them. . . . It has nothing to do with education. The theory is that if black kids sit next to white kids, they will learn better; it's insulting. I thought these people were liberals!
>
> *Reason:* You castigate liberals a lot. But aren't you a liberal Democrat?
>
> *Williams:* Labels do not tell you much about me. I'm not a liberal; I believe in what works.[23]

Targeting this school-choice initiative—and its successors in other places—on poor, minority, inner-city dwellers also brought tactical benefits. Because the program was thus confined, its cost was contained, at least at the outset. Because it operated for the benefit of kids who needed better school opportunities, not for schools needing pupils or revenues, it didn't look like "aid to private (much less parochial) schools." Because it was voluntary, with deployment of the vouchers wholly in parents' hands, it plausibly sidestepped First Amendment concerns about the state acting on behalf of "an establishment of religion." Because it was aimed at deserving youngsters who had undeniably been ill served by the traditional system, it was hard to wage a convincing moral battle against. (One person's exhortation on the sanctity and universality of public education could be trumped by another's sermon on the need to address the pressing educational needs of America's most distressed populations.) Because its beneficiaries were, by and large, minority group members residing in liberal urban districts, it was more awkward (though rarely impossible) for Democratic politicians to fight. Conversely, because it had little direct effect on white suburbanites, Republicans could afford to support it without alarming their constituents that *those* kids would flood into *their* schools.

Although the inclusion of religious schools in voucher programs created constitutional uncertainties (which lasted until the Supreme Court's 2002 *Zelman* decision), it had ample popular and social-scientific backing. Many parents favor Catholic, Lutheran, Jewish, and other church-related schools for their children even when they don't necessarily embrace that faith themselves, because such schools emphasize character, morals, values, behavior, and discipline as well as academics. That this kind of learning environment matters, particularly for disadvantaged youngsters, was meticulously shown once again by Anthony Bryk and his colleagues, whose important 1993 book, *Catholic Schools and the Common Good*, picked up where Coleman, Glenn, and Chubb and Moe had left off.[24] After a careful comparison of Catholic and public high schools, they concluded that parochial schools are indeed more effective in narrowing the learning gap between poor and middle-class students; that this is caused not only by sound curricula and effective teaching but also by their success in forging communities of learners; and that, ironically, they now come closer to the "common school ideal" of public education than do public schools themselves.

Before decade's end, the Ohio legislature would follow Wisconsin's lead and create a similar program for Cleveland children, and in 1998 Congress would (barely) pass—and Bill Clinton would veto—a smallish voucher program for the District of Columbia. Vouchers were no longer unthinkable in these United States. The question was where they would pop up next.

M ore insistently than before, prominent economists and management experts cautioned that future U.S. prosperity would hinge on people's education levels and skills. In 1992, for example, Lester Thurow predicted that competing successfully in the internationalizing economy of the twenty-first century would depend on "the education and skills of the workforce." The following year, Peter Drucker wrote that "the only long-term policy which promises success is for developed countries to convert manufacturing from being labor based into being knowledge based." [25]

At the same time, accumulating international data periodically shocked Americans with the message that their children were not learning as much as their peers across the sea—and that their schools were less effective.

In 1992, the prolific Harold Stevenson and his colleague James Stigler published *The Learning Gap.* Subtitled *Why Our Schools Are Failing and What We Can Learn from Japanese and Chinese Education*, this arresting book, as Ravitch has explained,

> pinpointed differences in classroom activities, parent attitudes and behavior, and cultural values that were amenable to change. Among these were, for example, his finding that parents in Asian societies value effort and thus expect their children to work hard in school, while American parents tend to value their children's innate abilities and thus excuse their mediocre academic performance.
>
> *The Learning Gap* was especially influential because it appeared at a time when there was a heated debate among education researchers about whether the performance of American students was or was not problematic. Defenders of the status quo claimed that critics of student performance were trying to "destroy" the public schools. They charged that international assessments—on which American students performed poorly, especially in high school—were technically flawed and therefore of no significance. . . . Into this debate, Stevenson waded with a mountain of unassailable empirical data comparing the results of the American educational system unfavorably to those in Asian countries. [26]

Stevenson and Stigler showed not only that schools do matter and that some are strikingly more effective than others, but also that a country's policies and institutional arrangements make a big difference, not just its cultural underpinnings. "The time has come," they concluded, "when the United States needs a national education policy. . . . We must decide who should control the curriculum. Are Americans willing to abdicate this function to textbook publishers? . . . Should curricula conform to a national standard . . . that all children are expected to meet? Or does state or local control . . . remain the most effective way to prepare students for the working world?"[27]

Three years later (1995) came the Third International Mathematics and Science Study (TIMSS), the largest comparative assessment yet, involving youngsters in five grade levels in forty countries. These data, too, gave ample cause for worry. At the end of middle school (eighth grade), for example, U.S. students scored twenty-eighth in math and seventeenth in science, lagging not only such Far Eastern pacesetters as Singapore, Korea, and Japan but also Russia, many of its former satellites, and much of western Europe.

The challenge was clearer than ever: to prosper in the global economy, to keep its culture vibrant, its defenses strong, and its civic life in good repair, America needed better-educated and more highly skilled adults—and many more of them—than its schools were producing.

The United States has tended to work around that problem rather than solving it directly. Via a relatively openhanded policy toward skilled immigrants (and a porous border for others), we have imported human capital from abroad. Our sprawling, diversified, and endlessly forgiving higher education system has allowed skill-seeking and career-changing Americans to come back (at bargain prices, thanks to taxpayer subsidies) to school at the university or community college level to acquire whatever training and credentials their primary-secondary schools did not provide. Our firms have deployed new technologies and other productivity enhancers to eke more from their present workforce. And many, of course, now outsource work to lower-wage and/or higher-skilled workers in other parts of the planet.[28]

Such coping mechanisms have helped to keep us prosperous, but they beg the question of whether we could, at lesser cost and with greater assurance, produce a better-educated and more highly skilled workforce of our own by graduating young people from the K–12 education system who possess more of the requisite knowledge and competencies—competencies that are themselves changing as today's "knowledge economy" calls for different skills than the industrial age required.[29]

At least since *A Nation at Risk* in 1983 (and arguably since Sputnik), anxiety about America falling behind the rest of the world, expressed primarily in economic terms, has been the mainspring of our education reform efforts, particularly the standards-based genre. That's mostly what's kept politicians and business leaders engaged with this oft-frustrating endeavor. Educators, however, are dismayed not just by the implicit (and sometimes explicit) criticism of their own work but also by seeing their mission justified in such crass, utilitarian terms.

I've come to terms with this, recognizing that perceived threats to American prosperity rouse more people and elicit greater energy to push for better schools and stronger pupil achievement than does lofty talk of an "educated citizenry." Yet this view of education reform also fosters tunnel vision: overemphasis on those skills and subjects most directly tied to economic competitiveness (e.g., math, technology, science) and inattention to the rest of the curriculum (literature, history, civics, the arts, character development, etc.) as well as to other vital outcomes of good education (a vibrant culture and civil society, a competent polity, decent communities, good neighbors, responsible parents, and more).

Can we keep the reformist energy of instrumentalism, better jobs, and economic growth while broadening our understanding of why society sends kids to school and what it means to be educated?

Behaviorism and Replication | Few educators like behaviorism any better than they like utilitarianism, but it, too, looms large in the externally driven reform strategies of the past two decades. After all, the main point of goals, standards, assessments, and accountability is to alter the behavior of institutions and individuals in the hope that this will yield stronger outcomes. Following on those management-style reforms, by the early 1990s some prominent thinkers were also developing psychological rationales for strategies of this sort.

In 1990, a private outfit called the National Center on Education and the Economy issued a report called *America's Choice: High Skills or Low Wages*. The product of a commission cochaired by two former labor secretaries, Democrat Ray Marshall and Republican Bill Brock, its most arresting insight was that young Americans did not study hard or learn much in school because they saw scant payoff for doing so. They visualized no better jobs or higher wages following from a rigorous, honors-level education than from a lax and mediocre one. So why hit the books?

That analysis owed much to the work of Cornell economist John H. Bishop, who has long pressed for school systems to incorporate greater incentives for students—and offer them more immediately tangible rewards. He perceived that standards, combined with tests and grades that would give young people feedback on how they were doing, plus employers who would compensate those they hired according to their skill level, could rev students' academic engines—akin to the stimulus of winning at competitive sports—and thereby boost their school results.

Bishop's reasoning was nakedly behaviorist: sweetening the incentives for young people will change how hard they work and how much they learn. In the domain of individual psychology, this matched the reasoning that was driving standards-based reform at the institutional level: create norms for schools to attain, measure their performance in relation to those norms, and reward or punish (or intervene in) them according to how well they do. It also paralleled an essential part of the logic of school choice: cause schools to improve by confronting them with competition from other schools that will exact market share and revenue from them as their students opt for higher-performing alternatives.

Behaviorism offends the sensibilities of educators who believe that the impulse to learn arises deep within, not from external pressure; that a child is more wildflower than cultivated plant; that a proper education is motivated by joy rather than coercion; that innate ability and interests count for more than effort in determining how much one ends up learning; and that effective pedagogy calls for children to "construct" their own knowledge rather than for ace teachers systematically to impart skills and knowledge to them. E. D. Hirsch evokes a dreamy educationist universe of naturalism and developmentalism, defiantly fending off outsiders more concerned with standards, effectiveness, productivity, accountability, utility, and skilled instruction. This clash of fundamental beliefs is at the core of educators' discomfort with both standards-based and choice-driven reforms and is, in fact, the chief reason that the push for such reforms comes mainly from the outside and that it encounters pushback within.[30]

In the view of some educators and a few politicians of the nineties, external standards also threatened to damage children's fragile self-esteem. Teachers and professors were given to excusing weak performance as the result of some psychic or emotional deficit in the learner, not a consequence of low expectations, poor instruction, or laziness.[31] Such reasoning also led them to argue that expecting more of such youngsters—especially low-income and minority kids—would further discourage them.

This caring but misguided view crept into the policy arena in California with the 1990 report of a legislatively mandated Self-Esteem Task Force inspired by assembly leader John Vasconcellos. That body recommended steps for schools to take to elevate young people's self-esteem, including specialized teaching and counseling. However, its own expert studies belied its recommendations: there turned out to be little correlation between self-esteem and anything important. Indeed, robust research by William Damon and others demonstrates that true self-esteem arises from true achievement, not from faked esteem-pumping, and also shows that kids with the highest self-esteem, particularly minority youngsters, often show distressingly low achievement levels as well as sundry social pathologies.

Other educators argued against the externally driven reform strategies beloved of elected officials and business leaders on grounds that such changes would make schools worse. The best schools, insisted Sizer and his colleagues, are self-directed, relatively autonomous, mission oriented, and blessed with like-minded teammates voluntarily tugging in the same direction. This was a sophisticated successor to the "effective schools" analyses of earlier years, which had identified similar characteristics in the best-functioning schools. Indeed, too much outside control and manipulation might even cause a successful school to forfeit the qualities that made it work—a telling point of convergence with the more recent choice-centered findings of Chubb and Moe.

Sizer was at least partly right about this—as were Chubb and Moe. The built-in frustration with such research and exhortation, however, was that governors, presidents, and business leaders could never find a sure path to creating *more* good schools. It was one thing to explain that they thrive amid autonomy and professionalism. But elected officials couldn't figure out a way to make this happen "at scale," or didn't think they could risk it politically. Certainly they were impatient with Sizer's inclination to liberate (and trust) educators to cause a thousand education flowers to bloom. They were more apt to clamp on standards and measurements (and occasionally to set free market forces) to *force* schools to change.

This understandably dismayed Sizer. "If there is one quality that best characterizes the American school system," he wrote in 1992, "it is mistrust.

The assumption is that no one can depend on anyone else. There must be 'independent accountability systems' at every turn. . . . Scores on thirty-minute tests are usually considered more reliable gauges of a child's merits than the opinions of his teachers. That is as sad as it is ludicrous."[32]

The schools he favored, and which he has labored for decades to encourage (at the secondary level) via his Coalition of Essential Schools and prolific writing and advocacy, would be painstakingly designed by their own professionals. While they might be old schools or new, while they would surely be mindful of the need to deliver stronger academic results (as gauged by educators, not standardized tests), and while doing these things would mean they required charter-like freedom to deviate and innovate, at day's end they would be schools created (or reshaped) by and belonging to professionals, not the work of elected officials or parents. Though accepting of school choice up to a point—Sizer had, after all, unveiled his own version of vouchers back in 1968—unlike such single-minded market advocates as Chubb, Moe, and Milton Friedman, he put most of his faith in educators to craft good schools that people would want to attend and that would also advance the public interest. Whether that faith is warranted depends in considerable measure on one's sense of urgency. After more than twenty years, Sizer's coalition contains barely two hundred "affiliate" schools, some of them private and many of them charters.

More Private Dollars | Sizer and Vartan Gregorian, then president of Brown University, turned up in 1993 as key advisers to mega-rich *TV Guide* publisher Walter Annenberg, a Reagan chum and former ambassador to the Court of St. James, who sought to repay his lifetime personal debt to public education with a munificent half-billion-dollar gift—the largest education philanthropy in U.S. history at the time—to nine large urban school systems and sundry national organizations committed to school improvement (including Lamar Alexander's New American Schools Development Corporation).

When Annenberg announced his gift, he explained that he was making it because of his concern over rising violence among young people. (This was six years before the Columbine High School shootings.) "We must ask ourselves whether improving education will halt the violence," the eighty-five-year-old Annenberg said, unveiling his largesse at a press conference with President Clinton at his side. "If anyone can think of a better way, we may have to try that. But the way I see the tragedy, education is the most wholesome and effective approach."

"Improving education" was a broad and nebulous goal, and so was the strategy adopted by the Annenberg Challenge program. Showing Sizer's influence, it began by seeking to foster the development of small, effective schools, linking them into networks, and prompting communities and school systems to support them. Rather than helping needy kids to end-run the system, as Walton and Forstmann did with their big gift of scholarships a few years later, Annenberg's program took for granted that intrasystem reforms would yield improved education in general and more student learning in particular. Yet it proffered no one model for a good school nor any uniform standards by which to appraise efforts to create more of them.

In time the Annenberg Challenge focused somewhat more on "systems" than on individual schools and voluntary networks.[33] Yet the venture remained firmly within the profession. Its theory of change was that, given enough resources and expert advice, educators could get the job done. And in the end, it left few lasting marks upon American public education—but it left plenty of lessons, some of them apparently unlearned, for later megaphilanthropists such as Bill and Melinda Gates, Eli Broad, and Michael Dell, whose generous benefactions to education reform may likewise underestimate the tenacity and inertia of this enterprise and the complacency of the public that pays for most of it.[34]

The glancing impact of their lavish and ambitious ventures is no surprise to analysts such as David Tyack and Larry Cuban, who, while cautiously optimistic about U.S. schools improving, insist that "educational reformers fail to give due weight to the resilience of schools as institutions." What they term the "grammar of schooling" incorporates "previous reforms that had, and continue to have, powerful political constituencies and a strong foundation in the social expectations about schooling held both by educators and by the general public." Altering that "grammar," particularly in millions of separate classrooms, is the single greatest challenge of education reform.[35] As in ancient archeological sites—Jericho and Rome come to mind—where layers of different civilizations have accumulated atop one another, changing what's under the surface is next to impossible; the likeliest effect of a contemporary reform is to add another layer on top.

Following my Education Department exit in late 1988, I rejoined the Vanderbilt faculty in the university's downtown D.C. office, which housed the Educational Excellence Network and its four-person staff. Every few weeks, I traveled to Nashville to co-teach a graduate seminar, and one summer I led a Washington internship-and-seminar program for under-graduates. These were pleasant, earnest, half-educated young people whose simplistic and ill-written summer research papers, by my norms, warranted Ds and Cs. Thinking myself incredibly kind and generous, I added a full letter grade to each, handing them back with Cs and Bs. Belatedly, I learned that their "human development" program back in Nashville was staffed by ed-school professors who believed that everyone deserved As for showing up. Hence my inflated grades were their first college marks lower than A. This naturally prompted wails from the students—and complaints from their full-time instructors. I was only too pleased not to be asked to do any-thing like that again.

Writing was more gratifying. It was more honest, as well as a way of trying to make sense of, and perhaps to influence, national affairs. In 1990, in the educators' journal *Phi Delta Kappan*, I suggested—the result of a midlife encounter with Thomas Kuhn's *Structure of Scientific Revolutions*—that America was struggling to redefine education itself:

> Under the old conception . . . education was thought of as process and system, effort and intention, investment and hope. To improve education meant to try harder. . . . Under the new definition . . . education is the result achieved, the learning that takes root when the process has been effective. *Only* if the process succeeds and learning occurs will we say that *education* happened.[36]

The following year brought *We Must Take Charge*, an extended portrait of America's education woes and the reforms needed. This was an angry book, a cri de coeur. I could picture the education system we should have—but from where I sat it was hard to see decisive steps being taken to get us there. Rather than the costly, overregulated, and poorly performing schools that surrounded us, I wrote,

We could live instead in a land where every young adult meets a high standard of skills and knowledge. Where we conduct our affairs on the basis of shared information and understanding. Where parents know how well their children and schools are doing. Where policymakers decide what the goals are, expert educators select effective ways to reach them, and families choose the schools that work best for their daughters and sons. Where everyone engaged in education is accountable for the results—and rewarded accordingly. Where schools are good at what they do and aren't expected to do things they're not good at. Where teaching promotes reason, which oils the wheels of our democracy and fosters both stability and civility. We could live in such a land.[37]

After forty-plus years in education, I still believe that. It's what gets me out of bed in the morning.

The Edison Project | Later in 1991, media entrepreneur Chris Whittle tracked me down and invited me to a seminar at Tennessee's rustic/posh Blackberry Farm, which, I later deduced, was an audition to gauge my fitness to join his nascent "Edison Project," an audacious effort to reinvent schools from scratch and then colonize American education with the new model.

Whittle is an inspiring visionary as well as the most charmingly convincing salesman I've ever met, and in time his vision, charisma, and persistence—plus a generous employment offer—induced me to take the plunge.

Again on leave from Vanderbilt, I joined a seven-member team of educators, scholars, journalists, and public-affairs types, to be captained by a secret figure whose identity would be made known to us and the world in due course. Several months later, during a planning session at Chris's spiffy weekend spot in the Hamptons, our leader was revealed to be Benno Schmidt, then president of Yale, who was leaving the ivy-clad walls of academe in order to re-create its feeder system. Benno turned out to be a genial raconteur, very smart, a smooth manager of high-strung, high-talent, high-need individuals, and unexpectedly devoted to this new calling.

Besides Whittle and Schmidt, the planning squad included John Chubb, who had recently coauthored that influential Brookings book on school choice; Dominique Browning, who today edits *House & Garden*; Lee Eisenberg, who had piloted *Esquire* magazine; Dan Biederman, who founded the Grand Central and 34th Street Partnerships in Manhattan; Nancy Hechinger, a gifted technology educator; and Sylvia Peters, previously the unquenchable principal of a successful elementary school on Chicago's troubled South Side.

We made a peculiar array as we traveled back and forth, sometimes via private jet, between New York, where Benno and Chris mostly lived, and Knoxville, where the firm was quartered in a grand complex known locally as "Colonial Whittlesburg." We also opened a Washington office, mainly for my benefit, though for months I commuted weekly to Tennessee.

Team members were never certain where Chris found the money for this luxe planning exercise, but we went at it hammer and tongs, running a sort of internal design competition in which pairs of us—Nancy Hechinger was my partner—fleshed out school plans and tested them on our colleagues.

Everything was fair game: calendar, staffing, curriculum, schedule, technology, school architecture, management structures, student grouping, pedagogy, and more. Whittle insisted that the garden-variety American public school of the late twentieth century was itself obsolete and thus incapable of becoming much more productive; that timid "reinvention" efforts (such as he foresaw emerging from the New American Schools venture) wouldn't be radical enough; and that because public education was apt to resist anything so venturesome, the "two thousand" new schools he pictured should launch in the private sector.

In the end, the Edison school design resembled an appealing amalgam of sound ideas and proven practices more than a radical breakthrough. We did a careful, creative job of integrating many promising features that drew from no one philosophy, that in combination resembled no extant school with which we were acquainted, and that, we believed, would boost achievement while also appealing to kids, educators, and parents. What's more, unlike NASDC and other cautious reinvention efforts then under way, we expected the dynamism of the private sector, fueled by eager investors, liberated educators, and zealous parents, plus freedom from the political and bureaucratic toils of public education, to help our new model sweep across the land.

Then two surprises hit. The less welcome was that Whittle's economic model hadn't adequately factored in the cost of new school facilities and that doing so almost certainly meant pricing these private schools beyond the reach of any but wealthy families, whose numbers were limited, who were generally content with their present education options, and whose unmet needs did not make a compelling moral or political case. The happier development was the simultaneous arrival of charter schools on the U.S. public-education scene. So we shifted gears. Why not, we asked, seize this new opportunity to mount our nifty school design in the public sector, at public expense, in publicly financed buildings?

And so by late 1993, joined by several terrific junior colleagues (Stacey Boyd, Richard Roberts, Ron Brady, Rodney Ferguson), I found myself cruising America's highways in search of communities that might be persuaded to take a chance on Edison's bold scheme, either under the charter umbrella or via an outsourcing agreement with the school system itself. (The firm's first deal—in 1995—involved a troubled Wichita public school that the superintendent asked Whittle to reconstitute.)

We logged many miles on Colorado's I-25 and its like, making innumerable community presentations and calling on school officials, board members, and local luminaries in places like Greeley, Castle Rock, Colorado Springs, and Pueblo, nourished by Daylight Donuts and Conway's Red Top hamburgers, as well as by the conviction that we had in fact engineered a better education mousetrap if only someone would buy it.

That, however, was no easy sell. Despite being joined by such charismatic and credible public educators as former Detroit superintendent Debra McGriff, the Edison brigade faced both the institutional inertia of U.S. public schooling and strident ideological and political objection to "privatization" in this sphere, particularly hostility to the notion that someone might make money from educating kids.

After two and a half intense years with Edison, the "core team's" work was essentially complete, and I began to get itchy. The school was designed—and that design, powerful if not revolutionary, was already being compromised by the need to assuage local politics and mollify interest group concerns. The company's future plainly belonged to salesmen, deal makers, publicists, lobbyists, and teachers. I was proud of what we had developed but mindful that convincing American public education to try anything so unfamiliar as a new school operated by a for-profit firm would be a long slog. Edison's prospects were both helped and hurt by the fact that another private outfit, Educational Alternatives, Inc., had fizzled after entering into high-profile contracts to run the public schools of Baltimore and Hartford. That precedent had acquainted the country with outsourced public schools run by private firms, so Whittle's central proposition no longer seemed outlandish. But EAI's failure also armed critics with "proof" that such a move was too risky.

A long slog indeed, yet the injection of improved school designs, private capital, unconventional talent, and entrepreneurial energy into K–12 education was a good and needed thing. America was beginning to outsource other kinds of work to firms deemed able to do a better or more efficient job. The year I joined Edison, David Osborne and Ted Gaebler published *Reinventing Government*, and in many parts of the public sector the idea took hold that state and municipal (and federal) agencies might save money and provide superior services by contracting with others. This logic was bound one day to hit public education, too. In reality, school systems had long turned to for-profit companies for their computers, textbooks, transportation, cafeteria operations, and sundry other services. It was, however, a leap to entrust such firms with responsibility for running entire schools and teaching their pupils, a leap that many public educators and their political allies were loath to make.

Edison struggled to make ends meet, depending for capital on investors who wanted too rich a return, having probably invested too much in our posh planning process, and finding its new customers and clients demanding in unforeseen ways. The company went public for a while, then was taken private again. It diversified its offerings and in pursuit of school management contracts made concessions in some communities that distorted its school model (by easing back on the longer day, for example, or agreeing to hire only teachers already employed by the system). Sooner or later, in my experience, every entrepreneurial education-reform venture finds itself pulling its punches, modifying its plans, or otherwise compromising with the public-school establishment that turns out to be its main client and/or regulator. Ironic, given that that's the very establishment the venture set out to transform, but inevitable, I've come to believe, for every attempt, public or private, to effect education change one school at a time.

Still and all, Edison now serves some 330,000 public-school students in various ways, about one-fifth of them enrolled full-time in 136 schools that it operates in twenty states, either as charters or under contract. Its educational results are uneven, generally good but not mind-blowing.[38] As for the company's profitability, that remains a bit of a mystery. Money is coming from somewhere, however, because late in 2006 Edison embarked on an ambitious effort to update its twelve-year-old school design, intending to make the most both of its on-the-ground experience and of fast moving developments in technology and public policy.[39]

Entrepreneurial organizations can do timely, agile things like that far better than government programs and bureaucracies. In K–12 education, however, they then face two big challenges: finding the talented and committed people—as executives, sure, but mainly as principals and teachers—who can successfully implement their models in an environment abounding in well-meaning mediocrity; and persuading public-sector decision makers to open the door for them despite heavy pressure from interest groups that want no intruders.

For me, Edison was another fantastic ride, plus a welcome financial boost while Arti and Aloke were in college. It also introduced me to the potential of charter schools—and the stiff resistance to them—and gave me close-up experience with the overwhelming challenge of school-level education reform. But continuing the inside-outside rhythm of my life, I was ready to return to an analyst's role where I could try to make sense of, and candidly comment on, the fast-changing world of U.S. schooling.

Think-tanking Again | My new venue was the Hudson Institute, the Washington (and Indianapolis) think tank then headed by old friend and fellow Moynihan graduate student Leslie Lenkowsky. He encouraged me to build an education policy program. With financial help from the John M. Olin Foundation, which years before had helped launch the Educational Excellence Network, we were able both to bring the network under Hudson's aegis and to make me a senior fellow there.

Education wasn't the whole of it. For example, when he left the cabinet after Clinton's election victory, Lamar Alexander entered into a Hudson affiliation that led to publication in 1995 of *The New Promise of American Life*, which he and I co-edited, aspiring to pick up where Herbert Croly had left off decades earlier. *Is There Life after Big Government?* was the title of a shorter Hudson monograph I co-authored that explored the potential of civil society and other nongovernmental responses to sundry domestic challenges. Tying philanthropy to civil society, Lamar also chaired, and I served on, the Bradley Foundation–supported National Commission on Philanthropy and Civic Renewal, which reported in 1998.

Most of what filled my plate was education, however, which got easier to chew once I was joined at Hudson by longtime colleague Bruno Manno and the brilliant young Scott Hamilton, himself also an Edison alumnus. The tantalizing new phenomenon known as charter schools swiftly became our foremost interest, leading to a major research project and in time to a book.

Plenty of other analysts were also on the education case. In 1994, Brookings published *Making Schools Work: Improving Performance and Controlling Costs*, written primarily by Rochester economist Eric A. Hanushek, which enumerated three principles that promised to boost school performance without increasing costs. These were "efficient use of resources, performance incentives, and continuous learning and adaptation." Hanushek and his associates contended that most school reform discussions proceeded entirely on the basis of prospective benefits and ignored costs, as if money and other resources either didn't matter or were infinite or could not be competently analyzed.[40]

They were right. Though concern about sluggish school "productivity" tacitly underlay most critiques of American education as well as most reform proposals, little attention had been paid to which changes might yield the most robust gains in cost-benefit terms and what performance increments might be eked out of current investments.

Thirty years after Coleman, it was indeed time to reopen this topic. School revenues had risen for as long as data were available, quintupling from $164 per pupil in 1890 to $772 in 1940 and more than quintupling again to $4,622 in 1990 (after adjusting for inflation). Yet nobody thought the educational returns on that investment were rising, and the weak performance of schools had placed the nation at risk. Productivity was surely a problem.

Coleman had changed the education world with his finding that the resources going into a school did not straightforwardly translate into stronger results—and almost three more decades of rising expenditures and lagging results now dramatized the squishiness of that link. Hanushek and colleagues were not arguing (as they are sometimes erroneously accused of) that "money doesn't matter" in education but, rather, that the nation ought to move forcefully to eke greater value from its immense education investments. They concluded that "the only real hope for improvement comes from strong and clear performance incentives. By rewarding individual people and schools for outstanding achievement, administrators can encourage the school system as a whole to match that achievement."[41]

This was behaviorism again, now on the fiscal front, with changed financial incentives meant to parallel and buttress the standards, tests, and accountability arrangements (and market forces) arising on the operational side. And it came, once again, from the august Brookings Institution.

Daffiness and Insight | Elsewhere in the academic world raged what James Atlas dubbed "the book wars," centered in the postmodern proclivities of university scholars but seeping, usually with bad effect, into the schools. The year 1995 brought, for example, *The End of Education* by trendy New York University professor Neil Postman, arguing not that schools were archaic or inefficient but that they worshipped the wrong "gods": cognitive science (he ridiculed the notion that research-based pedagogy might be more effective), economic utility, and technology. He pooh-poohed such reform ideas as school choice ("essentially engineering") and instead offered five "narratives" to inform the education of the future: "spaceship earth," human frailty, the "law of diversity," and so on.[42]

It's hard to know whether anyone took this stuff seriously, and it's no crime (much less a surprise) when professors inscribe foolishness onto paper. But the last thing serious K–12 reformers needed was further evidence that academics harbored daft notions about education. Worse, such silliness signaled to the politicians and business leaders at the helm that they could safely ignore, might even be wise to shun, the views of card-carrying intellectuals.

Some, though, were worth heeding, above all E. D. Hirsch, Jr., whose *Cultural Literacy* had been a powerful influence on school reform efforts in the 1980s and whose 1996 book, *The Schools We Need and Why We Don't Have Them*, was a brilliant intellectual hat trick. First, he offered a compelling explanation of why American youngsters aren't learning much: because their schools deploy ineffectual curricula and pedagogies based on the romantic, unscientific view that children learn "naturally" rather than by being systematically taught skills and knowledge. Second, he depicted "the schools we need," featuring "focused instruction leading to well-practiced operational skills in reading and mathematics, and well-stocked minds conversant with individual subject matters like history and biology." Finally, he explained how a complacent, insular, and defensive belief system, centered in colleges of education and politically bolstered by certification rules and insider-dominated "standards boards," fends off efforts to change its beliefs and practices while rebuffing external standards, testing, and accountability for schools and children on grounds that they chill the love of learning. "Education schools," Hirsch charged, "derogate such traditional practices in favor of the progressive program of individual pacing, discovery learning, thematic teaching, nonobjective testing, and so on. Their captive audiences, consisting of millions of teachers, are offered no intellectual alternatives. . . . The resulting pandemic of mistaken ideas may be the gravest barrier to America's educational improvement."[43]

Hirsch's insights curiously paralleled those of Tyack's and Cuban's *Tinkering Toward Utopia*, published the previous year. Just as they had found schools and classrooms to be nearly impervious to externally imposed reform schemes, Hirsch found the philosophical core of the profession Teflon-like in its capacity to shed outside ideas.

Yet ed school faculties weren't unique. It was now fashionable in the academy to do battle against "the canon" in literature, against "Eurocentrism" in history, against history itself in social studies, against the acquisition of knowledge per se (after all, it changes so fast), even against the search for truth as the proper end of education. (It all depends on your point of view.) This was damaging enough in higher education but posed a major threat to the K–12 curriculum, the more so when combined with pedagogies that insist on children figuring things out for themselves and on teachers coaxing and coaching but never actually instructing.

In 1989, a task force of the New York State Department of Education issued "A Curriculum of Inclusion," a racialist document that accused Empire State textbooks of Eurocentrism and held that minority youngsters exposed to such books would feel "alienated and devalued" even as "members of the majority culture are exclusionary and overvalued."

Two years later, the eminent liberal historian Arthur M. Schlesinger, Jr., deplored such trends in *The Disuniting of America*, a powerful, outraged book that said runaway multiculturalism imperiled America's identity and undermined its civic ideals.[44]

I kept scribbling, too. In *Commentary* in 1994, underwhelmed by the new Goals 2000 law ("no great advance"), I offered a six-part reform agenda of my own, including "major shifts of authority and control over resources from producers to consumers and from experts to civilians" and a combination of "supply-side pluralism" and "demand-side choice."[45] Two years later, as alarmed as Schlesinger by the schools' romance with separatist literature and "revisionist anti-American accounts of history," and again writing in *Commentary*, I urged a core "curriculum of national unity" and restoring "to the schools their vital role in fostering, reinforcing and transmitting the sense of a common civic culture."[46]

19 | *Clinton, Goals, and Testing*

Bill Clinton did not really need to prove himself an "education president." It was in his blood. Though Arkansans say that his and Hillary's reform efforts of the 1980s left few lasting marks—his boldest move as governor was a teacher-testing plan that was eventually softened to the point that nearly everyone passed—he arrived in Washington with a strong reputation as an education change agent. He had helped lead his fellow governors through sundry school-related ventures. He had burned the midnight oil in Charlottesville. Though his candidacy for the White House enjoyed the backing of both teachers' unions and he promised plenty more federal money for education, his campaign speeches also spoke eloquently of the need for standards and tests, more effective schools, and more choices for families.

A fabulously gifted but often rudderless political figure, in education as elsewhere he frequently sought to have it both ways, seeming to embrace radical reforms while not upsetting major applecarts. When, during the NGA's work on *Time for Results* in the mid-eighties, I traveled to Little Rock to speak at a symposium that he chaired on school leadership, Governor Clinton graciously received me and seemed to indicate through nods, winks, smiles, and body language that he agreed with my heretical notions about the principals of the future—why must they be former teachers?—but never actually uttered a word on this topic that anyone could quote back at him.

After the 1992 election, he chose South Carolina's respected former governor Dick Riley as education secretary. Their first major legislative proposal—to a Congress controlled by their party on both sides of the Hill—was called "Goals 2000: The Educate America Act." In many respects, it resembled Bush 41's and Lamar Alexander's America 2000 program. Though lawmakers had spurned the GOP version, Goals 2000, duly amended, was passed and signed into law fourteen months into Clinton's presidency.

Along the way, Congress added two goals to the six that had emerged from Charlottesville, addressing teacher quality and parental responsibility. They also tacked four more subjects (foreign languages, the arts, economics, and civics and government) onto the five that George H. W. Bush and the governors had specified. Though I fretted that home economics and drivers ed would soon get added, too, in fact Goals 2000 envisioned a broad, solid, even liberal-artsy K–12 education for young Americans.

At its heart was a new program of federal financial grants to underwrite states' development of standards and tests and their use by local school systems. This entailed few mandates but sought to build on extant state-level efforts at "systemic reform" and—more behaviorism—give laggard states incentives to climb aboard.

A few spurned the money at first, claiming that this was none of Washington's business and they preferred to handle education their own way. In time, however, all but two states joined; the program disbursed some $2 billion between 1994 and 1999; and a third of the country's fifteen thousand local systems wound up with Goals 2000 grants.

It was one thing to help states pay for the development of standards and tests. It was quite another to gauge whether these were any good. Here Clinton initially seized upon NCEST's proposal for a new National Education Standards and Assessment Council to evaluate and certify state-devised standards and tests, the thought being that such a body would gradually prod them toward uniform standards without Uncle Sam's heavy hand pressing down directly.

After much argument, Congress incorporated a variant of this scheme into Goals 2000, to be called the National Education Standards and Improvement Council (NESIC). This ill-fated panel's saga is extraordinarily convoluted, even for Washington. Suffice to say it became embroiled in one heated debate about the perils of a "national curriculum" and another about whether the proposed council would be responsible for school-input standards (e.g., class sizes, spending levels) as well as standards for student achievement. Who would appoint it? Who would oversee it? To whom was it accountable, and for what, exactly? Once the sobriquet "national school board" got attached to it, the 1994 midterm election was sure to foreshadow its demise. After that year's GOP victory and noises by Newt Gingrich's allies about getting the federal government entirely out of education (including another abortive move to abolish the Education Department), Clinton deferred naming anyone to NESIC, and by 1996 Congress had amended it out of existence.

Goals 2000 thus amounted to little more than a federal grant program in pursuit of state-led, standards-based reform. (That's why I pooh-poohed it in various writings, testimony, and speeches.) However, it was soon joined by a toothier measure called the Improving America's Schools Act (IASA), also the handiwork of the Democratic 103rd Congress—but just barely, as this one didn't pass until October 1994, days before the GOP election romp.

Formally, IASA was another renewal of the three-decade-old Elementary and Secondary Education Act. Its eleven titles, dozens of sections, and hundreds of pages sprawled across a vast landscape of programs and topics (including the new "public charter schools program"). Its centerpiece, however, was the requirement that, for a state to continue receiving money from the big Title I program, its "state plan" would henceforth have to describe the "challenging academic content standards" and "challenging student performance standards" that it would apply to "all students," as well as include a "description of the set of high-quality, yearly student assessments, including at least mathematics, and reading or language arts, in one grade in each school, that will be used as the primary means of determining the yearly performance of each local educational agency and school served under this part in enabling all children served under this part to meet the State's student performance standards." The secretary of education was authorized to set criteria by which such plans would or—in theory—would not be approved.

In such tortured prose did Congress begin to mandate standards-based reform, using the fiscal leverage of Washington's biggest K–12 school aid program to tug states into compliance.

In practice, the Clinton team did not enforce this mandate with great vigor. Many governors objected to its heavy-handedness—and the symbolic shift of reform leadership from state capitals to Washington. The new congressional GOP majority also contained powerful figures (including House education chairman Bill Goodling, a former public-school superintendent in small-town Pennsylvania) who saw red at the prospect of federal control of education. The swift elimination of NESIC from the Goals 2000 program underscored that wariness—and served to warn anyone in the executive branch who would second-guess state-level decisions with respect to standards and tests. And as the 2000 election neared, the White House backed off further, not wanting Vice President Gore's political prospects in key states such as California to be dimmed by Republican complaints that his administration was messing around with the schools.

Still, the combination of Goals 2000 and IASA propelled Washington into the school reform endeavor as never before and prefigured Bush 43's No Child Left Behind Act.

National Testing? | Clinton didn't rest. In his State of the Union address on February 4, 1997, he proposed "voluntary national tests" in fourth-grade reading and eighth-grade math. This was a departure from his second-term practice of offering small "feel good" initiatives such as promoting school uniforms—and fending off GOP efforts to trim the federal role in education. (He brilliantly succeeded in depicting Republicans as anti-education, including a jujitsu job in the 1996 campaign whereby Bob Dole's criticism of teachers' unions was refracted by Clinton as an attack on teachers.)

The president spoke compellingly of

> a national crusade for education standards, . . . representing what all
> our students must know to succeed in the knowledge economy of the
> 21st century. . . . To help schools meet the standards and measure their
> progress, we will lead an effort over the next 2 years to develop
> national tests of student achievement in reading and math. . . . Good
> tests will show us who needs help, what changes in teaching to make,
> and which schools need to improve.[47]

It was, in fact, a worthy idea that kindled a firestorm on both left and right, from "experts" and interest groups alike, and the administration's inept handling of its implementation added fuel to that blaze.

At first I thought Clinton might pull off a "Nixon goes to China" political feat, as a centrist who could unite liberals and conservatives behind an education breakthrough with much merit. It was—and today remains—absurd for a big modern country, seeking to advance its education performance via standards-based reforms, to continue using a patchwork testing system where nothing quite compares with anything else.

I expected the president to quell Democratic critics and, with Bill Bennett and Diane Ravitch, I worked to deliver some GOP support. But I also cautioned, "If this falls apart it will be because of liberals who hate 'testing' and conservatives who hate 'national.'"[48]

And that's pretty much what happened. Declaring that "we already have plenty of testing . . . why another measurement instrument to tell us what we already know?" chairman Goodling took up arms against the White House plan.[49] His nose was also out of joint because the administration was trying to do this unilaterally, without explicit congressional authority. Moreover, it was seeking to develop and implement the tests via a complicated edifice of panels and contracts answerable to Dick Riley's Education Department rather than the sort of independent, bipartisan structure that is the only approach with much chance of gaining credibility in a politically divided and turf-jealous Washington.

As had been obvious since Charlottesville eight years earlier, the United States lacked suitable mechanisms for setting national education objectives and managing progress toward them. This meant initiatives such as Clinton's testing plan would necessarily be jerry-rigged. This time, the main vehicle was a whopping federal contract to a consortium of test publishers.

In short order, the project headed down the wrong track. "Fuzzy" math and calculators crept into the math-testing plan, and political correctness into the reading test. By late summer, the whole project was falling apart. Senator Dan Coats tried to salvage it via a bill that would transfer responsibility to the independent National Assessment Governing Board, and Clinton and Goodling appeared to reach a shaky compromise around that approach. In September, Bennett and I endorsed their alternative in the *Washington Post*, declaring that the president's original scheme would "subvert the whole idea of national testing and has flaws so misguided as to be dangerous." [50]

NAGB was indeed assigned to develop the individual-level testing plan—a big change for an organization accustomed to a "sample" assessment that yields results only for state and nation—but nonstop congressional opposition, mainly from Republicans, plus the difficulty of redirecting a train that had already left the station, meant the project slowly ground to a halt and was in time abandoned. In February 1998, Deputy Secretary Marshall Smith pronounced it dead. Clinton by then had plenty of other woes and was probably glad to be rid of this little nightmare. The pity was the rancid taste it left on Washington's palate when it comes to national testing, the absence of which remains a major barrier to the success of NCLB in particular and standards-based reform in general.

What Happens to Goals Deferred? | The National Education Goals Panel, codified in the Goals 2000 legislation, faithfully tracked America's progress or lack thereof toward the goals set in Charlottesville (and reworked by Congress in 1994). It had a small, competent staff. Its lucid reports brimmed with examples of which states were gaining on the end-of-decade targets. Its detailed studies and analyses were often insightful, and its hearings and conferences frequently illuminating.

As the millennium neared its close, however, there was no disguising the fact that none of those ambitious goals would actually be reached by the year 2000.

That's not to say the "goals process" was pointless. To the contrary, its visibility and transparency, the peer pressure and competitiveness among states, the pep-rally spirit that sometimes enveloped discussions of progress toward the goals, the development of better indicators and more sophisticated analyses—all prodded the country in a positive direction and helped to maintain momentum even when key officials were replaced, electoral upheavals occurred, and other issues vied for attention. Moreover, the Goals Panel's own bipartisanship and its uniting of Congress, executive branch, and state leaders served to minimize political grandstanding.

In a 1998 paper written for the panel, Harvard professor Richard Elmore perceptively sketched America's education transformation since *A Nation at Risk*:

> We have moved from a system that emphasized the autonomy of local boards of education and the tailoring of all curriculum and instruction to the demands of local communities to a system that emphasizes the interdependence of states and localities on basic decisions about what students should know and be able to do and what schools should do for students. We have moved from a system in which states focused mainly on providing and monitoring inputs to schooling—financing, teacher certification, school facilities, etc.—to a system in which states are playing a much more assertive role in monitoring school performance and developing alternative structures for the delivery of schooling, including charter schools, vouchers and various other market-based choice schemes. We have moved from a system in which there was virtually no discussion among state and local political leaders of what students actually learn . . . to a system in which governors and state legislators routinely discuss student performance on statewide tests. . . . We have moved from a situation in which performance-based comparisons among schools, among states, or between the U.S. and its major industrialized competitors were discussed only in academic circles to one in which such comparisons are now a routine feature of political discourse.[51]

All good, to be sure, even revolutionary, and much of it ably chronicled and occasionally shoved forward by the Goals Panel, yet the goals themselves could not be met on the timeline that the president and governors had optimistically set. What to do?

The panel cogitated, consulted its experts, then solemnly declared in late February 1999 that the goals should go on forever, that they should be renamed "America's Education Goals" and the deadline for reaching them should henceforth be, well, nonspecific.

This smacked of a government unit near the end of its assignment seeking a way to justify its own immortality. Worse, it threatened to transform what had been a useful if unrealistic deadline for action into an open-ended statement of simple aspirations. Instead of saying, "This has been a worthy effort but we didn't achieve the desired result and now someone else should take responsibility for flogging American elementary-secondary education to shape up," the panel looked as if it was cravenly begging to be kept on the job indefinitely. Not a smart move. After the 2000 election, the Goals Panel found itself with few supporters in Washington, and the No Child Left Behind Act, for all its hundreds of pages and dozens of programs, did not renew the group's authorization.

The education profession continued to react to external pressure for change by revising the problem definition and expanding the solution. Even as Clinton boosted standards-based reform and others pressed for greater school choice, the third reformist strand was also strengthening. In 1994, Carnegie and Rockefeller teamed up to create the National Commission on Teaching and America's Future (NCTAF), now a permanent organization. Its keystone report, *What Matters Most: Teaching for America's Future*, appeared in 1996. Chaired by North Carolina governor Jim Hunt and led by prominent education scholar Linda Darling-Hammond, then at Teachers College, it was the progeny of the mid-eighties Carnegie task force that issued *A Nation Prepared*. (Hunt served on both.) Just as the earlier group strove to make teachers and their profession as prominent a reform focus as students and learning, so did NCTAF seek to bestow on teaching a status as worthy of the nation's attention.

"What teachers know and can do," they wrote, "is the most important influence on what students learn. Recruiting, preparing, and retaining good teachers is the central strategy for improving our schools. School reform cannot succeed unless it focuses on creating the conditions in which teachers can teach, and teach well." [52]

Those propositions seem obvious and unexceptional. On second viewing, however, a momentous shift was taking place. To declare that installing good teachers "is the central strategy for improving our schools" is a far different thing from insisting that standards and accountability, on the one hand, or choice and competition, on the other, is the straightest avenue to education reform. Those are "outside" strategies. Getting better teachers could be, too, but not the way NCTAF framed it. As with the earlier Carnegie panel, its recommendations, though couched in the language of quality and standards, would strengthen educators' own grip on the entire enterprise—always, of course, in the name of "professionalism."

By insisting on "accreditation" of all teacher preparation programs, for example, NCTAF would restrict pathways into public-school classrooms to those approved by the National Council for Accreditation of Teacher Education (NCATE), a veritable Noah's Ark of establishment interests. By urging every state to empower a "professional standards board" for education,

NCTAF would place teacher (and principal) licensure in the hands of bodies that consist mainly of people chosen by teachers' unions and ed schools. And by urging a huge expansion of the National Board for Professional Teaching Standards (NBPTS), NCTAF would reinforce a definition of teacher quality that has much to do with classroom practices but little to do with students' learning.

It was, in short, an inside job, a plan to empower educators to write the ground rules, to magnify the influence of ed school values, to equate school reform with the well-being of teachers, and to confer on the profession's favorite organizational arrangements a priority equal to the needs of students, parents, and employers.

It was also a brilliant maneuver that continues today and has, indeed, yielded a multifaceted reform agenda that seeks primarily to retain control of essential education decisions—above all, who gets to teach in public schools—within the very institutions and regulatory structures that caused many of the education woes that "outside" reformers are scrambling it rectify.

Educators understandably craved the stature, respect, and remuneration of professionals, and they weren't wrong about the central role that teachers play in schooling. Yet—I confess to a touch of schadenfreude here—the problems they hoped to solve via professionalism were largely of their own making. For too long, educators and their organizations (not just unions) had settled for mediocrity in their own ranks as well as lackluster learning by their pupils. They had focused on their own ends rather than the common good. And they paid a price for it—a price they now sought to lessen.

Some key figures were active both on externally driven reforms and on the professionalism front, saw no conflict between them, and easily crossed back and forth. Al Shanker and Jim Hunt illustrate the type—and deserve both kudos and brickbats for the roles they played.

Shanker, who passed away in 1997, was president of the American Federation of Teachers after 1974 and its driving force for more than three decades. His extraordinary intellect, passion, articulateness, vision, and political acumen caused him to tower above everyone else in the teachers' unions—including the far larger NEA—and indeed above just about everyone else in the field. His fingerprints can be found on every major advance toward standards-based reform between *A Nation at Risk* and his death.

Al was outspoken on America's need for higher expectations for children and teachers alike—and on the profession's need to accept that reality.

He was equally relentless on the nation's duty to improve, empower, and reward its educators. And while he deserves credit for helping to introduce the charter-school concept, he was doggedly effective in opposing most forms of school choice, especially vouchers and tax credits.

A canny strategist, Shanker willingly joined forces with other people and groups in pursuit of ends that they shared—and mercilessly battled the same people over proposals that divided them. He and I agreed, for example, about standards, about curriculum content (he lauded Hirsch's "Core Knowledge" program, for instance), about civics and democracy, and about foreign policy. The AFT and its parent AFL-CIO did superb work in Eastern Europe in the eighties to strengthen free trade unions, bring down communism, then assist in building a proper education system that included "education for democracy."[53]

We disagreed, however, about breaking the grip of the public-school monopoly, giving families more choices and control of their children's education, and including private schools in that universe of options. Al was a superb debater, a nonstop writer (especially his must-read weekly *New York Times* column), and a deft backroom operator. His side won more than a few battles. Though pro–school choice forces made gradual headway—not even Al could stop the tide of Republican governors and legislative majorities, or prevent inner-city parents from demanding better opportunities for their kids—he and his troops fought all the way.

Al was a central figure in both Carnegie-funded commissions that advanced the teacher-professionalism agenda and, especially, in his beloved National Board for Professional Teaching Standards (NBPTS), which was formed in 1987 and thrives today. This outfit has a huge board drawn from across the public-education establishment but dominated by teachers, which in practice means by their unions. It mission is to provide special recognition for teachers who meet its standards, which have so far been set in twenty-four fields. And it has succeeded in persuading policymakers to pony up extra money for "board-certified" teachers, sometimes in the form of extra pay or bonuses, sometimes in subsidies for the board's own costly vetting process, sometimes in priority for job opportunities, license renewals, and suchlike. Every state now confers some form of commendation or reward on these teachers, as do more than five hundred local districts. Delaware and North Carolina, for example, provide a permanent 12 percent salary boost to board-certified teachers.

NBPTS starts with the unassailable proposition that some teachers are better than others and should be recognized and compensated. The big issue is whether instructors identified by the board are truly the cream of the public-school classroom. NBPTS relies primarily on peer judgments rather than student outcomes. In other words, it checks to see whether what a teacher does in her classroom looks right to fellow educators, mostly by having the candidate submit a "portfolio" that includes videotapes and other evidence of her pedagogy. (There are also assessments of teachers' subject-matter knowledge.) What's missing is dependable proof that the pupils of board-certified teachers are actually learning what they should, indeed that board-certified teachers are more effective in producing such classroom outcomes than those who fail (or do not bother) to gain the board's endorsement.[54]

NBPTS is nonetheless the most appealing part of the teacher professionalism agenda because it's more about quality than control and because it accepts the proposition—Shanker insisted on this and overcame objections from the NEA—that some teachers are superior. The main complaint of its critics—I've been one—is that for it to meld into a regimen of standards-based reform it would need to focus on classroom effectiveness as gauged by student results. Perhaps one day it will.

Critics also chafe at its price tag. Over two decades, NBPTS has received more than $437 million in public and private dollars and certified about 55,000 teachers, a "unit cost" of almost $8,000, considerably more expensive than a straightforward system of ranking teacher performance by the achievement gains of their pupils.

More than a third of those monies have come from the federal government, which attests above all to the superb connections and lobbying prowess of Jim Hunt.

Hunt was governor of North Carolina from 1977 to 1985 and again from 1993 to 2001. A courtly, cagey southern attorney reminiscent of Senator Sam Ervin, he placed education and child development at the top of his agenda, primarily because, like other southern governors, he saw that these were vital for the Tarheel State to make real economic gains. He was an early conductor on the standards train and an eager participant in many NGA education projects (though he was out of office during the Charlottesville summit). His real passion, however, was "excellence in teaching," and his stamp, like Shanker's, is visible on innumerable panels, organizations, and commission reports that advanced the professionalism agenda. A gifted and well-wired politician with friends on both sides of the aisle—and a Democrat liked by voters in an increasingly Republican state—he functioned as chief Washington lobbyist and financial rainmaker for NBPTS, and it is primarily thanks to his devoted labors that that project has received upward of $159 million in federal grants, as well as almost twice that sum from many of the country's premier foundations and Fortune 500 corporations.

When I was assistant secretary of education in the late 1980s and NBPTS was new, I was sent to Capitol Hill to explain to the appropriations committees why the Reagan administration opposed federal funding for this enterprise. With Hunt and Shanker playing the Congress like a violin, I never stood a chance.

In 1995, pressed by GOP governor George Voinovich, Ohio's General Assembly enacted a voucher program for Cleveland children. It was confined to poor kids in grades K–3, with voucher amounts not to exceed $2,250 each. The vouchers could be taken either to private and parochial schools within Cleveland or to public schools in surrounding communities.

That something needed to be done for young Clevelanders was unarguable. The city's public school system was a disaster. While spending more per pupil than the state average, its dropout rate was twice the state average. Its passing rate on Ohio's ninth-grade proficiency test was in the single digits. The state auditor declared that the city's "educational delivery system is not accomplishing its purpose," and a federal judge ordered the state superintendent to assume control of the district's finances and administration.

Faced with this meltdown, Voinovich, a former mayor of Cleveland, persuaded legislators to act. Here is how he (now a U.S. senator) explained himself in a 2002 interview:

> I have always been a strong supporter of the non-public school system
> in Ohio, because I felt they were doing a terrific job. . . . I introduced
> a comprehensive program for improving schools, and a voucher
> program in Cleveland was part of it. I had originally asked that the
> voucher option be given to any school district in the state. . . . But,
> finally, the only way we were able to get it done was to restrict
> vouchers to just the Cleveland area. . . . The rationale was that the
> Cleveland system was in such bad shape and taking so much money
> out of the state that we ought to give them this opportunity to see if
> vouchers would make a difference. . . .
>
> At the time I did it, I got an enormous amount of flak from a
> whole lot of people, but my view was that it was constitutional. The
> money wasn't going to the school, it was going to the individual,
> just like the GI Bill. I also felt this was a reasonable educational
> program we ought to be trying out. The problem in government
> today, right across the board, is that we are not willing, as busi-
> nesses, to try new things. Too often, the reason we don't try new

things is because there are strong lobbies trying to preserve their turf.[55]

Upward of six thousand Cleveland children applied for vouchers in the first year, and about one-third received and used them. Fifty private schools, mostly religious, volunteered for the program—but not a single suburban school system. When the program's constitutionality reached the Supreme Court six years later—the landmark *Zelman* decision affirming vouchers arose here—critics objected that most voucher recipients took them to parochial schools. They didn't mention that suburban public schools wouldn't accept these inner-city kids or that the vouchers' value was too low for most other private schools to make ends meet.

In Ohio and elsewhere, the mid-nineties also brought more charter schools. By 1996, Arizona had 146 of them serving some 13,500 students—not a huge number, to be sure, but enough to be noticed and felt, particularly by such east-of-Phoenix suburban districts as Mesa, where many of the new schools opened.

At Hudson Institute, our little education-policy crew was tantalized by the charter phenomenon with its novel blend of public education, private initiative, and choice. With financial help from the Pew Memorial Trusts, we embarked in 1995 on a sizable research project dubbed "Charter Schools in Action." In January 1996, we issued our first report, itemizing start-up problems encountered by many of these schools, suggesting repairs to state charter laws, and acknowledging some surprises. For example, charters turned out to be overwhelmingly attended by minority youngsters and what we termed "square peg" kids with diverse problems who had fallen behind in conventional district schools—this in sharp contrast to charter foes' prediction that these schools would "cream" the most fortunate children and neglect the neediest. Just the opposite was happening.

The schools were interesting, too, and not nearly as flaky as critics had intimated. "The charter world is marvelously varied," we wrote,

> and we do not necessarily agree with the educational philosophy or curriculum of every school we have encountered. But we have seen none that seemed outside the pale of defensible (and in many respects familiar) educational thought and practice. We haven't stumbled on any witchcraft schools or Klan schools, for example. . . . In fact, most of the charter schools we have seen can be described either as variants

on "progressive" educational thought or versions of "traditional" education (with some interesting efforts to blend the two).[56]

Though many charters occupied sketchy facilities, most also had waiting lists, indicating greater demand than they could meet. We also found lots of involved parents and exceptional teachers:

> Some of them accept lower pay, and most want no involvement with the teachers' unions. . . . Some of these people are "square pegs," too—individuals with unconventional backgrounds and variegated careers who want to do something different from what is possible in ordinary public (and sometimes private) schools, who crave the chance to work with colleagues who share their philosophy and with the children of parents who also share it, and who are willing to make trade-offs, including minimal facilities and modest pay, for personal and professional fulfillment.[57]

Also promising, we judged, was the entrance of new organizational players into K–12 education. We had unearthed, for example,

> an Arizona charter school that operates in partnership with the juvenile corrections system, one sponsored by a Native American tribe, and one sponsored by a boys-and-girls club. We have been to a school in Minnesota that operates in partnership with the municipal parks department, one in Michigan that is closely tied to a fast-food company, one in Colorado whose new building is being financed by an office park developer, and one in Massachusetts where the education program is delivered by a for-profit firm.[58]

By 1999, almost 1,700 charter schools were operating, and more than a million children applied that year for the privately funded vouchers offered by the Children's Scholarship Fund, which had hustled matching dollars and recruited partners in dozens of communities.

In April of that year, the Florida legislature enacted Governor Jeb Bush's "A+" education reform plan, which ingeniously harnessed vouchers and choice to school accountability. Youngsters attending public schools that repeatedly earned "F" grades on the state rating system would be set free to attend other public *or* private schools if they wished, with the state covering their costs.

And America was also discovering "home schooling," the education option whereby kids don't attend regular schools at all but instead study with their parents or other adults at home or other informal settings.

This had been quietly going on forever, of course, sometimes with stellar results—the media periodically profile homeschooled youngsters who excel in prestige universities—and sometimes bad. (The impulse to educate one's kids at home does not always signal the capacity to do this well.)

Home schooling has two roots in American society. The better known is conservative and generally devout families that hope to shield their children from modern, liberal, secular influences and instead rear them in the parents' own God-fearing image. But home schooling's other root is on the left, in the "de-schooling" movement of the 1970s, in a broader rejection of state authority and social conformity, and in the writings of education critics such as John Holt, who concluded (in *How Children Fail*) that schools were stultifying and in 1977 started a magazine called *Growing Without Schooling.*[59]

Until the late 1990s, however, the larger education community paid scant attention to the home-schooling phenomenon. Then it started to emerge as a true option and drew greater scrutiny.

A 1999 study by Lawrence M. Rudner shone a spotlight on this shadowy K–12 sector. An independent analyst rather than a home-schooling partisan (although his project was underwritten by an advocacy group), he administered standardized tests to twenty thousand homeschooled youngsters and concluded that "achievement test scores of this group of home school students are exceptionally high—the median scores were typically in the 70th to 80th percentile; 25 percent of home school students are enrolled one or more grades above their age-level public and private school peers."[60]

Wary of government interference, home schoolers often refuse to fill out questionnaires or cooperate with surveys. But 1999 also brought the first earnest effort by the National Center for Education Statistics to enumerate them: approximately 850,000 youngsters. Though advocates said the true figure was bigger still, this was more than most people expected, indicating that almost two children out of every hundred were being educated at home, more than in charter schools.

And the count was sure to rise. Publishing companies were pumping out curricula and instructional materials for home schoolers, and technology was equipping parents who favored this option with online access to content and instructional materials. A tiny fissure thus began to emerge between the idea of *educating* children and the need for them to attend *school*.

Summiting | The 1989 Charlottesville education summit had proven memorable and consequential, so in March 1996 IBM CEO Louis V. Gerstner, Jr., and Wisconsin governor Tommy Thompson, who chaired the National Governors Association, convened another one. IBM played host at its swank conference center high on the Hudson Palisades, and forty-one governors turned up, as did innumerable corporate leaders, President Clinton, Secretary Riley, and a handful of educators (including me).

"Our goal," Thompson said, "is to leave here with a commitment by each of the governors to return to their states and set high standards for their schools within two years." [61]

Clinton did his usual peerless mind-meld with his audience, relating so empathically to his listeners that, were it not for the Secret Service presence, one might have imagined he was still a governor himself.

"In an increasingly global economy," Gerstner said, "I'm not liking our chances." [62] He invoked the international-competitiveness argument to enlist fellow CEOs in the education-reform cause and emerged from the summit with a whole new organization—Achieve, Inc., is its name—meant to join governors with captains of industry in pursuit of better schools. The group's precisely calibrated board is half governors (from both parties) and half corporate leaders. It got off to a strong start by selecting Robert Schwartz, formerly of the Harvard Ed School and the Pew Memorial Trusts (and another alumnus of Moynihan's Coleman seminar three decades earlier), to direct it.

Harnessing the energy and influence of corporate leaders to the education-reform cause had plenty of precedent. The Business Roundtable took this plunge shortly after Charlottesville, helping to lobby Goals 2000 through Congress, and some of its affiliates did solid work on behalf of standards-based reform in their states. The Committee for Economic Development had issued education reports and recommendations for years. Xerox's David Kearns had done (and continues to do) yeoman service in the cause of education reform, both in the private sector and while in government. But the charismatic and tireless Gerstner, combined with IBM's corporate stature, raised such engagement to a new level. I wondered whether businessmen might even fill one of the great vacuums in American education politics: the missing "consumers' lobby."

For as long as I've been involved with this field, it's been obvious that the public-school establishment with its alphabet soup of organizations, millions of dues-paying members, and platoons of lobbyists, publicists, and campaign strategists is superbly well organized on behalf of producers to stymie or re-shape reform initiatives that conflict with its interests, as well as to advance its own priorities via elections, legislative markups, and public relations. The far larger population of education consumers has no such army. The PTA was long since co-opted (I've come to describe it as "all T and no P"); kids don't employ lobbyists; and despite various "coalitions" of professional groups that would have you think otherwise, nobody really looks after the interests of parents, students, and taxpayers in the education policy arena.

Corporate chieftains can do some of this, but I've learned that they, too, have limits. IBM, for example, sells plenty of goods and services to schools, as do Microsoft and many others. It's not good for a company's im-age or balance sheet to be picketed by angry teachers. CEOs would rather be lionized than criticized. That's why most business leaders—capitalists though they plainly are—steer clear of divisive market-style reforms and usually shun efforts such as Chris Whittle's bid to run schools for profit. Such initiatives are too controversial, likelier to land them in hot water than get them thanked by grateful educators. So most confine themselves to the more mainstream agenda of standards and accountability, and many also sign up for the educators' cherished "professionalism" agenda.

On balance, they deserve two cheers.[63]

| In 1999, Gerstner and Achieve, Inc., decided it was time for yet another education summit on the tenth anniversary of the first one, and IBM again hosted the assembly. Lots of governors and corporate chiefs again showed up, and this time they also invited busloads of educators, including repre-sentatives of almost the entire congeries of organizations within the field. (Many had been miffed by their exclusion from the 1996 gathering.) In ad-dition, a dozen education policy types, myself included, were asked to take part as "resource" people.

Gerstner and Thompson again led the proceedings, and Clinton reap-peared to address the group. Adding bipartisan legitimacy, so did House education chairman Bill Goodling, the foremost congressional foe of national standards and testing.

Though this convocation drew much media attention and displayed all the bells and whistles of a major political event, it broke little new ground. Its main message was "stay the course" on standards-based education reform. "We have to bear the pain of this transition" to a standards-driven system, Gerstner declared. "We can't roll back to the input-driven system responsible for the problem."[64] Thompson reported, "We are seeing improvements already based on the work that has been done. But the simple truth we must face and address is that we are not making our schools better fast enough."[65]

Achieve, Inc., reported to attendees that forty-five states now *had* academic standards, up from fourteen in 1996. But to give those standards traction, Clinton told his rapt audience, it was vital to commit to "accountability," too, to actually rewarding people and schools (and districts and states) that attained the standards—and intervening in those that did not. Progress on that front had been far slower. "In 1996," the president said, "there were only 11 states with systems that identify and sanction low-performing schools. Today there are only 16. This is the hard part." Though he didn't say it, these facts also suggested that the pair of federal education laws that he had pushed through Congress five years earlier were not getting the job done.

In their joint communiqué, 1999's summiteers pledged themselves to a trio of reform strategies. As expected, the first of these would strengthen accountability as part of a continued push for standards-based reform.

Second, attendees committed to "provide all students access to high-quality instruction, curriculum and assessments aligned with standards, and the time and extra support they might need to meet the standards." Although this "access" included public-school choice and charter schools, it mostly meant furnishing schools and educators with resources and services of various kinds, a clear echo of the "opportunity to learn" standards that had helped to paralyze NCEST early in the decade and redolent of pre-Coleman thinking about school reform. One could feel the influence at this summit of the profession's innumerable "stakeholders."

Their participation was still more evident in the communiqué's third strand: "Improving educator quality." Declaring that "we cannot expect students to meet rigorous academic standards unless we have teachers equipped to teach to higher standards," summit participants pledged to "work together in our states to strengthen the entry and exit requirements of teacher-preparation programs and require them to demonstrate that graduates are prepared to teach to the state's academic standards, and are technologically literate."[66]

Yes, they demanded higher standards for teachers, not just fatter paychecks, and they even dipped a toe into the turbid waters of "pay for both skills and performance." But this time I descended from the Palisades unconvinced that mingling the insiders' priorities with the outsiders' strategy was a pure plus for the country. Was America's education renewal energy beginning to be redirected back into the system? Or did this summit herald an overdue coming together of political, business, and education leaders and a necessary if belated melding of their agendas?

22 | *Back to Dayton*

I held no full-time post in government in the 1990s, though I stayed active on its fringes via boards and panels such as NAGB, PEPAC, and NCEST and kitchen-cabinet work with Secretary Alexander. My day-job employers—Vanderbilt, the Edison Project, Hudson Institute, later the Manhattan Institute—were amenable, even grateful for the access and visibility that sometimes followed.

Since college, my jobs have cycled between "inside-action-participant" and "outside-analyst-writer." I crave both the excitement of doing and running things and the intellectual stimulus of trying to make sense of them. I need to write—books, articles, op-eds, testimony—but I also yearn for direct experience. And while I don't suffer from attention deficit disorder, I do grow restless. From 1969 to 1997, I never stayed put longer than three or four years; I chafe at too much repetition, and few jobs blend action with analysis or combine my own pot stirring with opportunities to taste and review what others have cooked up. (Yet despite changing roles and payrolls several times, between 1988 and today my principal workplace has never moved more than a few blocks in downtown D.C.)

The Thomas B. Fordham Foundation has turned out to be the exception, and I recently marked my tenth year at its helm.[67] It can do one thing in April and another in May, fight one sort of fire on Tuesday and a different kind on Wednesday. It combines real-world projects with research, joins nitty-gritty developments in Ohio to the abstractions of national policy, and gives me the freedom to cogitate, scribble, and stir all the pots I like, as well as time to lend a hand to outside projects and groups.

Tom Fordham was a Dayton industrialist who died the year I was born. My grandfather was his attorney, and my grandparents, then my parents, became close friends of his widow Thelma, who outlived him by a remarkable half century. In the early 1950s she created a foundation in his memory but, because she was supported (quite comfortably) by his estate, the foundation had little money during her lifetime and functioned primarily as a vehicle for her personal philanthropy. By the time she passed away in 1995, I had joined its small board, but that meant little more than a yearly lunch to determine how much to give to various Ohio charities.

When Thelma died without heirs, however, the full estate passed to the foundation, which suddenly found itself with $40–50 million and had to get serious. It now needed a proper board, staff, and a coherent program. We invited several thoughtful individuals to join its trustees and reflect with us on its mission. Because Thelma left no clear guidance, we had a free hand and soon resolved to devote this enterprise to reforming K–12 education, both nationally and in the Dayton area where she and Mr. Fordham had spent their lives.

The foundation's board asked if I would lead this venture and, after discussing it with Diane Ravitch, we agreed that Fordham could shoulder the mandate and adopt the credo of the Educational Excellence Network—a credo erroneously branded "conservative" by its critics though in fact it presages radical changes in primary-secondary schooling. We further enlarged the board (including Diane herself), hired a couple of outstanding young staffers, beginning with the estimable Gregg Vanourek, and entered into an agreement with Hudson Institute, later with the Manhattan Institute, whereby the foundation functioned as a sort of tenant in the think tank's Washington office and took advantage of its payroll system, benefits, and facilities.

By 1997, this new arrangement was operating in downtown D.C. with staffers making frequent trips to Dayton. (In 2003 we opened a tiny Dayton office, headed by the energized Terry Ryan, and in 2005 and 2006, with financial help from the Gates Foundation, we added a couple more staff members there plus one in Columbus.)

Though organized under the tax code as a private foundation, from the start Fordham did more than make grants to others.[68] Within the limits of an endowment whose annual yield is only in the $2–2.5 million range, we were entirely pro-active, devising projects rather than waiting for them to fly through the transom, coming up with our own ideas and seeking people, structures, and dissemination vehicles by which to execute them. At the national level, we quickly began to function as a mini–think tank in our own right, engaging scholars to conduct specific studies and analyses, then editing, publishing, and publicizing these. I've been blessed to have meticulous Marci Kanstoroom, then creative Justin Torres, then the multiply gifted Mike Petrilli lead this part of our work.

Fordham's first major study, in mid-1997, was Sandra Stotsky's expert review of state English standards, followed swiftly by reports across a host of topics: fifteen during our first two years. In that day before 24/7 Internet access to everything, we also continued to produce the monthly, then quarterly, compilation of education news and commentary that the Excellence Network had begun fifteen years earlier.

Fordham's rebirth in Dayton coincided with disillusionment among community leaders with that city's rickety, low-achieving school system and despair over prospects for setting it right. In the decades since I departed Colonel White High School, the Dayton Public Schools had a massive enrollment hemorrhage as almost everyone who could afford to leave fled into private and suburban public schools, leaving the city schools to poor families, black and white, with all the pathologies and challenges associated with high-poverty communities and dysfunctional urban systems. But schools were only the tip of a melting iceberg. Dayton's old manufacturing base had all but vanished, and increasingly its economy depended on the public sector (e.g., Wright Patterson Air Force Base, Wright State University, Sinclair Community College) and on service-industry institutions such as Miami Valley Hospital and the University of Dayton. Its physical infrastructure was in poor repair; its downtown was pretty much a wasteland after the daytime occupants of its office towers went home; and it no longer had many of the civic-minded leadership groups that my grandfather and father had taken part in, groups with optimistic, midcentury names such as the Area Progress Council.

The demographic, macroeconomic, and sociological reasons for this decay in a smallish rust-belt city like Dayton are fundamentally the same as in Canton, Pittsburgh, or Buffalo, and I won't rehearse them here. Suffice to say, returning on the Fordham Foundation's behalf to Dayton, a journey I had not made very often in the intervening years—my father still had a part-time residence there, but no other close relatives remained—was depressing. Yet it was also gratifying to be back, to think I might find a way—and have the means—to do something beneficial for the community that had been ground zero for the Finn family for a century, something that might also make use of what I had learned and done in my decades away. During these return visits of two or three days every month or so, though I usually slumbered in hotel rooms and got around by rental car, I would sometimes steal off to Riverview Cemetery and the peaceful, shady graves of my mother, grandparents, and great-grandparents. Those bittersweet moments deepened my awareness of my own roots and strengthened my sense of obligation to use Mr. Fordham's fortune to do some good for this city's children.

Making the rounds among those Dayton business leaders and philanthropists who still cared about K–12 education, seeking the right niche for Fordham, we resolved to try when we could to help reform the decrepit, change-resistant public school system but to place the lion's share of our hope, energy, and money on helping needy kids find decent alternatives. Several cities had started scholarship programs—privately funded voucher programs—to assist youngsters to attend private and parochial schools, and early evidence around the country indicated that these were working well. It happened that several of Dayton's wealthy businessmen were Catholic and keenly interested in the fate of the community's parochial schools. There, as in many cities, such schools were limping, underfunded and underenrolled, trying to serve the remaining Catholic youngsters in their neighborhoods but also doing a pretty good job with low-income non-Catholics, for whom they functioned as a haven from dismal public schools. The parochial schools had room for more such kids, but neither families nor parishes could afford to pay for them.

Some business leaders agreed to join with us—they even seemed to welcome the outside catalyst—in creating a scholarship program for needy Dayton youngsters, which we dubbed Parents Advancing Choice in Education, or PACE. It began with local funds but, coincidentally, 1998 brought the creation by Walton and Forstmann of the national Children's Scholarship Fund (CSF), which sought local matching funds and program operators. PACE swiftly became CSF's Dayton partner, and this infusion of national dollars enabled it to grow. By 2001–2, it was assisting some nine hundred Dayton kids to attend private schools that they could not otherwise swing; the schools were practically full; and the need for a lottery to determine which PACE/CSF applicants would be aided created a true experiment that enabled Harvard political scientist Paul Peterson to use Dayton, along with New York and Washington, as a site for studying the effects of vouchers on needy children. (His complex findings boiled down to this: vouchers and private schooling brought academic gains for black children but had little effect on the achievement of equally poor white and Hispanic youngsters.)[69]

Just as PACE was launching, legislators were enacting the Buckeye State's first charter-school law and soon extended it beyond Toledo to include opportunities for these new schools to arise in other Ohio cities, including Dayton. Because we were already examining the charter phenomenon at the Hudson Institute, we quickly deduced that this new program might create more school options for thousands of Dayton young-sters who still needed them and that, unlike private scholarships, this proj-ect could be carried out mainly with public dollars.

For Fordham, that meant finding ways to catalyze charter-school activ-ity in the Miami Valley. We made small seed grants to would-be school op-erators; we launched an "incubator" to help new schools open with solid governance, competent staffing, realistic business plans, and workable edu-cation programs; we supplied technical assistance to struggling schools via an "education resource center"; and we supported statewide efforts to pro-mote sound charter policy, thus creating an environment for such schools to succeed in Dayton and beyond.

We stumbled more than once while exploring this ill-mapped terrain, but by 2001–2 thirteen Dayton charter schools enrolled some four thousand youngsters, more than four times the number benefiting from the PACE scholarship program.

We also found a few small ways to help the school system and groups struggling to improve it. But our emphasis was creating options for chil-dren, and this turned out to have a transformative, if painful, effect on the system itself, far more potent than anything we or others could have done directly: in 2001, a competent four-woman "reform slate" was elected to a majority of seats on the Dayton school board, outgunning the dysfunctional crowd that had done so little. Most observers ascribe this shift to a sense of emergency created by the exodus of thousands of children from the school system into charter and private schools, causing a dramatic shrinkage of en-rollments and budgets among the schools they were leaving.

In this limited but important sense, school choice was working, and we at Fordham, helped by lucky breaks with national funders and state policy, were prompting reform within the system over the medium term even as we assisted children to escape into better options in the near term.

My Fordham role also gave me time to think and write. When possible, I scribbled at home in the morning—a pattern I still follow—and then dealt with foundation issues, meetings, and such in the office during the after-noon. Always something of a workaholic, I usually hit the office on Sun-days, too, and brought work home at night, but Renu and I would steal off several times a year to continue our touristic conquest of the planet.

Besides tangling with charter schools on the ground in Ohio, my Hudson/Fordham colleagues and I maintained a keen research interest in what could be learned from these new players on the public-education stage. Our original Pew-supported study led, at decade's end, to publication (by Bruno Manno, Gregg Vanourek, and me) of *Charter Schools in Action*, which profiled this rapidly spreading phenomenon and distilled some lessons by which it could be strengthened.[70]

Public policy wasn't my sole interest, however, nor necessarily the surest route to better education for young Americans. *The Educated Child* came out in 1999, co-authored with Bill Bennett and John Cribb.[71] It was a very different sort of book that sought to empower parents directly with insights and concrete advice to function as effective quarterbacks of their kids' education—and as discerning, demanding school consumers.

I was, in truth, a lucky guy, in most respects my own boss, largely free to pursue my own interests intellectually, locally, and nationally. My kids were nearly grown. My wife was successful—playing a role in cardiac medicine not unlike mine in education. My main employer had an endowment sufficient to cover its core work. Some of what I wrote and said got noticed. On the ground in Dayton, some of what we did was getting traction. As the millennium ended, my one large lament was that American education as a whole was still making scant progress and millions of other people's kids were still learning far too little.

Part V | *Today and Tomorrow*

The 2000 presidential election took education seriously. Al Gore ran on his and Bill Clinton's two-term record while George W. Bush highlighted his Texas gubernatorial performance. Both spoke often of education reform.

Yet campaign watchers had some difficulty distinguishing between them. Both platforms called for higher standards, greater accountability, better teachers, stronger discipline, more attention to character, and expanded choice among schools. The GOP took pains this time not to espouse formulaic right-wing positions or to urge cutbacks in federal programs. That stance hadn't served them well after 1994, and this presidential candidate styled himself a "compassionate conservative" bent on ending "the soft bigotry of low expectations." The Gore-Lieberman ticket sounded themes that would appeal to soccer moms even if they made the teacher unions a tad nervous. As a result, when the televised debates turned to education, viewers were hard-pressed to detect major disagreements. "Rhetoric aside," wrote *Education Week*'s Joetta Sack in early September, "what's clear is that both candidates are attaching high prominence to education and, when they aren't jabbing at each other, they can be heard espousing goals and policy proposals that sound surprisingly similar." [1]

Such convergence ordinarily means an issue is losing its electoral salience. But this time both sides *wanted* education to be an issue. Gore pushed for more federal spending, boasting about the progress made during the previous eight years and making much of Bush's alleged support for vouchers, which in fact was muted. The Bush team said that the Clinton-Gore years had left America in an "education recession" and accused the Democrats of being handmaidens to the establishment.

The closest thing to a real difference turned out to be conflicting interpretations of what had happened in Texas on Bush's watch.

The basic history was not in dispute. Ever since Mark White and Ross Perot steered the Lone Star State onto the school-reform path in the early 1980s, political leaders of both parties, abetted by the state's business elite, had maintained a steady focus on academic standards and tests, a slowly rising achievement bar for students, and plenty of sunshine on school performance, onto which was layered a good deal of school choice, including a fast-growing charter program. Few rewards or sanctions (other than publicity) were meted out at the state level, but districts were keenly aware of which schools weren't measuring up, and many moved locally to solve the problems.

A decade and a half later, it was fair to ask whether this strategy was working. The RAND Corporation, among others, said it was. A study published in July 2000, authored primarily by David W. Grissmer, high-lighted Bush's Texas (along with Jim Hunt's North Carolina) as a state whose NAEP scores had risen faster than the national average. When results were disaggregated by race, minority youngsters in Texas were among the highest scoring in the land.

The RAND analysts probed deeper:

The state-administered tests given to all students statewide showed similarly large gains in math scores in both states, providing an independent verification of the NAEP trends. . . . The study identified a set of similar systemic reform policies implemented in both states in the late 1980s and early 1990s as being the most plausible reason for the gains. These policies included developing state standards by grade, assessment tests linked to these standards, good systems for providing feedback to teachers and principals, some accountability measures, and deregulation of the teaching environment.[2]

The Bush-Cheney team was thrilled and the Gore-Lieberman forces alarmed by this independent confirmation that Texas deserved credit for bona fide achievement gains arising from its school-reform strategy. On October 24, however, two weeks before election day, RAND published *another* interpretation, this time a concise "issue paper" written primarily by analyst Stephen P. Klein and titled *What Do Test Scores in Texas Tell Us?* It cast doubt upon the Lone Star education miracle, indeed came close to alleging fraud when it said that gains on Texas's state tests were not matched by NAEP results. "Stark differences" was the phrase used to describe discrepancies between the two sets of scores. Klein suggested that drilling kids to pass the Texas tests accounted for the bounce shown there.[3]

RAND insisted that its July and October studies were not directly comparable, because the authors had used different methods. Still, this was a peculiar situation for a research organization, and many observers suspected that factions within RAND were using their institution's reputation for impartiality as a fig leaf for their own political agendas. RAND's CEO sought to split the difference. In an unusual, Solomon-like statement of his own, issued concurrently with the October report, James A. Thomson said, "The new paper suggests a less positive picture of Texas education than the earlier effort. But I do not believe that these efforts are in sharp conflict. Together in fact they provide a more comprehensive picture of key education issues."[4]

| Since 2000, both standards-based and choice-based reforms have made big gains and have begun to intersect in tantalizing ways, although both remain unloved by educators who favor their own "resources and professionalism" agenda and their one-school-at-a-time makeover efforts. But the establishment glacier is receding. Such influential groups as the Council of Chief State School Officers and the Council of the Great City Schools have either embraced or reconciled themselves to standards-based, results-driven education, though not yet to many forms of school choice. Ironically, even some of the continuing pushback demonstrates the triumph of post-Coleman thinking: critics now demand that eager reformers prove that their stratagems and novel arrangements—e.g., charter schools—yield superior outcomes. They hurl evidence of meager academic performance as proof that the reform was misguided or is being bungled. Sheer innovativeness and good intentions no longer cut it.

What's sauce for the goose should be sauce for the gander. Education change agents of every persuasion justify their schemes and nostrums by pointing to the shoddy results of schools-as-we-know-them. On closer inspection, however, a double standard looms. As stakes rise, protectors of the system have come to demand from those who would alter it proof of performance that they do not require of themselves. Reformers are challenged to prove that their plan will work flawlessly—boosting achievement with no one left behind and no adverse consequences—while existing schools and practices are given a pass, permitted to continue producing mediocre results and tolerating persistent inequities on grounds that that's the normal way of doing things from which only those who deviate must justify themselves. Because such justification is customarily demanded in advance of a reform's deployment, it poses a tall barrier, not necessarily because the reform is ill conceived or unsuccessful but because kids change slowly and new schools and other major education innovations commonly require a shakedown period. The whiff of a double standard is also yielding an unwelcome backlash as proponents of reforms such as charter schools are tempted to rationalize weak academic results on grounds that the insistence on high performance comes from enemies of change. Such trench warfare is not good for anyone.

One reason for escalating hostilities is that U.S. K–12 enrollment in the early twenty-first century is nearly flat: 47.2 million youngsters in public education (pre-K through high school) in 2000, 48.4 million in 2005, and 48.8 million expected by federal forecasters in 2010. As for private schools, nobody can accurately predict the future, but so far their pupil numbers look like a relatively stable 5 million, although urban Catholic schools are again closing left and right.

Demographic shifts are altering the ethnic composition of schools—by 2006, public school enrollments were 42% minority—and are redistributing youngsters from some parts of the country (the Northeast and Midwest, mostly) to others (South and West), as well as causing some districts to balloon while others deflate. Yet today's big picture approximates a zero-sum game in which more children moving into one sector (e.g., charter schools, home schooling) mean fewer for the sectors that they leave. That raises anxiety levels all around.

Competition to attract and retain pupils so as to keep one's budget up or one's school full of pupils also takes such forms as the push by public education to expand pre-K and kindergarten offerings, the quest to retrieve dropouts, and the complaint that escalating standards will drive more young people out of school.

Though standards-based reformers and choice advocates are still, by and large, different people and organizations, and though some policymakers, philanthropists, and business leaders, viewing these two strategies as incompatible, still think they must sign up for one and reject the other, in fact we see early signs that both approaches are compatible, even mutually dependent. A few places are imaginatively blending them, such as Florida, which deployed standards and tests to rank all its public schools on the basis of their effectiveness, then used exit vouchers, charter schools, and other choice-based mechanisms to assist youngsters to leave low-performing schools for more salubrious education settings.[5] Ohio's new statewide voucher program is similarly accessible only to students previously enrolled in persistently weak schools.

As those examples suggest, today's twin external reform strategies, far from undercutting one another, can compensate for each other's inherent frailties. Standards-based reform is notably better at identifying weak schools than at strengthening them.[6] The upshot is millions of youngsters stuck in ineffective schools that stay that way, year after year. Interventions intended to repair their schools mostly fail. One solution is to give those kids other options, that is, to deploy choice as a practical solution to the number one conundrum of standards-based reform. (This, of course, works only where an adequate supply of decent "schools of choice" exists or can be created.)

The buzzing school marketplace, by contrast, is full of hard-to-compare schools and ill-informed customers. It's a flawed market wherein novice parents, lacking objective information by which to make wise education choices for their kids, are easily beguiled by school claims or readily satisfied by verifiable aspects of a school (e.g., safety, location, "caring teachers") that may have little to do with its educational effectiveness. One remedy is obvious: clear, comparable data on schools' performance, data that come best from the workshop of standards-based reformers. Some parents still won't choose on this basis, but some will.

The No Child Left Behind (NCLB) Act is the tallest and shakiest tree in today's education-reform jungle, the one most apt to bend and sway in coming months as the 2008 presidential contenders (several of whom voted for it) find that disputes surrounding it occupy the heart of contemporary federal education policy and politics.

President Bush signed NCLB into law on January 8, 2002, a year after an elaborate White House debut where he unveiled the four principles of his pathbreaking plan:

First, children must be tested every year in reading and math. . . . Without yearly testing, we don't know who is falling behind and who needs help. Without yearly testing, too often we don't find failure until it is too late to fix. . . .

Secondly, the agents of reform must be schools and school districts, not bureaucracies. . . . One size does not fit all when it comes to educating the children in America. School districts, school officials, educational entrepreneurs should not be hindered by excessive rules and red tape and regulation. . . . If local schools do not have the freedom to change, they cannot be held accountable for failing to change. . . .

Third, many of our schools, particularly low-income schools, will need help in the transition to higher standards. When a state sets standards, we must help schools achieve those standards. . . .

Fourth, American children must not be left in persistently dangerous or failing schools. When schools do not teach and will not change, parents and students must have other meaningful options.[7]

The invited East Room audience (myself included) sensed that we were attending an Important Event. The freshly inaugurated president was signaling the significance of education reform by making it the first item on his agenda. He and his education secretary, Rod Paige (well-regarded former Houston superintendent, African-American, and Republican), strode in, both looking very Texan. All rose. Bush took command, and it was evident this wasn't just something he had been briefed on. This was a subject he knew well.

NCLB's main elements had accompanied him from Austin, where versions of them had been deployed with fair success before and during his six-year governorship. Applying himself to making them work in Texas (and getting them noticed and applauded), he had ample opportunity to master the issues. During the couple of policy and strategy sessions I took part in while he was governor, and a few more during his first year in the White House, I could see that he knew at least as much about K-12 education and its makeover as any number of experts in the room. Bush critics love to depict his mind as weak and his tongue as tied, but when grappling with elementary-secondary education—the only topic I've seen him discuss up close in private—he is well informed, articulate, confident, probing, decisive, and funny.

Which does not mean one can easily take state-level reforms and apply them nationally, although that's pretty much what the president was bent on doing. (Recall defense secretary–designate Charles Wilson's 1953 comment: "We at General Motors have always felt that what was good for the country was good for General Motors, and vice versa.") Maybe Texans find it easier than others to gloss over the challenge because they tend to view their vast state as a nation in its own right. Bush also recognized, however, that his plan was, in key respects, a souped-up extension of the education bills that Clinton had coaxed through Congress in 1994—and a lineal descendant of his father's America 2000 strategy.

As with Goals 2000 and IASA, the lure of federal billions would be the bait dangled before hungry states and educators. If they swallowed it—which, strictly speaking, was optional—they would find new hooks inside, tugging them in the direction of Texas. Yet the administration's proposal was cast in general terms, not dispatched to Capitol Hill as a draft bill. Bush wanted to work with Congress to craft a bipartisan measure based on his principles. Outwardly at least, the administration was relaxed about the details. White House emissaries were instructed to cooperate on both sides of the aisle.

Which they did—and much compromising and horse-trading ensued. Democrats would have nothing to do with vouchers, for example, and were loath to give states and districts much flexibility, certainly not the option of spending their Title I dollars on anything but poor kids. Many Republicans were jittery about the whole proposal, which struck them as an unwarranted extension of federal control in K–12 education. They strove to preserve freedom for states to set their own standards and devise their own tests—and even balked at using NAEP to double-check their progress. (In the end, states were required to administer NAEP every two years in fourth- and eighth-grade reading and math, but those results don't count in determining whether schools are making progress.) And everybody added, tweaked, expanded, or simply preserved favorite programs and projects.

The upshot was a tenuous but adequately bipartisan policy pudding that nearly everyone on Capitol Hill could talk themselves, or be talked, into voting for. (The House roll call in May 2001 was 384–45 in favor; the Senate vote in June was 91–8.) As enacted, NCLB (officially the latest reauthorization of LBJ's Elementary and Secondary Education Act) runs to more than a thousand pages and authorizes a staggering array of federal programs, good, bad, and indifferent. Perhaps the oddest raisin in this mighty pudding is "Exchanges with Historic Whaling and Trading Partners," a program inserted by Massachusetts senator Edward M. Kennedy that channels some $8.5 million annually into a handful of institutions in the Bay State plus Alaska and Hawaii.[8]

NCLB's core, however, is Title I, which houses most of the provisions that elicit cheers and lamentations. And at the core of that core is a key trade-off. On the one hand, states are required (if they want to continue receiving Title I funding, which amounts to hundreds of millions per year for most and billions for several) to agree that all their pupils in grades three through eight will become "proficient" in reading and math by 2014, and are obliged to put in place standards and measures that spell out what's meant by proficiency, how it will be measured, and how "adequate yearly progress" toward it will be monitored. On the other hand, states are free to define proficiency as they like, to set high, low, or middling standards, and to use whichever tests they wish (and whatever passing scores on those tests they deem reasonable or politically palatable) to track their progress.

In hindsight, Bush and his congressional partners got this backward. The law should have set uniform standards and measures for the nation, then freed states, districts, and schools to produce those results as they think best, perhaps even on timetables of their own devising. Lawmakers should also have insisted on school performance being judged primarily by how much a school causes its pupils' achievement to rise, not just how they're faring in relation to fixed standards. The way it came out, however, states face an almost irresistible temptation to lower their standards or ease their passing scores—and can do this in dozens of ways, some of them so techni-cal and obscure that stealthy dumbing down is hard to detect. Given the animus in Washington toward national standards and tests, without this Faustian compromise there likely would have been no bipartisan pact. Yet dealing with its awkward aftermath may prove the most volatile education issue in the 2008 election—and for the Congress that convenes in January 2009.[9]

Also in hindsight, lawmakers made a noble yet misleading promise when they declared that *no* child would be left behind and *all* would be-come proficient by 2014—a date that will actually arrive during the next president's second term. Reminiscent of Bush 41 and the governors an-nouncing in 1990 that U.S. schools would lead the world in math and sci-ence by decade's end, it's the sort of grand claim that politicians always make—imagine JFK proclaiming that America would get three-fourths of the way to the moon—but that everyone privately knows will not come true. For a host of reasons, some kids just won't attain a reasonable level of proficiency by 2014. If we do a fantastic job, their number will be small but it won't be zero. In truth, moving from today's 30 percent of children profi-cient to, say, 70 percent or 80 percent would be a transformative achieve-ment for the nation. But politicians cannot say things like that, lest they instantly be skewered with "Which 20 percent are you writing off?"

The main NCLB negotiators were Texas attorney and Bush confidant Sandy Kress on behalf of the White House, Senators Judd Gregg and Ted Kennedy, and Congressmen John Boehner and George Miller. They spent much time together, hammering out the specifics of this wide-ranging mea-sure, which also delves into teacher qualifications, school safety, "scientifi-cally based" reading programs, and much more. Although vouchers were quickly jettisoned (with no evident tears at the White House), youngsters whose public schools are deemed "in need of improvement" for two con-secutive years were given the right to switch to higher-performing dis-trict (or charter) schools. (A similar exit visa was authorized for students whose schools are "persistently dangerous.") After three such years, they also gained the right to claim a share of their Title I dollars as mini-vouchers with which to purchase "supplemental educational services"—free tutoring—from approved providers, which can include private vendors as well as the school system itself.[10]

Besides the risk that their pupils may depart for greener pastures (if such can be found within NCLB's cramped view of choice), schools "in need of improvement" are subject to a sequential cascade of prescribed interventions and "corrective actions" by their districts. (A parallel series of revampings by states is mandated for faltering districts themselves.) By spring 2006, some 1,750 schools had reached the bottom of the waterfall, that is, had needed—and not shown—improvement for so long (five years!) that they are now supposed to be "restructured." But that lengthening list of low-performing schools reveals another big flaw at the heart of NCLB: the assumption that the very districts that let these schools fail now possess the capacity and will to transform them—and that Washington can drive so long and loosely coupled a train.

Once a low-performing school proves incorrigible, NCLB gives its district five options. Four of these (outsourcing the school's operation, replacing the staff, converting it into a charter, getting the state to operate it directly) are fraught with personnel, political, fiscal, and management challenges. Which is why most districts choose the catch-all fifth option: "Any other major restructuring of the schools' governance arrangement that makes fundamental reforms."

This vague phrasing, unimpeded by clarifications from Washington, allows tepid, woolly interventions that are far less disruptive, hence easier to implement—and probably less effective. "Most schools are not doing radical things," comments Jack Jennings, a veteran House education aide who now heads the Center on Education Policy and has studied restructuring efforts in several states. "They are offering professional development, rethinking the curriculum, bringing coaches in, and trying to improve the school without wiping the slate clean." [11]

Nor is there much evidence that states are keen to intervene in failing districts. They may be even warier after the Maryland legislature in April 2006 thwarted the state board of education's move to take control of eleven long-failing Baltimore schools so as to bring them into compliance with NCLB.

The meager capacity of most state and local education agencies to mount such interventions is a corollary of a structural flaw in U.S. education federalism that NCLB inherited from earlier rounds of ESEA. Back in 1965, when lawmakers' main goal was to disburse federal dollars to schools for additional instructional services for poor kids, it made sense, indeed was practically inevitable, to hand those dollars down the familiar institutional ladder from Washington to state education agencies (SEAs) to local education agencies (LEAs). That was how state and local monies already flowed, and there was no reason to create another mechanism to move federal funds. While SEAs and LEAs weren't always diligent in following Uncle Sam's rules, it was in their interest to comply, if only because they and their schools then got the money, which came without so many strings as to disrupt what they were already doing.

Today, however, getting Washington's dollars to the right places is the lesser mission of ESEA. The law now deploys its funds and their attendant conditions, regulations, state plans, and oversight mechanisms to *transform* the system in fundamental ways, above all to boost student achievement and hold schools (and districts and states) to account for whether or not they accomplish this.

Thus arises a great paradox: Washington still relies primarily on SEAs and LEAs to do its bidding, yet now the point of federal programs is not to "help" them do more but to change what they do, often in ways they don't much want to be changed. In ways they judge contrary to their own interests. Ways that include admitting failure. And ways they may not be competent to handle, albeit ways that the public interest demands.

Why do federal policymakers assume that the very agencies that caused the system's problems (or, at least, allowed them to fester) now possess the will and capacity to solve them? The truth is, Congress and the White House never gave this any thought. When crafting NCLB, they simply clung to the assumption that has ruled ESEA for four decades: that working down the familiar ladder is how Washington does business in the K–12 sector.

Thus NCLB proceeds in the accustomed sequence, with Uncle Sam telling states what to do, states telling districts, and districts doing most of the work. That hierarchy remains the basic architecture of federal education policy today as in LBJ's time. But its engineers never pictured it supporting a results-based accountability system, making repairs to faltering schools, or functioning in an education environment peppered with such disruptive, nonhierarchical creations as charter schooling, home schooling, and distance learning. It's as if a high-tech firm was officed in an old foundry without anyone bothering to rewire, replumb, or even fumigate the structure.

For all its lofty ambitions, NCLB was thus constrained from the start. Having overpromised, it's now underdelivering (nobody should be surprised by that)—and spawning all manner of new compromises, end runs, deviations, and regulatory revisions.

Granted, no big, complicated federal law ever works perfectly from day one. Statutes need shakedown periods, too. Revisions, fine-tuning, and midcourse corrections are normal in Washington, and a cottage industry has arisen to spot weaknesses in NCLB and suggest legislative remedies when the time comes to reauthorize the statute. Strictly speaking, that was supposed to occur during 2007, and the first substantial committee hearing took place on schedule in March. Studies, commission reports, and interest group recommendations gushed forth. By mid-summer, bills were being filed by Democrats and Republicans alike. Yet so touchy, contentious, and politically freighted has this law become that renewed bipartisan consensus—if such is even possible—will likely have to follow the 2008 presidential election.

Congressional Democrats—and presidential candidates—are noisily unhappy with what they view as too little money for NCLB implementation in Bush's budgets, and many of their traditional backers in the public-education sector view NCLB as naïvely ambitious and painfully demanding. For their part, Republicans say they voted for the bill in 2001 only because it was important to their new president and that they never liked its "Washington knows best" approach to education reform, the ways it tramples on state and local control, and its weak-kneed school-choice provisions.

As the consensus that produced NCLB unravels, the executive branch has become somewhat more responsive to complaints. During Bush's first term, the White House was unbending. It wouldn't hear of changes that might make NCLB work better. Even when Secretary Paige and his lieutenants concluded that some damaging rigidities in the statute could be softened through regulatory revisions, exemptions, and waivers, the message from 1600 Pennsylvania Avenue was that the medicine may be bitter but states must swallow it. The main enforcer was chief domestic policy aide Margaret Spellings, another Texan and Bush loyalist who earnestly believes that standards, testing, and accountability are the remedy for whatever ails American education. (I stopped getting invited to White House meetings during this period. This Bush team has never been good at handling constructive criticism from friendly sources. They want you to be a hundred-percenter or go away. So I went.)

After the 2004 election, however, when Paige was rudely let go and Spellings took his place at the Education Department, flexibility and responsiveness became her watchwords. She eased back on some of NCLB's most onerous regulations (which had, for example, exempted too few

severely disabled youngsters from the standardized testing regimen) and allowed states to rework their accountability plans to reduce the number of
schools found "in need of improvement."

In some instances, such easing was warranted. Several states had pre-
existing accountability systems that were beginning to yield decent gains,
and NCLB mainly served to complicate their work. Florida, for example,
found itself puzzling schools by giving them high marks on the state rating
system while labeling them candidates for reconstitution under the federal
formula—and vice versa.

Spellings dug in her heels on waiver requests that plainly violated the
law—Connecticut's plea, for instance, to continue testing its students in alternate grades rather than annually. But mostly she sought to accommodate. This is a good thing in some situations—and would have been better
had Paige been given leeway to do it from day one—but in others it threat-
ens to turn NCLB into a paper tiger. For example, federal flexibility with
respect to how many children of any one race a school must enroll before
that subgroup's test scores "count" has led to millions of minority youngsters' performance being ignored by a law whose goal is to erase intergroup
achievement gaps.[12]

Despite the Education Department's newfound willingness to appease
and pacify, NCLB still has plenty of critics. The NEA is seeking through
the courts to overturn it. The American Association of School Administrators is urging that the "federal role in education be refocused on supple-
menting the efforts of states and school districts to overcome the many and
varied effects of poverty on student outcomes." Dozens of conservative Republicans have taken a similar tack, signing on to House and Senate bills
that would, in effect, let states opt out of NCLB's regulatory regimen without forfeiting their federal dollars. There's much grumbling that some provisions of the statute are having perverse effects (e.g., judging all schools
against fixed standards, rather than student gains) while others have proven
unenforceable. Public-school choice, for example, amounts to an empty
promise in cities with many schools flagged as "needing improvement" but
few openings for kids in higher-performing schools.

In August 2006, Spellings famously declared NCLB to resemble Ivory
Soap: "It's 99.9 percent pure. . . . There's not much needed in the way of
change." Yet few others love it as is. Indeed, five months later, the Bush administration itself recommended dozens of amendments. Weeks after that, a
high-status commission convened by the Aspen Institute, funded by the

Gates Foundation and chaired by two well-regarded former governors (Wisconsin's Tommy Thompson, Georgia's Roy Barnes) recommended more than seventy specific changes to NCLB—most of them calculated to *reduce* state flexibility and *tighten* the federal grip on U.S. schools.[13]

The 2006 election results probably portend big changes in NCLB. Although the Democratic chairs of the two key education committees (Messrs. Miller in the House and Kennedy in the Sente) were architects of the current law, they are under considerable pressure from their party's traditional constituencies to roll back, soften, or otherwise modify various elements of it, as well as to appropriate far more federal dollars to offset its costs.[14] With their president's term nearing its finale and themselves again in the minority on Capitol Hill, Republicans feel freer to vote their consciences—and look after *their* constituents—on highly charged issues. And if that did not create sufficient obstacles to future consensus, the nation's governors have indicated that this time around they want to participate in the legislative process.

| I've blown hot and cold on NCLB since it was enacted. I welcome the pressure on states to set and enforce academic standards and illuminate school results. But an awful lot of sawdust went into this sausage, and some of the provisions I felt most strongly about were omitted or emasculated. In 2003, when the Milken Family Foundation invited me to speak about NCLB at its gala teacher-awards conference, I asked whether they wanted me to be for it or against it. In fairness to the audience and my own ambivalence, I wound up literally debating myself: moving back and forth between two podiums as I gave first "pro" and then "con" views on ten elements of that law.

Four years later, the best thing about NCLB so far is the added light it casts upon the performance of schools, groups of children, districts, and states. Even where state standards and tests get monkeyed with, NAEP remains a reasonably steady gauge of progress. In time, I expect that the trove of new information and hard data on school performance now being accumulated and pumped out (at least for grades three through eight, at least in reading and math) will help state and local officials, citizens, and parents to wrestle with their schools, address shortcomings directly, and make wiser (or at least better-informed) choices, where choices exist to be made.

No Child Left Behind is not the whole of standards-based reform in the new millennium, nor is Uncle Sam the sole—even the primary—tiller of this field. Though fertilized and watered from Washington, the concept has taken root across most of the land that states *should* set standards for schools and students, *should* monitor performance in relation to those standards, and *should* deploy incentives, rewards, and interventions to effect greater achievement gains than would naturally occur.

That's the steady message when governors and business leaders gather. (Two more summits have been held, one in 2001 and a Gates-assisted one in 2005 that focused on high schools. They've been useful support groups for veteran "education governors" and opportunities for newcomers to sip the Kool-Aid of standards-based reform.) The public endorses it in surveys and opinion polls. Several key national education groups have made it part of their policy portfolio. And it has spread almost everywhere. Iowa was the last holdout, for years refusing to set statewide standards, but under the pressure of NCLB it, too, is moving in that direction, albeit jerkily.[15]

With the theory no longer in much doubt, attention now focuses on the pesky practice, and there we find much debate, considerable scrambling, and more than a little finagling. Although the impetus for standards-based reform almost always comes from outside the system, its implementation usually falls to those who run that system, typically the state's education chief, department, and board, and their district-level counterparts. This is akin to asking companies' senior executives to audit their own firms and poses an inherent risk that they will go easy on themselves in order to produce verdicts that make their stewardship appear successful. One recalls with alarm the "everybody above average" problem that Dr. Cannell exposed in the late 1980s when he showed how easy it was for state and district testing programs—and the test firms they hired—to color and contour their results.

A well-crafted standards regimen resembles a tripod. One leg consists of the standards themselves, aspirational statements of the skills and knowledge that children are supposed to acquire. Leg two is the assessments and other measures by which achievement and progress are gauged vis-à-vis those standards. Leg three, the behavior-changing part, is the incentives, rewards, sanctions, and interventions by which—it is hoped—greater progress is induced.

Let us look at the challenges of getting this tripod to stand straight.

Standards | The first requisite of standards-based reform, obviously, is academic standards, usually subject by subject and grade by grade. Since the tests are meant to be aligned with the standards (as are textbook content, teacher training, and much else), and since the rewards and sanctions of the accountability system are supposed to be triggered by the test results, the quality of the underlying standards is key.

When the Fordham Foundation cranked up in 1997, we saw that a pressing issue was whether the new state standards then beginning to emerge were capable of bearing such weight. We asked reading expert Sandra Stotsky to appraise the twenty-eight sets of language arts (i.e., English) standards that she was able to obtain.

The results were bleak: just five states deserved high marks. The rest ranged from so-so to dire. So we examined the other four subjects on the original national goals list. By 1998, Fordham analysts had completed reviews of math, science, history, and geography. The average grade was a dismal D+.

Other standards-reviewing outfits—the Council for Basic Education, the American Federation of Teachers—were less harsh, but their appraisals pointed toward the same alarming conclusion: with rare exceptions, the most significant education reform effort in the land, involving enormous effort, lots of money, and much attention by governors, presidents, and tycoons, rested on a cracked foundation.[16]

Despite the NCLB push, getting standards right continues to be an overwhelming challenge for many states. Some have come through with flying colors but, in the latest round of Fordham reviews, most again deserved low marks. Table 1, for example, shows the grades assigned to state science standards in 2005 by a team of scientists led by the eminent biologist Paul R. Gross.[17]

The reviewers itemized five widespread failings:

- *Excessive Length and Poor Navigability.* Sprawling, almost impenetrable documents, uncontrolled in size and poorly organized, are too common a result of a push to cover everything.

Table 1. Grading State Standards in Science, 2005

Grade	Number of States
A	7
B	12
C	9
D	7
F	15

Source: Paul R. Gross et al., *The State of State Science Standards 2005*, Thomas B. Fordham Institute

- *Thin Disciplinary Content.* States' zealous embrace of "inquiry-based learning" has squeezed real science content (astronomy, biology, chemistry, ecology, physics, etc.) out of the curriculum to make room for "process."
- *Do-It-Yourself Learning.* Many state standards documents take a very good idea—*Whenever practical, science learners should find things out for themselves*—and carry it to an absurd level, declaring that all knowledge should be "discovered" by the student rather than passed along by the teacher.
- *Good Ideas Gone Bad.* Too many states create a false dichotomy between "rote" and "hands-on" learning. Of course students should engage science in the laboratory or field, but they also must learn and memorize some things.
- *Shunning Evolution.* A disturbing and dangerous trend over the past five years, in response to religious and political pressures, is the effort to water down the treatment of evolution.[18]

Setting standards isn't easy. Every subject taught in U.S. schools is a crucible of controversies within the discipline, among educators, and sometimes in the broader public. Evolution is one example, phonics another. The treatment of innumerable ethnic and national interests in history curricula. The race and gender of authors of books and stories that students are expected to read, even of the short reading passages used in test items. And so on, into health (sex education) and phys ed (competitiveness versus individual fitness) and beyond.

Even when content battles can be won or a truce declared, do the standards relate to anything in the real world that young people will enter, or do they simply represent educators' fancy of what would be nice for students to know? What's the evidence, a teen or parent might reasonably ask, that learning these things will make a difference in my college or career? (And, if they won't, why should I study hard when there are so many things I'd rather do?) What's the evidence, an employer wonders, that standard-setters have attended to the actual skills and knowledge a worker needs to succeed in our firm, lab, or plant? Where's the proof, university professors skeptically inquire, that a young person who masters this state's K–12 standards is truly prepared for college-level work in the subjects we require on our campus?

Yet that real world seldom intrudes upon the sprawling committees and exquisitely "diverse" panels that states generally rely upon to establish their K–12 standards. Working out a modus vivendi among fractious education stakeholders normally takes precedence.

In 2001, Fordham teamed up with Achieve, Inc., the Education Trust, and five states to see if we could do a better job of tethering high-school exit standards in English and math to real-world expectations. Aided by money from the Hewlett Foundation—Fordham can start things like this but we don't have deep-enough pockets to support giant projects—we scrutinized those states' standards in relation to the skills and knowledge that universities expect in entering students and that modern employers demand of those embarking on careers in their firms. After much struggle, the "American Diploma Project" produced an ambitious set of twelfth-grade standards in those two subjects and, now assisted by the Gates Foundation, has set about both to recruit more states to join the venture and to assist them in persuading K–12 officials, universities, and major employers all to align their standards (and tests) to those we devised.[19] That work continues—getting high-school exit expectations to match university entrance norms is a steep climb all by itself—but the project has already shown that the ingredients exist for such alignment.

Testing | When (and if) its standards are sound, the next challenge a state faces is syncing its tests to them, setting ambitious but attainable performance expectations for students taking those tests, getting them quickly and accurately scored, and analyzing the results in actionable yet fair ways. Five assessment anxieties loom large:

■ Where to set the bar? In deciding whether a youngster meets a state's standards, one must determine whether he/she has *passed* the test. But where to locate the passing score? If too high, few will succeed and many will despair. If too low, passing signifies little. Is it fixed in place forever or a moving bar that (one hopes) rises over time? Is there a single passing score or (as on NAEP) several levels of attainment, ranging from minimal to proficient to distinguished?

Many jurisdictions have yielded to the temptation to set their bars low—nearly irresistible when one is, in effect, auditing oneself. Complying with NCLB's mandate to define "proficiency" in reading and math, for example, most states pegged it closer to NAEP's "basic" than "proficient" level. In the main, high-school graduation tests are also easy to pass, just as when legislators first mandated them in the seventies. In 2004, Achieve, Inc. evaluated six states' exit exams and concluded that students could succeed on them with math skills in the seventh- to eighth-grade range and English prowess around grades eight and nine.[20]

Still, not everyone passes. In California in 2006, after failing that state's undemanding graduation test multiple times, 11 percent of seniors were denied their diplomas. In Massachusetts, which has longer experience, 94 percent of the graduating class of 2005 eventually passed the state's somewhat more challenging test. (After factoring in dropouts, however, only 72 percent of Bay State youngsters graduate from high school with a standard diploma, including just 53 percent of black and 41 percent of Hispanic students.)

■ Because it's generally true in education that "what gets tested is what gets taught," too cramped a testing plan may narrow the curriculum. If only reading and math "count," for example, schools may focus overmuch on drilling youngsters in those skills and neglect history, civics, and science, not to mention art, music, and languages. (NCLB names ten "core" academic subjects, but its accountability scheme rests exclusively on reading and math test results.) If teachers can determine which topics will actually appear on the year-end test, they may further restrict what they cover in class.

"Teaching to the test" is widely deplored in education circles, although that complaint is easily answered: if the test faithfully mirrors the skills and knowledge set out in the standards—assuming those are sound, too—then preparing one's pupils to ace such a test is an honorable mission for educators.

Yet a 2006 study by the American Federation of Teachers concluded that just eleven states are using tests that are well aligned with strong content standards.[21] Moreover, because testing costs time and money, many states strive not to overdo it. That quickly leads to the kind of testing regime that fosters curricular thinning as well as mismatches between what kids should learn and what's actually assessed.

■ Is the testing program well run, trusty, and timely? While most states painstakingly construct their own standards, most then outsource their testing system to private firms, generally following procurement rules that obligate them to engage the lowest bidder. NCLB's insistence on annual assessment of every child expands the quantity of testing, which usually means finding cheap, uncomplicated instruments, often sloppily constructed and subject to sluggish (and sometimes flawed) reporting of results. It's common, for instance, for the results of April testing to come back after the next school year has begun, a damaging delay with repercussions for students, teachers, parents, and the entire accountability system. Ten states had such iffy assessments in place in mid-2006 that the Education Department initiated steps to punish them by withholding bits of their federal funding.

■ How much should hinge solely on test results? When judging a youngster via a high-stakes exam that determines promotion or graduation, how many chances should he/she have to pass? What if someone tests badly but has worked hard, completed the course, and done okay on homework assignments, class participation, research papers or labs, maybe even extra-credit opportunities? Does that student get held back or denied a diploma because of lacking a point or two on a test score? What if he/she is disabled or homeless, emotionally shaky, or a potential dropout? Such concerns have led most states both to give kids multiple test-taking opportunities and to permit alternate means of demonstrating their educational fitness.

■ Is a school's (or teacher's) performance best judged against fixed standards or in relation to the *gains* that students make over time? This dilemma sharpened after the development in the early 1990s of a "value-added" assessment system for Tennessee. Statistician William Sanders showed that it is possible both to calculate individual students' academic progress from year to year and to aggregate those increments in ways that shed light on the relative effectiveness of individual teachers (and schools). Today, perhaps the single biggest beef about NCLB is Washington's insistence that states use a fixed definition of "proficiency" and judge their schools by the fraction of students who reach that standard. Critics show how a suburban school may have plenty of kids scoring above the proficient level yet be teaching them little, while an inner-city school may add much academic value to its pupils yet not (so far) boost them over the proficiency bar. Moreover, if meeting a single standard is the only currency with value in the education kingdom, teachers may concentrate on youngsters slightly below that bar and neglect those who have already cleared it or are far from attaining it.[22] On the other hand, to focus solely on student gains and neglect absolute standards can lead to premature applause for those who have improved yet whose performance still leaves much to be desired.

Our daughter Arti, now in her mid-thirties, holds an MBA from a fine business school, is successfully working in retail marketing and business development, happily married, and the slightly harried mother of our spectacular granddaughter. Her act is nicely together.

But she didn't get there via test scores. She made it through pluck, hard work, good teaching and tutoring, a couple of lucky breaks, and the occasional parent intervention.

She was a diligent student but struggled for academic success in the early grades, though she attended one of Washington's most esteemed private schools. When a teacher suspected a mild learning disability, we had Arti tested, and the report came back that she had some difficulty putting a collection of pictures into the right sequence to tell a story. We didn't head down the special-ed path but got her some extra tutoring from the school itself, which seemed to help. Her grades were satisfactory, her teachers liked her, and she enjoyed school as much as any kid does.

Our move to Nashville came when she was eleven. We enrolled her (sixth grade) at the Harpeth Hall School for Girls, an old-line, private, single-sex "day school," complete with plaid skirts, school-prescribed blouses, and saddle shoes. My beautiful Punjabi daughter was one of just two kids in the entire school who weren't white Anglo-Saxons. (Half her classmates seemed to be named Tiffany or Ashley.)

Arti flourished there, with plenty of structured teaching from old-fashioned, serious-minded, and thoroughly competent teachers reminiscent of mine in Dayton three decades earlier. She had plenty of friends, too. (Making and keeping friends, then networking with their help, has always been one of her strengths.) We worried, though, that when high school began she might feel left out of the country-clubbish southern social scene, so we began to look into boarding schools. We tested the concept by sending her one year to a summer program at Connecticut's Choate-Rosemary Hall instead of back to camp. She loved it and did fine.

With prep-school applications, however, came the realization that Arti didn't knock the top off multiple-choice admission tests. Her scores were just okay. (This recurred when taking the SAT a few years later and the GMAT some years after that.)

In the summer of 1984, she and I toured a dozen New England boarding schools, and that fall she applied to four of them. One was Exeter, my (and my father's) alma mater, but I wasn't sure Arti could succeed there so made certain also to include some that were less demanding.

She labored over her essays, her Harpeth Hall teachers wrote good recommendations, and in time she was admitted to all four. We were pleasantly surprised, and Renu then joined Arti and me in revisiting the two top contenders. I felt really good about Loomis-Chafee, with whose excellent headmaster I was friendly and which seemed like the right sort of place for Arti.

The next day, however, we went to Exeter, and Renu promptly fell in love. After a walking tour of its impressive grounds and sitting in a couple of fast-paced classes, my-wife-the-doctor wistfully remarked that she wished she "could go to school again." Meanwhile, Arti overnighted in a dorm, and the next morning we had our solemn meeting with the admissions director. "Mr. Herney," asked our perpetually candid daughter, recently turned fifteen, "why did you admit me to this impossible school?" He cleared his throat for a few seconds before responding along the lines of—he was vastly more suave than this, of course—"We really value diversity here, we think you can do the work, and every class needs a bottom third."

Wrapped in our thoughts, the three of us silently drove the hour to Boston's Logan Airport and sat in a coffee shop to wait for our planes and deliberate about which school was right for Arti. Renu and I felt it was important that she make this decision—it had to be a place she felt good about going to—but much as we esteemed Exeter's education and reputation, we privately hoped she would opt for Loomis because we felt she had a better chance of succeeding there.

After what felt like a long while, Arti looked at us and said, "I want to go to Exeter." Tearing up, as I often do in emotional moments, I said, "Let's go call Grandpa" and escorted her to a pay phone so she could inform my elated father that a third generation of Finns was headed to Exeter.

Her first year there (tenth grade) was indeed rugged. She consumed much tutoring from faculty and peers. She leaned hard on her dorm adviser, history teacher Richard Schubart. She stayed up late and studied hard. If Exeter in 1985 were as unforgiving as it had been in 1960, I'm not sure she would have survived. But the help she needed was available, and she made the most of it. In time she graduated with high honors. Thence to Kenyon College, where "Schubes" had gone and, after a couple more large adventures, jobs, romances, and parental interventions, to business school at Kellogg and on to a promising career—not to mention a swell husband and the world's most perfect child.

Arti taught me plenty. She helped me realize that, while test scores are an efficient and reasonably accurate way to gauge the performance of schools, states, and groups of students, it's a mistake to read too much into the scores of any one individual—and certainly into any one test result. Some kids do fine on tests yet never amount to much. Others, like my daughter, rack up uninspiring scores but more than compensate via character and hard work. Sophisticated admissions offices know, but state accountability programs sometimes do not, that numbers tell just part of a person's story. When education reformers push "high-stakes" tests for individual kids—whether for high-school graduation, compulsory summer school, repeating grades, whatever—they need to move sensitively, giving students multiple chances to pass the test and, when warranted, other ways to demonstrate their academic prowess.

Accountability | The tripod's third leg is the accountability system itself: the incentives that a state or other authority creates for performance; the sanctions and interventions that it applies to nonperformance; and the student, teacher, school, and district practices that are meant to shift in response to this behaviorist approach to education change. Here, too, we face the problem of not having a true external judge or auditor. The system, in effect, chooses its own rewards and punishments.

Four concerns loom large.

| *First*: are the incentives and interventions credible—and powerful enough to trigger the desired changes? Can they be sustained politically? Even as some states hold fast to or toughen their graduation requirements, others ease their standards or defer the application of harsh consequences to kids (e.g., summer school, diploma denial) or to schools (e.g., curricular or staff changes). Here are three recent illustrations from the pages of *Education Week*:

> Faced with large percentages of failing students, the [Arizona] state board of education this month lowered the passing scores for the state's required graduation exams, which first affect the class of 2006. Students may now score as low as 59 percent in reading, down from 72 percent, and 60 percent on mathematics, down from 71 percent.
> —May 25, 2005[23]

> Utah students can receive a high school diploma even if they fail to pass all portions of the state's exit test, but those diplomas will specify that the students haven't passed the exam. That decision by the state board of education, made Jan. 12, comes as a growing number of states are grappling with whether to hold firm on high school graduation requirements even as many students fail to pass graduation exams.
> —January 25, 2006[24]

> The Missouri board of education approved new standards for its state tests last month that should result in more students scoring "proficient" and "advanced" at some grade levels this year. Committees of educators and citizens developed the unanimously approved guidelines. . . . The new standards are intended to ensure that at least 40 percent of students score at least at the proficient level.
> —February 1, 2006[25]

Lowering standards is so much easier than raising them. Though a few jurisdictions—notably Texas—embarked on this reform strategy by knowingly setting the bar low at first and then slowly lifting it, places that set fixed expectations have trouble boosting them later. Until mid-2006, for example, Massachusetts was widely expected to raise the passing level on its well-regarded MCAS tests. Then the state board of education backed off, saying it would be "unfair" to students to lift the bar for all and that the Commonwealth should instead devote itself to getting more young people over the present bar while creating different academic expectations for those who have cleared it.[26]

| *Second*: does the system fairly apportion responsibility—and mete out rewards and sanctions—among kids, adults, and institutions? States differ in their views of where accountability properly rests for academic performance. Half of them, for example, have some sort of statewide graduation test, but the rest do not—and most of the latter say they don't want one. Typically, schools are the accountability units—NCLB pushes in this direction—but individual teachers and principals are not much affected. It's reprehensible, however, to punish kids for what they fail to learn while exonerating those who fail to teach them. And it borders on the absurd to give the school a poor grade while maintaining unscathed the pay and tenure of its instructors and principal. But schools and kids don't belong to unions or employ lobbyists.

| *Third*: are those being held to account for results also being given a reasonable chance to attain them? This variant of the "opportunity to learn" debates of the early 1990s still resonates—and is turning up in courtrooms. If a youngster is denied a diploma because he fails the geometry portion of the statewide graduation test, for example, yet his school did not offer a proper geometry course (or he wasn't able to take it or its teacher didn't know much geometry), he likely has a cause of action. Certainly he has a grievance. Similarly, if a school is dinged because its students do poorly in science, yet it has no qualified science teacher or laboratory, it (and its parents and other teachers) may legitimately protest.

That was the reasoning followed by an Alameda County judge in mid-May 2006 when, with high-school graduation ceremonies looming, he nixed California's statewide exit exam. "There is evidence in the record," Judge Robert Freedman wrote, "that students in economically challenged communities have not had an equal opportunity to learn the materials." The state urgently appealed, and the Supreme Court agreed to stay his ruling, but the underlying legal issues are far from resolved, and the matter may drag on for years—ironic, especially since the present California graduation test, dealing only with basic competence in math and English, is almost laughably undemanding.[27]

| *Finally*: is the accountability system having perverse consequences along with whatever good ones it produces? Will test anxiety or fear of failure discourage or even drive out kids like Arti? With barely seven in ten young Americans graduating from high school at all—the rates among black and Hispanic students are just 52% and 56%—nobody wants to worsen the situation by pushing more kids to leave school in frustration over standards they doubt they'll ever reach.[28] Are skilled teachers exiting because of the added pressure? Are able leaders refusing to take principalships, especially in tough schools, for fear their schools will be fingered (or intervened in)? Are the best students and most-motivated families fleeing schools that may be harmed by their departure—or are weak students flooding into high-performing schools whose achievement level they may pull down? Does the cost of such unwanted effects outweigh the benefit of a standards-driven education system?

Taking Stock | Even as such quandaries beset standards-based reform, we are witnessing the growing pains of a very different education regime than I grew up with in the fifties and that still reigned in the schools of the seventies.

Almost every state has erected some sort of tripod, though many are rickety. Using a complex schema for appraising states' standards and accountability systems in 2006, *Education Week* assigned eleven A grades, twenty-three Bs, twelve Cs, four Ds, and one F (to Iowa).

Far less certain is whether the new regime will yield the gains in school effectiveness and student performance that America craves.

Surveying the results of standards-based reforms through 2005, *Education Week* editor Lynn Olson summed them up this way:

The conclusions are at once heartening and sobering. They're heartening because when looked at over this span from 1992 to 2005, student achievement has gotten better, particularly in mathematics and particularly for those students who started furthest behind. . . . At the same time, it would be hard to ignore the fact that progress has not come nearly far or fast enough. That's particularly true in reading, where average scores nationally have barely budged since 1992. It's also true that, despite the solid gains of poor, African-American, and Hispanic students during this period, the achievement gaps between those students and their more affluent and white peers remain disturbingly deep—at least 20 points in both grades and subjects, or the equivalent of two grade levels or more.[29]

In late 2006, Fordham's own analysis yielded gloomier conclusions. Far from finding "solid gains" among poor and minority youngsters, using NAEP's "proficient" level as the benchmark we spotted just eight states in which these kids had made even "moderate" progress over the past ten to fifteen years—and thirteen that showed no significant advances.[30]

Half a dozen other recent studies and data sources yield similar results. The National Center for Education Statistics reported that twelfth graders' reading performance in 2005 was worse than in 1992—and flat since 2002—even though high-school students are taking more difficult courses and getting better grades in them.[31] And in February 2007, the U.S. Chamber of Commerce concluded that, despite wide variation across the country,

> The academic performance of every state needs to improve. This is true for all demographic groups, but especially for poor and minority students. . . . To boost student achievement and thus help individual Americans achieve economic success and mobility in the 21st century workforce, we need to fundamentally rethink how we provide education in this country. That will require nothing less than restructuring the bureaucratic apparatus of American education.[32]

Not, overall, a very cheery picture, either of American academic performance or of the efficacy of innumerable reform efforts. "Despite concerted efforts by educators," *New York Times* reporter Sam Dillon summarized in November 2006, "the test-score gaps are so large that, on average, African-American and Hispanic students in high school can read and do arithmetic at only the average level of whites in junior high school. 'The gaps between

African-Americans and whites are showing very few signs of closing,' said assessment expert Michael T. Nettles." [33]

The thin silver lining in this cloud is that most of the states in which black and Hispanic youngsters *have* made significant gains (e.g., Florida, Delaware, Massachusetts, Texas) were early tripod builders. Fordham's analysts generally agreed with *Education Week* researchers who found "evidence of a consistently positive relationship between achievement gains and the implementation of standards-based policies related to academic-content standards, aligned assessments, and accountability measures. These associations are more robust for achievement in mathematics, compared to reading." [34]

The new regime is hard to sustain, however. For every example of stronger performance, we can cite an instance of backsliding or finagling. For the most part, educators still resist the behaviorism of standards-based reform and resent the heavy hands and instrumental values of the laymen who have imposed this strategy, as well as the embarrassing results that it often brings to light.

The political system is creaking, too. California won't be the only state whose graduation test is litigated. During the 2006 election campaign, gubernatorial candidates in bellwether states like Texas, Florida, Ohio, and Massachusetts sought to exploit public discontent with the test-based accountability regimen to advance their own political prospects. (Two of them won.)

Complex issues of federalism also arise as Washington interferes with state education decision-making and states tread on time-honored values of "local control." But that's not all. When standards and accountability are imposed upon an enterprise that never before had them, especially so universal an enterprise as public schooling, many people and institutions are discomfited. (Picture the sudden arrival of driver testing in a place that previously handed a license to anyone of suitable age who requested one.) In a democracy, that means elected officials will feel the heat of aggrieved constituents for whom the immediate pain is more palpable than the promised long-term benefit.

Thus far, despite all the discomfort and uncertainties, the flawed standards and poorly aligned tests, the paucity of conclusive proof, and the occasional misfires, wimp-outs, and retrenchments, this new regime persists. But I worry about its longevity as well as its success. Parents are growing skittish, the more so when it touches their own schools and children. Few educators love it. And while business leaders appear steadfast, more politicians are seeing electoral hay to be made from weakening it.

Much attention will focus on NCLB reauthorization dynamics as Congress faces the immense, possibly unmanageable, burden of resolving dozens of issues—most of which have good arguments and determined interest groups on at least two sides. The post-2006 divided government in Washington could yet generate another wave of bipartisanship in education policy, but it is as likely to lead to deadlock. That could cripple federal efforts to ramp up standards-based reform while also sending tremors through state-level accountability systems.

25 | *The Burden of Choice*

Easily 30% of U.S. children do *not* attend the district-operated public school in their neighborhood. Instead, they and their parents exercise their right to attend schools of their choice, public, private, and in between. As the Supreme Court held in 1925, "The fundamental theory of liberty upon which all governments in this Union repose excludes any general power of the State to standardize its children by forcing them to accept instruction from public teachers only. The child is not the mere creature of the State." [35]

Tax dollars increasingly pay for the exercise of these rights as the United States gradually embraces a radically different principle than underlay the schools of my childhood: government's obligation is to ensure that all youngsters get an education, not simply to operate a network of public schools and assign kids to them. Choice is close to being taken for granted in today's America—a massive conceptual shift—and most of today's fights are over which varieties of schooling qualify for public funding, the terms on which that funding is provided, and the constraints and conditions that accompany it.

In fact, the fraction of American children exercising some form of school choice exceeds 30 percent, for it properly includes millions more—24 percent of all K–12 families according to a recent federal survey—who attend a neighborhood school but whose parents moved into that neighborhood *because* of its schools. In other words, they chose the school first, the neighborhood second—and had the means to effect that choice. [36]

Yet the demand for school options continues to exceed the accessible supply, at least for families with limited means. That explains one of the most appalling practices in U.S. public education (in some of the many states and communities that lack open-enrollment policies): good school systems hiring guards and security firms to *prevent* families who live across the district line—usually poor families seeking respite from hopeless urban schools—from surreptitiously enrolling their kids. In 2006, KidsOhio reported that 21 percent of parents with children in the Columbus public schools would swiftly leave for other schools "if they get the chance" (and another 37 percent were receptive to doing so in the future). In mid-2007, a statewide survey indicated that just 41 percent of Ohio parents would prefer that their children attend district-operated public schools "if money were not an issue," compared with half who would opt for private schools (predominantly religious schools) and 5 percent who would choose charters.[37]

School choice now describes a spectrum of education offerings and arrangements, from plain-vanilla district and private schools to the exotic tang of home schooling. In between, we find at least ten flavors:

1 | *Magnet Schools.* Usually district based—Houston alone has more than a hundred—these are purpose-created specialty schools with distinctive themes: music and art, science and technology, Hispanic cultures, and sometimes the additional goal of racial integration. Some such schools are regional or statewide, often for gifted youngsters at the secondary level, such as northern Virginia's Thomas Jefferson High School for Science and Technology, serving students from a cluster of Washington suburbs, the Illinois Mathematics and Science Academy, and the North Carolina School of Science and Mathematics. (The latter two are residential.)

2 | *Alternative Schools.* Developed primarily for hard-to-handle youngsters and dropouts, these are not so much programs that parents select as schools that the district offers to young people who cause problems in regular classrooms.

3 | *Intradistrict Public School Choice.* A growing number of systems now permit families to select their schools within the district. Sometimes the options are circumscribed by court orders and desegregation formulas, as well as by capacity issues, complex rules for matching children with schools, and scant diversity in district offerings.

4 | *Interdistrict Choice.* More than twenty states have followed Minnesota's lead and passed open-enrollment or interdistrict transfer laws. The most generous of these permit kids, in effect, to enroll anywhere in the state. Some are limited to contiguous districts. Other transfers require the assent of the "sending" and/or "receiving" district. Often the right to move is constrained by the number of vacant classroom seats. Still, such policies can make a big difference. Some Michigan districts have lost a quarter of their students to interdistrict transfers (and charter schools). Which helps to explain the posting of guards at district borders to interdict youngsters whose transfer rights are not vouchsafed by state law.

5 | *Charter Schools.* As we have seen, these range from back-to-basics to Montessori methods to schools for disabled kids, with numerous variants along the way.[38] Today's four thousand charters are public schools with certain features of private schools—and they're all schools of choice, run by an impressive cast of civic, education, parent, and business groups, even by a teachers' union. (Attempting to revive, at least symbolically, Shanker's original vision of charters as teacher-created schools, New York's United Federation of Teachers has made much of the two charters it opened in Brooklyn in 2005 and 2006—even as it struggled in Albany to retain a tight cap on the number of such schools allowed statewide.)[39]

6 | *Schools within Schools.* A brick-and-mortar edifice can house more than one education program. This insight inspired the pioneering public-school-choice program in East Harlem's District 4 but is also suited to rural areas with few school buildings.

7 | *Minischools.* Encouraged by philanthropists, notably the megabucks Bill and Melinda Gates Foundation, intentionally small schools—usually high schools—are springing up, many cast in the "early college" mold that also seeks to palliate student ennui at the end of high school by providing college courses to those ready to attempt them. America now boasts some one thousand Gates-funded small schools (typically fewer than five hundred students).

8 | *Tech-Prep Schools.* Community colleges in many cities have joined with high schools to blend the last two years of K–12 education with the first two years of college, often leading to an associate's degree plus a high-school diploma. This arrangement is especially well suited to young people keener on jobs than on academic studies.

9 | *Virtual Schooling.* Need students come to school at all if it can come to them? Via Internet and e-mail, they can interact with teachers (and with lesson plans, homework assignments, etc.) without leaving home. In the old days, families living deep in the mountains or serving overseas could obtain mail-order curricula for their children from Baltimore's Calvert School and other suppliers. Today, technology makes possible innumerable "distance learning" options 24/7, often with online access to teachers. In late 2005, the North American Council for Online Learning listed 157

online learning programs in forty-two states. Thirty-two of these programs were "virtual charter schools." Some of the latter (the Pennsylvania Virtual Academy, for example) are statewide programs enrolling upward of five thousand students each. (We return to technology-driven education reforms in the next chapter.)

10 | *Hybrids.* Several states require public schools to allow homeschooled (and private-schooled) children to participate in any part of the program, from physics class to the soccer team. Some kids both attend school—perhaps a charter school—and study at home part-time. Some schools blend online learning with traditional classroom instruction. Several charter schools now specialize in this kind of arrangement, making it easier to obtain the best of both worlds.

Colorado's Hope OnLine Academy illustrates another hybrid model, legally a charter school but operating neither as conventional school nor as an online program accessed from home. It's more like a skein of learning centers—thirty-eight of them in May 2006—under various auspices where youngsters come by day to get an education.[40] Though this particular network of quasi schools has run into problems (some of its own making), the model itself holds considerable promise for tomorrow.

Tomorrow will bring still more options, such as the specialized "STEM" (science, technology, engineering, mathematics) high schools already under way in Texas and under eager consideration in other states as a "competitiveness" response to other countries' production of tech-savvy high-school and college graduates.

Something Old, Something New | What's striking about today's "schools of choice" in their many forms is how many are *new*, designed to carry out a distinctive mission or occupy a specialized niche.

Twenty years ago, America had practically no new schools save for replicas of old schools built to handle surging enrollments in Sunbelt communities and metropolitan exurbs. Schools were permanent institutions of brick and mortar. They didn't start from scratch and almost never closed.

That static picture faded as we realized that those immortal old schools often taught their students little and failed to keep pace with technological innovation, organizational breakthroughs, and fast-changing delivery systems.

Yet it's painful to make over existing schools—which is why NCLB-inspired efforts to "reconstitute" them so often take the form of mild interventions with limited payoff, why Sizer's Coalition of Essential Schools grew at a snail's pace, and why so many adopters of Hirsch's estimable "core knowledge" curriculum turn out to be pale shadows of the real thing. Established schools are set in their ways, beset by inertia, tenure, regulation, and politics, imbued with certain expectations and norms, and resistant to outside efforts to nudge them into doing things differently. Sure, new programs may be grafted on, sometimes so many that schools find themselves tugged apart by competing loyalties and "categorical" funding streams. More often, though, the core of the school proves nearly immune to change, and the new programs last only so long as their outside funders are willing to write checks.

If changing an old school is as arduous (Admiral Hyman Rickover once remarked) as moving a graveyard, yet the nation is at risk because of the weak performance of thousands of such schools, perhaps creating new ones holds greater promise. That doesn't necessarily mean lots of new buildings. Thanks to technology, the school-as-education-program can now be distinguished from school-as-physical-structure.

As for those buildings under whose roofs most youngsters still spend 180 or so days a year, we are beginning to view them more like temporary domiciles for education programs. New schools can inhabit old buildings (as well as storefronts, church basements, and warehouses). Multiple schools can cohabit. And, far from being permanent institutions, under a serious regimen of standards-based accountability they would continue only so long as they deliver the goods. If not, they might be closed by their sponsors or lose their clientele. They might, like a host of Philadelphia schools, be "outsourced" to private operators. Or they might, under state accountability plans or NCLB, be "reconstituted": their principal, teaching team, and curriculum replaced by different and (one hopes) more effective alternatives.

Nobody says a new or reconstituted school is inherently a good one, any more than an old one is automatically a failure. There are plenty of false starts and failed ventures. There are hucksters as well as earnest, decent people gripped by eccentric, unworkable instructional notions. There are start-ups that die and expansion efforts that falter. As the New American Schools and Edison ventures showed, there are ambitious plans to do things differently that turn out not to be all that different.

Early zealots of the charter-school movement, myself included, were naïve. We tended to assume that starting anew and putting a "charter" sign over the door signaled a different and perforce superior school. We were keener on the diversity, choice, and competition elements of the charter enterprise than on its academic achievement. Hence we paid too little attention to whether those vying to launch charter schools were up to the challenge, whether those authorizing them were performing due diligence and oversight, whether curricular and instructional plans were sound and accountability instruments adequate.

Then came results-based reform in the states and the added traction of NCLB nationally, together with clarity that (fairly or not) charters will be judged by the same metrics as district-operated schools. Academic achievement is indisputably the currency of the K–12 realm today, and by that measure some operators and authorizers of new schools are as impoverished as the worst of the old.

As with standards-based reform, "mixed" best describes the available evidence on pupil achievement in new schools and choice schemes. Early evaluations of the Gates Foundation's "small high schools" initiative, for example, showed so-so results.[41] And careful analyses of charter schools' overall academic results yield a similar verdict, albeit limited by a dearth of reliable, comparable data.[42]

No, new schools aren't easy to get right. Yet the opportunity to create them is drawing terrific folks into education; keeping some who would otherwise throw up their hands and head for the exit; and liberating others to range wider and do more than the old system allows. It's bringing in money as well, from both federal and state coffers and from entrepreneurs, venture capitalists, and major-league philanthropists such as the Walton Family Foundation (Wal-Mart), the Gates Foundation (Microsoft), the Don & Doris Fisher Foundation (The Gap), and the Lynde & Harry Bradley Foundation.

Some funders have grown wary of isolated "mom and pop" school start-ups but bullish about another new set of organizations on the K–12 landscape known as education management organizations (EMOs) and charter management organizations (CMOs). The former (examples include Edison and National Heritage Academies) seek to make a profit, while the latter (e.g., Green Dot, Aspire, and Big Picture) operate in the nonprofit sphere. Yet another genre, illustrated by the celebrated Knowledge Is Power Program (KIPP), does not directly manage the schools in its portfolio but helps them start, trains their leaders, troubleshoots them, and sets performance standards that they must meet in order to continue waving this coveted banner.

These entities represent one more evolution in the genome of American K–12 education. Part entrepreneurial private organization and part virtual school system, they are ways of creating and replicating schools according to specific models, supplying them with financial and human capital, providing them with needed business and curricular services, and branding them with names that are starting to win national recognition. Whereas Americans once thought of school systems as local and bureaucratic—the "Dayton Public Schools"—these new systems are far-flung. A child whose family moves from Baltimore to Denver may be able to transition smoothly from one Edison (or National Heritage, Achievement First, or Big Picture) school straight into another. The numbers of such schools are not yet huge—in 2006, some fifty EMOs ran 521 schools, most of them charters, enrolling 237,000 youngsters in twenty-eight states—but will surely grow.[43] The KIPP organization recently unveiled plans (and private funding) to grow its flagship Houston operation to forty-two schools—effectively creating an alternative public-school system for disadvantaged kids in the country's fourth-biggest city. Slowly, the U.S. education industry, like our hospitality and retailing industries, is developing recognizable brands that will spread across the nation and perhaps in time the world, not unlike Holiday Inn, Macy's, and CNN.

Meanwhile, in a pattern reminiscent of the 1970s, long-established parochial schools are shutting their doors in many cities, diminishing the supply of high-quality education options for needy kids. Some 127 Catholic schools closed in New York City alone over the past decade. The causes are multiple: the Church's fiscal woes (aggravated by the high price of settling its recent sex-abuse cases); the surging costs of operating such schools (in which essentially every teacher is now salaried); the continuing flight of tuition-capable Catholic families to the suburbs and beyond; the parochial schools' (and their parishes') unfamiliarity with marketing, planning, budgeting, and modern management; new competition from charter schools and other forms of government-assisted school choice; as well as the political and constitutional rigors of securing financial aid for low-income kids to access parochial-school classrooms.

Vouchers remain the bloodiest battleground in the school-choice wars, yet even here supporters have made slow headway. The Supreme Court opened a constitutional pathway in 2002. Two years later, Congress put the finishing touches on a Bush-backed voucher program for the District of Columbia (combined with new federal assistance for district and charter schools). The next year, 2005, brought both a lifting of the cap on Milwaukee's program and the expansion of Cleveland's to all of Ohio, and 2007 saw Utah legislators enact a "universal" voucher program. But there have been setbacks, too. The few decent studies to date indicate that some children—black youngsters in particular—benefit from the chance to attend private schools, but others don't. No ballot initiative on behalf of vouchers has won in any state; litigation is widespread; and courts in Colorado and Florida have invalidated those states' programs. Moreover, strictly worded "Blaine amendments" place voucher-style programs out of constitutional bounds in many states.

| Welcome to the Academy of the Pacific Rim, a freestanding charter school operating in an old factory building in Boston's Hyde Park neighborhood. Begun in 1995 by my young friend and protégé, entrepreneur Stacey M. Boyd, fresh from Harvard's business and public policy schools and an Edison Project alumna, and by some Bostonians of Asian origin who wondered why their children could not attend schools as powerful as those in their homelands, "Pac-Rim" now enrolls 350 youngsters in grades six through twelve. Its students are overwhelmingly minority and poor. It has high standards, long days and years, weekly feedback to parents, tons of tutoring and summer instruction, and gobs of parent involvement, as well as a challenging curriculum that features algebra in eighth grade and Mandarin for all. Its test scores are among the highest in town. A glowing profile of the school in *The New Yorker in* October 2004 had this to say:

Every student in the school's inaugural graduating class, of 2003, had passed the state math and literacy competency tests on the first try. (At the city's public schools, only the famed "exam" schools, like Boston Latin, matched this feat.) The entire class of

2003 now attends a four-year college. . . . By September of 2003, there were three hundred and thirty students; the new batch of sixth graders had been selected by lottery from a list of applicants four times that large. The faculty absorbed this growth with both pride and fear. School achievement is the key to ending racial inequality, they'd tell college friends who were now writing legal briefs or bundling bonds. It's the civil-rights issue of our time. Among themselves, they indulged in self doubt. While many Americans and the politicians who serve them concentrate on what inner-city kids shouldn't do— have babies, drop out, collect welfare, sell drugs—Pacific Rim emphasizes accomplishment, and not just in the form of a post-high-school job or a military enlistment. The school wanted to see every single student enter college, America's escalator to the middle and upper classes.[44]

| Welcome to The Accelerated School in South Central Los Angeles, a charter school founded in 1994 by two young and idealistic teachers named Johnathan Williams and Kevin Sved. The first year it enrolled 50 youngsters in the primary grades. Today, it's evolving into a "school multiplex" to serve 2,000-plus kids from prekindergarten through high school. At last report, its waiting list numbered 4,500 children. Named "elementary school of the year" by *Time* magazine in 2001, it loosely follows an education model developed by economist Henry Levin that treats all students as "gifted" and seeks to accelerate, rather than remediate, their learning. With 100% minority and virtually all low-income pupils, the school's ratings on California's Academic Performance Index are consistently strong. Delivering his first State of the City address from the school's campus in April 2006—and pleading for more control of Los Angeles's sprawling school system—Mayor Antonio Villaraigosa declared it a place that "demonstrates what you can achieve when you accelerate your ambitions."[45]

| Welcome to Any Old Charter School. I've been involved, via the Fordham Foundation, with far too many lackluster charter schools, mostly in southwestern Ohio. You walk in the door and nearly always find good will and child-centeredness, but it's as if the heart

were not connected to a brain or to much muscle. Many parents like these schools because they're welcoming, safe, convenient, often small, and staffed by caring adults. So the "marketplace" signals that all is well—and one must respect school attributes that parents value. Yet too many such schools lack coherent curricula, effective pedagogy, grade-specific standards, close attention to data, and a serious results orientation. Sometimes they're better at marketing themselves to inexperienced—maybe desperate—parents than at educating their children. They're usually on the state's watch list and rarely make "adequate yearly progress" under NCLB. Financially, they operate on the thin edge—and those run by EMOs are sometimes squeezed to generate profits. Their teaching staffs are inexperienced, ill paid, and subject to lots of turnover. Their compliant if well-meaning boards generally do whatever the school director wants. And their authorizers pay scant attention to academic results and provide little help or external discipline. This is by no means the norm—Ohio, too, has outstanding charter schools—but it's way too common.

Some charter schools are stunningly effective educational institutions that prove what can be done in tough settings with challenging kids. (KIPP's motto, borrowed from Kant, is "The actual proves the possible.") They are places that reshape the life prospects of poor youngsters. What that usually requires is extraordinary leadership, fantastic teacher commitment, and tons more time, enough to overpower the dysfunctional culture of the streets—and disprove the determinists of left and right who insist that this cannot be done.[46] Watching the first "graduating class" of eighth graders from the KIPP DC Academy walk across the stage of the ornate U.S. Chamber of Commerce building in early summer 2005—headed to high school at places like Andover and St. Albans—reaffirmed my faith in education reform. Schools like this would be far less able to succeed if forced to work "inside the system"—or if students were assigned to them. Choice is crucial to their success, as is the freedom to function as they think best. Yet neither choice nor freedom guarantees quality. Any Old Charter School has those elements, too, but scant learning occurs in its classrooms. How much simpler education reform would be if changing the ground rules were enough. Changing them does create new and perhaps more favorable *opportunities* for schools to succeed. But that's about all. The resulting schools may be innovative or not, effective or not.

Choice enthusiasts sometimes become so enamored of the market's invisible hand—or so keen to explain why families line up to enroll in the schools they run, despite sagging test scores and weak curricula—that they brush off accountability systems that also demand academic results. Some are sublimely confident that if the statutory structures and policies can be set right, quality will inexorably follow.

That's false. They and other "structural" reformers err when they disregard what goes on *inside* classrooms. Particularly in the NCLB era, academic results count. Which means the quality of curriculum, pedagogy, and teachers cannot be ignored.

Parents aren't always discerning about this. In schools of choice, as well as district-run neighborhood schools, they're apt to be content with *their* child's school even when critical of others. This is partly for emotional reasons—nobody wants to think they've done badly by their own kids— and partly because they seldom have access to clear information about how their school is doing compared with other schools and in relation to objective standards. And sometimes they just kid themselves. Surveys show that 60–70 percent of parents of U.S. high-school students believe—despite ample evidence to the contrary—that their daughters and sons will emerge with the skills to succeed in college and the workforce. Moreover, families keenest to move their child to a different school—typically low-income city dwellers—are often consumed by such urgent considerations as safety that it's almost unfair to expect them to weigh long-term abstractions like academic achievement. Parents and students alike voice greater concern about violence in school than about low standards. Choice critics are apt to conclude that "families don't pick schools for the right reasons." Not so.[47] But market forces alone will not speedily lead to stronger academic achievement.

The other big fly in the choice ointment is political compromise, leading to too few options, too many constraints, and too little money for a proper test of the market's capacity to boost both quality and efficiency. Most state charter laws are so confining—and the funding for these schools, typically about 70 percent of the per pupil sums going to local district schools, is so meager—that one can fairly argue that chartering hasn't yet had such a test.[48] Why? Because while breaking up monopolistic schoolsystems and creating options for kids may be a good and necessary thing to do, the erstwhile monopoly does its utmost via political means, courtroom grandstanding, harassment, constitutional challenge, electioneering, and dirty tricks to minimize and cripple the upstart competitors. Indeed, Frederick M. Hess's careful case studies of the effects of (smallish) voucher programs in three cities during the 1990s indicate that, to the dismay of school-choice advocates and market theorists who hope that competition will cause traditional school systems to improve, the monopoly's actual response is akin to that of Richard II, redoubling its efforts to strangle these new rivals while they're small.[49]

After all these years, the hypocrisy and convoluted politics in much of this still amazes me. Many tireless foes of expanding school options for poor kids are upper-middle-class professionals who take for granted that their own daughters and sons will enroll in private or carefully selected public schools. Others are Democrats whose inner-city constituents stand to benefit the most from additional choices. Equally remarkable, though, are Republican politicians who support choice measures so long as they're *confined* to poor kids and thus pose no threat to their upscale suburban constituents or the high-status schools their children attend.

Perhaps we shouldn't be surprised that the ensuing compromises often yield Potemkin reforms, surface changes unaccompanied by the more wrenching structural, fiscal, and social shifts without which these reforms can seldom flourish.

26 | *Technology and Governance*

For years I scoffed at technology's potential to transform education. I recalled the late Ralph Tyler, one of the twentieth century's grandees of education psychology, then in his eighties, remarking that he had witnessed at least ten technological innovations touted as education breakthroughs but that the only one with staying power was the overhead projector, "because it doesn't require any special skill to operate and the teacher doesn't have to turn her back on her students to use it."

Since then, lots of computers and software have been installed in lots of schools. Billions of dollars have changed hands. Most schools now intersect with the "information highway." Yet in most essentials, the typical American school of 2007 still resembles the schools of Dayton in the 1950s. Technology remains an add-on, another handy supplement like the overhead projector. That's probably why scant attention was paid in the early nineties to Lewis Perelman's visionary book, *School's Out*.[50] Well before the Internet conquered the planet, he foresaw the replacement of traditional schools by "a universe of new technologies" that at remarkably low cost (and delivered mostly via private enterprise) would equip people for success in the economy of the twenty-first century.

I didn't pay much heed, either. I was trying to reform real schools, and such woolly futurism struck me both as politically irrelevant to the task at hand and as a high-tech cousin of the "de-schooling" arguments that I hadn't liked in the sixties.

Today I see that Perelman was onto something: the combination of computer technology, the Internet, and wireless communications has the power to revolutionize primary-secondary education in five essentials:

■ It severs the link between education and schooling and makes it possible to be taught and to learn almost anything at any time or place. That doesn't mean little kids no longer need grown-ups to help, coax, and supervise. But the adults in the room might be family members, tutors, day-care workers, teacher aides, or camp counselors. The main instructor might be across the state or globe. And the lesson is as easily "delivered" at ten p.m. on Sunday as at noon on Tuesday.

■   It multiplies one's options. One can change schools—or curricula, lesson plans, or teachers—not just by moving from one building to another but also by flipping channels, entering a different URL, or inserting a new DVD. Instead of selecting one's education provider from physical places within reasonable travel time, one may choose from a near-infinite array of options.

■   It enables parents and students to circumvent and augment formal schooling. They can buy, rent, borrow, or download instructional options that enrich (or contradict) what the classroom provides. This is a way to bootleg music instruction, religion, and foreign languages into a child's education. To engage tutors thousands of miles away to help prep for an exam or review something that the teacher glossed over. What's more, learning can continue in the summer, at one's workplace, whenever. "Lifelong learning" has long been a dream of starry-eyed educationists, but technology makes it real. (At sixty-three, I'm learning much history while composing this book by "surfing" for information that was neither in my head nor on my bookshelf.)

■   It empowers teachers, liberating them from the textbook and their own training to acquire material and ideas and develop lessons on their own, to "chat" with others about proven ways to present concepts, eras, places, or literary works, to exchange and refine lesson plans with the help of their peers, to turn their pupils into active researchers, to receive, comment upon, and return students' written work, to communicate with parents, and to track which kids met what standards this week.

■   It also empowers principals. Whether one is monitoring the school's yearly progress for federal overseers, evaluating teacher effectiveness, managing the school budget, providing bulletins to parents and superintendent, keeping up on the latest education news, recording attendance, adjusting the schedule, or communicating swiftly with faculty and board members, technology saves time and extends one's reach.

The kids are different, too. Fast-changing images on the screen, addictive computer games, compulsive instant-messaging, and impatient Web surfing are not altogether good for them. The American Academy of Pediatrics recommends *no* television before age two because of evidence that it interferes with the early development of the brain and nervous system. Today's epidemic of "attention deficit disorder" in kids likely results from neuro-wiring better adapted to following actions on a screen than words on a page. (That's why Emma Finn at three has seen almost no TV.)

Yet today's kids *are* accustomed to learning things via computer and television, and every grown-up knows how agile they are with such gadgets. They're used to near-constant visual and aural stimulation. They are "in touch" 24/7 with their friends, with entertainment, with the world. This inevitably affects how they approach formal education and must influence how that education approaches them if we want it to register.

Schools, however, are slow to change, and educators and their organizations may get palpitations from technology and its staffing implications. Many states and districts have found overwhelming challenge in simply computerizing their pupil databases. Besides the usual technical glitches and the nervousness that adults often feel in a high-tech environment, instruction via computer also has downsides. It simplifies cheating and plagiarism. (Disreputable Internet firms not only edit one's research paper but will sell you a complete draft. Others sell college degrees on the basis of one's "life experience" plus a credit card number.) It raises questions about children's physical fitness and interpersonal skills, if much of their "school" experience is alone with a screen and keyboard. And its extensive use in K–12 education portends big personnel changes. America's long-running love affair with smaller classes, for example, which has employed many thousands more teachers, could easily reverse if "virtual schooling" really takes off. The fact that a single virtual charter school may enroll thousands of kids across an entire state or nation heralds a sea change in how schools are organized, staffed, financed, governed, and led.

The policy dilemmas that accompany such changes are legion. For example, at what level (if any) should the taxpayer spring for what looks from afar like "home schooling" but from the consumer's standpoint is simply another education option? What happens to locally generated education tax dollars when a kid enrolls in a statewide (or international) virtual school?

Yet technology strengthens both choice-based and standards-based reform in myriad ways. In most states, Web-based school-level report cards are now available (though not always user-friendly) by which a school's performance can be monitored and compared by parents and public officials—and by realtors, journalists, pressure groups, and aspiring politicians.[51]

National outfits such as Just for the Kids and SchoolMatters.com provide careful analyses and comparisons at the school, district, and state level.[52] Others, such as GreatSchools.net, supply information designed specially for parents.[53] And any number of private firms offer programs and software to schools and districts keen to use data to drive instruction, boost performance, and simplify administration.[54]

We oughtn't to be gaga about technology. The Internet brings no quality assurances. It invites scams and shysters. But we shouldn't be Luddites, either. Just as travel, banking, communications, and entertainment are being radically transformed before our eyes, this will surely happen to schooling as well.

From eight years beginning in 1999, I served as a director and education-advisory committee chairman of K12, a for-profit "virtual school" firm started by Bill Bennett, Lowell Milken, and Ron Packard. Loosely based on Bennett's, Cribb's, and my book, *The Educated Child*, and on Hirsch's Core Knowledge curriculum, K12 today supplies a high-quality education program from kindergarten through high school, now educating more than twenty-seven thousand kids in a dozen states, mostly in virtual charter schools.[55] The firm's Web-based lessons in core subjects are generally first-rate, supplemented both by live teachers (usually reached via phone or e-mail) and by cartons of instructional materials that arrive on students' doorsteps. K12's test scores are respectable. Far from enrolling only home schoolers, its program turns out to meet a spectrum of human needs, including those of medically fragile youngsters, transients, and rural families whose school choices are otherwise scant. Lately, K12 has branched out to provide high-tech curricula (primarily in science, where expert teachers are scarce) for brick-and-mortar schools. And it's becoming profitable.

Getting there, however, has meant untold compromises, political scuffles, and lawyering. Myriad public-education interests are threatened, and they wield much power as rule makers, political heavyweights, and potential customers. For me, the most painful moment came when a pair of urban school systems told K12 they wouldn't do business with it if Bennett remained board chairman. Outspoken as ever, he had made an ill-considered remark on his radio show that angered some black activists with enough influence upon their school systems to force his exit. I wished the company had told those prospective customers to shove it. But the private sector is political, too.

Structure and Governance | Intriguing innovations can also be glimpsed in the governance of American public schooling. They're scattered and patchy, and we cannot yet know how they will turn out, but they signal newfound openness in some communities to experimenting with unconventional arrangements, all worth trying and some, to my eye, holding fair promise.

Three kinds of changes are particularly notable: the intervention of mayors, the hiring of noneducators in leadership roles, and fresh efforts to decentralize and diversify control to the school level.

What governors were to education reform in the late twentieth century, mayors may turn out to be in the early twenty-first, at least in urban America. Boston's Thomas Menino, New York's Michael Bloomberg, and Chicago's Richard Daley exemplify the strong-willed municipal executives who determined that they should run—and be responsible for—their cities' school systems rather than preserving yesterday's parallel governance system of board and superintendent. In Cleveland, the mayor appoints the school board from a slate generated by a nominating panel. Philadelphia's five-member "school reform commission" is named partly by the mayor and partly by Pennsylvania's governor. In 2006, after a huge brouhaha, Los Angeles mayor Antonio Villaraigosa won partial control of the country's second-largest school system—only to lose it months later when the state supreme court declared the arrangement unconstitutional. The District of Columbia's dynamic young mayor Adrian Fenty has wrested substantial authority over the woeful public schools of the nation's capital and Newark's Cory Booker is bent on taking charge of his city's bleak K–12 education system as well. In several settings—Oakland, Indianapolis, Milwaukee—where mayors have not been able to gain much traction on the traditional system itself, they have energetically promoted charter schools and via that mechanism have created a sort of alternative education system.

Such arrangements are not necessarily stable. Detroit, for example, had a mostly state-appointed school board from 1999 to 2006, but Motor City voters rejected proposals to convert that to mayoral control and opted instead to return to a conventional elected board. This has, however, proven immensely exasperating to Mayor Kwame Kilpatrick, now an ardent booster of charter schools as a source of decent educational alternatives for youngsters currently stuck in Detroit's crumbling district system.

The chief rationale for mayoral engagement in urban schools is that the traditional governance scheme is broken in many places besides Detroit. Though the late-nineteenth-century civic reformers who devised it hoped to keep politicians' grubby fingers off the pristine body of public education, and though that theory may still apply in parts of suburban and rural America, in many big cities it has become a joke. Their schools are faltering. Their kids aren't learning. The superintendent's office is entered and swiftly exited via a revolving door. Far from attracting the community's wisest and most selfless leaders, the school board is itself a warring mix of interest group agents (the teachers' union above all), aspiring politicians for whom it's a stepping stone to the legislature or other office, and individuals seeking to impose idiosyncratic ideas or redress personal grievances by gaining leverage on the public schools.

Faced with such challenges, and sometimes also with nepotism and fiscal shenanigans, some states moved to seize control of vexed urban school systems, and some mayors sought to take them over. (The Illinois legislature handed control of Chicago's schools to Mayor Daley almost as a dare.) If my city is blighted by dreadful public schools, these mayors reason, if employers shun us because they cannot hire the talent they need and middle-class families are fleeing to the suburbs, I must find a way to solve this problem or my other efforts to brighten the city's future will come to naught.

When mayors gain control, and sometimes when they don't, urban school systems have been experimenting with "nontraditional" executives. New York schools chancellor Joel Klein is an attorney and former Justice Department trustbuster. Los Angeles's Roy Romer was governor of Colorado. (His successor in the City of Angels was a navy admiral.) Mayor Fenty's choice for education chancellor in the District of Columbia, the young and hard-charging Michelle A. Rhee, had led a national teacher recruitment-and-placement project. Chicago's Arne Duncan was a professional basketball player and head of a small nonprofit group. Paul Vallas, the new head of New Orleans's schools after high-profile, take-few-prisoners superintendencies in both Chicago and Philadelphia, was once the Windy City's budget director. Former Jacksonville superintendent John Fryer had been an air force general. Former San Diego superintendent Alan Bersin (who went on to serve as California's secretary of education) is an attorney who coordinated federal law enforcement along the Mexican border. Denver superintendent Michael Bennet, also an attorney, had an earlier career in business and government, including a stint as the mayor's chief of staff.

The hypothesis here is that leading a complex modern school system is dauntingly difficult and that, to have a fighting chance of success, it's more important to be a great executive and astute political operator than a veteran educator.[56] This makes better sense in theory, however, than sometimes works out in practice. Such superintendents (or chancellors, CEO's, whatever the title may be) usually hasten to hire a veteran educator as their top deputy, and sometimes they make dubious choices. (This happened to both Klein and Bersin.) Sometimes they knuckle under to community pressures akin to those that press upon conventional school leaders, believing they must yield on some fronts in order to press ahead on others. (While in Philadelphia, Vallas agreed to mandate the study of African history by every high-school student in the city, black, white, or brown.) Sometimes they're defeated by dysfunctional systems and nonstop politics. Retired army general Julius W. Becton, for instance, was overwhelmed by the rival power centers and inept bureaucracy of the District of Columbia public schools and resigned in April 1998 after eighteen months at that system's helm. Despite a background in business himself, Seattle's Joseph Olchefske was undone by a whopping "surprise" deficit in 2002, three years after he succeeded highly popular ex–army general John Stanford (who died) as head of that city's schools.

A few school systems have experimented with even more esoteric leadership arrangements. In 2003, faced with fiscal crisis as well as low-performing schools, St. Louis engaged a private management firm to run its system. (Minneapolis and Hartford had made similar arrangements in the mid-1990s.) Louisiana and New Orleans officials have commenced a radical makeover of public education in the Big Easy, including charter status for nearly all schools, a huge transformation made possible in the aftermath of the devastation wrought by Hurricane Katrina and now to be led by the dynamic Vallas.

American public education has also been toying again with "site-based management," "building-level control," and kindred restructurings. It's part of the professional-empowerment reform agenda as well as an effort to adapt sound corporate practices to public education, with less top-down regulation, slimmer middle management, and more authority vested in the units that are accountable for results. So far, it hasn't amounted to much. Here is how Frederick M. Hess, one of the sagest biographers of urban school-reform efforts, describes this history:

> Site-based management [SBM] proposals seek to shift decision-making from the central administration to individual school sites. . . . SBM is politically ideal because it creates the impression of dramatic change,

while permitting policymakers to pursue this reform with only minimal disruption of school routines. . . . A 1990 review . . . found "little evidence that school-based management alters relationships, renews school organizations, or develops the qualities of academically effective schools." Neither was there evidence that SBM improves "the attitudes of administrators and teachers or the instructional component of schools" or "student achievement." . . . SBM measures tend to be piecemeal, only partially implemented, and more symbolic than concrete.[57]

In the past few years, however, energized (and increasingly accountable) superintendents in a dozen cities, egged on and subsidized by major philanthropists, have extended this heretofore tepid practice in interesting new directions, devolving greater authority to individual schools, outsourcing schools or clusters of schools to external managers, and deploying the charter option to reconstitute or start new schools.[58] They are gingerly testing the ideas of Paul Hill, Ted Kolderie, Tom Vander Ark, and others who argue that, instead of "school systems" of the familiar bureaucratic and quasi-monopolistic sort, America needs "systems of schools" and "portfolio" arrangements whereby local boards enter into diverse relationships—not just "command-and-control"—with the variegated schools for which they are ultimately responsible.[59] Most such initiatives also tap into the principle of school choice, and some include creative chartering of schools by districts as well as other sponsors.[60]

Thus we find, for example, Chicago's Renaissance 2010 project promising to create or re-create a hundred of that city's schools, mostly as charters or under contract with outside operators. In mid-2006, the Texas legislature voted that, after four consecutive years of weak performance, schools must be outsourced to nonprofit organizations with a record of successful school "turnarounds." Vallas entrusted more than fifty Philadelphia schools to a half-dozen private managers. New York's Bloomberg announced in June 2006 that almost a quarter of the schools in that sprawling system would become "empowerment schools" with added authority over personnel, budget, and curriculum—in return for their principals' promise to meet performance standards. (In his State of the City address in January 2007, Bloomberg proposed further expansion of principals' control.)

Personnel, budget, and curriculum are the three domains where principals most need to be in charge but all too often are not. Absent such authority, it's hard to picture many of them producing the stronger results for which they are being held to account—and the best of them, painfully aware of this tension, are frustrated, while others settle for the mediocre results that the "system" practically compels them to produce. In most U.S. school districts, these crucial managerial domains are constrained by state laws, regulations, and funding formulas; by bureaucratic procedures imposed by the superintendent's office; by restrictions and privileges built into the teachers' contract; by other reforms (such as districtwide curricula) intended to boost achievement; and by anxiety about litigation if the principal takes forceful action. Staffing, in particular, is encumbered by contracts, tenure laws, seniority systems, citywide salary schedules, state certification procedures, and more. It's extremely difficult even to get the downtown human-resources department to do the bidding of a change-minded superintendent, much less to devolve chunks of its mandate to principals and others at the building level.[61]

Budget authority is just as hard to shift. Most school-system dollars are spent on personnel, these monies are typically allotted as "slots" rather than dollars per school, and the system itself has limited control of its own budget, much of which is shaped by state and federal distribution formulas as well as multiyear employee contracts. (Not just teachers. Custodians, bus drivers, sometimes even principals and assistant principals often work under collectively bargained agreements.) Analysts may devote months to determining how much money is actually spent in which schools within a system.[62] Insofar as they succeed, they typically unearth the alarming finding that schools attended by the neediest children get the least money. This problem has myriad origins, starting with the fact that the most senior teachers, bearing the largest salaries, usually opt to work in middle-class schools rather than tougher environs with more challenging pupils.[63] Poor children, it follows, are most apt to be taught by lower-paid, novice instructors.

True decentralization, therefore, the foremost analyst/advocate of which is UCLA management professor William G. Ouchi, means reallocating the budget on a more equitable basis (preferably "weighting" state and district (and even federal) per pupil payments according to students' differing needs and making those payments fully portable from school to school) as well as placing fiscal authority in principals' hands—and installing individuals in those key roles who are competent and eager to handle such responsibilities. Strides in this direction have been made by Seattle, Houston, and New York City, as well as Edmonton, Alberta.[64]

Critics charge that devolving so much authority to individual schools runs big risks because many current principals aren't up to executive-style challenges and because some decisions—which early-grade reading program to use, for example—are better made centrally than left to the whims of school-level teams. Moreover, many of today's principals, while discontented with their limited span of control over key areas, have in fact accommodated to these constraints and are now more apt to view themselves as middle managers in a vast bureaucracy than as executives or change agents. (Charter-school and private-school principals generally relish their greater authority.)[65]

Funding mechanisms, organizational structures, governance schemes, and technology seem sterile and technocratic. But they're not going away. Indeed, in December 2006, a blue-ribbon "commission on the skills of the American workforce" framed what chairman Charles Knapp termed "a major reorganization of the states' education and training systems."[66] Critics such as my colleague, Diane Ravitch, contend that the panel's recommendations and kindred "structural" reforms involve dangerous risks and typically neglect crucial issues of curriculum and pedagogy. Larry Cuban says they are little more than ripples on the system's surface that overpromise on what schools can accomplish while failing to alter what happens in the classroom. Certainly such rearrangements lack the easy familiarity and sex appeal of issues like testing and vouchers. Yet in the long run I believe they matter as much. They are to education reform what girders, pipes, wires, and water supply are to architecture: the infrastructure that determines whether an edifice will be sturdy and habitable.

27 | Teachers, Time, and Money

Besides the obligations that NCLB laid on schools and students to make "adequate yearly progress," the federal statute insisted that every teacher of a core academic subject—it flagged ten of these—be "highly qualified" by 2006. In Washington's eyes, that meant a teacher must be fully certified by his/her state and also demonstrate that he/she knows the relevant subject(s).

This provision, which states are responsible for enforcing and which has proven exceedingly difficult to honor, is having mixed effects. On the plus side, it underscores the importance of subject mastery by teachers. But it also vests even greater authority in state certification mechanisms, which are the foremost barriers to entry into public-school classrooms and which were beginning to be waived and circumvented in order to draw talented but unconventional individuals into teaching and to free charter schools and others to staff themselves as they see fit.

Certification is disputed terrain in contemporary education reform. It is cherished by ed schools—their chief claim upon students and revenues—and by teachers' unions and other groups that flaunt it as evidence of professionalism and exclusivity. What, after all, is one's mark of priestly status and unique knowledge if anybody can don the vestments and perform the sacraments?

Yet there is no convincing evidence that certified teachers are more effective in the classroom or that ed-school-based training helps.[67] That being so, why erect such entry barriers and hike the cost of becoming a teacher? Besides, private schools appear to do fine—perhaps better—without being compelled to hire state-certified teachers. So do many charter schools. Why not also open up district classrooms and empower principals to hire the individuals they think will be most effective (and dismiss any who turn out not to be), while holding the principal to account for the school's success?[68]

Education's intrepid professionalizers prefer to strengthen the "qualifications" of teachers in the hope that this will boost their skills and status and in the certainty that it will make them scarcer, more valuable, and hence more generously paid. Yet the long-term trend of American K–12 education has been to employ more teachers rather than better—or better paid—instructors.[69]

Since the mid-1950s, in round numbers the pupil nose count in U.S. K–12 education has risen by half while the number of teachers has nearly tripled. Spending per student has tripled, too. If the teaching force had simply kept pace with enrollments, if school budgets had risen as they did, and if nothing else changed, today's average teacher would earn upward of $100,000, plus generous benefits. Starting pay would be $50,000–$60,000. The most senior teachers would receive $170,000 or so. We'd have a radically altered view of the job, which would attract different sorts of people who might also be more likely to stick with it.

Instead, what America has done these past fifty years is invest in many more teachers rather than abler ones, even as attractive career options have multiplied for the talented and well-educated women who once poured into public-school classrooms. No wonder teaching salaries have barely kept pace with inflation, despite escalating education budgets. No wonder this occupation (with blessed exceptions) draws people from the lower ranks of our lesser universities.[70] No wonder there are teacher shortages in key fields. No wonder there is much turnover.[71] When you employ 3 million people, you don't pay them very well (though there's good job security), you treat them all alike, and you don't reward excellence, it's hard to keep a field fully staffed, especially in locales (remote towns, tough neighborhoods) that aren't alluring and in subjects such as math and science where well-qualified individuals can earn big bucks doing something else. The tears that come to the eyes of the fifty or so teachers honored each year by the Milken Family Foundation are not due entirely to the handsome $25,000 checks that accompany their recognition. They also flow from the yearning of someone who is doing an especially good job to have others notice and say thanks.

That's also why NCLB's "highly qualified teacher" provision seemed like a good idea at the time. But when the deadline arrived in May 2006, not a single state had met it—so the Education Department gave them all a one-year extension.

Why did America triple its teaching force instead of paying more to fewer but superior instructors? Three reasons.

First, the seductiveness of smaller classes. Teachers want fewer kids in their classrooms, and parents also think their children will be better off, despite scant evidence that students learn more in smaller classes, particularly from less gifted instructors.

Second, institutional interests that profit from a larger teaching force, above all dues-collecting (and influence-seeking) unions and colleges of education, whose revenues (tuition, state subsidies) and size (all those faculty slots) hinge on their enrollments.

Third, societal, legal, and political forces that press schools to treat children differently from one another, creating one set of classes for the gifted, others for children with handicaps, those who want to learn Japanese, who seek full-day kindergarten, or who crave more community-service opportunities. The arrival of "special" education and its high teacher-student ratios accounts for a goodly share of swelling staff numbers.

Few resisted. It was not in anybody's immediate interest to keep teaching ranks sparse, while many interests were served by helping them balloon. Today, we pay the price: gobs of money spent on schooling, primarily for salaries, but schooling that, at the end of the day, depends on the knowledge, skills, and commitment of an army of teachers who don't earn much and cannot see that they ever will.

This situation helps explain the quest to restore "teacher professionalism" and the alphabet soup of organizations that have arisen to further that agenda. But it also helps explain why the stiffer entrance barriers high on that agenda are dysfunctional for schools that need lots of teachers today and are under the gun to get better ones wherever they can find them.

One of the recent success stories of American education has been the Teach for America (TFA) program, which since 1990 has brought more than 17,000 talented young people—mostly newly minted graduates of prestigious colleges and universities—into public-school classrooms, mainly in challenging inner-city settings, after a fast summer of training and almost always without conventional certification. Several studies have shown that TFA teachers are at least as effective as conventionally trained-and-licensed instructors, again raising the question why America should impose such opportunity costs on people wanting to enter public-school classrooms.[72] Teach for America continues to grow in popularity, with 19,000 applicants in 2006—including 10 percent or more of the senior class at Amherst, Yale, Dartmouth, and Notre Dame—for 2,400 slots.

Although many TFA-ers exit the classroom after their two-year stints, about two-thirds remain in education, and their alumni/ae ranks have proven to be a rich lode of talent and commitment from which now come a large fraction of charter-school heads and reform entrepreneurs. This is also a lesson worth noting by educators fretful about teacher retention. In contemporary America, young people typically change jobs a number of times and sample various career options before "settling down," if they ever do.

There is no reason to expect young teachers to behave differently. While teachers do become more effective after several years in the classroom—it's not clear that this edge keeps widening with further experience—we will need to structure different kinds of career paths and compensation schemes for educators if we're serious about keeping them in the field. We will also need to devise school-staffing plans that make effective use of short-termers as well as careerists, much as the military finds ways of deploying both those who enlist for a few years and those who sign up for twenty or more.

End Runs and Bottlenecks | Partly because traditional teaching credentials display such a shaky relationship to classroom effectiveness, partly because of shortages (especially in math, science, and special ed), and partly because of the folly of barring knowledgeable individuals who are keen to teach in public-school classrooms yet never attended ed school, most states have developed some sort of "alternate path" into this field. According to the National Center for Alternative Certification, by 2006 "48 states and the District of Columbia . . . were implementing . . . 124 actual alternative routes to teacher certification."[73]

Alas, many such programs are shams. They impose virtually the same hoops, hurdles, and requirements—even the same ed school courses—as conventional certification programs, but allow a candidate to go through them while also earning a teacher's salary rather than doing it all in advance. Some, though, are true alternatives, more like apprenticeships than campus course-taking, and give greater weight to demonstrated effectiveness than to paper credentials. Many of the latter are managed by school systems, not universities. This riles professionalizers who do not want education to be viewed as a craft and who insist on the value of university training and the quality control that they claim is afforded by strict state regulation.

State regulation is also their surest mechanism for safeguarding their own interests. A key player is the National Council for Accreditation of Teacher Education (NCATE), which has persuaded many states to make its accreditation a prerequisite for state approval of preparation programs, which in turn is a prerequisite for individual certification to teach.[74] Here is where things stood in summer 2005:

> NCATE has partnerships with 50 states, including the District of Columbia and Puerto Rico. In 17 partnership states, all public teacher

education institutions are NCATE accredited. In 28 partnership states, a majority of all the teacher education institutions are NCATE accredited. Twenty-five states have adopted or adapted NCATE Unit standards as their own and apply them to all institutions for purposes of state approval. Twenty-five states rely on NCATE's program review process in lieu of their own for purposes of NCATE accreditation and state approval.[75]

Such deference means states are ceding to professional groups the authority to determine which teacher-prep programs are legitimate, despite no evidence that this boosts teacher quality. To be accredited by NCATE to prepare history teachers, for example, a training program must be blessed by the National Council for the Social Studies, which has a "contemporary problems" view of the curriculum in which history is just one of ten "strands" that prospective social-studies teachers are supposed to master— meaning they are not really required to know much history.

Further, the official apparatus by which many states make such decisions is also squarely in the hands of educators. As of December 2004, reports ECS,

> Forty-six states have some type of [education] professional standards board. Fifteen states have *autonomous* boards; six states have *semi-autonomous* boards; and 25 states have *advisory* boards. . . . For example, the professional standards board may decide criteria for certification, issue licenses and may be funded in part through certification fees.[76]

Though the word "independent" is typically used in conjunction with such statewide credentialing boards and their members are ordinarily appointed by the governor, the statutes establishing these bodies usually specify their makeup. Oregon's seventeen-member Teacher Standards and Practices Commission, for example, must by law contain four elementary teachers, four secondary teachers, one elementary principal, one secondary-school administrator, one city superintendent, one county superintendent, one faculty member each from an "approved" private teacher-education institution and a state university, one local school board member, and two representatives of the "general public." The statute further requires that all but three of the commission members "must have been actively engaged in teaching, supervising or administering in the public schools or in approved

teacher education institutions in Oregon for the period of five years immediately preceding appointment."[77]

This approach to licensure pretty much assures that those charged with
deciding who can teach in a state's public schools themselves represent unions,
ed schools, and other establishment organizations.

Is there another approach? During Rod Paige's tenure as secretary, the
U.S. Department of Education used discretionary dollars to seed the creation
of the American Board for Certification of Teacher Excellence (ABCTE). I
helped author the successful application and served on the project's original
board and executive committee. Its core proposition is that, besides graduating from college and weathering a criminal-background check, all that
should be required of individuals before giving them a teaching license is
passing a rigorous test of knowledge of their subjects. ABCTE has developed
several such tests and, while there remains plenty of opposition to accepting
this straight path into teaching, by early 2007 six states had agreed to do so.
Preliminary evidence from the small number of teachers possessing such certification indicates that it works as well—and at far less cost in time and
money—as the old curvy path.

Watching over these tussles from Olympian heights between 2003 and
2006 was the Teaching Commission, a private blue-ribbon group led by the
indefatigable Lou Gerstner, former CEO of IBM, brilliantly assisted by the
late Gaynor McCown. Its excellent first report in 2004, *Teaching at Risk*,
argued for both a higher bar—in terms of teachers' subject-matter
knowledge—and fewer hoops and hurdles. It pleaded for more alternate
paths into teaching, better and more accountable preparation programs, and
compensation keyed to one's specialty and effectiveness—as well as higher
base salaries.[78]

In its final report, issued in March 2006, the commission voiced disap-
pointment, conferring mostly Cs and Ds upon states for their paltry advances on these fronts. "If teaching remains a second-rate profession,"
Gerstner said, "America's economy will be driven by second-rate skills. We
can wake up today—or we can have a rude awakening sooner than we
think."[79]

Though most energy in this domain flows toward the 3 million member teaching occupation, America's 100,000 school principals—and their
preparation and licensure—have also drawn attention. With the principal's
burden mounting, particularly under pressure for school-level accountability, with ever longer hours and more challenging duties, and with pay for

principals barely higher than for senior teachers, veterans are exiting the principal's office, and new talent is harder to find. Moreover, there is widening doubt that traditional preparation regimens for principals are suited to today's task.

In 2005, Teachers College president Arthur Levine harshly criticized university-based administrator-training programs for curricular disarray, low standards, weak faculty, poor research, and inadequate clinical training—for starters. Coming from the pen of a major ed school leader, this appraisal was especially telling.[80]

I'm persuaded that principals should be seen more as CEOs than instructional leaders and that they need not be former teachers. (They do, however, need education expertise on their teams.)[81] Most educators, however, still insist that "principal teacher"—as they say in England—is the proper way to construe the school head's role.

One small project is trying to do for principals what Teach for America does for teachers: recruit and place unconventional individuals in these roles. Called New Leaders for New Schools, to date it has deployed several hundred people in principals' chairs in selected communities. Los Angeles philanthropist Eli Broad also supports a number of programs to prepare and place nontraditional executives in leadership roles in urban school systems, up to and including the superintendent's office.

Why all these efforts to circumnavigate the ed schools? In part, it's that traditional campus-based preparation programs drain much time and money from candidates who may not benefit from the experience—and from taxpayers who generously subsidize most of them. In large part, though, it's that these institutions are out of step with the needs of American education, and the priorities of those struggling to reform it. Rejecting international competitiveness and prosperity as rationales for changing schools and boosting educational productivity, even as they reject behaviorist methods for effecting such changes in schools and kids, their professors also put little stock in traditional views of classroom behavior and learning. Rather, they keep time to what the research firm Public Agenda called *A Different Drummer*, the title of an important 1997 study. It found that

> nearly eight in ten teachers of teachers (79%) believe the public's approach toward learning is "outmoded and mistaken," and suggest a different path for American education. In sharp contrast to the concerns expressed by typical Americans . . . , small percentages of

education professors feel maintaining discipline and order in the classroom (37%), stressing grammar as well as correct spelling and punctuation (19%), and expecting students to be on time and polite (12%) are "absolutely essential" qualities to impart to prospective teachers. . . . Their emphasis on a love of learning leads them to downplay more traditional educational practices. Fifty-nine percent, for example, think academic sanctions such as the threat of flunking or being held back are not important in motivating kids to learn.[82]

It's no coincidence that, in appraising 1,200 college-based teacher-preparation programs in 2006, Levine found only a quarter of them doing a good job.[83] Perhaps even more dismaying, a majority of U.S. teacher-prep programs shun scientific evidence regarding effective instructional methods—akin to medical schools avoiding discussion of bacteria and antibiotics. A revealing 2006 study by the National Council on Teacher Quality found that fewer than 15% of the ed school programs that train primary teachers provide even minimal exposure to the "science of reading" and that most instead encourage methods of reading instruction that are apt to leave millions of elementary pupils illiterate.[84]

Time | The teaching corps isn't the only growth area in education today. The whole enterprise is expanding in five directions from the classic twelve grades, 180-day years, and six-hour days of my youth.

| *First*: more is happening earlier in kids' lives. Kindergarten is becoming ubiquitous—and likelier to be full- than half-day—and prekindergarten is spreading fast. Part of the impetus is working parents' need for child care. Part is the belief that children are more apt to succeed in school if they've had preschool. Part is greed on the part of school systems, unions, and private preschool providers, all seeking to grow their enrollments and revenues. The upshot is that in 2006 all but a dozen states paid for some sort of pre-K program—far fewer offered "universal" access—and such programs served 20% of American four-year-olds. Yet more than two-thirds of all four-year-olds (and two-fifths of three-year-olds) were enrolled in some sort of "preprimary" program—most often paid for by their parents and frequently amounting only to "day care."

Arguments persist as to how much this added time in preschool pays off later—the research is ambiguous, and the programs' quality varies widely— as well as how much of this is the government's business and how much should occur under the public-school roof. Still, governors seem to be tumbling over one another in their zeal to expand such offerings.[85] My own view is that preschool is important for disadvantaged kids, and I have no objection to the universal version, either, so long as it meets three criteria: it must be voluntary for families, it must be delivered by diverse providers (not just school systems) among which parents can choose, and it must be a true pre-_school_ with a curriculum and expectations related to the skills that small children need to succeed in kindergarten and thereafter.

| _Second:_ although the official U.S. school day and year haven't changed much in forty years—there's some district-to-district variation—a number of superintendents and state officials are making serious noises about lengthening these.[86] Moreover, before- and after-school, extended day, and summer programs are booming.[87] Part of the reason is to close gaps and boost pupil achievement but, as with preschool, much of the push comes from an appetite for child care rather than more teaching and learning. Hence much of the added time is spent in nonacademic pursuits.

| _Third:_ as discussed in the previous chapter, technology now makes it far easier for kids to learn outside school. Sometimes what they are learning is salutary— instructional software and educational programs selected by their parents, term-paper research via the Internet—and sometimes it's wasteful, narcissistic, or damaging (e.g., MTV, YouTube, porn sites). But anyone who has observed young people glued to their computer screens, video games, and TV sets, even to the detriment of their physical fitness and social contact, knows that eager minds pursuing knowledge or pleasure now have infinite round-the-clock opportunities.

| _Fourth:_ some of the charter (and other) schools that are most serious about closing learning gaps and putting disadvantaged children onto a trajectory to success have enlarged their portion of those kids' lives. Recognizing—as has been noted by analysts from James Coleman in the 1960s to Richard Rothstein in the early twenty-first century—that socioeconomic conditions, family background, and peer influence have potent effects on kids'

prospects, they strive to overwhelm those effects by magnifying the school's influence. So they start early and run until sundown. They operate weekend and summer programs or year-round calendars. (The well-regarded "Achievement First" charters, for example, add ninety minutes to the typical school day as well as mandatory summer programs.) They provide teachers' cell-phone numbers so kids can call at odd hours for help with homework or personal problems. They follow their students through high school and help them apply to college. Rarely (e.g., the District of Columbia's SEED School) they even operate as boarding schools. Where the school's regular funding doesn't cover these added costs—it usually does not—they package monies from other government programs and engage in extensive private fund-raising, as well as extracting plenty of sweat equity from earnest young teachers. Besides lengthening teaching-and-learning time, they envelop their pupils in a different culture and set of values than those of the 'hood.

| *Fifth*: today's assumption that just about every high-school graduate (and some nongraduates) will eventually attend college, while in part a costly adaptation to the weak K–12 education that many young people get, is increasingly borne out by reality. In 1971, just one-third of twenty-five- to twenty-nine-year-old Americans had completed any college (and 17% possessed a bachelor's degree). Three decades later, almost three in five had matriculated, and nearly 30% had a bachelor's degree. One practical effect of this is to enlarge the total amount of formal learning time of young Americans at the back end of K–12 education, much as pre-school is doing at the front.

I believe the United States ought to focus more on the quality of its education than on its quantity and should concern itself more with effectiveness, productivity, and results than with time and money spent. But there is no gainsaying that education remains a growth industry in today's America and is occupying more of people's lives. This could be turned to greater advantage if we made sure that the added time were more fruitfully employed.

Judges and Money | The executive and legislative branches of state and federal governments aren't the only shapers of education policy and practice. The courts frequently push into the K–12 action, too. During the fifties and sixties, their primary influence came in the realm of school desegregation, then (mostly at the college level) affirmative action. Slowly, though, the scope of education litigation widened to include school discipline, special ed, prayer, freedom of speech, church-state boundaries, student testing, personnel practices, physical and sex abuse, and finance.

One result is educators who feel shackled and fearful, unable to do what's in the best interests of their students and schools because of anxiety about being hauled into court. A 2003 study by Public Agenda found that "for many principals and superintendents, avoiding lawsuits and fulfilling regulatory and due process requirements is a time-consuming and often frustrating part of the job. Special education, discipline and sexual harassment, and staff issues" proved most vexing for them. Teachers reported that "the possibility of being sued or being accused of physical or sexual abuse of a student is ever-present in their minds," leading them to "completely avoid touching students or being alone with them." Maintaining classroom and school discipline, too, has been complicated by judicial interventions and mandates that make it difficult to punish or suspend out-of-line students—a problem exacerbated when students are also disabled and thus covered by special-education and civil-rights protections.[88]

Judges have reshaped public-school finance, too, causing many more billions to be expended. All states have constitutional clauses obligating them to provide education, clauses that can be cited by plaintiffs alleging that governor and legislature are not doing this fairly or adequately. New Jersey, for example, calls for a "thorough and efficient" education system, while Washington State speaks of "ample provision for the education of all children."

A series of lawsuits in the 1970s and 1980s sought more evenhanded funding of public education for children throughout a state by imploring judges to decree new finance formulas (and taxes) to compensate for disparities in local wealth and revenue-generating capacity. Most such suits succeeded, though legislators often dragged their feet in complying. Because it is politically unthinkable almost everywhere to "level down," that is, to take money away from districts that want to spend more on their schools, states usually found themselves "leveling up," which meant a heavier fiscal burden for public education and, usually, higher state taxes.[89]

I applaud more-equitable school funding and have no problem with shifting more of the cost to the state (mindful that, in a democracy, there is no practical way to stop communities or parents who can afford to from spending *additional* money on their kids' education). This would be consistent with statewide standards, tests, and accountability and with opening up school choices across district borders. Donning my troublemaker fedora, I've even suggested doing away entirely with school boards, superintendents, and districts themselves—the middle management of this enormous enterprise—and facing the reality that K–12 education is a state responsibility best discharged via autonomous (but accountable) individual schools.

I also welcome additional education spending—so long as it buys different results. The problem is that plumping today's school-system budgets typically yields either more disruptive new programs or across-the-board salary boosts for the same teachers, principals, and bureaucrats who weren't getting the job done yesterday. An enormous study of school finance in California, completed in 2007 by topflight Stanford economists, concluded that "meaningful reform to meet student outcome goals may well require substantial new investments. . . . But financial investments will only significantly benefit students if they are accompanied by extensive and systemic reforms. Without accompanying policy reforms, the substantial gains in student outcomes that Californians need are unlikely to accrue."[90]

Judges seldom think this way—or know how to craft remedies accompanied by "systemic reforms," though they definitely know how to order other branches of government to spend. Beginning in Montana and Kentucky in 1989, the same year the Charlottesville education summit started to forge a new federal-state partnership around standards, state courts (prompted by astute attorneys funded by prominent national foundations) advanced the concept of educational *adequacy*. Most judges construed this in terms of budgets and services. A few, however, went further. The Kentucky Supreme Court, for example, ruled the state's entire public school system unconstitutional and admonished the legislature to "re-establish a new system of common schools." "Every child in this Commonwealth," declared the judges, "must be provided with an equal opportunity to have an adequate education. . . . The children of the poor and the children of the rich, the children who live in poor districts and the children who live in rich districts must be given the same opportunity and access."[91]

It should have stopped there, but the court went on to spell out seven competencies ("learning goals") that public schools of the Bluegrass State must see that children acquire. These included "sufficient oral and written communication skills to enable students to function in a complex and rapidly changing civilization" and "sufficient knowledge of economic, social, and political systems to enable the student to make informed choices."[92]

The Kentucky judges and those following their lead in other venues should be faulted for superseding the duties of lawmakers *and* educators and setting themselves up as masters of a complex enterprise that they do not possess the competence to manage well, a point made strongly by New York's highest court in November 2006 in a decisive school-adequacy decision that said, "We must avoid intrusion on the primary domain of another branch of government." [93]

Yet jurists who spell out learning outcomes for children are at least singing from the post-Coleman hymnal that the president and governors were using for choir practice, focusing on school results rather than simple inputs.

In sum, judges have both advanced and retarded the pursuit of standards-based education in America. They have occasionally boosted it by construing the state's obligation in terms of what children should learn. They have more often slowed it by seeking to manipulate the policy lever that's easiest for them to grasp: spending. Few judges know how to command the executive branch to make children read or cipher. But many contemporary jurists show no more restraint when ordering dollars to be expended in vague pursuit of that objective than when messing with school operations and tying educators' hands in discipline cases.

Some initiatives work better than others. Some flame out. Besides the American Board for Certification of Teacher Excellence, I worked to launch the National Council on Teacher Quality, which keeps contrarian views and data on teacher quality in public view. In 1995, I assisted several dissident state superintendents (including Arizona's Lisa Keegan, Pennsylvania's Eugene Hickok, Colorado's Bill Moloney, Florida's Frank Brogan) to form the Education Leaders Council (ELC), an in-your-face alternative to the mainstream Council of Chief State School Officers. A decade later, I helped Howard Fuller craft the National Alliance for Public Charter Schools out of the wreckage of two previous efforts to establish an effective charter-school voice in Washington. Very slowly, the alphabet soup of "establishment" organizations is being matched by an array of smaller groups that push reformist approaches. Not all succeed, however. The Ohio Charter School Association ran out of gas (a successor group recently launched), and the ELC folded in 2005 amid charges of misuse of federal funds.

I've been part of all these and many more. Yet my main perch remains the Fordham Foundation, which furled its Manhattan Institute umbrella in 2002 and began to manage its own affairs, including full-fledged offices in Dayton and Washington and a wee outpost in Columbus. We have also developed links with Stanford's Hoover Institution and launched the companion Fordham Institute, which raises grant support from other funders and thereby expands our work beyond what the income from our endowment can pay for.

Expertly led by Eric Osberg, Mike Petrilli, and Terry Ryan, our little band issues reports and studies every month or so on national issues large and medium, plus (since 2001) a weekly electronic newsletter called the *Education Gadfly* that blends heavy combat in the war of ideas with humor, irreverence, and a bit of unpredictability. Fordham remains, to my knowledge, the only Washington education think tank cum advocacy group that's equally interested in standards-based and choice-based reforms—and from time to time we roam in other directions, such as teacher quality, education philanthropy, and school finance. We work hard and produce enough that outsiders are often startled to learn how few people—fewer than a dozen—work at Fordham.

We're also one of the few organizations that engage in both national and local work. Assisted by the Gates Foundation, our Ohio operation has diversified, particularly in the charter-school realm. Dayton is arguably ground zero of the charter movement, with nearly 30% of all the kids in town now attending several dozen such schools. Some are fine indeed—and in recent years larger percentages of charter pupils passed state proficiency tests in reading and math than did district students. But that's a low hurdle, and in Dayton, as throughout Ohio, too many charter schools are educational mediocrities or worse.

One reason is that their sponsors were inattentive—and for most schools their original sponsor was the Ohio Department of Education. That agency performed so badly that the legislature withdrew this mandate from it in 2002 and handed sponsorship duties instead to an array of other organizations, including nonprofit groups that meet certain requirements. Fordham qualifies, and so, with misgivings, we entered into the hands-on role of charter sponsorship, while spinning off a separate organization to handle schools' "back office" needs (business management and such at first, now slowly evolving into a full-fledged charter management organization.) We've gradually spread our sponsorship work across southwestern Ohio and already operate statewide on education policy issues, of which Ohio has no shortage.[94]

Climbing down from the ivory tower and grappling with tangible challenges involving real schools and people has been good for us; it grounds our think-tank work at both state and national levels, which in turn yields valuable information, connections, and leads that we can feed back into Ohio. But it's heavy going. Of the ten charter schools that Fordham sponsored in 2005–6, for example, just half performed academically at an acceptable level; four faced grave organizational, governance, fiscal, and leadership difficulties; one left us for a new sponsor because it thought we were too demanding with regard to changes needed at the school; the founder and moving spirit behind three of them departed under a legal cloud; nearly all of "our" schools have periodic emergencies, agitated parents, or aggrieved teachers, and other crises that we get pulled into; and we're losing our financial shirt, investing far more time, energy, and expertise (including pricey outside consultants) in this work than the schools' sponsorship fees begin to cover. Were it not for Fordham's own endowment and help from Gates, we could not function as a charter sponsor in Ohio, at least not at the level of intensity that we judge essential to our goal, which is for charter schools to be sound education options for families, not just options.

Getting up close and personal with schools has also reinforced for me just how difficult it is to make the finest of theories work on the ground. For example, a central tenet of the charter concept is that sponsors will close bad schools. And so, of course, they should. Now that Fordham is a sponsor, however, we're enmeshed in the complexities, subtleties, and human (and political) nuances of such decisions. For example, should one close a school midyear, stranding its pupils? What if—no matter the school's failings—these kids have nowhere better to go? What if they and their parents are content with the school despite its management problems, fiscal woes, and crummy test scores? And what if the school itself is tied to important community institutions? One of the low-performing charters that Fordham sponsors, for example, is a project of the largest African-American church in its city.

Some wag defined a think tank as "a place where reality is studied to see if it conforms to theory." I'm coming to understand that reality is a place where nifty theories get ambushed—and charter-school sponsorship in particular is a crucible in which some of them simply melt.

The "war of ideas" is hard, too, but less messy and, perhaps because it has no metrics as revealing as kids' faces and schools' test scores, it's easier in this realm to persuade ourselves that we're making a difference. (A 2006 survey of education-policy "influentials" by *Education Week* indicated that others agree.)[95]

With the help of a terrific staff and trustees, including Rod Paige and Bruno Manno, and nonstop exchanges of ideas and drafts (and humor) with Diane Ravitch, I do my best, via op-eds, *Gadfly* editorials, articles, books, and the occasional speech to state the truth and stir the policy pot without much regard for political correctness or approbation. I also try, via Fordham studies and commentaries, to appraise events and issues in clear-eyed fashion, usually testing them against core principles that have changed little since Diane and I laid them out a quarter century back.[96]

Most of this is serious, but occasionally I'm reminded that solemnity isn't always the best way to reach Americans. The annual "April Fool" issue of the *Gadfly* is by far the most appreciated. And a father-daughter stroganoff recipe that Arti had us submit to the Father's Day issue of *Real Simple*, the Time-Warner magazine where she then worked and which appeared in June 2005 with a cute photo of us, drew more attention than any five of my op-eds or articles on burning education issues. The briefest appearance on TV invariably gets more comment than anything I write.

Part of me remains a teacher, which now mostly takes the form of mentoring (and challenging, editing, explaining to) young Fordham staff members and a host of not-quite-so-young alumni/ae in whose lives and careers I stay involved. I relish talking with the groups of students and interns who occasionally pass through our office for seminars. And except when facing a truly hostile audience—in which case I seek a plump honorarium—I enjoy speaking with conference attendees and symposium participants. Though panels are usually a windy bore, I work at being clear, even outspoken, and enjoy mixing it up with people who think otherwise. I've made a personal specialty of moderating panels and emceeing events—the lesson there is to focus on the audience's experience, not the speakers' egos—and am not bad at giving talks myself. My résumé lists hundreds of "groups spoken to."

But there, too, I sometimes blunder—and not because I crave more trouble. My greatest public-speaking gaffe to date occurred at a Captiva Island education conference where I borrowed a well-worn Bill Bennett line to the effect that in today's America one faces swifter and more severe consequences for serving a single rotten hamburger in a luncheonette—the local health department shuts you down and padlocks the door—than from serving up a rotten education to thousands of kids year after year. The point is valid and the imagery vivid, but when I said it the audience gasped. Turns out I had forgotten that the event was sponsored by Burger King, and a big poster over my head said something like "happiness is a hamburger."

Occasionally you just want to vanish into the rostrum. Mostly, though, I stay unflummoxed and welcome the repartee. Everyone thinks himself an education expert, of course, because everyone went to school and has or knows kids. Almost every audience contains someone who asks "Isn't it really the parents' fault?" and another who is convinced that paying all teachers more would work wonders, and yet another who is sure that schools' greatest failing is their inattention to art (or character, foreign languages, discipline, uniforms, environmentalism, patriotism, you name it).

Besides my own writing and lecturing, more and more I find myself orchestrating and editing other people's work. In 1998, Hoover Institution director John Raisian set out to elevate the education-policy profile of that imposing and mostly conservative West Coast think tank. With funds from the San Francisco–based Koret Foundation, he invited eleven prominent education analysts to form a panel, which in time I found myself chairing.

The Koret Task Force on K–12 Education is a lively, brainy, and accomplished bunch whose twice-yearly meetings are the site of some of the most stimulating conversations that any of us has. We've undertaken group studies of a host of national and state policy challenges, mostly organizing our advice under the trinitarian headings of standards, choice, and transparency. Perhaps most striking about the task force is that only one member—psychologist Herbert Walberg—is primarily associated with a college of education. The other ten are economists (Eric Hanushek, Caroline Hoxby), political scientists (Paul Peterson, John Chubb, Terry Moe), think-tankers (Bill Evers, myself), a literary scholar (E. D. Hirsch), a historian (Diane Ravitch), and a broad-gauged "public policy" analyst (Paul Hill). This squares with my sense that today's ed schools are pools of conventional thinking and the real intellectual energy for reforming the K–12 enterprise comes from elsewhere.

The Koret Task Force also serves as the editorial board for a journal that Paul Peterson and I conceived in 1999 and first produced in 2001 under the name *Education Matters*. Today, after a pesky trademark dispute, it's called *Education Next*. Paul is chief editor; my title is "senior editor," and the rest of the team consists of sharp, imaginative young thinker/writers who themselves don't mind causing the occasional blip of trouble.

Now circulating to about fifteen thousand readers, *EdNext*, as it's known, has caused a stir in the previously staid precincts of education journalism. Using edgy, clever graphics, delving into unexpected as well as familiar topics, written in plain English, reasonably adept at getting itself noticed, and open to an array of viewpoints and ideas, it fills a real niche: a readable, feisty, yet responsible, nonestablishment quarterly accessible to educators, policymakers, and scholars alike. For many years, Irving Kristol's standard advice to anyone stewing over an intractable policy problem was "start a magazine." That's pretty much what we did with *Education Next*, and it's going gangbusters.

And If I'm Wrong? | Education reform is lifetime employment. I don't worry that one day I'll wake up to find all the schools purring like atomic clocks and myself with nothing to do. I do worry, though, that it's a bigger project than Americans will tolerate, and from time to time I have nightmares that my approach to it could even be wrong—maybe not wrong in theory but unable to be implemented satisfactorily on the ground.

Yes, after all these years that's like a bishop muttering doubts about his faith or Dylan despairing about song. But I must be honest. Though I don't harbor misgivings about my education values or principles, and I know today's schools aren't accomplishing what America needs from them, I entertain plenty of angst about the efficacy of today's reform efforts, including those in which I'm most engaged. Here are my top ten sources of misgiving.

| *First, parent problems.* Some U.S. parents—yuppies and immigrants come to mind—obsess over their kids' education, occasionally to a fault, but way too many are complacent about their current schools, uncritical shoppers for different schools, inattentive to homework, indulgent about TV, and far too apt to take the kid's side rather than close ranks with the teacher when a school problem (discipline, grades, etc.) crops up. This poses obvious challenges to choice-based reform plans while also undermining the standards-accountability edifice. Asian parents are definitely better education partners.

| *Second, teacher problems.* Until trumped by technology—which one day will surprise a lot of people—the classroom teacher is still where the education rubber hits the road. The "professionalizers" are right about this and right to want teachers to be respected experts. Yet in no small part thanks to teachers' own unions and the ed school cartel, we've created a set of inane policies and dysfunctional practices whereby getting a large number of well-educated, first-rate instructors into our public schools is next to impossible. Getting the best of them into the classrooms of those who need them most is harder still. And paying the really good ones what they deserve to earn may be hardest of all.[97]

| *Third, idea problems.* Bad ideas persist, no matter what social science does to debunk them. Parents and teachers favor smaller classes. Educators favor constructivist pedagogies, nonjudgmentalism, real-life relevance, and skills over knowledge. Employers and families favor long summer vacations. Never mind that all these practices—and dozens more—do more harm than good to student achievement.[98]

| *Fourth, market failures.* Choice supporters hate to admit that the K–12 market is flawed on both the supply and demand sides. (Those who concede the point also respond, with some justice, that choice foes have shrewdly blocked

these markets from doing what they do best.) On the supply side we see, for example, that charter schools are hard to open and harder to do well—and only a fraction of the bad ones get closed down. Private schools are susceptible to daft curricular ideas, and the best of them are loath to serve more kids. On the demand side, parents (and other school choosers) lack accurate and comparable information by which to select wisely—and are too readily taken in by educators' claims and contented with relatively superficial school features.

| *Fifth, standards woes.* Getting standards right via the political process is the exception not the rule, and installing good tests and real behavior-changing accountability systems may be more than our democracy can manage. It's us whose behavior we're trying to alter, and everyone knows how hard that is. It's now twenty-two years since Diane wrote *The Schools We Deserve.* I worry that we still have them today and that, when it comes to reforming them, we, like Pogo, are our own worst enemies.

| *Sixth, governance challenges.* K–12 education remains a loosely coupled system that's stubbornly unresponsive to policy change. It's good to have fifty laboratories of democracy, and some states make much of this opportunity, yet it's still ridiculous for a big, modern country to decentralize major-league decisions about things like standards, testing, and school choice. Washington, however, suffers from policy gridlock and inept implementation of overly ambitious yet egregiously compromised programs. Real decentralization should occur at the building level, yet, even when given the authority, too few school leaders are up to its effective exercise. Key mechanisms are missing, and their absence jeopardizes our prospects for bringing American K–12 education successfully into the twenty-first century. For example, almost two decades after Charlottesville, we still have no means to promulgate sound national standards, much less to deploy national tests aligned with them—if we had the will to do so. And we have no satisfactory source of comparable consumer information on school effectiveness. Such lacunae cause both standards-based and choice-based reform to remain hard to execute, as if we had terrific blueprints but no hammers or saws.

| *Seventh, political problems.* Most education money goes into the salaries of adults. Collective-bargaining contracts buttress the status quo and block almost every important change. Democrats say they care about poor people,

but most of them sleep with the unions; Republicans say they care about standards and choices, but their own constituents are at best smug about today's schools and, at worst, hostile to reforms that might help poor and minority kids to enter their suburban enclaves. Both parties have screwy ideas about how to balance freedom and regulation in the K–12 domain, with Republicans shunning uniform standards but tolerating government micromanagement while Democrats seem to care more about where the money goes than whether kids are learning. Liberals and conservatives alike burden the schools with too many extraneous responsibilities, whether it's ending drug abuse or fostering tolerance for gender diversity. In effect, they are embracing incompatible—and ultimately unworkable—versions of "big government." Any durable reform of American K–12 education—the kind that won't elicit a "this, too, shall pass" response from educators and parents—will need to be broad based, yet that grows ever harder in the ever more partisan arenas of Washington and most state capitals.

| *Eighth, disputes among experts.* Structural reformers are inattentive to curriculum while content aficionados pay scant attention to structure. Besides entrenched education forces that want nothing to change, we find activists narrowly focused on their own pet schemes, heedless of their limitations and jealous of their rivals—sometimes more envious of fellow reformers than determined to smite their common foes. Getting the structural arrangements right accomplishes little if the standards are bad, the curriculum ill conceived, and the teachers inept. On the other hand, getting the instructional elements right is nearly impossible so long as the system's political impediments and regulatory hurdles block change. Reformers are too often at each others' throats. I'm reminded of Franklin's admonition that revolutionaries must hang together, else hang separately.

| *Ninth, persistence problems.* Most of the education reforms that engage Americans today have so far yielded only modest results, despite decades of promising and years of heavy lifting. If this meager track record continues, people may lose faith in those strategies for change and perhaps lose hope for the renewal of K–12 education itself.

| *Tenth, and perhaps most important, kids really do differ, one from the next.* They learn at different speeds in different ways. They have different interests, talents, passions, and hatreds. They have different hang-ups and needs. They

develop at different rates. Their home environments differ. No one-size re-form fits all 50 million of them equally well.

Why, then, do I remain moderately bullish about the future of K–12 education in America? Admittedly, I couldn't look in the mirror if I saw no chance of improvement. But I don't think I'm deceiving myself. Beyond the wheel spinning, the status-quo-ism, and the political pushbacks, I see prog-ress in mounting both a widening array of choice strategies and a strength-ening battery of standards, tests, and accountability schemes. Some dubious ideas (middle schools, for example) are losing appeal, while good ones (e.g., more kids should take Advanced Placement courses) are gaining. Our schools still do a decent job with their top students, as they have for ages, and many educators now agree that they could do a better job with more. I see steadfastness about reform among business leaders, pundits, and some thoughtful professionals. I see the power of bipartisanship—rare as it is—to enact such revolutionary measures as NCLB at the federal level and voucher programs for Milwaukee and the District of Columbia, not to mention doz-ens of charter laws and thousands of charter schools. As I write, at least two prominent candidates for president in 2008 have served time as education reformers and take this issue seriously. Although most of the oomph still comes from outside the education profession, there have always been excep-tions within the field (e.g., Al Shanker), and today we see such constructive leaders as New Orleans's Vallas, Boston's Tom Payzant, the Council of the Great City Schools' Mike Casserly, even a promising ed school dean or two. (Hunter College's David Steiner is a fine example.)

I also see some heartening convergence across the three leading reform agendas with, for example, a few states edging (sometimes even with union assent) toward extra pay for highly effective teachers as gauged by student achievement and school results. A new generation of change-minded politi-cal leaders has emerged, too, willing to push hard to overcome the system's torpor. It's bipartisan, featuring governors like Jeb Bush (R-FL) and Tim Pawlenty (R-MN) but also Eliot Spitzer (D-NY) and Bill Richardson (D-NM) and mayors such as Cory Booker (D-Newark), Richard Daley (D-Chicago), and Bart Peterson (D-Indianapolis).

While the education enterprise continues to display staggering inertia, while the "grammar of schooling" is more set in its ways than that of the English language, while far too many peripheral problems are brought to school in search of solutions, while adult interests remain self-absorbed and greedy, while there is backsliding in some places and unrealistic ambitions in others, and while I cannot yet point to dramatic gains by way of results, we're slowly pouring the foundation of a very different kind of enterprise than I grew up with in Dayton, one that looks to me to be better attuned to the challenges America faces in the new century.

Best of all, this remains a resourceful, inventive, and dynamic country that bravely rises to challenges domestic and international, and will follow competent leaders when they can be found. Especially in education, the need for change is well understood. In the world we now inhabit, full of economic transformations, speedy globalization, stiffening competition, technology advances, and terrorist threats, if America is bent on staying out front, it must devise means to deliver a world-class education to all its children. We know we need to do that, we know what such mechanisms look like, and for the most part we know why we're not deploying them today. That's the beginning of wisdom.

EPILOGUE | *Two Little Girls*

Emma Finn is now three, the cutest little girl in the known universe. I've always liked kids, usually more than I like their parents, but becoming Emma's "papa" is the best thing that's happened to me in ages.

She recently entered nursery school, an upscale, Upper West Side preschool with competitive admissions and inflated tuition. I don't much care for the education craziness that overcomes yuppie parents in places like New York, questing after viable alternatives to decrepit public schools while also clawing their kids' way into classrooms that they view as the beginning of a conveyor belt to Brown or Stanford, then law school—but that seems to be the way it is. Socially, Emma would benefit from a public-school experience but for that also to be an education success she and her parents would probably have to relocate outside the city.

Emma is looking to the future, too, in her way. "I'm getting big soon," she remarked while "snuggle-buggling" with me early one morning. (Not too soon, I hope. Right now she's pushing the limits of what aging grandparents can lift and hug.) From nursery school entry in September 2006 until June 2025, when she will graduate from college (if she follows the classic sequence), she'll be in the grip of America's formal education system. She'll probably fare okay there. She seems smart and is undeniably fortunate, with successful and adoring adults lavishing every sort of help and encouragement upon her and navigating her way across the education map with options at nearly every intersection. But most kids lack those advantages.

Ana Aguilar is such a child. Four years old and living across the continent from Emma, she's the daughter of my friend and mentee Martin Aguilar, now twenty-four. Those names are pseudonyms because Martin is an illegal immigrant who I don't want to get into trouble and, as I write, Congress has again failed to act on long-overdue and sorely needed immigration-reform legislation. He is, please understand, an illegal immigrant of the blameless kind, having been brought into the United States from Guatemala as an infant by his fourteen-year-old mother. He and his siblings—born here and therefore legal—grew up in the barrio of South Central Los Angeles. We met while making a documentary film in which Martin's tale was the compelling human story while I was a talking head. He turned out to be a terrific young man, talented, perceptive, smart, an eager learner who had been treated miserably by the Los Angeles Unified School District, which cared not a whit about him and more or less discarded him. As in Emma's New York, it's *possible* to get a good education from the public schools of Los Angeles, but the odds are stacked against it, the more so when there's little backup at home.

Martin is no quitter, though, and with a little advice and encouragement from the documentary producer and me, he wrestled his way back to a diploma via "extension" and "adult ed" courses and is now studying (with tuition help from Renu and me) in a decent California community college and hoping in time to earn a university degree, even as he holds down a responsible nursing-home job and looks after his own wife and little Ana. He is one great guy, with American values and aspirations. He sounds and thinks like an American. He is, in fact, a loyal and patriotic American. But under our daft immigration regime, he cannot (yet) be a legal American. Which means no legitimate Social Security number, no legitimate driver's license, indeed no legitimate employment—and the constant fear of being caught and possibly deported.

Having been born in California, Ana doesn't face legal challenges to her presence on these shores. But she confronts others. Ana and Emma have much in common, starting with being total sweethearts. They both have plenty of innate curiosity, boundless capacity to learn, and adoring parents who will do all they can to secure their education and welfare.

Yet Ana's future depends more profoundly on the quality and effectiveness of U.S. public education—on what "the system" has to offer. In this she differs from Emma, whose family can insulate her from the failings of that system, supplement it, even circumnavigate it. Emma's parents and grandparents are practiced education consumers who can appraise their options with relative ease and call in plenty of reinforcements. Her ace in the hole is her family's ability to pay for private alternatives.

Ana's family is just as loving and eager, but her parents live close to poverty's edge, renting their (shared) apartment, getting around sprawling Orange County by bus (or foot), and somehow riding out emergencies with no savings. They, too, will pay what they can for Ana's education. Indeed, they have enrolled her in a private Church of Christ prekindergarten near their home, which they're pleased with. Ana attends full-time, four days a week, at a weekly cost of $94—a big chunk of Martin's take-home pay and one reason he and his wife can't save money. They're convinced that it's worth the price, however. The school is "not the greatest looking," Martin says, but "the teachers are dedicated, loving, and educated." He and his wife "have noticed a huge increase in Ana's vocabulary, speech, interaction, and overall social skills" since she started there. "She can count up to her late twenties," he reports, "recognizes shapes, colors and the alphabet as well. Her confidence level increases daily. She has friends which is a big deal to her, and she is learning basic Christian principles."

Martin hopes to keep Ana in this private program through kindergarten, but in time, barring a big shift in his circumstances, her formal education will be in the hands of the public schools, followed, most likely, by state colleges. Her family can't afford many housing alternatives, so cannot easily widen her school options by moving to a different neighborhood or town. If what the local system provides is not satisfactory, however, they can look to charter schools—California has lots of them now—and other taxpayer-financed choices, assuming those are decent. They will, of course, keep doing all they can at home.

But that has limits, too. Money is tight, both parents work hard, and there are no other family members ready and able to read to Ana, check her homework, take her places, or buy nifty software programs, books, and DVDs. Much of what supplements her formal education is what enters the apartment via TV and what happens on the streets outside.

Guidance is hard to come by, too. When navigating the complexities of America's formal and informal education system, one yearns for the equivalent of a dashboard GPS. But none exists. My kids had a workable substitute, as does Emma, via family and plugged-in friends. Martin, however, has struggled to get accurate information on such elemental questions as which high-school "extension" programs actually yield a recognized diploma and which community-college courses count both toward a marketable associate's degree and for transfer credit to a four-year institution. Without his own doggedness plus the informal guidance that we've supplied (including pointing him toward the college's own counseling office—where he sometimes gets inconsistent information), he could become disillusioned and, like so many of his contemporaries, abandon college in frustration. Motivation isn't the issue. Martin craves more education. But he lacks the support system to help him find his way through a daunting maze. As Ana begins her education, she faces similar challenges.

By nature, Ana, Emma, and millions of other little ones are education black holes, sucking in information, good and bad examples, skills, phrases, habits, and observations every second that they're awake. If they don't learn a lot and stay curious and eager to learn, it's the grown-ups' fault. If they don't learn the right stuff, it's because their schools and families fail to teach it to them.

This starts early. I'm staggered by how much there is to learn before kindergarten. In *The Educated Child*, Bill Bennett and John Cribb and I made a list of "kindergarten readiness" skills that fills more than 3 book pages. Florida's standards for its new statewide pre-K program fill 150 pages! Society has to take seriously how, where, and by whom these things will be taught. Emma can expect to get most of them from family. Ana will get a lot there, too, more than many kids, because her parents strive to make up via caring and energy what they lack in cash, sophistication, and direct experience. But it's going to be a rockier path for Ana.[1] And what about everybody else?

After kindergarten the rocks multiply, and the path grows steeper. Parental influence slowly wanes, and peers matter more. By the time the middle grades arrive, school safety is an issue—and those youngsters who didn't get a solid grounding in the basics during their primary years fall ever farther behind. Many kids falter along the way. Thirty percent don't complete high school on time—almost half of minority youngsters like Ana. Among high-school graduates, barely a third are truly prepared for what follows in their own lives and ready to help their country do what it must in the twenty-first century. Among twenty-five- to twenty-nine-year-old Americans of Hispanic origin like Ana and Martin, barely 11 percent possess a bachelor's degree (versus 34 percent among whites in the same age group and 18 percent of blacks).

Responsibility for this disaster belongs in many places: lazy children, heedless parents, messed-up families, drug dealers and gangs, a host of other social and economic problems. But the education system is dysfunctional, too, and cannot be excused on grounds that there's something wrong with the kids or communities.

Hence this reform enterprise, this several-decades-old push from outside the system both to create alternatives for Ana and Emma and to impose standards for all.

I wrote in the introduction that the turbos of education reform in twenty-first-century America are recognizing parents' right to choose their children's schools and holding schools to account for their students' academic achievement. I said that these twin engines of change are gradually altering primary-secondary schooling in America, and I predict that, in the years ahead, they will transform it. Call me an optimist.

But how long must we wait? Emma and Ana are starting school now.

GLOSSARY

ABCTE. American Board for Certification of Teacher Excellence, nonprofit organization furnishing an alternate route to teacher certification via exams.

Achieve, Inc. Bipartisan, nonprofit organization founded in 1996 by governors and CEOs to encourage and assist states in raising academic standards.

ACT. American College Testing program, nonprofit testing organization best known for college entrance exams widely used, particularly in the Midwest, as an alternative to the SATs.

AERA. American Educational Research Association.

AFT. American Federation of Teachers, the second-largest teachers' union.

Alexander-James Panel. A blue-ribbon panel, named for chairman Lamar Alexander and vice chairman H. Thomas James, that made recommendations in 1988 ("Alexander-James Report") for overhauling the National Assessment of Educational Progress.

American Achievement Tests. National tests proposed by President George H. W. Bush as part of America 2000 but not enacted.

America 2000. President George H. W. Bush's and Education Secretary Lamar Alexander's strategy for attaining the national education goals set in 1990.

AP. Advanced Placement, the college-level end-of-course exams for high-school students offered by the College Board.

AYP. Adequate yearly progress, the benchmark for state and school achievement under the No Child Left Behind Act.

BEOGs. Basic Educational Opportunity Grants, now known as "Pell Grants," federally financed college scholarships first enacted in 1972.

CMO. Nonprofit charter (school) management organization.

Council of Chief State School Officers (CCSSO). National organization based in Washington, D.C., representing almost all state education superintendents and departments.

Council of the Great City Schools. National organization based in Washington, D.C., representing 66 large urban school systems.

CSF. Children's Scholarship Fund, nonprofit organization founded by John Walton and Theodore Forstmann to provide scholarships for low-income children to attend private schools.

EAI. Educational Alternatives, Inc., for-profit firm that contracted to manage the public schools of Baltimore and Hartford in the early 1990s.

ECS. Education Commission of the States, national organization based in Denver, belonged to by state-level education policymakers.

Edison Project. Now Edison Schools, for-profit firm founded by Christopher Whittle in 1992 to develop a new model for U.S. schools.

EMO. Education management organization, for-profit firm operating primarily charter schools.

ESEA. Elementary and Secondary Education Act, first passed in 1965, the omnibus statute containing Title I and many other federal programs for K–12 education.

ETS. Educational Testing Service, large, Princeton-based nonprofit testing organization.

Excellence Commission. The National Commission on Excellence in Education, source of 1983 report *A Nation at Risk.*

Goals 2000. Enacted in 1994, federal law proposed by President Bill Clinton to encourage and assist states to make progress toward national education goals.

HEA. Higher Education Act, first passed by Congress in 1965, the omnibus statute containing many federal higher-education programs.

HEW. Department of Health, Education, and Welfare, cabinet agency that in 1980 was divided into today's Department of Education and Department of Health and Human Services.

IASA. Improving America's Schools Act, 1994 reauthorization of ESEA, with new emphasis on state standards and assessments.

KIPP. Knowledge Is Power Program, a network of intense, college-preparatory public schools, predominantly charter middle schools.

Koret Task Force. Eleven-member group of education-policy experts associated with Stanford's Hoover Institution.

K12. Private firm founded by William J. Bennett, Lowell Milken, and others to develop instructional materials and lessons, delivered primarily via the Internet in "virtual" charter schools.

K–12. Kindergarten through twelfth grade, shorthand for "elementary and secondary education."

LEA. Local education agency, i.e., local "school system."

MAT. Master of Arts in Teaching, graduate degree program, predominantly for prospective high-school teachers.

MCAS. Massachusetts Comprehensive Assessment System, statewide testing program including high-school exit exam.

MCT. Minimum competency testing, generally state-level tests meant to assure that high-school graduates possess basic skills.

MPS. Milwaukee Public Schools.

NAE. National Academy of Education, selective membership organization of education scholars.

NAEP. National Assessment of Educational Progress, also known as "The Nation's Report Card," since 1969 America's principal federally funded testing program.

NAGB. National Assessment Governing Board, independent "board of directors" for NAEP, members appointed by U.S. secretary of education.

NASDC. New American Schools Development Corporation (later "New American Schools"), nonprofit organization formed in 1991 to develop innovative school designs.

NBPTS. National Board for Professional Teaching Standards, nonprofit organization formed in 1987 to develop standards for accomplished teaching and certify teachers who meet those standards.

NCATE. National Council for Accreditation of Teacher Education, nonprofit organization that accredits teacher preparation programs.

NCES. National Center for Education Statistics, primary federal agency (within Department of Education) for gathering, analyzing, and disseminating education data.

NCEST. National Council on Education Standards and Testing, Congressionally created bipartisan commission that reported in 1992 on ways of advancing standards and assessments.

NCLB. No Child Left Behind, enacted in 2001, a reauthorization of ESEA, containing many provisions that address academic standards, tests, and progress as well as teacher quality and other issues.

NCTAF. National Commission on Teaching and America's Future, nonprofit organization established in 1996 to advance teacher professionalism and quality.

NCTM. National Council of Teachers of Mathematics, membership organization of U.S. K–12 math teachers.

NDEA. National Defense Education Act, law passed by Congress in 1958 to use federal financial aid to strengthen education, primarily in science, math, and foreign languages.

NEA. National Education Association, largest teachers' union.

NEGP. National Education Goals Panel, bipartisan body of federal and state officials formed in 1990 to track progress toward national education goals. Ended in 2002.

NEH. National Endowment for the Humanities, federal agency to advance the humanities.

NESAC. National Education Standards and Assessment Council, a never-formed organization proposed by NCEST to vet and approve state academic standards and tests.

NESIC. National Education Standards and Improvement Council, authorized by Congress in 1994 to evaluate state academic standards and tests; members never appointed.

NGA. National Governors Association.

NIE. National Institute of Education, federal agency that existed from 1972 to 1985 to conduct education research.

OCR. Office for Civil Rights, federal civil rights enforcement agency, formerly housed in Department of HEW, now in Department of Education.

OECD. Organisation for Economic Co-operation and Development, international organization of 30 developed countries committed to "democratic government and the market economy."

OEO. Office of Economic Opportunity, former federal "War on Poverty" agency.

OERI. Office of Educational Research and Improvement, unit within the Department of Education formerly responsible for research, statistics, and assessment. In 2002, these functions were taken over by the Institute for Education Sciences.

OMB. Office of Management and Budget, unit within the Executive Office of the President that is responsible, among other things, for the federal budget.

PACE. Parents Advancing Choice in Education, Dayton-based nonprofit organization providing scholarships for private-school attendance and other forms of assistance to families seeking to exercise school choice.

PBHA. Phillips Brooks House Association, Harvard undergraduate-student volunteer and social-service organization.

PEPAC. President's Education Policy Advisory Committee, advised President George H. W. Bush.

SAT. Scholastic Aptitude Tests, now Scholastic Assessment Tests, college entrance exams administered by the College Board.

SBM. Site-based management, devolves certain education responsibilities to the school level.

SEA. State education agency.

SREB. Southern Regional Education Board, organization of 16 states, founded in 1948 to advance education in the region.

TFA. Teach for America, nonprofit organization that recruits and places recent college graduates for two-year terms in public schools serving disadvantaged children.

TIMSS. Third International Math and Science Study, renamed Trends in International Math and Science Study, conducts comparative assessments of student achievement in many countries, including an influential 1995 study.

Title I. The principal federal elementary-secondary education assistance program and the centerpiece of ESEA and NCLB, intended to strengthen the achievement of disadvantaged children.

UNESCO. United Nations Educational, Scientific, and Cultural Organization.

USIA. United States Information Agency, former federal international agency (now part of State Department) providing news, information, and cultural exchanges from the United States to other countries.

USOE. United States Office of Education, until 1980 and establishment of the Department of Education, the principal federal agency (within the Department of HEW) responsible for education, headed by a commissioner of education.

Virtual charter school. Charter school that provides curriculum and instruction primarily via the Internet.

Zelman decision. The 2002 *Zelman v. Simmons-Harris* U.S. Supreme Court decision (536 U.S. 639) holding that the Cleveland school-voucher program did not violate the First Amendment's "establishment of religion" clause.

NOTES

Part I | *Early Days*

1. Chapter 421, Laws of the State of New York (1874), 532.

2. Susan B. Carter, Michael R. Haines, Richard Sutch, and Gavin Wright, "Race and Ethnicity: Population, Vital Processes, and Education," *Historical Statistics of the United States, Millennial Edition,* February 2003, 10, http://www .economics.ucr.edu/papers/papers03/03-11.pdf.

3. We assume the family changed its name along the way, but no one recalls when or from what. Today the Ukraine—the part of Russia from which they came—is a separate nation.

4. A lively debate continues among experts such as E. D. Hirsch, Jr., who contend that "progressive" ideas and practices were so widespread in U.S. schools by the 1950s—and remain so today—that only a handful of critics even noticed them; historians such as the late Lawrence Cremin (and, in some of her writings, Diane Ravitch), who saw the progressive education "movement" collapsing even as its postwar critics were putting pen to paper; and chroniclers such as David Tyack and Larry Cuban, who argue that progressivism, like waves of other theories and later reforms, crashed without much lasting impact upon the rocky shore of established school practice. I do not expect to settle the matter in these pages.

5. Jeffrey Mirel, "The Traditional High School," *Education Next* 6, no. 1 (2006), http://www.hoover.org/publications/ednext/3212486.html.

6. Critics such as I. L. Kandel and William C. Bagley had been making similar arguments since 1930.

7. Milton Friedman, interviewed by Nick Gillespie, "The Father of Modern School Reform," *Reason Online,* December 2005, http://www.reason.com/ 0512/fe.ng.the.shtml.

8. You could, for example, be tested in the seventh month of fourth grade and have your score (in, say, reading or vocabulary) reported as "eighth grade, sixth month." This meant your performance in that subject was equivalent to the average performance of students across the country who were two-thirds of the way through grade eight. This sort of thing often happened to me, causing my head to swell.

9. In retrospect, I wonder whether this exposure to "manual arts" and "home economics" in the middle grades was meant to help us have a better basis for selecting our high-school "track."

10. At the high-school level, there were some statewide graduation requirements—certain mandatory courses to be taken—and selective colleges

published their admission prerequisites, also in the form of courses to be taken.

11. E. D. Hirsch, Jr., *The Schools We Need And Why We Don't Have Them* (New York: Random House, Inc., 1999), 50.

12. Diane Ravitch, *Left Back: A Century of Failed School Reform* (New York: Simon & Schuster, 2000), 395–96.

13. Diane Ravitch, *The Troubled Crusade: American Education, 1945–1980* (New York: Basic Books, 1983), 175.

14. Debra Viadero, "Race Report's Influence Felt 40 Years Later," *Education Week,* June 21, 2006, http://www.edweek.org/ew/articles/2006/06/21/41coleman.h25.html?qs=Coleman&levelId=2300.

15. Frederick Mosteller and Daniel P. Moynihan, eds., *On Equality of Educational Opportunity* (New York: Random House, 1972), 5.

16. Ibid., 44.

17. Viadero, "Race Report's Influence Felt 40 Years Later."

18. Debate has long raged over the proper interpretation of the decline in average SAT scores that commenced in the mid-sixties, with some analysts—and the College Board itself—favoring explanations having to do with changes in the test-taking population rather than deteriorating school performance. We can't finally resolve this, but I am persuaded by Christopher Jencks's analysis—based in part on a close look at score slippage in "white bread" Iowa—that kids were truly learning less than before. Hirsch, *The Schools We Need,* 179.

Part II | *The Seventies*

1. Thomas Toch, *In the Name of Excellence* (New York: Oxford University Press, 1991), 4.

2. As noted in chapter 2, Scholastic Aptitude Test (SAT) scores are an imperfect gauge of educational achievement. Not everyone takes them, and the test-taking population has changed over time. The test changes, too, from time to time, and the College Board further complicated matters in 1995 when it "recentered" SAT scores based on student performance in 1990, versus the earlier scale calibrated to performance in 1941. Some analysts, such as Richard Rothstein, assert that demographic changes among test takers are a better explanation for long-term shifts in average performance than deterioration in school quality and that, in fact, the achievement of students in each group improved even as national averages declined. See, for example, Richard Rothstein, *The Way We Were? The Myths and Realities of America's Student Achievement* (New York: Century Foundation Press, 1998). Others, such as E. D. Hirsch and Christopher Jencks, conclude that the SAT

decline bespoke true deterioration in the performance of U.S. schools and students. In the event, these scores are one of the few records of student performance available before 1970, and the perception that they fell dramatically after the mid-sixties had a catalytic effect on American education and education policy.

3. Chris Pipho, *Seven Lessons Learned from Minimum Competency Testing*, Education Commission of the States, http://www.ecs.org/clearinghouse/32/67/3267 .htm.

4. Gerald R. Ford, quoted in Michelle R. Davis, "Ford's Legacy Includes a Special Education Law He Signed Despite Worries," *Education Week*, January 30, 2007, http://www.edweek.org/ew/articles/2007/01/03/18ford_web.h26 .html.

5. Diane Ravitch, *The Troubled Crusade: American Education, 1945–1980* (New York: Basic Books, 1983), 273.

6. Ibid., 299.

7. A friend who grew up in Anniston, Alabama, recently described her dismay at what has happened to public education in that small city, which formerly operated a competent (albeit segregated) "dual" system for both blacks and whites but from which most of the latter have exited over the past several decades and in which few of the former are now succeeding.

8. Ravitch, *The Troubled Crusade*, 176.

9. Toch, *In the Name of Excellence*, 5.

10. Douglas Schoen, *Pat: A Biography of Daniel Patrick Moynihan* (New York: Harper & Row Publishers, 1979), 163.

11. Gareth Davies, *See Government Grow: Education Politics from Johnson to Reagan* (Lawrence, KS: University Press of Kansas, 2007), chapter 4.

12. Richard M. Nixon, "Special Message to the Congress on Education Reform," (March 3, 1970), quoted in Chester E. Finn, Jr., *Education and the Presidency* (Lexington, MA: Lexington Books, 1977), appendix A.

13. Ibid.

14. Ibid.

15. Ibid., appendix B.

16. Ibid., 69.

17. Raymond Wolters, *The Burden of Brown: Thirty Years of School Desegregation* (Knoxville, TN: University of Tennessee Press, 1984), 163. Gareth Davies concurs, noting that, while Nixon never got credit for major strides toward southern school desegregation—partly because his enemies truly saw no good in him, partly because he declined to characterize the federal role in moral terms—"[I]t seems likely that Nixon's emphasis on carrying out the law—on obeying the Constitution, rather than carrying out a moral obligation—was

precisely what was needed to bring about the peaceful desegregation of the South." Davies, *See Government Grow*, chapter 5.

18. In 1970, the race for New York's U.S. Senate seat turned into a three-way contest among Ottinger, incumbent liberal Republican Charles Goodell, and Nixon-backed conservative James Buckley (who won). Several times that autumn I found myself bemusedly taking the Ottinger kids on expeditions to ball games while their parents campaigned, even as my White House superiors did their utmost to foil the congressman's ambition. Six years later, Pat Moynihan foiled Buckley's reelection.

19. I had no idea that Nixon saw my memo, much less commented on it. I owe thanks to Oxford historian Gareth Davies, who came upon it three decades later in Nixon's presidential papers and was kind enough to send me a photocopy.

20. Schoen, *Pat*, 166.

21. Ibid., 167–68.

22. I borrow this observation, and the quote from Nixon's memoirs, from Davies, ibid.

23. Gareth Davies also notes that "Nixon was the first President in 120 years to assume office with the opposition party in control of Congress." Davies, *See Government Grow*, chapter 4.

24. Chester E. Finn, Jr., "What the NIE Can Be," *Phi Delta Kappan*, February 1972, 349.

25. Chester E. Finn, Jr., "The National Foundation for Higher Education: Death of an Idea," *Change* 4, no. 2 (March 1972): 31.

26. Schoen, *Pat*, 184.

27. James M. Tooley, "Private Schools for the Poor," *Education Next*, Fall 2005, http://www.educationnext.org/20054/22.html.

28. Chester E. Finn, Jr., and David W. Breneman, *Public Policy and Private Higher Education* (Washington, DC: The Brookings Institution, 1978), 34.

29. Ibid., 52.

30. Chester E. Finn, Jr., *Scholars, Dollars & Bureaucrats* (Washington, DC: The Brookings Institution, 1978), 3.

31. Hugh Davis Graham, *The Uncertain Triumph: Federal Education Policy in the Kennedy and Johnson Years* (Chapel Hill: University of North Carolina Press, 1984), 22.

32. Ibid.

33. Eugene Eidenberg and Roy D. Morey, *An Act of Congress: The Legislative Process and the Making of Education Policy* (New York: W. W. Norton and Company, 1969), 87.

34. Testimony of Antonin Scalia, *Tuition Tax Relief Bills* (Washington, DC: Government Printing Office, 1978), 284.

35. Daniel Patrick Moynihan, *Counting Our Blessings* (Boston, MA: Little, Brown and Company, 1980), 172.

36. Ibid., 237–38.

37. Joseph A. Califano, Jr., *Governing America* (New York: Simon and Schuster, 1981), 303.

38. Godfrey Hodgson, *The Gentleman from New York* (Boston: Houghton Mifflin Company, 2000), 290.

39. Beryl A. Radin and Willis D. Hawley, *The Politics of Federal Reorganization: Creating the U.S. Department of Education* (New York: Pergamon Press, 1988), 41.

40. Carter made another exception within weeks of his inauguration, proposing creation of the cabinet-level Department of Energy on March 1, 1977, and signing the enabling legislation just five months later. With the nation facing an "energy crisis," little controversy attended this measure.

41. Rufus E. Miles, Jr., *A Cabinet Department of Education: The Time Is Now* (Washington, DC: Heldref Publications, 1977).

42. Califano, *Governing America*, 277.

43. Ibid.

44. Ibid., 277–78.

45. Ibid., 280.

46. Carter did not spell out precisely what this was another "major step" toward, but he implied that it would help bring about better-organized and more-efficient government.

47. *Legislative History of Public Law 96-88* (Washington, DC: Government Printing Office, 1980), 784–87.

48. Ibid.

49. Ibid., 784.

50. Albert Shanker, "Where We Stand," *New York Times,* April 29, 1979, http://source.nysut.org/weblink/index.asp?DocumentID=1356&FolderID=485&SearchHandle=0&DocViewType=ShowImage&LeftPaneType=Hidden&dbid=0&page=1.

51. Califano, *Governing America*, 287.

52. Ibid., 289.

53. Lyndon B. Johnson, "Remarks in Johnson City, Texas, Upon Signing the Elementary and Secondary Education Bill" (speech, Johnson City, TX, April 11, 1965), http://www.lbjlib.utexas.edu/johnson/archives.hom/speeches.hom/650411.asp.

54. It pains me to recall that Kozol's evocative first book tugged at my twenty-one-year-old emotional (and career) strings, as his recent influence on American education has been almost entirely malign.

(He is also one of the meanest and most ad hominem individuals I have ever dealt with.)

55. Irving Kristol, "Forty Good Years," *The Public Interest*, Spring 2005, http://www.findarticles.com/p/articles/mi_m0377/is_159/ai_n13779487.

56. Terrel H. Bell, *The Thirteenth Man: A Reagan Cabinet Memoir* (New York: The Free Press, 1988), 44.

Part III | *The Eighties*

1. Terrel H. Bell, *The Thirteenth Man: A Reagan Cabinet Memoir* (New York: The Free Press, 1988), 114–15.

2. *A Nation at Risk: The Imperative for Educational Reform* (Washington, DC: Government Printing Office, 1983), 5.

3. Ibid.

4. Thomas Toch, *In the Name of Excellence* (New York: Oxford University Press, 1991), 14.

5. Edmonds appeared to be headed for an important place in education-reform circles but died young in 1983. His own work was foreshadowed by a thoughtful British scholar named Michael Rutter, whose 1979 book, *Fifteen Thousand Hours: Secondary Schools and Their Effects on Children*, caused a mild sensation in the ed schools. It, too, identified school characteristics that correlated with higher and lower student achievement. Later in the eighties, this kind of analysis was expertly extended by Stanford's Marshall Smith and colleagues. The problem with nearly all of the "effective schools" research was that, while it excelled at retrospectively describing the qualities of good schools, it wasn't very helpful to reformers seeking surefire means of creating more of them.

6. Toch, *In the Name of Excellence*, 29.

7. Reflecting on his tenure as education secretary, Terrel H. Bell himself called in 1987 for a "major Marshall-plan type of effort" to remake American education. See http://www.edweek.org/ew/articles/1987/10/28/07330004.h07.html?qs—arshall+plan. And the analogy continues two decades later. In January 2007, Stanford professor Linda Darling-Hammond urged "a Marshall plan for teaching." See Linda Darling-Hammond, "A Marshall Plan for Teaching," *Education Week,* January 10, 2007, http://www.edweek.org/ew/articles/2007/01/10/18hammond.h26.html?qs=Marshall+Plan.

8. Jimmy Carter, *Keeping Faith* (New York: Bantam Books, Inc., 1982), 76.

9. Bell, *The Thirteenth Man*, 95–96. In his superb new history of federal education policymaking, Oxford scholar Gareth Davies depicts Bell as politically astute and given to telling various audiences what they wanted to

hear, indicating to "movement" conservatives that he stood foursquare for eliminating the Education Department and reducing its budget while signaling to educators (and Democrats) that he believed no such thing. Davies also suggests that abolishing the Education Department, while important to some White House aides and conservative supporters, was never a particularly high priority for Ronald Reagan himself. Gareth Davies, *See Government Grow: Education Politics from Johnson to Reagan* (Lawrence KS: University Press of Kansas, 2007), chapter 10.

10. This saga is methodically recounted in Davies, *See Government Grow.*

11. Toch, *In the Name of Excellence*, 17.

12. Gardner later raised his total to nine intelligences, adding "naturalist" and "existential" intelligences to the original list.

13. Joseph Adelson and Chester E. Finn, Jr., "Terrorizing Children," *Commentary* 79, no. 4 (April 1985): 29.

14. Carnegie Forum on Education and the Economy, *A Nation Prepared: Teachers for the Twenty-first Century* (New York: Carnegie, 1986).

15. Ernest L. Boyer, *High School: A Report on Secondary Education in America* (New York: Harper & Row Publishers, 1983). While on the Vanderbilt faculty in the early eighties, I did some consulting—researching, brainstorming, drafting, reacting, editing—for Boyer and his colleagues, based at the Carnegie Foundation for the Advancement of Teaching, next to Brookings. I welcomed the expense-paid trips from Nashville to Washington.

16. Theodore R. Sizer, *Horace's Compromise: The Dilemma of the American High School* (Boston, MA: Houghton Mifflin Company, 1984).

17. John I. Goodlad, *A Place Called School: Prospects for the Future* (New York: McGraw-Hill Book Company, 1984).

18. Toch, *In the Name of Excellence*, 29.

19. Allan Bloom, *The Closing of the American Mind* (New York: Simon & Schuster, 1987), and E. D. Hirsch, Jr., *Cultural Literacy: What Every American Needs to Know* (Boston, MA: Houghton Mifflin Company, 1987).

20. Charter schools, commonly defined as independently operated public schools of choice, are discussed at greater length in chapters 16 and 25.

21. Diane Ravitch and Chester E. Finn, Jr., *What Do Our 17-Year-Olds Know?* (New York: Harper & Row, 1987), 16–17.

22. *Time for Results: The Governors' 1991 Report on Education* (Washington, DC: National Governors Association Center for Policy Research and Analysis, August 1986), 4.

23. Diane Ravitch, "The State of Standards," *Network News & Views*, December 1996, http://www.edexcellence.net/foundation/publication/publication.cfm?id=228.

24. Toch, *In the Name of Excellence*, 55–56. Other "academics" named by Toch were Joseph Adelson, Nathan Glazer, Denis Doyle, Edward A. Wynne, and Gerald Grant.

25. Chester E. Finn, Jr., "The Future of Education's Liberal Consensus," *Change* 12, no. 6 (September 1980): 25–32.

26. Chester E. Finn, Jr., "Giving a Boost to Quality Education," *Wall Street Journal*, June 1, 1981.

27. E. J. Dionne, "American in Paris Who's Disenchanted by UNESCO," *New York Times,* April 21, 1983, http://select.nytimes.com/gst/abstract.html?res= F30B10FD3C5C0C728EDDAD0894DB484D81&n=Top%2fReference%2fTimes %20Topics%2fOrganizations%2fU%2fUnited%20Nations%20.

28. Lamar Alexander, "To Bring Out the Best in America," interviewed by *Democracy in Action,* September 29, 1998, http://www.gwu.edu/~action/ alexint.html.

29. *Time for Results.* Twenty years later, the jury remains out as to whether competition, at least on the limited scales undertaken to date, actually changes district school systems in desirable ways or simply impels them to fight harder to maim, contain, and erase their unwanted competitors. See, for example, Frederick M. Hess, *Revolution at the Margins* (Washington, DC: The Brookings Institution, 2002).

30. James S. Coleman, Thomas Hoffer, and Sally Kilgore, *High School Achievement: Public, Catholic, and Private Schools Compared* (New York: Basic Books, 1982), and James S. Coleman and Thomas Hoffer, *Public and Private Schools: The Impact of Communities* (New York: Basic Books, 1987). Drawing on the same data set and coming to similar conclusions was Andrew M. Greeley, *Catholic High Schools and Minority Students* (New Brunswick, NJ: Transaction Books, 1982).

31. Bell, *The Thirteenth Man*, 139.

32. Toch, *In the Name of Excellence*, 37.

33. Chester E. Finn, Jr., "What the NIE Cannot Be," *Phi Delta Kappan*, February 1983. The "regional educational laboratories" and university-based education research centers date back to the mid-1960s, when they were begun as a network of federally funded institutions meant to advance education R&D and its translation into school practice, somewhat in the mode of national laboratories working on nuclear weaponry and agricultural productivity. As might have been predicted, once established they did not want to forfeit their hold on a sizable fraction of federal education research dollars, despite repeated evaluations indicating that they were accomplishing little.

34. This structure changed even more radically in 2002 when the Education Sciences Reform Act established, within the Education Department, the

Institute of Education Sciences, modeled in part on the old OERI but larger and somewhat more independent. See http://www.ed.gov/about/offices/list/ies/index.html?src=oc.

35. *What Works: Research About Teaching and Learning* (Washington, DC: Government Printing Office, 1986).

36. Daniel B. Levine, ed., *Creating a Center for Education Statistics: A Time for Action* (Washington, DC: National Academy Press, 1986), 4.

37. *The Nation's Report Card* (Cambridge, MA: National Academy of Education, 1987).

38. Lynn Olson, "Bennett Panel Urges Major Expansion of NAEP," *Education Week*, March 25, 1987, http://www.edweek.org/ew/articles/1987/03/25/26naep.ho6.html?qs=Bennett+NAEP+Kirst&levelId=2300.

39. Ibid.

40. Ibid.

41. "Groups Oppose Expansion of Federal Test," *Education Week*, February 10, 1988, http://www.edweek.org/ew/articles/1988/02/10/07440033.ho7.html?qs=NAEP+PTA+1988.

42. Chester E. Finn, Jr., "Policy, Interest Groups and the 'Gang of 237,'" *Education Week*, May 10, 1989, http://www.edweek.org/ew/articles/1989/05/10/08290016.ho8.html?qs=gang+of+237&levelId=2300.

43. Stephen A. Smith, ed., *Preface to the Presidency: Selected Speeches of Bill Clinton, 1974–1992* (Fayetteville, AR: University of Arkansas Press, 1996), 33–34.

44. Maris A. Vinovskis, "The Road to Charlottesville: The 1989 Education Summit" (National Education Goals Panel, December 1999), 26, http://govinfo.library.unt.edu/negp/reports/negp30.pdf.

45. Ibid., 25.

46. Ibid., 28.

47. Ibid., 35.

48. Ibid., 38.

49. Bill Clinton, *My Life* (New York: Alfred A. Knopf, 2004), 350.

50. Charles Kolb, *White House Daze* (New York: The Free Press, 1994), 135.

51. *America 2000: An Education Strategy, Sourcebook* (Washington, DC: U.S. Department of Education, 1991), 62.

52. *The Second International Science Study*, IAEA, April 1982–86, http://www.iea.nl/siss.html.

53. *Japanese Education Today* (Washington, DC: Government Printing Office, 1987), 61.

54. Cheri Pierson Yecke, *The War Against Excellence: The Rising Tide of Mediocrity in America's Middle Schools* (Westport, CT: Praeger Publishers, 2003), 29.

55. Cheri Pierson Yecke, *Mayhem in the Middle: How Middle Schools Have Failed America, and How to Make Them Work* (Washington, DC: Thomas B. Fordham Institute, 2005).

56. Bill Honig, *Teaching Our Children to Read: The Role of Skills in a Comprehensive Reading Program* (Thousand Oaks, CA: Corwin Press, 1995). The "reading wars" still rage, despite the seemingly definitive scientific findings of the National Reading Panel in 2000. Seven years later, the federal Reading First program was engulfed in crisis due in large part to its managers' insistence on funding only those early-reading programs that rested on a solid scientific foundation.

57. Diane Ravitch, *National Standards in American Education: A Citizen's Guide* (Washington, DC: The Brookings Institution, 1995), 125.

58. In an attempt to shed more light than heat on math and to bring to bear whatever scientific evidence could be found, in April 2006 President George W. Bush named a National Mathematic Advisory Panel, composed of leading mathematicians and educators, and charged it to report by early 2008. See http://www.ed.gov/about/bdscomm/list/mathpanel/about.html.

59. America's foremost authority on the theory of charters and chartering and their evolution, as well as a major contributor himself to these ideas, is Ted Kolderie, currently associated with a Minnesota-based reform group called Education Evolving. Its website (http://www.educationevolving.org/) contains much valuable background reading, including Kolderie's 1993 paper titled "Charter Schools: The States Begin to Withdraw the Exclusive" (http://www.educationevolving.org/pdf/Withdraw_exclusive.pdf) and his 2005 writings on Ray Budde and the origins of the charter concept: http://www.educationevolving.org/pdf/Ray_Budde.pdf.

60. Charles L. Glenn, Jr., *The Myth of the Common School* (Amherst, MA: University of Massachusetts Press, 1988). Charles Glenn, "Fanatical Secularism," *Education Next* 3, no. 1 (Winter 2003).

61. This story is superbly told by Daniel McGroarty in *Break These Chains: The Battle for School Choice* (Rocklin, CA: Prima Publishing, 1996).

62. John E. Chubb and Terry M. Moe, *Politics, Markets, and America's Schools* (Washington, DC: The Brookings Institution, 1990), 165.

63. Ibid., 167.

Part IV | *The Nineties*

1. Charles Kolb, *White House Daze* (New York: The Free Press, 1994), 39.
2. *America 2000: An Education Strategy, Sourcebook* (Washington, D.C.: U.S. Department of Education, 1991), 3–4.
3. Diane Ravitch, *Left Back: A Century of Failed School Reforms* (New York: Simon & Schuster, 2000), 432.

4. Ibid., 433.

5. *America 2000*, 25.

6. Jeffrey Mirel, *Evolution of the New American Schools: From Revolution to Mainstream* (Washington, D.C.: Thomas B. Fordham Foundation, 2001), 1, http://www.edexcellence.net/foundation/publication/publication.cfm?id=44&pubsubid=679&doc=pdf.

7. Ibid., 8.

8. Mark Berends, Susan J. Bodilly, and Sheila Nataraj Kirby, *Facing the Challenges of Whole-School Reform* (Santa Monica, CA: RAND, 2002), xxxvi.

9. *Raising Standards for American Education* (Washington, D.C.: Government Printing Office, 1992), 14.

10. Robert B. Schwartz and Marian A. Robinson, "Goals 2000 and the Standards Movement," in Diane Ravitch, ed., *Brookings Papers on Education Policy 2000* (Washington, D.C.: The Brookings Institution, 2000), 179.

11. *Raising Standards for American Education*, 13.

12. Diane Ravitch, *National Standards in American Education: A Citizen's Guide* (Washington, D.C.: The Brookings Institution, 1995), 143–44.

13. Robert Rothman, "Standards and Testing Report Is Hailed, Criticized," *Education Week*, February 5, 1992, http://www.edweek.org/ew/articles/1992/02/05/20test.h11.html?qs=Theodore+R+Sizer.

14. Maris A. Vinovskis, "Overseeing the Nation's Report Card" (National Assessment Governing Board, 1998), 45. This valuable paper can be found in full on the NAGB website: http://www.nagb.org/pubs/95222.pdf. To develop a "consensus" behind each performance level for each subject in the relevant grades, we adopted a standard-setting process known as the "modified Angoff method"; it and some alternatives to it and their virtues and weaknesses are exhaustively examined in Gregory J. Cizek and Robert J. Sternberg, eds., *Setting Performance Standards: Concepts, Methods, and Perspectives* (Mahwah, NJ: Lawrence Earlbaum Associates, 2001).

15. A careful analysis by Gary Phillips of the American Institutes of Research indicates that a substantially larger proportion of youngsters in other "advanced" countries are in fact performing at or above NAEP's "proficient" level and that, while it may be unrealistic to expect all children to attain that level, it is a reasonable standard to aim for and one that far more U.S. students could attain than the 25–30% that typically do so today. See Gary W. Phillips, *Linking NAEP Achievement Levels to TIMSS* (Washington, D.C.: American Institutes for Research, 2007), http://www.air.org/news/documents/naep-timss.pdf.

16. Charter authorizing is explained in depth in Paul T. Hill and Chester E. Finn, Jr., "Authorizing: The Missing Link," in Paul Hill, ed., *Charter Schools*

Against the Odds: An Assessment of the Koret Task Force on K–12 Education
(Stanford, CA: Hoover Institution Press, 2006), 103–26.

17. Although some suspect that the charter option serves mostly to create opportunities for "traditional" school models, Dick Carpenter's research shows otherwise. See *Playing to Type?* (Washington, D.C.: Thomas B. Fordham Institute, 2006), http://www.edexcellence.net/doc/Carpenter %20ProjectV2.pdf. And for a discussion of a specific "progressive" charter school, see Louis Pugliese, "Surviving as a Progressive Charter School—Is It Possible?" *Education Week,* March 7, 2007, http://www.edweek.org/ew/ articles/2007/03/07/26pugliese.h25.html?qs=pugliese.

18. For a useful typology of charter schools, see *Playing To Type?,* http://www .edexcellence.net/doc/Carpenter%20ProjectV2.pdf.

19. Paul T. Hill, "Introduction," in *Charter Schools Against the Odds,* 1–14.

20. Chester E. Finn, Jr., Bryan C. Hassel, and Sheree Speakman, *Charter School Funding: Inequity's Next Frontier* (Washington, D.C.: Thomas B. Fordham Institute, August 2005), http://www.edexcellence.net/doc/Charter%20School %20Funding%202005%20FINAL.pdf.

21. Besides Clinton, Riley, and Romer, happy exceptions included legislators such as Minnesota's John Brandl and Ember Reichgott and Pennsylvania's Dwight Evans, U.S. senator Joe Lieberman, and Indianapolis mayor Bart Peterson.

22. The late Mike Joyce had earlier led the John M. Olin Foundation, which supplied the first grant to Ravitch's and my Educational Excellence Network in the early eighties.

23. Polly Williams, interviewed by John H. Fund, "Champion of Choice: Shaking Up Milwaukee's Schools," *Reasononline,* http://reason.com/williamsint .shtml.

24. Anthony S. Bryk, Valerie E. Lee, and Peter B. Holland, *Catholic Schools and the Common Good* (Cambridge, MA: Harvard University Press, 1993).

25. Ravitch, *National Standards,* 114.

26. Diane Ravitch, "Harold Stevenson: In Memoriam," *The Education Gadfly* 5, no. 29 (August 25, 2005), http://www.edexcellence.net/institute/gadfly/issue .cfm?id=204&edition=#2434.

27. Harold W. Stevenson and James W. Stigler, *The Learning Gap: Why Our Schools Are Failing and What We Can Learn from Japanese and Chinese Education* (New York: Summit Books, 1992), 202.

28. Robert J. Samuelson, "How We Dummies Succeed," *Washington Post,* September 6, 2006, http://www.washingtonpost.com/wp-dyn/content/ article/2006/09/05/AR2006090501131.html.

29. This argument is made persuasively by a number of economists, including Frank Levy and Richard J. Murnane in such works as *The New Division of*

Labor: How Computers Are Creating the Next Job Market (Princeton, NJ: Princeton University Press, 2004) and *Teaching the New Basic Skills: Principles for Educating Children to Thrive in a Changing Economy* (New York: The Free Press, 1996).

30. This aversion to behaviorism is not total. Many educators are quick to distribute "gold stars" to second graders who do well in school; to reward attendance with trips to theme parks; to give pizzas to youngsters who read extra books; even to pay cash to high-school students who take Advanced Placement courses.

31. Today's version of that sort of determinism, albeit arising from a very different direction, is Charles Murray's contention that IQ, not schooling, is the chief determinant of what kids learn. See Richard J. Herrnstein and Charles Murray, *The Bell Curve: Intelligence and Class Structure in American Life* (New York: Simon & Schuster, 1996), as well as Murray's several 2007 essays in the *Wall Street Journal*. *Education Week*'s annual *Quality Counts* publication also slipped into determinism in 2007. See http://www.edweek.org/ew/toc/2007/01/04/index.html/. For critical comments thereon, see "Quality doubts" in *The Education Gadfly*, January 11, 2007, http://www.edexcellence.net/foundation/gadfly/issue.cfm?edition=&id=272#3198 and Kati Haycock, letter to the editor, *Education Week,* March 7, 2007, http://www.edweek.org/ew/articles/2007/03/07/26letter-1.h26.html?qs=Haycock.

32. Theodore R. Sizer, *Horace's School: Redesigning the American High School* (Boston, MA: Houghton Mifflin, 1992), 188–89.

33. A six-year board member—and several-year chairman—of the Chicago Annenberg Challenge was Barack Obama, the U.S. senator from Illinois who at this writing is running for president.

34. "Citizens Changing Their Schools: A Mid-term Report of the Annenberg Challenge," http://www.annenberginstitute.org/Challenge/pubs/citizens_changing/intro.html. The Fordham Foundation also engaged expert observers to conduct case studies of the Annenberg Challenge program in New York, Philadelphia, and Chicago and published their findings in *Can Philanthropy Save Our Schools?* http:www.edexcellence.net/foundation/publication/publication.cfm?id=41. Additional observations on education philanthropy can be found in Chester E. Finn, Jr., and Kelly Amis, *Making It Count: A Guide to High-Impact Education Philanthropy,* http://www.edexcellence.net/ foundation/publication/publication.cfm?id=39, and Frederick M. Hess, *With the Best of Intentions: How Philanthropy Is Reshaping K–12 Education* (Cambridge, MA: Harvard Education Press, 2005).

35. David Tyack and Larry Cuban, *Tinkering Toward Utopia: A Century of Public School Reform* (Cambridge, MA: Harvard University Press, 1995), 134–35.

36. Chester E. Finn, Jr., "The Biggest Reform of All," *Phi Delta Kappan* 71, no. 8 (April 1990): 586.

37. Chester E. Finn, Jr., *We Must Take Charge: Our Schools and Our Future* (New York: The Free Press, 1991), xvi.

38. CSRQ Center Report on Education Service Providers (Washington, D.C.: American Institutes of Research, 2006), http://www.csrq.org/documents/ESPCSRQReport-Full_000.pdf and http://www.edisonschools.com/design/d23.html. The other students served by Edison are mostly participants in tutoring and other ancillary programs.

39. Since late 2003, when the Edison firm was again "taken private," nearly all its stock has been owned by the Florida state retirement system—more than a little ironic (and controversial) inasmuch as the primary beneficiaries of that system are public-school teachers whose unions cannot abide Edison.

40. Eric A. Hanushek, *Making Schools Work: Improving Performance and Controlling Costs* (Washington, D.C.: The Brookings Institution, 1994), xv.

41. Ibid., 154.

42. Neil Postman, *The End of Education: Redefining the Value of School* (New York: Alfred A. Knopf, 1995). During the "revolutions" of the late sixties, the ever-timely Postman had published *Teaching as a Subversive Activity*.

43. E. D. Hirsch, Jr., *The Schools We Need and Why We Don't Have Them* (New York: Doubleday, 1996), 230.

44. Arthur M. Schlesinger, Jr., *The Disuniting of America* (New York: W. W. Norton & Co., 1998).

45. Chester E. Finn, Jr., "What to Do about Education: The Schools," *Commentary* 98, no. 4 (October 1994): 33–35.

46. Chester E. Finn, Jr., "Can the Schools Be Saved?" *Commentary* 102, no. 3 (September 1996): 45.

47. William J. Clinton, "Address Before a Joint Session of the Congress on the State of the Union" (speech, Washington, DC, February 4, 1997), http://www.presidency.ucsb.edu/ws/index.php?pid=53358.

48. "National Testing: Prepare for a Battle," *Education World*, September 15, 1997, http://www.educationworld.com/a_admin/admin/admin020.shtml.

49. Rene Sanchez, "House Republicans Fail to See the Need for Clinton's National Test Plan," *Washington Post*, August 19, 1997, http://www.washingtonpost.com/wpsrv/politics/special/testing/stories/ed081997.htm.

50. William J. Bennett and Chester E. Finn, Jr., "National Tests: A Yardstick to Learn By," *Washington Post*, September 15, 1997, http://www.washingtonpost.com/wpsrv/politics/special/testing/stories/op091597.htm.

51. Richard F. Elmore, "The National Education Goals Panel: Purposes, Progress, and Prospects," http://govinfo.library.unt.edu/negp/reports/elmoref.htm.

52. *What Matters Most: Teaching for America's Future* (New York: National Commission on Teaching and America's Future, 1996), 10, http://www.nctaf.org/documents/nctaf/WhatMattersMost.pdf.

53. Diane Ravitch and I and our Educational Excellence Network cooperated in various ways with these worthy endeavors, including speaking tours and seminars in Eastern Europe under the AFT's aegis.

54. The evidence to date is mixed. See http://www.nbpts.org/resources/research/browse_studies?ID=167, http://www.nbpts.org/resources/research/browse_studies?ID=164, http://www.caldercenter.org/research/publications.cfm, and Bess Keller, "National Board Teachers No Better Than Other Educators, Long-Awaited Study Finds," *Education Week,* May 9, 2006, http://www.edweek.org/ew/articles/2006/05/09/37nbpts_web.h25.html#. For additional studies commissioned by the NBPTS, see http://www.nbpts.org/resources/research/impact_of_certification.

55. George V. Voinovich, interviewed by George A. Clowes, "Together We Can Do It: An Exclusive Interview with U.S. Senator George V. Voinovich," *School Reform News*, October 1, 2002, http://www.heartland.org/Article.cfm?artId=10434.

56. Louann Bierlein Palmer, Chester E. Finn, Jr., and Bruno V. Manno, *Charter Schools in Action: A First Look* (Washington, DC: Hudson Institute, January 1997), http://www.edexcellence.net/foundation/publication/publication.cfm?id=82.

57. Ibid.

58. Ibid. This passage also illustrates the extent to which even practiced charter watchers confuse school operators with school "sponsors." The latter refers to the entities that license these schools to operate, a far different role than running the schools themselves. Charter authorizing is explained in depth in Paul T. Hill and Chester E. Finn, Jr., "Authorizing: The Missing Link," in *Charter Schools Against the Odds*, 103–26.

59. A good overview of home schooling can be found in Isabel Lyman, "Home-schooling: Back to the Future?" Cato Policy Analysis No. 294, The Cato Institute, January 7, 1998, http://www.cato.org/pubs/pas/pa-294.html.

60. Lawrence M. Rudner, *The Scholastic Achievement and Demographic Characteristics of Home School Students in 1998*, Home School Legal Defense Association, http://www.hslda.org/docs/study/rudner1999/Rudner0.asp.

61. "President Clinton Delivers Message of 'High Standards and High Accountability'" (U.S. Department of Education, No. 35, May 1996), http://www.ed.gov/G2K/community/96-05.html.

62. Charles Bierbauer, "Now That Johnny Can Read, Can He Get a Job with IBM?" *CNN*, March 26, 1996, http://www.cnn.com/US/9603/education_summit/index.html.

63. Extraordinary exceptions in recent years have included the late John Walton, Theodore Forstmann, and Don and Doris Fisher, generous supporters of school choice in myriad forms.

64. Louis V. Gerstner, Jr., "1999 Summit Address" (speech, 1999 Education Summit, IBM Conference Center, Palisades, NY, September 30–October 1, 1999).

65. Tommy G. Thompson, "1999 Summit Address" (speech, 1999 Education Summit, IBM Conference Center, Palisades, NY, September 30–October 1, 1999).

66. "Action Statement" (paper, 1999 Education Summit, IBM Conference Center, Palisades, NY, September 30–October 1, 1999), http://www.achieve.org/achieve.nsf/1999Summit_ActionStatement?OpenForm.

67. In December 2006, *Education Week* published a perceptive summary of the Fordham Foundation's ten-year track record. See Lesli A. Maxwell, "Finn Basks in Role as Standards-Bearer, Gadfly," *Education Week,* December 20, 2006, http://www.edweek.org/ew/articles/2006/12/20/16fordham.h26.html?qs=Thomas+B.+Fordham+Foundation.

68. Strictly speaking, on January 1, 2007, the Thomas B. Fordham Foundation became a "supporting organization" for the Thomas B. Fordham Institute rather than a conventional private foundation.

69. The detailed findings can be found in William G. Powell and Paul E. Peterson, *The Education Gap: Vouchers and Urban Schools* (Washington: Brookings Institution Press, 2006) and in William G. Howell, Patrick J. Wolf, Paul E. Peterson and David E. Campbell, "Test Score Effects of School Vouchers in Dayton, Ohio, New York City, and Washington, DC," http://www.ksg.harvard.edu/pepg/research.htm#2000.

70. Chester E. Finn, Jr., Bruno V. Manno, and Gregg Vanourek, *Charter Schools in Action: Renewing Public Education* (Princeton, NJ: Princeton University Press, 2000).

71. William J. Bennett, Chester E. Finn, Jr., and John T. E. Cribb, Jr., *The Educated Child: A Parent's Guide from Preschool Through Eighth Grade* (New York: The Free Press, 1999).

Part V | *Today and Tomorrow*

1. Joetta L. Sack, "Candidates' K–12 Policies Share Themes," *Education Week,* September 6, 2000, http://www.edweek.org/ew/articles/2000/09/06/01election.h20.html?qs=Joetta+Sack.

2. David W. Grissmer, Ann Flanagan, Jennifer H. Kawata, and Stephanie Williamson, "Trends in State Scores," *Improving Student Achievement: What State NAEP Scores Tell Us* (RAND Education, 2000), 59, http://www.rand.org/pubs/monograph_reports/MR924/MR924.chap5.pdf.

3. Stephen P. Klein, Laura S. Hamilton, Daniel F. McCaffrey, and Brian M. Stecher, *What Do Test Scores in Texas Tell Us?* (RAND Education, 2000), http://www.rand.org/pubs/issue_papers/IP202/index2.html.

4. "Statement of RAND President and CEO, James A. Thomson" (speech, RAND, October 24, 2000), http://www.rand.org/news/texas.html.

5. In 2005, the Florida Supreme Court invalidated the voucher part of the state's "A+" accountability system on grounds that it violated the "uniformity" clause of the state constitution. But other voucher programs continue in the Sunshine State, including a sizable one whereby disabled youngsters are able to carry state funding to the private schools of their choice.

6. The track record of school interventions, reconstitutions, and other "turnaround" strategies in American education is uneven at best. Ronald C. Brady, *Can Failing Schools Be Fixed?* (Washington, DC: Thomas B. Fordham Foundation, 2003), http://www.edexcellence.net/doc/failing_schools.pdf.

7. "Press Conference with President George W. Bush and Education Secretary Rod Paige to Introduce the President's Education Program" (Washington, DC, January 23, 2001), http://www.whitehouse.gov/news/releases/2001/01/20010123-2.html.

8. "Educational, Cultural, Apprenticeship, and Exchange Programs for Alaska Natives, Native Hawaiians, and Their Historical Whaling and Trading Partners in Massachusetts," U.S. Department of Education, Office of Innovation and Improvement, http://www.ed.gov/programs/whaling/index.html.

9. As I write in mid-2007, the White House and some Capitol Hill leaders assert that NCLB's reauthorization can and will be completed by the 110th Congress, but most of the "smart money" in Washington says this is a fantasy and the task will await the next president and the 111th Congress.

10. An excellent explanation of NCLB's workings can be found in Frederick M. Hess and Michael J. Petrilli, *No Child Left Behind* (New York: Peter Lang Publishing, 2006).

11. Jack Jennings, quoted in Ben Feller, "Rising Number of Schools Face Penalties," Associated Press, May 9, 2006.

12. Lynn Olson and Linda Jacobson, "Analysis Finds Minority NCLB Scores Widely Excluded," *Education Week*, April 26, 2006, http://www.edweek.org/ew/articles/2006/04/26/33exclude.h25.html?levelId=2300.

13. See Commission on No Child Left Behind, *Beyond NCLB: Fulfilling the Promise to Our Nation's Children* (Washington, DC: The Aspen Institute, 2007), http://www.aspeninstitute.org/atf/cf/%7BDEB6F227-659B-4EC8-8F84-8DF23CA704F5%7D/NCLB_Book.pdf, and U.S. Department of Education, *Building on Results: A Blueprint for Strengthening the No Child Left Behind Act*

(Washington, DC: U.S. Department of Education, 2007), http://www.ed
.gov/policy/elsec/leg/nclb/buildingonresults.pdf.

14. These costs are widely misunderstood. In fact, NCLB does not require
students to learn more; it requires only that states set standards, administer
tests, report results, and intervene in various ways in low-performing
schools. Current Title I appropriations are sufficient to cover the costs of
those activities. What may carry a larger price tag is the combination of
better schools, stronger teachers, and additional tutoring needed actually
to boost pupil proficiency, though one may fairly ask why America is
spending so much money on education today without reaping better
results.

15. Nebraska has resisted statewide testing, relying instead on district-level
testing, thus putting the Cornhusker State in semi-perpetual conflict with the
Education Department over NCLB's testing requirements. See Rhea R.
Borja, "Nebraska Swims Hard Against Testing's Tides," *Education Week*,
February 21, 2007, http://www.edweek.org/ew/articles/2007/02/21/
24nebraska.h26.html.

16. When the American Federation of Teachers re-examined state content
standards in 2006—using less-demanding criteria than the Fordham
Foundation—it concluded that barely half of state reading standards were
acceptable and just eighteen states had standards in every subject and grade
that satisfied the reviewers. *Smart Testing: Let's Get It Right,* policy brief no. 19
(Washington, DC: American Federation of Teachers, July 2006), http://www
.aft.org/pubs-reports/downloads/teachers/Testingbrief.pdf.

17. Paul R. Gross, Ursula Goodenough, Lawrence S. Lerner, Susan Haack,
Martha Schwartz, and Richard Schwartz, *The State of State Science Standards
2005* (Washington, DC: Thomas B. Fordham Institute, 2005), 16.

18. Ibid., 6.

19. American Diploma Project, *Ready or Not: Creating a High School Diploma That
Counts* (Washington, DC: Achieve, Inc., 2004), http://www.achieve.org/
files/ADPreport_7.pdf.

20. *Do Graduation Tests Measure Up? A Closer Look at State High School Exit Exams*
(Washington, DC: Achieve, Inc., June 2006), http://www.achieve.org/files/
TestGraduation-FinalReport.pdf.

21. *Smart Testing.*

22. An example of such triage in upscale Montgomery County, Maryland, was
reported in the *Washington Post* in March 2007. See Daniel de Vise, "A
Concentrated Approach to Exams," *Washington Post,* March 4, 2007, http://
www.washingtonpost.com/wp-dyn/content/article/2007/03/03/
AR2007030301372.html.

23. "Arizona Class of 2006 Gets Break on Graduation Exams," *Education Week*, May 25, 2005, http://www.edweek.org/ew/articles/2005/05/25/38cap-b1.h24 .html?qs=Arizona.

24. Lynn Olson, "Utah to Give Diplomas to Students Who Fail State Exit Exam," *Education Week*, January 25, 2006, http://www.edweek.org/ew/ articles/2006/01/25/20utah.h25.html?qs=Utah.

25. "Missouri Board Eases Test Targets," *Education Week*, February 1, 2006, http://www.edweek.org/ew/articles/2006/02/01/21testing.h25.html?qs= Missouri.

26. Massachusetts is devising a more advanced course of study for those high-school students who easily clear the testing bar, creating what will, in effect, be a two-tiered system of achievement standards.

27. "Judge Grants Injunction Against H.S. Exit Exams," *CBS 5/AP,* May 12, 2006, http://cbs5.com/education/local_story_132152507.html. In August 2006, a panel of judges of the California Court of Appeals overruled Freedman but the plaintiffs vowed to carry the matter to the state supreme court.

28. Endless debate, discrepant definitions, and incompatible statistics beset all discussions of high-school graduation and dropout rates, despite efforts by the National Governors Association and others to standardize these measures across states. Reasonable data can be found in *Diplomas Count*, an annual research publication of *Education Week*. http://www.edweek.org/ew/toc/ 2007/06/12/index.html.

29. Lynn Olson, "A Decade of Effort," *Education Week*, January 5, 2006, http:// www.edweek.org/ew/articles/2006/01/05/17overview.h25.html.

30. *How Well Are States Educating Our Neediest Children?* (Washington, DC: Thomas B. Fordham Foundation, 2006), http://www.edexcellence.net/ foundation/publication/publication.cfm?id=363&pubsubid=1399, especially table 9.

31. Kathleen Kennedy Manzo, "Students Taking More Demanding Courses," *Education Week*, February 23, 2007, http://www.edweek.org/ew/articles/ 2007/02/23/25naep.h26.html?qs=NAEP+12th+grade.

32. *Leaders and Laggards: A State-by-State Report Card on Education Effectiveness* (Washington, DC: U.S. Chamber of Commerce, 2007), 72, http://www .uschamber.com/icw/reportcard/default.

33. Sam Dillon, "Schools Slow in Closing Gaps Between Races," *New York Times,* November 20, 2006, http://www.nytimes.com/2006/11/20/education/ 20gap.html?hp&ex=1164085200&en=50afd2f22c6d95fa&ei=5094&partner= homepage.

34. Christopher B. Swanson, *Making the Connection: A Decade of Standards-Based Reform and Achievement"* (Washington, DC: Editorial Projects in Education

Research Center, January 2006), 9, http://www.edweek.org/media/ew/qc/
2006/MakingtheConnection.pdf. Eric A. Hanushek and Margaret E.
Raymond have found a similar association. See "Does School Accountability
Lead to Improved Student Performance?", National Bureau of Economic
Research, Working Paper 10591, June 2004, http://papers.nber.org/papers/
w10591.

35. *Pierce v. Society of Sisters*, 268 U.S. 510 (1925).

36. "Contexts of Elementary and Secondary Education: School Choice, Indicator
36," *Condition of Education 2006* (Washington, DC: National Center for
Education Statistics, 2006), http://nces.ed.gov/programs/coe/2006/section4/
indicator36.asp.

37. *Ohioans' Views on Education 2007* (Washington, DC: Thomas B. Fordham
Institute, 2007), http://edexcellence.net/foundation/publication/publication
.cfm?id=369, question 38; "The Painful Truth," *Columbus Dispatch,* May 9,
2006, http://www.kidsohio.org/NewsMediaArticle.asp?ID=36; and Ignazio
Messina, "Area School Districts Draw the Line on Illegal Enrollees; Officials
Target Boundary Hoppers," *Toledo Blade,* February 28, 2007, http://www
.toledoblade.com/apps/pbcs.dll/article?AID=/20070218/NEWS04/702180304.

38. For a useful typology, see Dick Carpenter, *Playing to Type?* (Washington,
D.C.: Thomas B. Fordham Institute, 2006), http://www.edexcellence.net/
doc/Carpenter%20ProjectV2.pdf.

39 In mid-2007, UFT head Randi Weingarten announced that her union would
also team up with the California-based "Green Dot" charter management
organization to open a charter school in New York City. Green Dot is well
known because of its leader's willingness to welcome unionized teachers in
his schools, albeit teachers working under a far more flexible collective
bargaining contract than is the norm in American public education.

40. Learn more from the website of the Hope On-line Learning Academy Co-op
at http://www.hopeco-op.org.

41. Erik W. Robelen, "Gates High Schools Gets Mixed Review in Study,"
Education Week, November 16, 2005, http://www.edweek.org/ew/articles/
2005/11/16/12gates.h25.html. Unfortunately, the foundation then terminated
this series of evaluations. Debra Viadero, "Foundation Shifts Tack on
Studies," *Education Week*, October 25, 2006, http://www.edweek.org/ew/
articles/2006/10/25/09gates.h26.html?qs=Gates,+American+Institutes+of+
Research,+small+schools.

42. See, for example, Robin J. Lake and Paul T. Hill, eds., *Hopes, Fears, & Reality:
A Balanced Look at American Charter Schools in 2006* (Seattle, WA: Center on
Reinventing Public Education, 2006), http://www.ncsrp.org/cs/csr/view/csr
_pubs/8.

43. Alex Molnar, David R. Garcia, Margaret Bartlett, and Adrienne O'Neill, *Profiles of For-profit Education Management Organizations: 2005–2006,* eighth edition (Tempe, AZ: Arizona State University, May 2006), http://www.asu.edu/educ/epsl/CERU/CERU_2006_emo.htm.

44. Katherine Boo, "The Factory," *The New Yorker,* October 18, 2004, http://www.pacrim.org/documents/APR%20in%20TNY.pdf.

45. Antonio Villaraigosa, "Accelerating Our Ambitions" (State of the City address, Los Angeles, CA, April 18, 2006), http://www.lacity.org/mayor/myrspeech/mayormyrspeech246937252_04212006.pdf.

46. Abigail Thernstrom and Stephan Thernstrom, *No Excuses: Closing the Racial Gap in Learning* (New York: Simon & Schuster, 2003).

47. Paul Teske, Jody Fitzpatrick, and Gabriel Kaplan, *Opening Doors: How Low-Income Parents Search for the Right School* (Seattle, WA: Center on Reinventing Public Education, 2007).

48. Chester E. Finn, Jr., Bryan Hassel, and Sheree Speakman, *Charter School Funding: Inequity's Next Frontier* (Washington, DC: Thomas B. Fordham Institute, August 2005), http://www.edexcellence.net/institute/charterfinance/.

49. Frederick M. Hess, *Revolution at the Margins* (Washington DC: The Brookings Institution, 2002).

50. Lewis J. Perelman, *School's Out: Hyperlearning, the New Technology, and the End of Education* (New York: William Morrow, 1992).

51. For an example of such a state-issued school report card, see Ohio's report on Lexington's Central Elementary School for the 2004-5 school year at http://www.ode.state.oh.us/reportcardfiles/2004-2005/BUILD/005496.PDF.

52. See a specimen school-level report on a Colorado middle school from Just For the Kids (and its sponsor, the National Center for Educational Accountability) at http://www.just4kids.org/jftk/index.cfm?st=COLORADO&loc=School%20Search%20Defined&tabtype=prof&studentgrp=ALL&campus_id=09002226&tabfam=M. See a specimen state report (Georgia) from Standard & Poors at http://www.schoolmatters.com/pdf/error_band/EB_Georgia.pdf.

53. For an example of a parent-friendly school report (in this case for a Tucson elementary-middle school) from GreatSchools.net, see http://www.greatschools.net/modperl/browse_school/az/1600/.

54. Two examples of such firms are "Schoolnet" and IBM's "Insight at School" program, about which more can be learned at http://www.schoolnet.com/ and http://www-03.ibm.com/industries/education/doc/content/solution/309650310.html.

55. K12 is by no means the only such firm in the "virtual charter school" space. Another excellent program already operating in a dozen states is Baltimore-based Connections Academy: http://www.connectionsacademy.com/.

56. The daunting challenges facing urban superintendents are laid out in Howard Fuller's 2003 report, *An Impossible Job? The View from the Urban Superintendent's Chair*, with Christine Campbell, Mary Beth Celio, James Harvey, John Immerwahr, and Abigail Winger (Seattle, WA: Center on Reinventing Public Education, University of Washington, July 2003), http://www.crpe .org/pubs/introImpossibleJob.shtml.

57. Frederick M. Hess, *Spinning Wheels: The Politics of Urban School Reform* (Washington, DC: Brookings Institution Press, 1999), 113–14.

58. Catherine Gewertz, "Easing Rules Over Schools Gains Favor," *Education Week,* March 16, 2007, http://www.edweek.org/ew/articles/2007/03/16/28 autonomy.h26.html.

59. Paul Hill's thoughtful presentation of the "portfolio" approach to school district organization and management can be found, inter alia, in Paul T. Hill, "Put Learning First: A Portfolio Approach to Public Schools", Progressive Policy Institute, 2006, http://www.ppionline.org/documents/Portfolio _Districts021006.pdf. One early approach followed by the giant Bill and Melinda Gates Foundation entailed the creation of "portfolios" of high schools, many of them smaller than the American norm. That strategy is explained in a foundation publication, "Creating a Portfolio of Great High Schools," http://www.gatesfoundation.org/nr/downloads/ed/GreatHigh Schools.pdf. Experience showed, however, that "small" is no more reliable a signpost to academic success than "charter"; that a school's performance is determined by much more than its size—and that if one adopts a loopy curriculum or hires weak teachers, one's school isn't going to produce great results. See Thomas Toch, *High Schools on a Human Scale: How Small Schools Can Transform American Education* (Boston, MA: Beacon Press, 2003).

60. Eliminating the school board's "exclusive franchise" to create and operate public schools is a key element of lasting reform, according to the visionary and persistent Ted Kolderie, whose organization, Education Evolving, is a rich source of this kind of thinking. See http://www.educationevolving.org/. Meanwhile, vigorous debates continue over the educational effectiveness of such structural reforms as "outsourcing" public schools to private managers. See, for example, Brian Gill, Ron Zimmer, Jolley Christman, and Suzanne Blanc, *State Takeover, School Restructuring, Private Management, and Student Achievement in Philadelphia* (RAND Corporation, 2007), http://www.rand .org/pubs/monographs/2007/RAND_MG533.pdf, and Paul Peterson, "The Philadelphia Story," *Wall Street Journal,* February 23, 2007, http://www.ksg .harvard.edu/ksgnews/Features/opeds/022307_peterson.html.

61. Christine Campbell, Michael DeArmond, and Abigail Schumwinger, *From Bystander to Ally* (Seattle, WA: Center on Reinventing Public Education,

April 2004), http://www.crpe.org/pubs/pdf/BystanderToAlly_reportweb.pdf,
and Bradley Portin with Paul Schneider, Michael DeArmond, and Lauren
Gundlach, *Making Sense of Leading Schools* (Seattle, WA: Center on Reinventing Public Education, September 2003), http://www.crpe.org/pubs/pdf/
MakingSense_PortinWeb.pdf.

62. The weakness and opacity of school-finance data in states and districts pose
enormous barriers to reformers who want to leverage current and future
dollars into more productive and higher-need uses. For thoughtful discussions of this problem, see *Creating a World-Class Education System in Ohio*
(Washington, DC: Achieve, Inc., 2006), 49–56, http://www.achieve.org/
files/World_Class_Edu_Ohio_FINAL.pdf, and *Charter School Funding:
Inequity's Next Frontier* (Washington, DC: Thomas B. Fordham Institute,
August 2005), 16, http://www.edexcellence.net/doc/Charter%20School
%20Funding%202005%20FINAL.pdf.

63. Marguerite Roza and Paul T. Hill, "How Within-District Spending Inequities Help Some Schools to Fail," in *Brookings Papers on Education Policy: 2004,*
ed. Diane Ravitch (Washington, DC: The Brookings Institution, 2004) 201–
18, http://www.crpe.org/pubs/pdf/InequitiesRozaHillchapter.pdf. Occasionally one encounters salary-linked innovations that succeed in drawing veteran
teachers into tough schools and keeping them there. See Letitia Stein,
"Veteran Educators Step Up to the Challenge," *St. Petersburg Times,* March 5,
2007, http://pqasb.pqarchiver.com/sptimes/access/1227519811.html?dids=
1227519811:1227519811&FMT=FT&FMTS=ABS:FT&date=Mar+5%2C+2007
&author=LETITIA+STEIN&pub=St.+Petersburg+Times&edition=
&startpage=1.B&desc=Veteran+educators+step+up+to+the+challenge.

64. William G. Ouchi, *Making Schools Work* (New York: Simon & Schuster,
2003). See also Marguerite Roza, "Many a Slip 'tween Cup and Lip:
District Fiscal Practices and Their Effect on School Spending," (Washington, DC: The Aspen Institute, February 2005), http://www.crpe.org/
workingpapers/pdf/Roza_AspenInstitute.pdf. In June 2006, the Fordham
Institute released a "manifesto" urging fully portable weighted student
funding. A long and bipartisan list of public officials and educators affixed
their names to *Fund the Child: Tackling Inequity & Antiquity in School Finance,*
which can be found at the website of the Thomas B. Fordham Foundation,
http://www.100percentsolution.org/.

65. Steven Adamowski, *The Autonomy Gap* (Washington, DC: Thomas B.
Fordham Institute, 2007), http://edexcellence.net/foundation/publication/
publication.cfm?id=368.

66. National Center on Education and the Economy, *Tough Choices or Tough
Times: The Report of the New Commission on the Skills of the American Workforce*
(San Francisco, CA: Jossey-Bass, 2006).

67. This territory is indeed contested, although a 2006 report by Arthur Levine, the longtime president of Teachers College, Columbia, pounded a big nail into the coffin of ed school–based teacher preparation. See Arthur Levine, *Report #2 Educating School Teachers* (Washington, DC: Education Schools Project, 2006), http://www.edschools.org/teacher_report.htm. In 2006, Thomas Kane and colleagues "use[d] six years of data on student test performance to evaluate the effectiveness of certified, uncertified, and alternatively certified teachers in the New York City public schools. On average, the certification status of a teacher has at most small impacts on student test performance. However, among those with the same certification status, there are large and persistent differences in teacher effectiveness." See Thomas J. Kane, Jonah E. Rockoff, Douglas Staiger, "What Does Certification Tell Us About Teacher Effectiveness? Evidence from New York City", National Bureau of Economic Research Working Paper W12155, April 2006, http://www.nber.org/papers/w12155. Other examples of responsible criticism can be found in several publications of the Baltimore-based Abell Foundation (http://www.abell.org/pubsitems/ed_cert_summary_1101.pdf, http://www.abell.org/pubsitems/ed_cert_rejoinder_1101.pdf, http://www.abell.org/pubsitems/ed_cert_appendix_1101.pdf) and in Kate Walsh, "Teacher Certification: Coming Up Empty", Thomas B. Fordham Foundation, 2006, http://www.edexcellence.net/doc/Teacher%20Education%20fwd.pdf. Spirited defenses of traditional teacher training and certification can be found, inter alia, at Linda Darling-Hammond, "The Research and Rhetoric on Teacher Certification: A Response to 'Teacher Certification Reconsidered'," National Commission on Teaching and America's Future, 2001, http://www.nctaf.org/resources/research_and_reports/nctaf_research_reports/index.htm; Michael Allen, "Eight Questions on Teacher Preparation: What Does the Research Say?", Education Commission of the States, 2003, http://www.ecs.org/ecsmain.asp?page=/html/educationIssues/teachingquality/tpreport/index.asp; and Linda Darling-Hammond, Deborah J. Holtzman, Su Jin Gatlin, Julian Vasquez Heilig, "Does Teacher Preparation Matter? Evidence About Teacher Certification, Teach for America, and Teacher Effectiveness," Education Policy Analysis Archives, 2005, http://epaa.asu.edu/epaa/v13n42/.

68. This very different approach to the credentialing and deployment of teachers has been set forth in many places, including *The Teachers We Need and How To Get More of Them: A Manifesto*, Thomas B. Fordham Foundation, 1999, http://www.edexcellence.net/foundation/publication/publication.cfm?id=16; Frederick M. Hess, "Tear Down This Wall: The Case for a Radical Overhaul of Teacher Certification," White House Conference on Preparing Tomorrow's

Teachers, http://www.ed.gov/admins/tchrqual/learn/preparingteachers conference/hess.html; and Frederick M. Hess, Andrew J. Rotherham, Kate Walsh, "Finding the Teachers We Need," WestEd *Policy Perspectives*, http://www.wested.org/online_pubs/pp-05-01.pdf.

69. Much of the next several paragraphs appeared originally in the *Wall Street Journal* (Chester E. Finn, Jr., "Teacher Can't Teach," March 11, 2005) and in the *Education Gadfly*: http://www.edexcellence.net/foundation/gadfly/issue .cfm?edition=&id=186#2222.

70. *Teaching at Risk: A Call to Action* (New York: The Teaching Commission, 2004), 17–18, www.csl.usf.edu/teaching%20at%20risk.pdf.

71. The turnover and attrition issue is also overblown. Americans in general follow different career patterns today than did their parents and grandparents and are far more apt to explore multiple lines of work before—if ever— settling into one. A few years of teaching might well fit in before or after one does other things, or between other things. A well-functioning education system would make sensible—and grateful—use of the short-timers while intelligently deploying its career educators in roles that most need them and bring them the greatest reward.

72. For the most careful study of the instructional effectiveness of Teach for America corps members, see Paul T. Decker, Daniel P. Mayer, and Steven Glazerman, *The Effects of Teach for America on Students: Findings from a National Evaluation* (Princeton, NJ: Mathematica Policy Research, Inc., 2004), http://www.teachforamerica.org/assets/documents/mathematica_results_6.9.04.pdf.

73. "Overview of Alternative Routes to Teacher Certification" (Washington, DC: National Center for Alternative Certification, 2006), http://www .teach-now.org/overview.cfm.

74. Levine, *Report #2 Educating School Teachers*, 68. Levine's landmark study of teacher preparation found "no difference in student math or reading achieve- ment by students taught by teachers educated for certification at NCATE- and non-NCATE-accredited institutions."

75. National Council for Accreditation of Teacher Education, "NCATE and the States," http://www.ncate.org/states/NCATEStates.asp?ch=95.

76. Molly Burke, "Professional Standards Boards—State Policies," Education Commission of the States, December 2004, http://www.ecs.org/clearinghouse/ 57/05/5705.htm.

77. *Teachers and Other School Personnel,* Oregon Legislative Statute 9, chapter 342, 2005 edition, http://www.leg.state.or.us/ors/342.html.

78. The Teaching Commission, "Teaching At Risk: Progress and Potholes," Final Report, Spring 2006, www.nctq.org/nctq/images/ttc_teachingatrisk .pdf. The public-school teaching ranks having swollen to 3.1 million people;

even a $1,000 across-the-board boost in teacher pay would cost more than $3 billion; $10,000 more per teacher would mean a bill to the taxpayer totaling $31 billion. Meanwhile, there is preliminary evidence that performance-based merit-pay schemes for teachers do lead to (slightly) higher pupil achievement. See Debra Viadero, "Study Links Merit Pay to Slightly Higher Student Scores," *Education Week*, January 10, 2007, http://www.edweek.org/ew/articles/2007/01/10/18merit.h26.html.

79. Teaching Commission, *Teaching at Risk: Progress & Potholes,* Spring 2006, http://www.theteachingcommission.org/press/2006_03_22_pr.html.

80. Arthur Levine, *Report #1 Educating School Leaders* (Washington, DC: Education Schools Project, 2005), http://www.edschools.org/pdf/NewsRelease _050315.pdf.

81. See, for example, *Better Leaders for America's Schools: A Manifesto*, Thomas B. Fordham Institute and The Broad Foundation, 2003, http://www.edexcellence .net/foundation/publication/publication.cfm?id=1.

82. *A Different Drummer* (New York: Public Agenda, October 1997), http://www .publicagenda.org/press/press_release_detail.cfm?report_title=Different %20Drummers.

83. See Levine, *Report #2 Educating School Teachers.*

84. *What Education Schools Aren't Teaching about Reading and What Elementary Teachers Aren't Learning* (Washington, DC: National Council on Teacher Quality, 2006), http://www.nctq.org/nctq/.

85. W. Steven Barnett, Jason T. Husted, Laura E. Hawkinson, and Kenneth B. Robin, *The State of Preschool 2006* (New Brunswick, NJ: National Institute for Early Education Research, 2006), http://nieer.org/yearbook/pdf/yearbook .pdf.

86. Diana Jean Schemo, "Failing Schools See a Solution in Longer Days," *New York Times,* March 26, 2007, http://www.nytimes.com/2007/03/26/us/ 26schoolday.html.

87. In 1994, the National Education Commission on Time and Learning estimated that "in their final four years of secondary school, according to our estimates, French, German, and Japanese students receive more than twice as much core academic instruction as American students." U.S. Department of Education, *Prisoners of Time* (Washington, DC: U.S. Department of Education, 1994), http://www.ed.gov/pubs/PrisonersOfTime/Lessons.html. See also Aaron Benavot, "Instructional Time and Curricular Emphases: U.S. State Policies in Comparative Perspective," Thomas B. Fordham Institute, December 12, 2006, http://www.edexcellence.net/doc/Beyond_The_Basics-Benavot _Long.doc; Elena Silva, *On the Clock: Rethinking the Way Schools Use Time* (Washington, DC: Education Sector, 2007), http://www.educationsector.org/

usr_doc/OntheClock.pdf; and Kate Walsh, "Time in School: Opportunity to Learn," Thomas B. Fordham Institute, December 12, 2006, http://www.edexcellence.net/doc/Beyond_The_Basics-Walsh_Long.doc.

88. Jean Johnson and Ann Duffett, *"I'm Calling My Lawyer": How Litigation, Due Process and Other Regulatory Requirements Are Affecting Public Education* (New York: Public Agenda, 2003), http://www.publicagenda.org/research/pdfs/im_calling_my_lawyer.pdf. See also Richard Arum, *Judging School Discipline: The Crisis of Moral Authority* (Cambridge, MA: Harvard University Press 2003).

89. In the late 1990s, Vermont undertook to redistribute local tax dollars from wealthy high-spending districts like Stowe to a larger number of less prosperous communities, producing outrage and fury in the former and allegations of "class warfare."

90. "Overview Paper," in *Getting Down to Facts: A Research Project Examining California's School Governance and Finance Systems,* 5 (Stanford, CA: Institute for Research on Education Policy & Practice, 2007), http://irepp.stanford.edu/projects/cafinance.htm.

91. *Rose v. Council for Better Education*, 790 S.W.2d 186, 60 Ed. Law Rep. 1289 (1989), http://www.wku.edu/library/kera//rose.htm.

92. Ibid.

93. Eric Hanushek, ed., *Courting Failure: How School Finance Lawsuits Exploit Judges' Good Intentions and Harm Our Children* (Palo Alto, CA: Hoover Institution Press, 2006).

94. Erik W. Robelen, "A Think Tank Takes the Plunge," "Fordham's Connections to School That It Sponsors Spark Concerns," and "School's Troubles Take Fordham by Surprise," *Education Week*, December 20, 2006.

95. Christopher B. Swanson and Janelle Barlage, *Influence: A Study of the Factors Shaping Education Policy* (Bethesda, MD: Editorial Projects in Education Research Center, December 2006).

96. "Mission Statement," Thomas B. Fordham Foundation, http://www.edexcellence.net/foundation/global/page.cfm?id=6.

97. Florida's 2006 performance-based bonus program for teachers began eroding within months in the face of Governor Jeb Bush's departure, inept district implementation, and nonstop union hostility, much as, two decades earlier, Lamar Alexander's "career ladder" began to crumble when he vacated the Tennessee governor's chair.

98. For a provocative expose of dubious but persistent ideas about education, see Jay P. Greene, *Education Myths: What Special-Interest Groups Want You to Believe About Our Schools and Why It Isn't So* (Lanham, MD: Rowman & Littlefield, 2005).

Epilogue |

1. It recently got rockier. Since I wrote this, Martin's wife left him, taking Ana with her, making his life miserable and curbing access to his daughter, a painful but not unusual amplification of the challenges Ana (and millions of other youngsters) will face in years to come and the difficulty—and urgency—of securing her the kind of education she deserves.

INDEX

educators (*continued*)
multiple intelligences and, 108;
performance and, 114–15; politics and,
109–11; power struggles and, 109–11;
professionalism agenda and, 109–11;
progressive/pragmatic ideals and, 7–8,
14; propaganda and, 108–9; real wages
and, 284; reform and, 108–17; as shapers,
110; short-term, 343n71; strikes and,
15–16, 39, 110; subsidies and, 69–70;
support groups and, 115–17; teacher-
testing plan and, 204; Teach for America
(TFA) program and, 285–86; teaching to
the test and, 250–51; unions and, 15–16,
38–39, 75, 79, 109–10 (*see also* unions);
wall chart and, 114–15

effective schools research, 101–2

Ehrlichman, John, 42–44, 52

Eidenberg, Eugene, 70

Eisenberg, Lee, 196

Elementary and Secondary Education Act
(ESEA), 17–18, 38, 47, 70, 87, 206,
239–42

Elliott, Emerson, 130, 133

Elmore, Richard, 209

End of Education, The (Postman), 201

Engler, John, 106

English standards, 225, 247

equity, 36, 38, 46–47, 96, 292; educators
and, 108; information quality and, 147;
politics and, 90–93, 178; private schools
and, 68, 71; Tennessee and, 118, 121

Ervin, Sam, 214–15

Escalante, Jaime, 146

essentialists, 8, 14

Eurocentrism, 202

Evers, Bill, 300

evolution, 248

excellence movement, 96, 98–99, 119, 194;
American Educational Research
Association (AERA) and, 143–45;
Bennett and, 134–48; business groups
and, 128–29, 138; Charlottesville and,
151–54; curriculum issues and, 150;

Education Department and, 114–15;
educators and, 108–17, 211–15; governors
and, 104–7, 115–17, 126–29, 150;
information quality and, 134–45;
National Assessment of Educational
Progress (NAEP) and, 136–43; No Child
Left Behind Act and, 106; quality and,
101–7; standards issues and, 150–57;
Thomas B. Fordham Foundation and,
224–29

Fairbanks, Charles, 122

Family Assistance Plan, 42, 52

Fannie Mae, 41

Featherstone, Joseph, 14–15

Fenty, Adrian, 277–78

Ferguson, Rodney, 197

*Fifteen Thousand Hours: Secondary Schools
and Their Effects on Children* (Rutter),
324n5

fifties: *Brown* decision and, 8–9; Conant
studies and, 9–10; economic robustness
of, 10; Eisenhower era and, 7; population surge of, 8; post perception of, 7;
progressive/pragmatic ideals and, 7–8;
school choice and, 10–11; shifting high
school function and, 9–10; Sputnik and,
8–9; television and, 12–13

Finance Committee, 72

Finch, Robert, 42, 44

Finn, Aloke, 118, 160–63, 199

Finn, Arti, 118, 162, 199, 252–55, 298

Finn, Chester E., Jr.: American Educational Research Association (AERA)
and, 143–45; blackballing and, 91;
Brookings Institution and, 62–64, 66;
Colorado Outward Bound School and,
22–23; current activities of, 296–300; as
Democrat, 87–90; Edison Project and,
195–99, 224; Education Department
and, 129–31; as educator, 26–31, 194;
Ehrlichman and, 43–44, 52; Exeter and,
20–22, 24; family background of, 4–6,
11–13; global travels of, 56; grading by,

194; Harvard and, 23–25, 28; Hudson Institute and, 199–201, 224; in India, 59–62; Moynihan and, 41 (*see also* Moynihan, Daniel Patrick); national standards and, 194–95; neoconservatism and, 88–91; Nixon administration and, 30–31; qualifying paper of, 31; as Republican, 87–93; return to Washington, 129–33; Sargent and, 56–57; schools working group and, 44–47; Tennessee and, 118–24; Thomas B. Fordham Foundation and, 224–29; volunteering of, 23–25; White House days of, 41–55

Finn, Emma, ix, 275, 307, 310–11

Finn, Renu, 61–62, 65, 91–93, 118, 129, 131, 161, 253

Finn, Samuel, 4–5

First Amendment, 70

First Lessons report, 147

Flanigan, Peter, 42

Florida, 218–19, 259, 310

Ford, Gerald, 38, 96

Ford Foundation, 16

Fordham, Thelma, 224–25

Fordham, Thomas B., 224–25

Forstmann, Theodore J., 167, 193

Frames of Mind (Gardner), 108

Freedman, Robert, 257

Freeman, Roger, 42

Friedman, Milton, 10–11, 39, 192

Fryer, John, 278

Fuller, Howard, 296

Gaebler, Ted, 198

Galbraith, John Kenneth, 31, 59

Gans, Herbert J., 23

Gardner, David P., 98

Gardner, Howard, 108, 178

Gardner, John W., 9

Garrity, Arthur, 37, 56

Gates, Bill, 193

Gates, Melinda, 193

Gates Foundation, 245, 249, 266, 297

Geiger, Keith, 178

General Education Board, 3

General Revenue Sharing, 57

geography, 2, 11, 153, 173, 247

George Peabody College for Teachers, 91

Gerstner, Louis V., Jr., 220–22, 288

Giamatti, Bart, 98

GI Bill, 7, 216

"gifted and talented" programs, 11

Gilligan, Carol, 108

Gingrich, Newt, 205

Glazer, Nathan, 31, 88

Glenn, Charles, 158–59

globalization, 168, 273

Goals 2000: The Educate America Act, 166, 178, 202–10, 220, 238

Goldberg, Milt, 133–34

Goldwater, Barry, 72

Goodlad, John I., 112, 178

Goodling, Bill, 206, 208, 222

Goodman, Paul, 15

Gore, Al, 206, 232

government, x; Catholic schools and, 71–76; Coleman study and, 17–19; Family Assistance Plan and, 42; GI Bill and, 7, 216; home schooling and, 219; Moynihan and, 41 (*see also* Moynihan, Daniel Patrick); National Foundation for Higher Education and, 48–49; National Institute of Education (NIE) and, 45–47; school choice and, 10–11; tax credits and, 72–76; Watergate and, 34. *See also* policy

governors, 104–7, 166, 211, 277, 304; America 2000 and, 172; business groups and, 220–21; Charlottesville and, 151–54; charter schools and, 183; Clinton and, 204; education summits and, 151–54, 220–23; excellence movement and, 115–16, 126–29; Goals 2000 and, 204–5; National Council on Education Standards and Testing (NCEST) and, 176–78; National Governors Association (NGA), 115–16, 123, 126, 151–54, 204, 214, 220; No Child Left Behind Act and, 244–45

liberals, 121, 205, 207, 219, 303; Department of Education and, 81; Finn and, 87–88; private schools and, 70; quality and, 101; vouchers and, 183–86
Life magazine, 59, 90
Light, Richard, 28
Lindsay, John V., 16
Linkletter, Art, 51
local education agencies (LEAs), 241–42
Long, Russell, 27, 74
Lowell, A. Lawrence, 4
Lynde & Harry Bradley Foundation, 266

MacArthur foundation, 138
Macchiarola, Frank J., 128
McCown, Gaynor, 288
McElroy, Neil, 42
McGovern, George, 53, 59, 72
McGriff, Debra, 197
McIntyre, James, 81
magnet schools, 16–17, 262
Making Schools Work: Improving Performance and Controlling Costs (Hanushek), 200
Making the Grade (Twentieth Century Fund), 102
Manhattan Institute, 296
Manno, Bruno, 133, 170, 200, 229, 298
Marshall, Ray, 189–90
Massachusetts, 2, 56, 259
mathematics, 9, 34, 201, 233, 297, 328n58; educators and, 116, 124, 284, 286; national standards and, 154–57, 173; No Child Left Behind Act and, 237, 239–40, 245; quality and, 102, 134, 146, 150; reform and, 154–57, 173, 180; school choice and, 262, 264, 268; skill assessment in, 188–89, 206–8, 247, 249–50, 255, 257–59; types of intelligence and, 108
Maximum Feasible Misunderstanding (Moynihan), 39
mayors, 277, 304
Meese, Ed, 97, 103
Menino, Thomas, 277

Michigan, 8, 277–78
Microsoft, 266
Milken, Lowell, 113, 276
Milken Family Foundation, 245
Miller, George, 240
Milliken decision, 126
Miner, Joshua L., 22
minimum competency testing (MCT), 35
Minnesota, 127, 158, 182, 184, 262
Mirel, Jeffrey, 9–10, 175
Mitchell, Parren, 85
Moe, Terry M., 159–60, 175, 186, 191, 300
Moloney, Bill, 296
Mondale, Walter, 77–78, 80, 85
Morey, Roy, 70
Morgan, Edward L., 43–44, 47, 52–53
Mosteller, Frederick, 18–19
Moynihan, Daniel Patrick, 20, 24, 29, 54–55, 103, 118, 120, 130; as ambassador to India, 59–62; cabinet promotion of, 43; Catholic schools and, 71–72; Coleman Report and, 18–19; Education Department and, 83–84; Family Assistance Plan and, 52; Finance Committee and, 66–67; Harvard and, 18, 58; Kissinger and, 60; memo leak and, 53; methods of, 66, 89–93; National Foundation for Higher Education and, 48–49, 57–58, 63, 83, 89–90; National Institute of Education (NIE) and, 45–47; national urban policy and, 52; Nixon administration and, 30–31; schools working group and, 44–47; Stockman and, 90–91; tax credits and, 72–76; team of, 66; UN third committee and, 59; urban affairs and, 41–42; welfare reform and, 42
Moynihan, Elizabeth, 30, 59–60, 93
multiculturalism, 108–9
multiple intelligences, 108
music, 11, 250, 262, 274
Musick, Mark, 116

Osberg, Eric, 296

Osborne, David, 198

Other America, (The Harrington), 23

Ottinger, Betty Ann, 51

Ottinger, Dick, 51

Ouchi, William G., 281

Our Children Are Dying (Hentoff), 15

Outward Bound, 22–23, 30

Owings, Nathaniel, 52

Packard, Ron, 276

Packwood-Moynihan bill, 73–74

Paige, Rod, 237, 243, 288, 298

parents, 105; assessment metrics and, ix–x; blaming, 299; charter schools and, 218; disabled children and, 56–57; home schooling and, 219–20; influence of, 291–92; judges and, 293–94; national standards and, 259–60; problems of, 301; school choice and, 157–60, 261–72, 310–11 (*see also* school choice); technology and, 274

Parents Advancing Choice in Education (PACE), 227–28

Pataki, George, 183

Pawlenty, Tim, 304

Payzant, Tom, 135, 304

Peace Corps, 22–24, 30

Pearlstein, Mitch, 133

peer review, 143

Pell grants, 47

Perelman, Lewis, 273

Perot, Ross, 106

Perpich, Rudy, 106, 127

Peters, Sylvia, 196

Peterson, Bart, 304

Peterson, Paul, 102, 227, 300

Petrilli, Mike, 225, 296

Pew Memorial Trusts, 217, 220

Phi Delta Kappan journal, 194, 326n33

philanthropists, 167, 192–93, 245, 249, 266, 280, 289

Phillips Brooks House Association (PBHA), 24, 29

Phillips Exeter Academy, 5, 20–22, 24, 60, 253–54

Pinkerton, Jim, 151

Pipho, Chris, 35

Place Called School, A (Goodlad), 112

Podhoretz, Norman, 88–89

Politics, Markets and America's Schools (Chubb and Moe), 159

Porter, Roger, 152, 169, 178

Postman, Neil, 201

postmodernism, 108–9

poverty, 23; achievement gap and, 57–58; Catholic schools and, 68; education and, 87–89; Family Assistance Plan and, 42, 52; Johnson's War on Poverty and, 16, 17, 24, 29–30, 69, 87; school choice and, 39; Southern States and, 105–6; subsidies and, 69–70; Upward Bound program and, 30; vouchers and, 185–86

prekindergarten, 290–91

prep schools, 5, 20–22

President's Education Policy Advisory Committee (PEPAC), 169–70, 178, 224

Price, John, 41

private schools, 2–3, 8, 235; British-style, 61; politics of aiding, 66–76; tax credits and, 72–76, 86; think-tanks and, 195–99

privatization, 197

professionalism agenda, x, 109–11, 301

Progressive Education Association, 14

PTA, 12, 221

Public Agenda, 289–90, 293

Public Interest, The (journal), 88–89, 155

public schools, 2, 8; desegregation and, 7, 37–38, 42, 44, 47, 49, 85, 126, 262, 293; Irish influence and, 28–29

Pursuit of Excellence, The (Gardner), 9

quality: block grants and, 103–4; certification and, 283–90, 296; educators and, 108–17; effective schools research and, 101–2; governors and, 104–7; of information, 134–45; Internet and, 276; No Child Left Behind Act and, 106;

quality (*continued*)
  reports on, 101–2. *See also* excellence
  movement